Fan Fare!
Best of Bridge
Cookbook

Brand-New Volume
Brand-New Recipes

Robert
ROSE

For complete cataloguing information, see page 340.

Disclaimer
The recipes in this book have been carefully tested by our kitchen and our tasters. To the best of our knowledge, they are safe and nutritious for ordinary use and users. For those people with food or other allergies, or who have special food requirements or health issues, please read the suggested contents of each recipe carefully and determine whether or not they may create a problem for you. All recipes are used at the risk of the consumer.

We cannot be responsible for any hazards, loss or damage that may occur as a result of any recipe use.

For those with special needs, allergies, requirements or health problems, in the event of any doubt, please contact your medical adviser prior to the use of any recipe.

Design and Production: Joseph Gisini/PageWave Graphics Inc.
Editor: Sue Sumeraj
Recipe editor: Jennifer MacKenzie
Proofreader: Sheila Wawanash
Indexer: Gillian Watts
Photographer: Colin Erricson
Associate Photographer: Matt Johannsson
Food Stylist: Kathryn Robertson
Prop Stylist: Charlene Erricson

Cover image: Chicken Med (page 174)

We acknowledge the financial support of the Government of Canada through the Book Publishing Industry Development Program (BPIDP) for our publishing activities.

Published by Robert Rose Inc.
120 Eglinton Avenue East, Suite 800, Toronto, Ontario, Canada M4P 1E2
Tel: (416) 322-6552 Fax: (416) 322-6936
www.robertrose.ca

Printed and bound in China

3 4 5 6 7 8 9 PPLS 19 18 17 16 15 14 13 12 11

CONTENTS

INTRODUCTION

ASK ANY OF THE BEST OF BRIDGE LADIES AND THEY'LL TELL YOU — THIS IS THE WAY TO WRITE A COOKBOOK. SALLY, WHO CAME ON BOARD TWO YEARS AGO, SPENDS ENDLESS HOURS IN THE KITCHEN DEVELOPING GREAT NEW RECIPES. MEANWHILE, WE GET TO TEST, TASTE AND PROVIDE FEEDBACK ON ALL THE FRESH IDEAS AND FLAVORS, AND CONTRIBUTE SOME OF OUR OWN RECIPES. THE PROCESS IS GREAT FUN, AND WE CONTINUE TO DELIGHT IN SALLY'S ENTHUSIASM, HER SENSE OF HUMOR AND HER EXTENSIVE FOOD KNOWLEDGE. SHE "GETS" US, SO IT'S A MATCH MADE IN CULINARY HEAVEN!

OUR FANS OFTEN ASK, "HOW DO YOU COME UP WITH ALL THOSE NEW RECIPES?" SOMETIMES IT STARTS WITH A CONVERSATION. WE'LL SAY SOMETHING LIKE, "WE TASTED A TERRIFIC COUSCOUS SALAD THE OTHER DAY. IT HAD CRANBERRIES, ALMONDS, FETA CHEESE AND A REALLY DELICIOUS DRESSING. CAN YOU CREATE A RECIPE LIKE THAT?" AND SALLY REPLIES, "I'M SURE I CAN. GIVE ME A COUPLE OF DAYS AND I'LL GET BACK TO YOU." OR SHE'LL BE IN THE SUPERMARKET, CHECKING OUT NEW PRODUCTS AND INGREDIENTS, AND NOTICE AN ARRAY OF NEW SALAD DRESSINGS. AFTER CONSIDERING THE FLAVOR COMBINATIONS, SHE'LL SAY, "I CAN MAKE THAT — AND IT'LL BE HEALTHIER AND COST A LOT LESS MONEY!"

THIS NEW COLLECTION OF RECIPES FEATURES LOTS OF MEALS AND TIPS TO HELP YOU DEAL WITH THE MIDWEEK MADNESS OF MEAL PREPARATION. YOU'LL FIND NEW CHAPTERS, SUCH AS FAST FAMILY FAVORITES AND ALL-DAY BREAKFAST, THAT WILL HELP YOU MAKE FAST MEALS WHEN YOU DON'T HAVE A LOT OF TIME. AS ALWAYS, THE DISHES ARE MADE USING INGREDIENTS THAT ARE READILY AVAILABLE AT YOUR LOCAL SUPERMARKET.

SALLY AND "THE LADIES" WISH YOU CONTINUED FUN AND SUCCESS IN YOUR KITCHEN, AND HOPE YOU ENJOY THIS DELICIOUS NEW COOKBOOK.

WHILE THE BEST OF BRIDGE LADIES HAVE HAD
TWO JOYFUL YEARS OF GRANDMOTHERING AND
TRAVELING, WE HAVE BEEN GREATLY SADDENED BY THE
RECENT LOSS OF OUR DEAR FRIEND AND PARTNER, KAREN
BRIMACOMBE. SHE HAD A QUICK WIT, A TALENT
FOR LANGUAGE, A PASSION FOR SHOES ("I HAVE NO
INTENTION OF TAKING UP ANY SPORT THAT CAN'T BE
DONE IN HIGH HEELS") AND, OF COURSE, SHE WAS A
GREAT COOK. WE WILL ALWAYS MISS HER.

ALL-DAY BREAKFAST

OVERNIGHT EGGS JALAPEÑO

ASSEMBLE BEFORE BED, SET THE ALARM AN HOUR EARLY AND POP THE EGGS IN THE OVEN. THEN ENJOY ANOTHER SNOOZE WHILE BREAKFAST BAKES. USE LESS JALAPEÑO PEPPER IF YOU PREFER — OR INCLUDE THE SEEDS IF YOU'RE LOOKING FOR A FIERY START TO THE DAY.

6	EGGS	6
2	JALAPEÑO PEPPERS, SEEDED AND CHOPPED (SEE TIP, BELOW)	2
1 CUP	SOUR CREAM	250 ML
3/4 CUP	SHREDDED SHARP (OLD) CHEDDAR CHEESE	175 ML
3/4 CUP	SHREDDED JALAPEÑO MONTEREY JACK CHEESE	175 ML
	SALT AND FRESHLY GROUND BLACK PEPPER	

BUTTER A 9-INCH (23 CM) SQUARE BAKING DISH. IN A LARGE BOWL, WHISK TOGETHER EGGS, JALAPEÑOS, SOUR CREAM, CHEDDAR AND MONTEREY JACK. SEASON WITH SALT AND PEPPER. TRANSFER TO PREPARED BAKING DISH, COVER AND REFRIGERATE OVERNIGHT.

PREHEAT OVEN TO 350°F (180°C). UNCOVER EGGS AND BAKE FOR ABOUT 1 HOUR OR UNTIL SET AND LIGHTLY BROWNED. SERVES 4.

TIP: GREEN JALAPEÑOS ARE THE MOST COMMON, BUT THERE IS ALSO A RED VARIETY. FOR A MILDER FLAVOR, REMOVE THE RIBS AND SEEDS. WHEN HANDLING FRESH CHILE PEPPERS, BE CAREFUL NOT TO TOUCH YOUR EYES OR OTHER SENSITIVE PARTS — IT WILL BURN! WASH YOUR HANDS AND SCRUB UNDER YOUR NAILS THOROUGHLY AFTER CHOPPING FRESH CHILES.

SMOKED SALMON AND ARTICHOKE QUICHE

1	9-INCH (23 CM) FROZEN DEEP-DISH PIE SHELL	1
6 OZ	SMOKED SALMON FILLETS, CHOPPED	175 G
1/2	CAN (14 OZ/398 ML) ARTICHOKE HEARTS, DRAINED AND CHOPPED	1/2
1/3 CUP	CRUMBLED GOAT CHEESE	75 ML
1/4 CUP	CHOPPED FRESH CHIVES	60 ML
4	EGGS	4
3/4 CUP	HEAVY OR WHIPPING (35%) CREAM	175 ML
	FINELY GRATED ZEST OF 1/2 LEMON	
	FRESHLY GROUND BLACK PEPPER	

PREHEAT OVEN TO 375°F (190°C). REMOVE PIE SHELL FROM FREEZER, PLACE ON A BAKING SHEET (IN ITS FOIL PAN) AND LET THAW FOR 15 MINUTES. PRICK BOTTOM AND SIDES WITH A FORK. BAKE FOR 12 TO 14 MINUTES OR UNTIL LIGHTLY BROWNED. CHECK A COUPLE OF TIMES WHILE IT'S BAKING; IF THE BOTTOM IS PUFFING UP, LIGHTLY PRICK IT WITH A FORK A FEW MORE TIMES. LET COOL COMPLETELY ON RACK. REDUCE OVEN TEMPERATURE TO 350°F (180°C).

IN A BOWL, COMBINE SALMON, ARTICHOKES, GOAT CHEESE AND CHIVES. SPOON INTO COOLED PIE SHELL. IN ANOTHER BOWL, WHISK TOGETHER EGGS, CREAM AND LEMON ZEST. SEASON WITH PEPPER. SLOWLY POUR EGG MIXTURE INTO PIE SHELL, ALLOWING EGG TO SETTLE IN AND AROUND THE SALMON MIXTURE. BAKE FOR 30 MINUTES OR UNTIL SLIGHTLY PUFFY AND SET. THE QUICHE MIGHT FALL SLIGHTLY AFTER IT COMES OUT OF THE OVEN. SERVES 6.

SUNRISE APPLE BACON STRATA

HERE'S A MAKE-AHEAD BREAKFAST OR SUPPER
DISH THAT'S READY BEFORE YOU ARE. SERVE WITH
MAPLE SYRUP FOR BREAKFAST OR WITH
APPLESAUCE AND A GREEN SALAD FOR SUPPER.

6	SLICES BACON, CHOPPED	6
6	EGGS	6
1 CUP	HALF-AND-HALF (10%) CREAM OR MILK	250 ML
2 TSP	CHOPPED FRESH THYME (OR $1/4$ TSP/1 ML DRIED)	10 ML
1 TSP	DIJON MUSTARD	5 ML
$1/2$ TSP	SALT	2 ML
	FRESHLY GROUND BLACK PEPPER	
4 CUPS	CUBED WHITE BREAD (1-INCH/2.5 CM CUBES)	1 L
4	GREEN ONIONS, CHOPPED	4
2	RED APPLES (UNPEELED), GRATED	2
2 CUPS	SHREDDED SMOKED GOUDA OR SHARP (OLD) CHEDDAR CHEESE	500 ML

GREASE AN 8-INCH (20 CM) SQUARE BAKING DISH.
IN A LARGE NONSTICK SKILLET, SAUTÉ BACON OVER
MEDIUM-HIGH HEAT UNTIL CRISP. USING A SLOTTED
SPOON, TRANSFER TO A PLATE LINED WITH PAPER
TOWELS. IN A LARGE BOWL, WHISK TOGETHER EGGS,
CREAM, THYME, MUSTARD AND SALT. SEASON WITH
PEPPER. SCATTER HALF THE BREAD CUBES IN PREPARED
BAKING DISH. ARRANGE COOKED BACON, GREEN ONIONS,
APPLES AND 1 CUP (250 ML) OF THE CHEESE ON TOP.
POUR IN HALF THE EGG MIXTURE AND SCATTER WITH THE
REMAINING BREAD. POUR IN THE REMAINING EGG MIXTURE.

SPRINKLE THE REMAINING CHEESE ON TOP. COVER AND REFRIGERATE FOR AT LEAST 4 HOURS OR UP TO 12 HOURS.

PREHEAT OVEN TO 350°F (180°C). BAKE, COVERED, FOR 30 MINUTES. UNCOVER AND BAKE FOR 20 TO 30 MINUTES OR UNTIL PUFFY AND GOLDEN BROWN. SERVES 6.

TIP: STRATAS ARE A GREAT WAY TO USE UP BREAD THAT'S 1 OR 2 DAYS OLD. STALE BREAD LENDS STRUCTURE TO THE STRATA AND PREVENTS IT FROM BECOMING TOO SOGGY.

VARIATION
SUNRISE APPLE SAUSAGE STRATA: REPLACE THE BACON WITH 6 BREAKFAST LINK SAUSAGES, CHOPPED SMALL. BROWN THEM IN A SKILLET BEFORE ADDING THEM TO THE BAKING DISH.

I'M SO OLD THAT BARTENDERS
CHECK MY PULSE INSTEAD OF MY ID.
— LOUISE BOWIE

RUSTIC MUSHROOM HAM TART

SERVE WITH A GREEN SALAD FOR A DELICIOUS
LATE-NIGHT SUPPER — THE BOOK CLUB WILL LOVE IT.

1	PACKAGE (14 OZ/398 G) FROZEN PUFF PASTRY, THAWED	1
3 TBSP	OLIVE OIL, DIVIDED	45 ML
1 CUP	FINELY CHOPPED ONION	250 ML
4 CUPS	SLICED CREMINI OR WHITE MUSHROOMS (SEE TIP, PAGE 229)	1 L
	SALT AND FRESHLY GROUND BLACK PEPPER	
1 TO 2 TBSP	COLD WATER (IF NEEDED)	15 TO 30 ML
2	CLOVES GARLIC, MINCED	2
1/2 TSP	DRIED OREGANO	2 ML
4 OZ	BLACK FOREST DELI HAM, CHOPPED	125 G
3/4 CUP	FRESHLY GRATED PARMESAN CHEESE, DIVIDED	175 ML
1/4 CUP	CHOPPED FRESH PARSLEY (OPTIONAL)	60 ML
2 TBSP	LIGHT SOUR CREAM OR HALF-AND-HALF (10%) CREAM	30 ML
2 TSP	BALSAMIC VINEGAR	10 ML
1/2 CUP	SHREDDED GRUYÈRE OR OTHER SHARP SWISS CHEESE	125 ML

PREHEAT OVEN TO 450°F (230°C). LINE A LARGE BAKING
SHEET WITH PARCHMENT PAPER. ON A LIGHTLY FLOURED
SURFACE, ROLL OUT PASTRY INTO A 12- BY 10-INCH (30 BY
25 CM) RECTANGLE. TRANSFER TO PREPARED BAKING
SHEET. WITH THE TIP OF A PARING KNIFE, LIGHTLY SCORE
A 1/2-INCH (1 CM) WIDE BORDER (DO NOT CUT THROUGH THE
PASTRY) AROUND THE INSIDE EDGES OF THE PASTRY, SO
IT LOOKS LIKE A PICTURE FRAME. BRUSH THE PASTRY WITH

1 TBSP (15 ML) OF THE OIL. BAKE FOR ABOUT 12 MINUTES OR UNTIL PUFFY AND LIGHT BROWN. REMOVE FROM OVEN, LEAVING OVEN ON, AND GENTLY PUSH DOWN THE PUFFED-UP CENTER.

MEANWHILE, IN A LARGE NONSTICK SKILLET, HEAT THE REMAINING OIL OVER MEDIUM HEAT. SAUTÉ ONION FOR ABOUT 5 MINUTES OR UNTIL SOFTENED. ADD MUSHROOMS, $\frac{1}{2}$ TSP (2 ML) SALT AND $\frac{1}{4}$ TSP (1 ML) PEPPER; SAUTÉ FOR 5 TO 7 MINUTES OR UNTIL MUSHROOMS ARE BROWNED. IF THE PAN GETS TOO DRY, ADD COLD WATER AS NEEDED. ADD GARLIC AND OREGANO; SAUTÉ FOR 15 SECONDS OR UNTIL FRAGRANT. REMOVE FROM HEAT AND LET COOL FOR 10 MINUTES. STIR IN HAM, $\frac{1}{2}$ CUP (125 ML) OF THE PARMESAN, PARSLEY, SOUR CREAM AND VINEGAR. TASTE AND ADJUST SEASONING WITH SALT AND PEPPER, IF DESIRED.

SPRINKLE THE REMAINING PARMESAN OVER PARBAKED CRUST. SPREAD MUSHROOM MIXTURE OVER CRUST, LEAVING $\frac{1}{2}$-INCH (1 CM) BORDER. SPRINKLE GRUYÈRE OVER TOP. BAKE FOR 10 TO 12 MINUTES OR UNTIL EDGES OF CRUST ARE GOLDEN BROWN, TOPPING IS HEATED THROUGH AND CHEESE IS MELTED. SERVES 4 TO 6.

MAKE AHEAD: THE MUSHROOM MIXTURE CAN BE PREPARED UP TO 2 DAYS IN ADVANCE. LET COOL, THEN REFRIGERATE IN AN AIRTIGHT CONTAINER.

VARIATION: ADD 12 UNCOOKED THINLY SLICED SLENDER ASPARAGUS STALKS TO THE MUSHROOM MIXTURE BEFORE SPREADING IT ON THE PARBAKED CRUST.

SWEET POTATO AND CHORIZO HASH

THIS HEARTY SKILLET SCRAMBLE IS PERFECT FOR BRUNCH OR A QUICK FAMILY SUPPER. SERVE IT WITH SALSA AND SOUR CREAM ON THE SIDE. USE OTHER VARIETIES OF SAUSAGE, SUCH AS MILD ITALIAN OR HERB, INSTEAD OF THE CHORIZO, IF YOU PREFER. WITH MILDER SAUSAGES, MAPLE SYRUP, APPLESAUCE, MUSTARD OR KETCHUP ARE MORE SUITABLE CONDIMENTS.

2 LBS	SWEET POTATOES, PEELED AND CUT INTO 1-INCH (2.5 CM) CUBES (ABOUT 3 CUPS/750 ML)	500 G
4	FRESH CHORIZO OR HOT ITALIAN SAUSAGES, CASINGS REMOVED, COARSELY CHOPPED	4
1	RED ONION, CHOPPED	1
1	RED BELL PEPPER, CHOPPED	1
2	CLOVES GARLIC, MINCED	2
1/2 CUP	HOMEMADE VEGETABLE STOCK (SEE RECIPE, PAGE 90) OR REDUCED-SODIUM CHICKEN BROTH	125 ML
4	EGGS	4
2 TBSP	CHOPPED FRESH CILANTRO	30 ML

PLACE SWEET POTATOES IN A LARGE POT OF SALTED WATER AND BRING TO A BOIL OVER HIGH HEAT. REDUCE HEAT AND SIMMER FOR ABOUT 4 MINUTES OR UNTIL FORK-TENDER. DRAIN AND SET ASIDE. IN A LARGE NONSTICK SKILLET OVER MEDIUM-HIGH HEAT, SAUTÉ CHORIZO FOR 2 TO 3 MINUTES OR UNTIL IT STARTS TO RELEASE SOME FAT. ADD RED ONION AND RED PEPPER; SAUTÉ FOR ABOUT 5 MINUTES OR UNTIL CHORIZO IS BROWNED AND VEGETABLES ARE SOFTENED. ADD GARLIC

AND SAUTÉ FOR 15 SECONDS OR UNTIL FRAGRANT. REDUCE HEAT TO MEDIUM. STIR IN RESERVED SWEET POTATOES AND STOCK. COOK, WITHOUT STIRRING, FOR ABOUT 4 MINUTES OR UNTIL BOTTOM OF HASH STARTS TO BROWN. WITH A SPATULA, FLIP PORTIONS OF THE HASH, MIXING IN THE BROWNED BITS. LIGHTLY PACK HASH DOWN WITH SPATULA. COOK FOR 6 TO 8 MINUTES, REPEATING THE FLIPPING PROCEDURE A COUPLE OF TIMES, UNTIL POTATOES ARE TENDER, BROWNED AND CARAMELIZED. WITH SPATULA, MAKE 4 INDENTATIONS IN THE HASH. BREAK AN EGG INTO EACH INDENTATION. COVER, REDUCE HEAT TO LOW AND COOK FOR ABOUT 5 MINUTES OR UNTIL EGGS ARE SET (OR UNTIL DESIRED DONENESS). SPRINKLE WITH CILANTRO. CUT INTO 4 WEDGES, WITH AN EGG IN EACH PORTION, AND SERVE IMMEDIATELY. SERVES 4.

TIP: THIS HASH DOESN'T SET LIKE AN OMELET, SO DON'T WORRY IF IT LOOKS A LITTLE RUSTIC WHEN SERVED — ENJOY THE CASUAL DINING EXPERIENCE.

MAKE AHEAD: COOK SWEET POTATOES AS INSTRUCTED. LET COOL AND REFRIGERATE IN AN AIRTIGHT CONTAINER FOR UP TO 2 DAYS.

YOU ONLY LIVE ONCE, BUT IF YOU DO IT RIGHT,
ONCE IS ENOUGH.
— MAE WEST

— LEMON RICOTTA PANCAKES —

THESE ARE THE FLUFFIEST PANCAKES YOU'VE EVER
TASTED. SERVE WITH WARM BLUEBERRY COMPOTE
(PAGE 334) OR MAPLE SYRUP AND FRESH BLUEBERRIES
FOR A SUNDAY MORNING TREAT. OR SIMPLY HEAT
YOUR FAVORITE RASPBERRY, BLACKBERRY OR BLUEBERRY
JAM IN THE MICROWAVE FOR A FEW SECONDS
UNTIL IT IS LOOSE ENOUGH TO POUR.

I CUP	ALL-PURPOSE FLOUR	250 ML
I TBSP	GRANULATED SUGAR	15 ML
1/2 TSP	BAKING SODA	2 ML
1/8 TSP	GROUND NUTMEG	0.5 ML
PINCH	SALT	PINCH
3	EGGS, SEPARATED	3
I CUP	RICOTTA CHEESE	250 ML
I CUP	SOUR CREAM	250 ML
	FINELY GRATED ZEST OF I LEMON	
2 TBSP	FRESHLY SQUEEZED LEMON JUICE	30 ML
	VEGETABLE OIL	

PREHEAT OVEN TO 200°F (100°C). IN A BOWL, WHISK
TOGETHER FLOUR, SUGAR, BAKING SODA, NUTMEG AND
SALT. IN A LARGE BOWL, BEAT EGG YOLKS, RICOTTA AND
SOUR CREAM. IN ANOTHER BOWL, WITH CLEAN BEATERS,
BEAT EGG WHITES UNTIL JUST STIFF. (YOU'LL KNOW THEY
ARE READY BECAUSE YOU'LL BE ABLE TO HOLD THE BOWL
UPSIDE DOWN AND THE EGG WHITES WILL STAY PUT!) ADD
FLOUR MIXTURE TO RICOTTA MIXTURE AND STIR GENTLY
TO JUST COMBINE. STIR IN LEMON ZEST AND LEMON
JUICE. CAREFULLY FOLD IN BEATEN EGG WHITES. (DO NOT

OVERMIX. YOU SHOULD STILL BE ABLE TO SEE FLECKS OF EGG WHITES IN THE BATTER.)

MEANWHILE, IN A LARGE NONSTICK GRIDDLE OR SKILLET, HEAT ABOUT 1 TBSP (15 ML) OIL OVER LOW TO MEDIUM HEAT. POUR ABOUT $\frac{1}{4}$ CUP (60 ML) BATTER ONTO HOT GRIDDLE AND COOK PANCAKE FOR 1 TO 2 MINUTES PER SIDE OR UNTIL LIGHT GOLDEN BROWN. TRANSFER PANCAKE TO AN OVENPROOF PLATE AND KEEP WARM IN OVEN. REPEAT WITH THE REMAINING BATTER, ADDING MORE OIL AND ADJUSTING HEAT AS NECESSARY. MAKES ABOUT 12 PANCAKES.

TIP: RICOTTA IS A FRESH ITALIAN CHEESE THAT RESEMBLES SMOOTH COTTAGE CHEESE. YOU'LL FIND IT IN THE DAIRY AISLE OF THE SUPERMARKET. YOU CAN SUBSTITUTE COTTAGE CHEESE, BUT PURÉE IT IN A BLENDER OR FOOD PROCESSOR UNTIL SMOOTH BEFORE USING IT IN THIS RECIPE. TO USE UP LEFTOVER RICOTTA, TRY MAKING GLAZED ITALIAN COOKIES (PAGE 290).

MAKE AHEAD: LET PANCAKES COOL COMPLETELY. PLACE BETWEEN LAYERS OF WAXED PAPER IN FREEZER BAGS AND FREEZE FOR UP TO 1 MONTH. REHEAT IN THE TOASTER.

MANY A MAN OWES HIS SUCCESS TO HIS FIRST WIFE, AND HIS SECOND WIFE TO HIS SUCCESS.

BAKED APPLE PANCAKE

PUFFY AND GOLDEN WHEN IT COMES OUT OF THE OVEN, THIS SIMPLE, DELICIOUS BRUNCH CLASSIC IS A REAL SHOW-OFF DISH THAT CAN ALSO BE SERVED AS A QUICK DESSERT. SERVE WITH MAPLE SYRUP, CARAMEL SAUCE AND/OR WHIPPED CREAM.

4 TBSP	BUTTER, DIVIDED	60 ML
4 CUPS	THINLY SLICED PEELED CORED TART APPLES, SUCH AS GRANNY SMITH	1 L
2 TBSP	PACKED BROWN SUGAR	30 ML
1 TSP	GROUND CINNAMON	5 ML
$1/8$ TSP	GROUND NUTMEG	0.5 ML
2 TBSP	FRESHLY SQUEEZED LEMON JUICE	30 ML
$1/2$ CUP	TOASTED SLICED OR SLIVERED ALMONDS (OPTIONAL)	125 ML
	CONFECTIONERS' (ICING) SUGAR	

BATTER

1 CUP	ALL-PURPOSE FLOUR	250 ML
1 TBSP	GRANULATED SUGAR	15 ML
PINCH	SALT	PINCH
4	EGGS	4
1 CUP	MILK	250 ML
1 TSP	ALMOND OR VANILLA EXTRACT	5 ML

IN A LARGE NONSTICK SKILLET, MELT HALF THE BUTTER OVER MEDIUM HEAT. SAUTÉ APPLES, FLIPPING OCCASIONALLY, FOR 8 TO 10 MINUTES OR UNTIL JUST TENDER. SPRINKLE WITH BROWN SUGAR, CINNAMON, NUTMEG AND LEMON JUICE; SAUTÉ FOR 2 MINUTES. REMOVE FROM HEAT.

BATTER: PREHEAT OVEN TO 450°F (230°C). IN A LARGE BOWL, WHISK TOGETHER FLOUR, SUGAR, SALT, EGGS, MILK AND ALMOND EXTRACT. (OR PULSE A FEW TIMES IN A FOOD PROCESSOR OR BLENDER.)

PLACE A 13- BY 9-INCH (33 BY 23 CM) METAL BAKING PAN IN THE PREHEATED OVEN FOR 5 MINUTES. (THIS IS IMPORTANT.) REMOVE PAN FROM OVEN, ADD THE REMAINING BUTTER AND SWIRL UNTIL MELTED. SPREAD APPLES EVENLY ON BOTTOM OF PAN. POUR BATTER OVER APPLES. SPRINKLE WITH ALMONDS (IF USING). BAKE UNTIL VERY PUFFY AND BROWNED. SPRINKLE WITH CONFECTIONERS' SUGAR AND SERVE IMMEDIATELY. SERVES 6.

TIP: THIS PANCAKE CONTAINS NO BAKING POWDER OR OTHER LEAVENER. IT RELIES ON THE VERY HOT OVEN TO TURN THE LIQUID INTO STEAM, WHICH CREATES AIR THAT CAUSES THE PANCAKE TO RISE — MUCH LIKE A YORKSHIRE PUDDING. IT'S ESSENTIAL TO USE A METAL BAKING PAN, AS IT HEATS UP FASTER THAN A GLASS OR CERAMIC BAKING DISH. CLASSICALLY, THIS PANCAKE IS BAKED IN A CAST-IRON SKILLET. IF YOU HAVE ONE, USE IT, REDUCING THE OVEN TEMPERATURE TO 425°F (220°C). COOK THE APPLES IN THE CAST-IRON SKILLET ON THE STOVETOP, POUR IN THE BATTER AND THEN BAKE ACCORDING TO THE DIRECTIONS ABOVE.

TIP: ALTHOUGH THIS BAKED APPLE PANCAKE IS BEST EATEN HOT FROM THE OVEN, THE COLD LEFTOVERS MAKE A GREAT TREAT TO TUCK INTO A LUNCHBOX.

SASSY CORNBREAD

SUN-DRIED TOMATOES, PISTACHIOS AND PARMESAN CHEESE PUT A FRESH SPIN ON THIS COUNTRY CLASSIC.

1½ CUPS	ALL-PURPOSE FLOUR	375 ML
1 CUP	YELLOW CORNMEAL	250 ML
½ CUP	FRESHLY GRATED PARMESAN CHEESE	125 ML
¼ CUP	GRANULATED SUGAR OR PACKED BROWN SUGAR	60 ML
3 TBSP	CHOPPED FRESH BASIL (OR 1 TSP/5 ML DRIED)	45 ML
2 TSP	BAKING POWDER	10 ML
½ TSP	SALT	2 ML
¼ TSP	BAKING SODA	1 ML
2	EGGS	2
1 CUP	BUTTERMILK	250 ML
¾ CUP	CANNED CREAMED CORN	175 ML
½ CUP	CHOPPED DRAINED OIL-PACKED SUN-DRIED TOMATOES	125 ML
¼ CUP	BUTTER, MELTED AND COOLED, OR VEGETABLE OIL	60 ML
½ CUP	PISTACHIOS OR PINE NUTS	125 ML

PREHEAT OVEN TO 400°F (200°C). GREASE AN 8-INCH (20 CM) SQUARE BAKING PAN AND LINE BOTTOM WITH PARCHMENT PAPER. IN A BOWL, WHISK TOGETHER FLOUR, CORNMEAL, PARMESAN, SUGAR, BASIL, BAKING POWDER, SALT AND BAKING SODA. IN ANOTHER BOWL, WHISK TOGETHER EGGS, BUTTERMILK, CORN, SUN-DRIED TOMATOES AND BUTTER. ADD WET INGREDIENTS TO DRY INGREDIENTS AND STIR UNTIL JUST COMBINED. STIR IN PISTACHIOS. POUR BATTER INTO PREPARED PAN AND LEVEL THE TOP WITH A SPATULA. BAKE FOR 20 TO 25 MINUTES

OR UNTIL A TESTER INSERTED IN THE CENTER COMES OUT CLEAN. LET COOL IN PAN ON A WIRE RACK FOR 5 MINUTES. CUT INTO 8 SQUARES. SERVE WARM. MAKES 8 SQUARES.

TIP: FOR AN EXTRA-CRUSTY EXTERIOR, BAKE THE CORNBREAD IN A BUTTERED 8-INCH (20 CM) CAST-IRON FRYING PAN.

MAKE AHEAD: LET COOL COMPLETELY AND STORE IN AN AIRTIGHT CONTAINER AT ROOM TEMPERATURE FOR UP TO 2 DAYS. OR WRAP TIGHTLY IN PLASTIC WRAP, PLACE IN AN AIRTIGHT CONTAINER AND FREEZE FOR UP TO 2 WEEKS. TO SERVE, THAW, WRAP IN FOIL AND REHEAT IN 325°F (160°C) OVEN FOR ABOUT 10 MINUTES.

THE TROUBLE WITH LIFE IN THE FAST LANE IS THAT YOU GET TO THE OTHER END IN AN AWFUL HURRY.
— JOHN JENSEN

LAZY DAYS BUTTERMILK BISCUITS

2 CUPS	ALL-PURPOSE FLOUR	500 ML
2 TSP	BAKING POWDER	10 ML
1 TSP	SALT	5 ML
1/2 TSP	BAKING SODA	2 ML
1/3 CUP	COLD UNSALTED BUTTER, ROUGHLY CUT INTO 6 TO 8 PIECES	75 ML
1 1/2 CUPS	BUTTERMILK	375 ML

PREHEAT OVEN TO 450°F (230°C). LIGHTLY GREASE 2 LARGE BAKING SHEETS OR LINE WITH PARCHMENT PAPER. IN A LARGE BOWL, SIFT TOGETHER FLOUR, BAKING POWDER, SALT AND BAKING SODA. ADD BUTTER AND RUB FLOUR MIXTURE THROUGH YOUR FINGERTIPS UNTIL IT RESEMBLES LARGE, COARSE CRUMBS ABOUT THE SIZE OF SMALL PEAS. (ALTERNATIVELY, USE A PASTRY BLENDER OR TWO KNIVES TO CUT IN THE BUTTER.) ADD BUTTERMILK AND MIX WITH A FORK OR SPATULA JUST UNTIL DRY INGREDIENTS ARE MOISTENED. DO NOT OVERMIX. DROP BY HEAPING DESSERTSPOONFULS (THE KIND IN YOUR CUTLERY DRAWER) ONTO PREPARED BAKING SHEETS, SPACING THEM ABOUT 3 INCHES (7.5 CM) APART. BAKE IN UPPER AND LOWER THIRDS OF PREHEATED OVEN FOR 12 TO 15 MINUTES, SWITCHING PANS ON RACKS HALFWAY THROUGH, UNTIL PUFFY AND LIGHTLY BROWNED. SERVE IMMEDIATELY. MAKES ABOUT 12 BISCUITS.

TIP: DON'T TRY TO SUBSTITUTE ANYTHING FOR THE BUTTERMILK — IT'S WHAT MAKES THESE BISCUITS SO GOOD. ALSO, IT'S IMPORTANT TO USE COLD BUTTER AND TO BAKE IMMEDIATELY AFTER MIXING; OTHERWISE, THE DOUGH WILL SPREAD AND WON'T RISE AS WELL.

AWESOME APPLE PECAN COFFEE CAKE

THIS SCRUMPTIOUS CAKE IS BEST FRESH FROM THE OVEN — YOUR BRUNCH GUESTS WILL RAVE.

2 CUPS	ALL-PURPOSE FLOUR	500 ML
2 TSP	BAKING POWDER	10 ML
I TSP	GROUND CINNAMON	5 ML
¼ TSP	SALT	I ML
⅛ TSP	GROUND NUTMEG	0.5 ML
⅛ TSP	GROUND CARDAMOM (OPTIONAL)	0.5 ML
1¾ CUPS	GRANULATED SUGAR	425 ML
3	EGGS, AT ROOM TEMPERATURE (SEE TIP, PAGE 289)	3
I CUP	BUTTER, MELTED AND COOLED	250 ML
I TSP	VANILLA EXTRACT	5 ML
5	GALA OR GOLDEN DELICIOUS APPLES, PEELED AND CHOPPED	5
I CUP	CHOPPED PECANS	250 ML

PREHEAT OVEN TO 350°F (180°C). GREASE A 13- BY 9-INCH (33 BY 23 CM) BAKING PAN AND LINE WITH PARCHMENT PAPER. IN A LARGE BOWL, SIFT TOGETHER FLOUR, BAKING POWDER, CINNAMON, SALT, NUTMEG AND CARDAMOM. IN ANOTHER LARGE BOWL, WHISK TOGETHER SUGAR AND EGGS. WHISK IN BUTTER AND VANILLA. POUR EGG MIXTURE OVER FLOUR MIXTURE. SPRINKLE WITH APPLES AND PECANS. STIR UNTIL JUST MOISTENED. SPREAD IN PREPARED PAN, LEVELING THE TOP WITH A SPATULA. BAKE FOR 35 TO 40 MINUTES OR UNTIL GOLDEN BROWN AND A TESTER INSERTED IN THE CENTER COMES OUT CLEAN. LET COOL IN PAN ON A WIRE RACK FOR 20 MINUTES. CUT INTO BARS. MAKES ABOUT 12 GENEROUS BARS.

RHUBARB GINGER STREUSEL COFFEE CAKE

MAKE THIS CAKE WHEN YOUR RHUBARB PATCH (OR YOUR NEIGHBOR'S) IS FLOURISHING, BECAUSE IT DOESN'T WORK WITH FROZEN RHUBARB. YOU CAN SUBSTITUTE OTHER RIPE SEASONAL FRUITS, SUCH AS PEACHES, PLUMS OR PEARS. THIS CAKE IS BEST EATEN WARM THE DAY IT IS MADE. SERVE WITH WHIPPED CREAM OR ICE CREAM.

4 CUPS	CHOPPED RHUBARB	1 L
2 TBSP	GRANULATED SUGAR	30 ML

BASE

3/4 CUP	ALL-PURPOSE FLOUR	175 ML
1 TSP	BAKING POWDER	5 ML
1 TSP	BAKING SODA	5 ML
1 TSP	GROUND GINGER	5 ML
PINCH	GROUND NUTMEG	PINCH
3/4 CUP	GRANULATED SUGAR	175 ML
3/4 CUP	BUTTER, SOFTENED (SEE TIP, PAGE 289)	175 ML
2	EGGS, AT ROOM TEMPERATURE	2
2 TBSP	SOUR CREAM (SEE TIP, OPPOSITE)	30 ML

STREUSEL TOPPING

2/3 CUP	PANKO (SEE TIP, PAGE 319) OR DRY BREAD CRUMBS	150 ML
1/3 CUP	ALL-PURPOSE FLOUR	75 ML
1/3 CUP	PACKED BROWN SUGAR	75 ML
1/3 CUP	CHOPPED TOASTED PECANS (SEE TIP, PAGE 127)	75 ML
1/3 CUP	BUTTER, MELTED AND COOLED	75 ML

PREHEAT OVEN TO 375°F (190°C). GREASE A 10-INCH (25 CM) SPRINGFORM PAN AND LINE THE BOTTOM WITH PARCHMENT PAPER. WRAP FOIL UNDER THE BOTTOM AND UP THE SIDES OF THE PAN TO PREVENT LEAKS. SET PREPARED PAN ON A LARGE BAKING SHEET. IN A LARGE BOWL, TOSS RHUBARB WITH SUGAR. SET ASIDE.

BASE: IN A BOWL, WHISK TOGETHER FLOUR, BAKING POWDER, BAKING SODA, GINGER AND NUTMEG. IN ANOTHER BOWL, CREAM SUGAR AND BUTTER UNTIL LIGHT AND FLUFFY. BEAT IN EGGS, ONE AT A TIME. STIR IN FLOUR MIXTURE ALTERNATELY WITH SOUR CREAM, MAKING THREE ADDITIONS OF FLOUR AND TWO OF CREAM. SPREAD BATTER OVER BOTTOM OF PREPARED PAN. SPOON RHUBARB MIXTURE OVER BATTER.

STREUSEL TOPPING: IN A BOWL, COMBINE PANKO, FLOUR, BROWN SUGAR, PECANS AND BUTTER. THE MIXTURE WILL CLUMP SLIGHTLY. SPRINKLE OVER RHUBARB.

BAKE FOR 45 TO 60 MINUTES OR UNTIL TOPPING IS GOLDEN BROWN AND CRISPY AND RHUBARB IS TENDER. (IF TOPPING STARTS TO BROWN TOO MUCH, COVER PAN LOOSELY WITH FOIL.) LET COOL IN PAN ON A WIRE RACK FOR AT LEAST 20 MINUTES. RELEASE SPRING AND UNMOLD CAKE. SERVE WARM. SERVES 8.

TIP: YOU CAN USE FAT-FREE, LOW-FAT OR REGULAR SOUR CREAM TO MAKE THIS CAKE.

APPROACH LOVE AND COOKING WITH RECKLESS ABANDON.

APPLE BLUEBERRY BRAN MUFFINS

THESE MUFFINS ARE SO GOOD — AND SO GOOD FOR YOU.

1 1/2 CUPS	NATURAL BRAN	375 ML
1 CUP	ALL-PURPOSE FLOUR	250 ML
1/2 CUP	PACKED BROWN SUGAR	125 ML
1 1/2 TSP	BAKING POWDER	7 ML
1 TSP	GROUND CINNAMON	5 ML
1/2 TSP	BAKING SODA	2 ML
1/4 TSP	GROUND NUTMEG	1 ML
PINCH	SALT	PINCH
2	EGGS	2
1 CUP	UNSWEETENED APPLESAUCE	250 ML
1/2 CUP	PLAIN OR VANILLA-FLAVORED YOGURT	125 ML
1/2 CUP	BUTTER, MELTED, OR VEGETABLE OIL	125 ML
1 1/2 CUPS	FRESH OR FROZEN BLUEBERRIES (NO NEED TO THAW)	375 ML

PREHEAT OVEN TO 400°F (200°C). GREASE A 12-CUP MUFFIN PAN OR LINE WITH PAPER LINERS. IN A LARGE BOWL, WHISK TOGETHER BRAN, FLOUR, BROWN SUGAR, BAKING POWDER, CINNAMON, BAKING SODA, NUTMEG AND SALT. IN ANOTHER BOWL, BEAT EGGS, APPLESAUCE, YOGURT AND BUTTER. POUR EGG MIXTURE OVER FLOUR MIXTURE AND STIR UNTIL JUST COMBINED. GENTLY STIR IN BLUEBERRIES. SPOON INTO PREPARED MUFFIN CUPS, DIVIDING EQUALLY. BAKE FOR 15 TO 18 MINUTES OR UNTIL A TESTER INSERTED IN THE CENTER OF A MUFFIN COMES OUT CLEAN. *MAKES 12 MUFFINS.*

COCONUT PINEAPPLE MUFFINS

EXOTIC ISLAND FLAVORS COMBINE
IN A SWEET AND MOIST MUFFIN.

1½ CUPS	ALL-PURPOSE FLOUR	375 ML
1 CUP	UNSWEETENED SHREDDED COCONUT, TOASTED (SEE TIP, PAGE 127)	250 ML
½ CUP	GRANULATED SUGAR	125 ML
1½ TSP	BAKING POWDER	7 ML
½ TSP	BAKING SODA	2 ML
¼ TSP	SALT	1 ML
2	EGGS	2
¾ CUP	COCONUT MILK (SEE TIP, PAGE 209)	175 ML
¼ CUP	BUTTER, MELTED, OR VEGETABLE OIL	60 ML
1 TSP	VANILLA EXTRACT	5 ML
	FINELY GRATED ZEST AND JUICE OF 1 LIME	
1 CUP	CHOPPED DRIED PINEAPPLE	250 ML

PREHEAT OVEN TO 400°F (200°C). GREASE A 12-CUP MUFFIN PAN OR LINE WITH PAPER LINERS. IN A LARGE BOWL, WHISK TOGETHER FLOUR, COCONUT, SUGAR, BAKING POWDER, BAKING SODA AND SALT. IN ANOTHER BOWL, WHISK TOGETHER EGGS, COCONUT MILK, BUTTER, VANILLA, LIME ZEST AND LIME JUICE. POUR EGG MIXTURE OVER FLOUR MIXTURE AND STIR UNTIL JUST COMBINED. GENTLY STIR IN PINEAPPLE. SPOON INTO PREPARED MUFFIN CUPS, DIVIDING EQUALLY. BAKE FOR 15 TO 18 MINUTES OR UNTIL A TESTER INSERTED IN THE CENTER OF A MUFFIN COMES OUT CLEAN. MAKES 12 MUFFINS.

CAPPUCCINO MUFFINS

*THESE SWEET MUFFINS WILL
START YOUR DAY OFF RIGHT.*

TOPPING

1/4 CUP	ALL-PURPOSE FLOUR	60 ML
3 TBSP	PACKED BROWN SUGAR	45 ML
PINCH	GROUND NUTMEG	PINCH
2 TBSP	BUTTER, MELTED AND SLIGHTLY COOLED	30 ML

BATTER

2 CUPS	ALL-PURPOSE FLOUR	500 ML
1/2 CUP	GRANULATED SUGAR	125 ML
1/2 CUP	PACKED BROWN SUGAR	125 ML
2 TSP	BAKING POWDER	10 ML
1 TSP	GROUND CINNAMON	5 ML
PINCH	SALT	PINCH
3 TBSP	INSTANT COFFEE GRANULES	45 ML
2 TSP	COLD WATER	10 ML
1	EGG	1
1 CUP	MILK	250 ML
1/2 CUP	BUTTER, MELTED (SEE TIP, OPPOSITE), OR VEGETABLE OIL	125 ML
1 CUP	WHITE CHOCOLATE CHIPS	250 ML

PREHEAT OVEN TO 375°F (190°C). GREASE A 12-CUP MUFFIN PAN OR LINE WITH PAPER LINERS.

TOPPING: IN A SMALL BOWL, WHISK TOGETHER FLOUR, BROWN SUGAR AND NUTMEG. STIR IN BUTTER. SET ASIDE.

BATTER: IN A LARGE BOWL, WHISK TOGETHER FLOUR, GRANULATED SUGAR, BROWN SUGAR, BAKING POWDER,

CINNAMON AND SALT. IN A MEDIUM BOWL, COMBINE COFFEE AND COLD WATER, STIRRING UNTIL DISSOLVED. ADD EGG, MILK AND BUTTER; WHISK UNTIL BLENDED. POUR COFFEE MIXTURE OVER FLOUR MIXTURE AND STIR UNTIL JUST COMBINED. STIR IN WHITE CHOCOLATE CHIPS. SPOON INTO PREPARED MUFFIN CUPS, DIVIDING EQUALLY. SPRINKLE TOPPING OVER MUFFINS. BAKE FOR 20 TO 25 MINUTES OR UNTIL A TESTER INSERTED IN THE CENTER OF A MUFFIN COMES OUT CLEAN. MAKES 12 MUFFINS.

TIP: TO MELT BUTTER, PLACE IN A MICROWAVE-SAFE MEASURING JUG OR BOWL AND HEAT IN 20-SECOND INCREMENTS UNTIL MELTED.

MAKE AHEAD: LET MUFFINS COOL COMPLETELY, TRANSFER TO AN AIRTIGHT CONTAINER AND STORE AT ROOM TEMPERATURE FOR UP TO 2 DAYS, OR WRAP INDIVIDUALLY IN PLASTIC WRAP AND FREEZE FOR UP TO 2 WEEKS.

DANCE AS THOUGH NO ONE WHO IS
QUALIFIED TO COMMIT YOU IS WATCHING.

CHEESE AND ONION MUFFINS

A HANDFUL OF SAVORY SATISFACTION TO NIBBLE WITH YOUR MID-MORNING COFFEE OR LUNCHTIME SOUP. BEST SERVED WARM FROM THE OVEN OR REHEATED FOR 20 SECONDS IN THE MICROWAVE.

1	PACKET (1 OZ/28 G) ONION SOUP MIX	1
1 CUP	MILK	250 ML
1½ CUPS	ALL-PURPOSE FLOUR	375 ML
1 TBSP	BAKING POWDER	15 ML
1 TBSP	GRANULATED SUGAR	15 ML
1 CUP	SHREDDED SHARP (OLD) CHEDDAR CHEESE	250 ML
1	EGG, LIGHTLY BEATEN	1
¼ CUP	VEGETABLE OIL	60 ML
¼ CUP	FRESHLY GRATED PARMESAN CHEESE	60 ML

PREHEAT OVEN TO 375°F (190°C). GREASE A 12-CUP MUFFIN PAN OR LINE WITH PAPER LINERS. IN A BOWL, WHISK TOGETHER ONION SOUP MIX AND MILK; SET ASIDE FOR 5 MINUTES. IN ANOTHER BOWL, WHISK TOGETHER FLOUR, BAKING POWDER AND SUGAR. STIR IN CHEDDAR. WHISK EGG AND OIL INTO ONION MIXTURE. POUR ONION MIXTURE OVER FLOUR MIXTURE AND STIR UNTIL JUST COMBINED. SPOON INTO PREPARED MUFFIN CUPS, DIVIDING EQUALLY. (THE MIXTURE MIGHT FILL ONLY 11 CUPS; IF SO, HALF-FILL THE EMPTY CUP WITH WATER.) SPRINKLE PARMESAN OVER MUFFINS. BAKE FOR ABOUT 15 MINUTES OR UNTIL GOLDEN BROWN. MAKES 11 OR 12 MUFFINS.

VARIATION: BAKE IN A 24-CUP MINI MUFFIN PAN AND SERVE AS APPETIZERS. REDUCE THE BAKING TIME TO 10 TO 12 MINUTES.

APPETIZERS

SAUSAGE PUFFS

THESE BITE-SIZED APPETIZERS ARE GREAT BEER FOOD. SERVE THEM WARM BY THEMSELVES OR WITH A DOLLOP OF YOUR FAVORITE PLUM SAUCE.

1	PACKAGE (14 OZ/398 G) FROZEN PUFF PASTRY, THAWED (SEE TIP, OPPOSITE)	1
8	MILD OR HOT ITALIAN SAUSAGES, CASINGS REMOVED BUT SAUSAGES LEFT WHOLE	8
1	EGG, LIGHTLY BEATEN	1

PREHEAT OVEN TO 375°F (190°C). LINE 2 LARGE BAKING SHEETS WITH PARCHMENT PAPER. CUT THE BLOCK OF PASTRY IN HALF (THERE IS USUALLY A LINE DOWN THE MIDDLE). ON A FLOURED SURFACE, ROLL OUT EACH OF THE PASTRY HALVES TO A 10-INCH (25 CM) SQUARE. IF NECESSARY, TRIM EDGES TO MAKE THEM NEAT. USING A SHARP KNIFE, CUT SQUARES IN HALF WIDTHWISE SO YOU HAVE FOUR 10- BY 5-INCH (15 BY 12.5 CM) PIECES WITH THE LONG SIDES FACING YOU. PLACE 2 SAUSAGES END TO END ALONG THE LONG SIDE OF ONE STRIP, LEAVING A $\frac{1}{2}$-INCH (1 CM) BORDER AT THE BOTTOM. IF NECESSARY, GENTLY SQUEEZE THE SAUSAGES TO MAKE THEM FIT THE LENGTH OF THE PASTRY. FOLD BOTTOM OF PASTRY UP ONTO SAUSAGES, THEN ROLL UP. BRUSH TOP EDGE OF PASTRY STRIP WITH EGG AND PRESS GENTLY TO SEAL. TURN SEALED EDGE DOWN AND BRUSH TOP WITH EGG. CUT INTO 8 PIECES. REPEAT WITH THE REMAINING PASTRY AND SAUSAGES. PLACE ON PREPARED BAKING SHEETS, SEAM SIDE DOWN AND ABOUT 1 INCH (2.5 CM) APART. BAKE

FOR 20 TO 25 MINUTES OR UNTIL PUFFED AND GOLDEN. IMMEDIATELY TRANSFER SAUSAGE PUFFS FROM THE PANS TO WIRE RACKS AND LET COOL SLIGHTLY. MAKES 32 PUFFS.

TIP: THAW PUFF PASTRY IN ITS ORIGINAL PACKAGING OVERNIGHT IN THE REFRIGERATOR. DO NOT ATTEMPT TO DEFROST IT IN THE MICROWAVE, AS THIS WILL CAUSE IT TO BECOME GLUEY. SOME PACKAGES MAY BE SLIGHTLY LARGER THAN 14 OZ (398 G), BUT WILL WORK FINE IN THIS RECIPE; THE PASTRY WILL JUST BE A LITTLE THICKER.

MAKE AHEAD: AFTER ASSEMBLING THE SAUSAGE PUFFS, PLACE THEM BETWEEN LAYERS OF WAXED PAPER IN AN AIRTIGHT CONTAINER AND REFRIGERATE FOR UP TO 1 DAY. OR BAKE, LET COOL AND FREEZE IN AN AIRTIGHT CONTAINER FOR UP TO 1 MONTH. REHEAT FROM FROZEN IN A PREHEATED 425°F (220°C) OVEN FOR ABOUT 20 MINUTES.

VARIATION: USE A GOOD-QUALITY HERB SAUSAGE OR ANOTHER FLAVORED SAUSAGE. REMEMBER TO REMOVE THE CASINGS.

AHHH, A NEW BABY: NO MORE HOT DINNERS
AND NO MORE COLD DRINKS!

CRANBERRY PECAN TURKEY MEATBALLS

PERFECT — A YUMMY MEATBALL AND SAUCE APPETIZER. ALWAYS A HIT WITH THE YOUNG CROWD AND MANY GROWN-UPS TOO!

CRANBERRY SAUCE

2 CUPS	UNSWEETENED CRANBERRY JUICE	500 ML
2 TBSP	PACKED BROWN SUGAR	30 ML
PINCH	CAYENNE PEPPER	PINCH
I TBSP	PORT, DRY SHERRY OR BRANDY (OPTIONAL)	15 ML

MEATBALLS

2	CLOVES GARLIC, MINCED	2
1/4 CUP	DRY BREAD CRUMBS OR CRACKER CRUMBS	60 ML
2 TBSP	DRIED CRANBERRIES, FINELY CHOPPED	30 ML
2 TBSP	CHOPPED FRESH SAGE (OR I TSP/5 ML DRIED CRUMBLED SAGE)	30 ML
I TSP	SALT	5 ML
1/4 TSP	FRESHLY GROUND BLACK PEPPER	I ML
I	EGG, BEATEN	I
I LB	LEAN GROUND TURKEY	500 G
I CUP	FINELY CHOPPED TOASTED PECANS (SEE TIP, PAGE 127)	250 ML

CRANBERRY SAUCE: IN A MEDIUM SAUCEPAN, BRING CRANBERRY JUICE TO A BOIL OVER HIGH HEAT. REDUCE HEAT AND SIMMER FOR ABOUT 30 MINUTES OR UNTIL JUICE IS REDUCED BY ABOUT THREE-QUARTERS. ADD BROWN SUGAR, CAYENNE AND PORT, STIRRING UNTIL SUGAR IS DISSOLVED. SET ASIDE. (AT THIS POINT, THE

SAUCE CAN BE COOLED, TRANSFERRED TO AN AIRTIGHT CONTAINER AND REFRIGERATED FOR UP TO 5 DAYS.)

MEATBALLS: PREHEAT OVEN TO 375°F (190°C). LINE A LARGE BAKING SHEET WITH PARCHMENT PAPER OR GREASED FOIL. IN A LARGE BOWL, WHISK TOGETHER GARLIC, BREAD CRUMBS, CRANBERRIES, SAGE, SALT, PEPPER AND EGG; LET STAND FOR 5 MINUTES. ADD GROUND TURKEY AND, USING CLEAN HANDS, MIX THOROUGHLY. SHAPE INTO 30 MEATBALLS. ROLL MEATBALLS IN PECANS, PRESSING LIGHTLY TO ADHERE. DISCARD ANY EXCESS PECANS. PLACE MEATBALLS IN A SINGLE LAYER ON PREPARED BAKING SHEET. BAKE FOR 15 TO 20 MINUTES, TURNING ONCE, UNTIL NO LONGER PINK INSIDE.

MEANWHILE, POUR CRANBERRY SAUCE INTO A LARGE NONSTICK SKILLET AND BRING TO A BOIL OVER HIGH HEAT. REDUCE HEAT AND SIMMER FOR 2 OR 3 MINUTES OR UNTIL SAUCE IS SYRUPY AND WILL LIGHTLY COAT THE BACK OF A SPOON. ADD MEATBALLS AND TOSS TO COAT. TRANSFER TO A WARM SERVING DISH, DRIZZLING SAUCE OVER TOP. MAKES 30 MEATBALLS.

MAKE AHEAD: PLACE COOKED AND COOLED MEATBALLS ON A FOIL-LINED BAKING SHEET AND FREEZE, UNCOVERED, FOR ABOUT 2 HOURS OR UNTIL HARD. TRANSFER TO FREEZER BAGS, SEAL TIGHTLY AND FREEZE FOR UP TO 3 WEEKS. THAW IN THE REFRIGERATOR AND REHEAT BY SIMMERING MEATBALLS IN CRANBERRY SAUCE.

QUIT WORRYING ABOUT YOUR HEALTH. IT WILL GO AWAY.
– ROBERT ORBEN

SHRIMP WITH ROMESCO SAUCE

ROMESCO SAUCE

3 TBSP	OLIVE OIL, DIVIDED	45 ML
2	CLOVES GARLIC, HALVED	2
1/2 CUP	FINELY CHOPPED ONION	125 ML
1 TSP	SWEET SMOKED PAPRIKA (SEE TIP, OPPOSITE)	5 ML
PINCH	CAYENNE PEPPER	PINCH
1	SLICE WHITE BREAD (SUCH AS SANDWICH, FRENCH OR ITALIAN), WITH CRUST, TOASTED AND TORN INTO COARSE CHUNKS	1
1	CLOVE GARLIC, MINCED	1
1	ROASTED RED BELL PEPPER (SEE TIP, PAGE 54), DRAINED AND COARSELY CHOPPED	1
1	LARGE TOMATO, COARSELY CHOPPED	1
1/2 CUP	SLIVERED OR SLICED ALMONDS, TOASTED	125 ML
3 TBSP	CHOPPED FRESH PARSLEY	45 ML
1/2 TSP	SALT	2 ML
2 TBSP	SHERRY VINEGAR OR RED WINE VINEGAR	30 ML
1 TO 2 TSP	LIQUID HONEY (OPTIONAL)	5 TO 10 ML

SHRIMP

2 LBS	EXTRA-LARGE SHRIMP (21 TO 25 COUNT), PEELED WITH TAILS LEFT ON AND DEVEINED, THAWED IF FROZEN	1 KG
2 TSP	SALT	10 ML

ROMESCO SAUCE: IN A LARGE NONSTICK SKILLET, HEAT 1 TBSP (15 ML) OF THE OIL OVER MEDIUM HEAT. SAUTÉ GARLIC HALVES AND ONION FOR 5 TO 7 MINUTES OR UNTIL SOFTENED AND GOLDEN. ADD PAPRIKA AND CAYENNE; SAUTÉ FOR 30 SECONDS OR UNTIL FRAGRANT. TRANSFER TO A FOOD PROCESSOR OR

CONTINUED ON PAGE 37...

Sweet Potato and Chorizo Hash (page 14)

Lemon Ricotta Pancakes (page 16)

Asparagus Parmesan Bites (page 40)

Artichoke Lemon Bruschetta (page 46)

BLENDER. ADD BREAD CHUNKS, MINCED GARLIC, ROASTED PEPPER, TOMATO, ALMONDS, PARSLEY, SALT, THE REMAINING OIL AND VINEGAR; PROCESS UNTIL A PASTE FORMS. TRANSFER TO AN AIRTIGHT CONTAINER AND REFRIGERATE FOR AT LEAST 24 HOURS OR FOR UP TO 2 DAYS.

SHRIMP: PLACE SHRIMP IN A SINGLE LAYER IN A LARGE, SHALLOW BOWL OR BAKING DISH. SPRINKLE WITH SALT. IN A KETTLE OR LARGE SAUCEPAN, BRING 8 CUPS (2 L) WATER TO A FULL ROLLING BOIL OVER HIGH HEAT. POUR BOILING WATER OVER SHRIMP, ENSURING THEY ARE IMMERSED. COVER AND LET STAND FOR 5 TO 7 MINUTES OR UNTIL SHRIMP ARE PINK AND OPAQUE. IF ANY GRAY PATCHES REMAIN ON SHRIMP, TOP UP BOWL WITH BOILING WATER AND STIR GENTLY UNTIL ALL SHRIMP ARE PINK. DRAIN INTO A COLANDER AND COOL UNDER COLD RUNNING WATER. TRANSFER TO AN AIRTIGHT CONTAINER AND REFRIGERATE FOR AT LEAST I HOUR OR FOR UP TO 24 HOURS.

BEFORE SERVING, TASTE THE SAUCE AND ADJUST THE SEASONING AS NECESSARY WITH SALT AND CAYENNE. IF DESIRED, SWEETEN WITH HONEY TO TASTE. (THE SWEETNESS WILL DEPEND ON THE QUALITY OF THE VINEGAR.) TRANSFER SAUCE TO A SMALL BOWL. SET BOWL ON A SERVING PLATTER AND ARRANGE CHILLED SHRIMP AROUND IT. SERVES A CROWD.

TIP: SPANISH SMOKED PAPRIKA LENDS A WARM, SMOKY BACON FLAVOR TO FOOD. IT COMES IN THREE LEVELS OF INTENSITY: SWEET, BITTERSWEET AND HOT. IT IS AVAILABLE ON THE SPICE SHELF AT MOST MAJOR SUPERMARKETS. YOU CAN SUBSTITUTE REGULAR SWEET PAPRIKA IN THIS RECIPE, BUT EXPECT A MILDER RESULT.

DIVINE DEVILED EGGS

THE SECRET TO DEVILED EGGS IS TO KEEP THE FILLING SIMPLE AND GARNISH WITH BIG FLAVORS. NOW YOU'RE ABOUT TO LEARN HOW TO PRODUCE THE PERFECT HARD-COOKED EGG.

12	EGGS	12
1/2 CUP	LIGHT OR REGULAR MAYONNAISE	125 ML
1 TBSP	FRESHLY SQUEEZED LEMON JUICE	15 ML
1 TSP	DIJON MUSTARD	5 ML
	SALT, CAYENNE PEPPER AND FRESHLY GROUND WHITE PEPPER	
	PAPRIKA	
	FINELY CHOPPED SMOKED SALMON, HAM, OLIVES AND/OR CAPERS	
	FINELY CHOPPED FRESH DILL, CHIVES OR TARRAGON	
	ALFALFA OR BROCCOLI SPROUTS	

PLACE EGGS IN A SINGLE LAYER IN A LARGE SAUCEPAN OF COLD WATER. BRING WATER TO A BOIL OVER HIGH HEAT. IMMEDIATELY REMOVE FROM HEAT AND COVER. LET STAND FOR 15 MINUTES. GENTLY DRAIN INTO A COLANDER. TAP EGGS LIGHTLY WITH A SPOON TO CRACK SHELLS. TRANSFER EGGS TO A LARGE BOWL AND SET UNDER GENTLY RUNNING COLD WATER FOR 2 MINUTES. LET STAND IN COLD WATER FOR 5 MINUTES. PEEL EGGS. CAREFULLY CUT EGGS IN HALF LENGTHWISE AND REMOVE THE YOLKS, LEAVING WHITES INTACT. (NOW CONGRATULATE YOURSELF — THERE'S NO GRAY RING ON THE YOLKS!) PLACE WHITES CUT SIDE UP ON A WORK SURFACE. USING THE SMALLEST HOLES OF A BOX GRATER,

GRATE YOLKS INTO A BOWL. (OR MASH THEM WITH A FORK, BUT THE FILLING WON'T BE AS SMOOTH.) IF ONE OR TWO WHITES HAVE BROKEN, GRATE THEM WITH THE YOLKS. STIR IN MAYONNAISE, LEMON JUICE AND MUSTARD. SEASON TO TASTE WITH SALT, CAYENNE AND WHITE PEPPER. SPOON OR PIPE YOLK FILLING INTO WHITES, MOUNDING SLIGHTLY. DUST WITH PAPRIKA. GARNISH WITH YOUR CHOICE OF TOPPINGS AND HERBS. ARRANGE ON A BED OF ALFALFA SPROUTS ON A SERVING PLATTER. MAKES 24 PIECES.

TIP: FOR A SNAPPIER PRESENTATION, REMOVE RESIDUAL SPECKS OF YOLK FROM THE WHITES BY GENTLY RINSING THEM IN COLD WATER. TURN THEM CUT SIDE DOWN ON PAPER TOWELS TO DRAIN BEFORE FILLING.

MAKE AHEAD: COOK THE EGGS AND MAKE THE YOLK FILLING. TRANSFER WHITES TO ONE AIRTIGHT CONTAINER AND FILLING TO ANOTHER; REFRIGERATE FOR UP TO 24 HOURS. ALTERNATIVELY, THE EGGS CAN BE FILLED, COVERED AND REFRIGERATED FOR UP TO 6 HOURS.

VARIATION: STIR $\frac{1}{4}$ CUP (60 ML) FRESHLY GRATED PARMESAN CHEESE INTO THE YOLK MIXTURE BEFORE FILLING THE WHITES.

A FOOL AND HIS MONEY ARE MY KIND OF GUY.

ASPARAGUS PARMESAN BITES

*THESE ELEGANT PUFF PASTRY NIBBLES
ARE OUR NEW FAVORITE APPETIZER.*

3 TBSP	OLIVE OIL, DIVIDED	45 ML
10	THIN ASPARAGUS SPEARS, TRIMMED AND CUT INTO 1/2-INCH (1 CM) LONG PIECES	10
1	SHALLOT OR SMALL ONION, FINELY CHOPPED	1
1/4 TSP	SALT, DIVIDED	1 ML
	FRESHLY GROUND BLACK PEPPER	
1/3 CUP	FRESHLY GRATED PARMESAN CHEESE, DIVIDED	75 ML
2 TBSP	MASCARPONE OR CREAM CHEESE, SOFTENED	30 ML
1 TSP	FINELY GRATED LEMON ZEST	5 ML
1/2	PACKAGE (14 OZ/398 G) FROZEN PUFF PASTRY, THAWED (SEE TIP, PAGE 33)	1/2

PREHEAT OVEN TO 375°F (190°C). LINE 2 LARGE BAKING
SHEETS WITH PARCHMENT PAPER. IN A NONSTICK
SKILLET, HEAT 1 TBSP (15 ML) OF THE OIL OVER MEDIUM
HEAT. SAUTÉ ASPARAGUS AND SHALLOT FOR ABOUT
3 MINUTES OR UNTIL ASPARAGUS IS TENDER-CRISP.
SEASON WITH 1/8 TSP (0.5 ML) SALT AND PEPPER
TO TASTE. TRANSFER TO A PLATE AND LET COOL
COMPLETELY. IN A BOWL, COMBINE 3 TBSP (45 ML) OF
THE PARMESAN, MASCARPONE, LEMON ZEST AND THE
REMAINING SALT. SEASON WITH PEPPER TO TASTE. ON
A LIGHTLY FLOURED SURFACE, ROLL OUT PASTRY TO A
10-INCH (25 CM) SQUARE. IF NECESSARY, TRIM EDGES TO

MAKE IT NEAT. USING A SHARP KNIFE, CUT INTO 2-INCH (5 CM) SQUARES. SPREAD CHEESE MIXTURE OVER PASTRY SQUARES, LEAVING A NARROW BORDER. DIVIDE ASPARAGUS MIXTURE AMONG PASTRY SQUARES. USING A SPATULA, TRANSFER TO PREPARED BAKING SHEETS. DRIZZLE SQUARES WITH ABOUT $\frac{1}{4}$ TSP (1 ML) OF THE REMAINING OIL PER SQUARE. BAKE FOR 20 TO 25 MINUTES OR UNTIL CRISP AND BROWN. SPRINKLE WITH THE REMAINING PARMESAN. SERVE WARM OR AT ROOM TEMPERATURE. MAKES 25 PIECES.

SWEET AND SALTY BACON BITES

THESE ARE GREAT WITH BEER. MAKE LOTS.

1	PACKAGE (12 OZ/375 G) PORK BREAKFAST SAUSAGE LINKS (ABOUT 14 SAUSAGES)	1
14	SLICES BACON	14
$\frac{3}{4}$ CUP	PACKED BROWN SUGAR	175 ML

PREHEAT OVEN TO 350°F (180°C). LINE 2 LARGE BAKING SHEETS WITH GREASED FOIL. CUT SAUSAGES AND BACON IN HALF CROSSWISE. WRAP EACH SAUSAGE HALF IN A PIECE OF BACON, OVERLAPPING THE BACON AT THE END. PRESS TO SEAL. PLACE BROWN SUGAR IN A SHALLOW DISH. GENTLY PRESS AND ROLL WRAPPED SAUSAGES IN SUGAR. ARRANGE IN A SINGLE LAYER ON PREPARED BAKING SHEETS. BAKE FOR 30 TO 40 MINUTES OR UNTIL BROWN AND NICELY STICKY. SERVE IMMEDIATELY. MAKES 28 PIECES.

SWEET POTATO SAMOSAS

SERVE WARM WITH YOUR FAVORITE MANGO CHUTNEY.

I	LARGE SWEET POTATO (ABOUT 1¼ LBS/625 G)	I
I TBSP	VEGETABLE OIL	15 ML
½ CUP	FINELY CHOPPED ONION	125 ML
2	CLOVES GARLIC, MINCED	2
2 TSP	GRATED GINGERROOT	10 ML
2 TBSP	MILD OR MEDIUM INDIAN CURRY PASTE (SEE TIP, PAGE 109)	30 ML
2 TBSP	COLD WATER	30 ML
½ CUP	FROZEN BABY PEAS, THAWED	125 ML
2 TBSP	CHOPPED FRESH CILANTRO	30 ML
I TBSP	LIQUID HONEY	15 ML
	SALT (OPTIONAL)	
8	SHEETS FROZEN PHYLLO PASTRY, THAWED (SEE TIP, PAGE 323)	8
½ CUP	BUTTER, MELTED	125 ML

PRICK SWEET POTATO ALL OVER WITH A FORK. MICROWAVE ON HIGH FOR 5 TO 7 MINUTES OR UNTIL TENDER. SET ASIDE UNTIL COOL ENOUGH TO HANDLE.

MEANWHILE, IN A NONSTICK SKILLET, HEAT OIL OVER MEDIUM HEAT. SAUTÉ ONION FOR ABOUT 5 MINUTES OR UNTIL TRANSLUCENT. ADD GARLIC, GINGER, CURRY PASTE AND COLD WATER; COOK, STIRRING, FOR 2 MINUTES.

HALVE SWEET POTATO AND SCOOP FLESH INTO A LARGE BOWL; DISCARD SKIN. STIR IN ONION MIXTURE, PEAS, CILANTRO AND HONEY. TASTE AND ADJUST SEASONING WITH SALT, IF DESIRED. (CURRY PASTE CAN BE QUITE SALTY, SO IT MAY NOT BE NEEDED.) LET COOL COMPLETELY.

PREHEAT OVEN TO 375°F (190°C). LINE 2 LARGE BAKING SHEETS WITH PARCHMENT PAPER. CAREFULLY UNROLL PHYLLO PASTRY AND COVER WITH A CLEAN TEA TOWEL. PLACE ONE PHYLLO SHEET ON A WORK SURFACE, WITH A LONG SIDE FACING YOU, AND BRUSH WITH BUTTER. TOP WITH ANOTHER PHYLLO SHEET AND BRUSH WITH BUTTER. CUT CROSSWISE INTO 4 STRIPS, EACH SLIGHTLY MORE THAN 4 INCHES (10 CM) WIDE. PLACE 1 TBSP (15 ML) SWEET POTATO MIXTURE ABOUT $\frac{1}{2}$ INCH (1 CM) FROM THE BOTTOM RIGHT-HAND CORNER OF EACH STRIP. FOLD THAT CORNER OVER THE FILLING SO THAT THE BOTTOM EDGE OF THE PHYLLO MEETS THE SIDE EDGE TO FORM A TRIANGLE. FOLD TRIANGLE UPWARDS. CONTINUE FOLDING TRIANGLE SIDEWAYS AND UPWARDS UNTIL YOU REACH THE END OF THE STRIP. WORKING QUICKLY, REPEAT WITH THE REMAINING STRIPS. REPEAT WITH THE REMAINING PHYLLO AND FILLING. PLACE TRIANGLES, SEAM SIDE DOWN, ABOUT 1 INCH (2.5 CM) APART ON PREPARED BAKING SHEETS AND BRUSH LIGHTLY WITH BUTTER. BAKE FOR ABOUT 15 MINUTES OR UNTIL GOLDEN. (IF THE BOTTOMS BROWN TOO QUICKLY, PLACE EACH BAKING SHEET ON TOP OF A SECOND UNGREASED BAKING SHEET. THIS IS CALLED DOUBLE PANNING.) MAKES 16 SAMOSAS.

MAKE AHEAD: AFTER ASSEMBLING THE SAMOSAS, PLACE THEM BETWEEN LAYERS OF WAXED PAPER IN AN AIRTIGHT CONTAINER AND REFRIGERATE FOR UP TO 1 DAY OR FREEZE FOR UP TO 2 MONTHS. BAKE FROM FROZEN IN A PREHEATED 425°F (220°C) OVEN FOR 15 TO 20 MINUTES OR UNTIL GOLDEN AND HEATED THROUGH.

PISTACHIO CHEESE TRUFFLES

SO GOOD AND SO EASY, THESE TRUFFLES LOOK
IMPRESSIVE AS PART OF A CHEESE PLATTER.
SERVE WITH CRACKERS.

I CUP	UNSALTED PISTACHIOS, SKINNED AND FINELY CHOPPED (SEE TIP, BELOW)	250 ML
8 OZ	MILD BLUE CHEESE (SUCH AS STILTON)	250 G
4 OZ	CREAM CHEESE, SOFTENED	125 G

SPREAD PISTACHIOS ON A WIDE RIMMED PLATE. IN A BOWL,
BEAT TOGETHER BLUE CHEESE AND CREAM CHEESE. ROLL
MIXTURE BETWEEN YOUR PALMS TO FORM 24 BALLS. ROLL
BALLS IN PISTACHIOS, PRESSING LIGHTLY TO ADHERE.
COVER AND REFRIGERATE FOR AT LEAST I HOUR OR FOR UP
TO 2 DAYS. MAKES 24 PIECES.

TIP: IT'S WORTH MAKING THE EFFORT TO REMOVE THE
REDDISH-BROWN SKINS OF PISTACHIOS TO REVEAL THE
ATTRACTIVE, BRIGHT GREEN NUT. PLACE PISTACHIOS
IN A SMALL SAUCEPAN AND COVER WITH COLD WATER.
BRING TO A BOIL FOR 15 SECONDS, THEN DRAIN. PLACE
PISTACHIOS ON A CLEAN KITCHEN TOWEL, FOLD TOWEL
OVER AND RUB TO LOOSEN THE SKINS.

WELL-BEHAVED WOMEN RARELY MAKE HISTORY.

SPICY CHICKPEA NIBBLES

CRUNCHY, LOW-FAT AND PACKED WITH PROTEIN, THESE SNACKS WILL GROW ON YOU. SERVE THEM WITH DRINKS OR TUCK SOME IN YOUR BAG FOR AN ANYTIME NIBBLE.

1	CAN (19 OZ/540 ML) CHICKPEAS, DRAINED AND RINSED	1
1 TSP	PAPRIKA	5 ML
1/2 TSP	GARLIC POWDER	2 ML
1/2 TSP	SALT	2 ML
1/4 TSP	CAYENNE PEPPER (OR TO TASTE)	1 ML
1 TBSP	OLIVE OIL	15 ML

PREHEAT OVEN TO 400°F (200°C). LINE A LARGE RIMMED BAKING SHEET WITH GREASED FOIL. SPREAD CHICKPEAS ON A LARGE PLATE AND BLOT DRY WITH PAPER TOWELS. IN A LARGE BOWL, COMBINE PAPRIKA, GARLIC POWDER, SALT, CAYENNE AND OIL. ADD CHICKPEAS AND TOSS TO COAT. SPREAD CHICKPEAS IN A SINGLE LAYER ON PREPARED BAKING SHEET. BAKE FOR ABOUT 40 MINUTES, SHAKING THE PAN TWO OR THREE TIMES, UNTIL CHICKPEAS ARE GOLDEN BROWN AND STARTING TO CRISP. TURN OVEN OFF AND LEAVE CHICKPEAS IN THE OVEN FOR 10 TO 20 MINUTES TO CRISP. REMOVE FROM OVEN AND LET COOL SLIGHTLY ON BAKING SHEET. MAKES 1 1/2 TO 2 CUPS (375 TO 500 ML).

MAKE AHEAD: COMPLETELY COOL BAKED CHICKPEAS. STORE IN AN AIRTIGHT CONTAINER FOR UP TO 3 DAYS.

VARIATION: EXPERIMENT WITH OTHER SEASONINGS, SUCH AS CURRY POWDER, SMOKED PAPRIKA OR CAJUN SPICE BLEND.

ARTICHOKE LEMON BRUSCHETTA

BRUSCHETTA IS AN ITALIAN APPETIZER OF TOASTED
BREAD BRUSHED WITH OLIVE OIL AND TOPPED WITH A
VARIETY OF SAVORY NIBBLES. MAKE THE TOASTS AND
TOPPING A DAY OR TWO AHEAD FOR EASY ENTERTAINING.

1	BAGUETTE (FRENCH STICK), CUT DIAGONALLY INTO $\frac{1}{2}$-INCH (1 CM) THICK SLICES	1
	OLIVE OIL	

TOPPING

1	CAN (14 OZ/398 ML) ARTICHOKE HEARTS, DRAINED AND FINELY CHOPPED	1
1	ROASTED RED BELL PEPPER (SEE TIP, PAGE 54), DRAINED AND FINELY CHOPPED (ABOUT $\frac{1}{4}$ CUP/60 ML)	1
1	CLOVE GARLIC, MINCED	1
2 TBSP	DRAINED CAPERS	30 ML
2 TBSP	CHOPPED FRESH PARSLEY	30 ML
$\frac{1}{4}$ TSP	SALT	1 ML
2 TBSP	OLIVE OIL	30 ML
2 TBSP	FRESHLY SQUEEZED LEMON JUICE	30 ML
$\frac{1}{2}$ CUP	FRESHLY GRATED PARMESAN CHEESE	125 ML
	SHAVED PARMESAN CHEESE (SEE TIP, OPPOSITE)	

PREHEAT OVEN TO 375°F (190°C). LIGHTLY BRUSH BOTH SIDES
OF EACH BAGUETTE SLICE WITH OIL. ARRANGE IN A SINGLE
LAYER ON 2 BAKING SHEETS. BAKE FOR 10 TO 12 MINUTES OR
UNTIL GOLDEN BROWN. TRANSFER TOASTS FROM THE PAN
TO A WIRE RACK AND LET COOL COMPLETELY. (THE COOLED
TOAST CAN BE STORED IN AN AIRTIGHT CONTAINER AT
ROOM TEMPERATURE FOR UP TO 2 DAYS.)

TOPPING: IN A LARGE BOWL, COMBINE ARTICHOKES, ROASTED PEPPER, GARLIC, CAPERS, PARSLEY, SALT, OIL AND LEMON JUICE. STIR IN GRATED PARMESAN. COVER AND REFRIGERATE FOR AT LEAST 4 HOURS OR FOR UP TO 2 DAYS.

PREHEAT OVEN TO 400°F (200°C). SPOON TOPPING ONTO TOASTS AND ARRANGE ON AN OVENPROOF SERVING PLATTER OR A BAKING SHEET. GARNISH WITH SHAVED PARMESAN. BAKE FOR 10 MINUTES OR UNTIL WARMED THROUGH. MAKES ABOUT 24 PIECES.

TIP: TO MAKE ATTRACTIVE PARMESAN SHAVINGS, USE A VEGETABLE PEELER TO SHAVE SMALL, THIN SLICES OFF A WEDGE OF FRESH PARMESAN CHEESE.

VARIATION: YOU CAN ALSO SERVE THE BRUSCHETTA WITHOUT HEATING IT. REMOVE THE TOPPING FROM THE REFRIGERATOR AND LET STAND AT ROOM TEMPERATURE FOR 30 MINUTES BEFORE SPOONING IT ONTO TOASTS AND GARNISHING.

I AM FAIRLY CERTAIN THAT GIVEN A CAPE AND A NICE TIARA, I COULD SAVE THE WORLD.

SWISS AND OLIVE FLATBREADS

*CARAMELIZED LEEK, ONION AND FENNEL TOPPED
WITH OLIVES AND MELTED SWISS CHEESE TURN
PITAS INTO TAPAS. CUT INTO THIN WEDGES
AND SERVE WITH DRINKS.*

4 TBSP	OLIVE OIL, DIVIDED	60 ML
I	FENNEL BULB, THINLY SLICED (SEE TIP, OPPOSITE),	I
I	ONION, THINLY SLICED	I
I	LEEK, WHITE AND LIGHT GREEN PARTS ONLY, THINLY SLICED (SEE TIP, PAGE 269)	I
I TO 2 TBSP	COLD WATER (IF NEEDED)	15 TO 30 ML
4	7-INCH (18 CM) GREEK-STYLE PITAS (NO POCKETS) OR MINI PIZZA SHELLS	4
1/2 CUP	FRESHLY GRATED PARMESAN CHEESE	125 ML
2 CUPS	SHREDDED SWISS CHEESE	500 ML
1/2 CUP	KALAMATA OLIVES, HALVED AND PITTED	125 ML
I TSP	DRIED OREGANO	5 ML
	SNIPPED FRESH FENNEL FRONDS OR FRESH DILL	

IN A LARGE NONSTICK SKILLET, HEAT 2 TBSP (30 ML) OF
THE OIL OVER MEDIUM HEAT. ADD FENNEL BULB, ONION
AND LEEK, STIRRING TO COAT WITH OIL. REDUCE HEAT
TO LOW, COVER AND COOK, STIRRING OCCASIONALLY, FOR
15 MINUTES OR UNTIL VEGETABLES ARE VERY SOFT BUT
NOT BROWNED. IF VEGETABLES START TO STICK, ADD
COLD WATER AS NEEDED. UNCOVER, INCREASE HEAT TO
MEDIUM AND COOK, STIRRING, FOR 5 TO 7 MINUTES OR
UNTIL VEGETABLES ARE GOLDEN. TRANSFER TO A BOWL

AND LET COOL SLIGHTLY. MEANWHILE, PREHEAT OVEN TO 375°F (190°C). PLACE PITAS ON 2 LARGE BAKING SHEETS. BRUSH TOPS WITH THE REMAINING OIL AND SPRINKLE WITH PARMESAN. SPREAD FENNEL MIXTURE OVER PITAS. SPRINKLE WITH SWISS CHEESE, OLIVES AND OREGANO. BAKE FOR ABOUT 15 MINUTES OR UNTIL CHEESE IS BUBBLING AND PITAS ARE BROWNED AND CRISP ON THE BOTTOM. CUT EACH PITA INTO 8 THIN WEDGES. SPRINKLE WITH FENNEL FRONDS. SERVE IMMEDIATELY. MAKES 32 PIECES.

TIP: IF THE FENNEL BULB HAS FEATHERY STALKS ATTACHED, TRIM THEM OFF ABOUT 1 INCH (2.5 CM) ABOVE THE BULB. RESERVE SOME OF THE FRONDS FOR GARNISH — THEY TASTE LIKE DILL. CUT THE BULB IN HALF VERTICALLY AND REMOVE THE WOODY CORE FROM EACH HALF. CUT EACH HALF CROSSWISE INTO VERY THIN SLICES.

MAKE AHEAD: LET THE COOKED VEGETABLE MIXTURE COOL COMPLETELY. TRANSFER TO AN AIRTIGHT CONTAINER AND REFRIGERATE FOR UP TO 2 DAYS.

VARIATION: SPREAD THE TOPPING ON A 12-INCH (30 CM) PIZZA CRUST TO SERVE AS A LIGHT SUPPER FOR GROWN-UPS OR ADVENTUROUS KIDS.

SIGN ON TEACHER'S DESK:
THE DOG ATE MY LESSON PLAN.

NO-FUSS HUMMUS

THIS VERSION OF HUMMUS USES SESAME OIL INSTEAD OF TAHINI. THE RESULT IS LIGHT AND CREAMY.

1	CAN (19 OZ/540 ML) CHICKPEAS, DRAINED AND RINSED	1
1 TO 2	CLOVES GARLIC, MINCED	1 TO 2
2 TBSP	CHOPPED FRESH PARSLEY, CILANTRO OR DILL	30 ML
1/2 TSP	GROUND CUMIN	2 ML
1/2 TSP	SALT	2 ML
1/4 CUP	WATER	60 ML
3 TBSP	FRESHLY SQUEEZED LEMON JUICE	45 ML
2 TBSP	LOW-FAT (2%) COTTAGE CHEESE OR LIGHT SOUR CREAM	30 ML
1 TSP	TOASTED SESAME OIL (SEE TIP, BELOW)	5 ML
1 TSP	ASIAN CHILI PASTE (SEE TIP, PAGE 207)	5 ML

IN A FOOD PROCESSOR, COARSELY CHOP CHICKPEAS. ADD GARLIC, PARSLEY, CUMIN, SALT, WATER, LEMON JUICE, COTTAGE CHEESE, SESAME OIL AND CHILI PASTE; PURÉE UNTIL SMOOTH. TASTE AND ADJUST SEASONING WITH SALT, LEMON JUICE AND CHILI PASTE AS DESIRED. MAKES ABOUT 2 CUPS (500 ML).

TIP: SESAME OIL COMES IN TWO TYPES. TOASTED SESAME OIL (OFTEN LABELED "DARK") IS MADE FROM TOASTED SESAME SEEDS AND HAS A DISTINCT NUTTY FLAVOR. A LITTLE GOES A LONG WAY. LIGHT SESAME OIL IS PALER IN COLOR AND MILDER IN TASTE. REFRIGERATE SESAME OIL TO PREVENT IT FROM BECOMING RANCID, AND TASTE IT BEFORE USING TO TEST ITS FRESHNESS.

MAKE AHEAD: STORE IN AN AIRTIGHT CONTAINER IN THE REFRIGERATOR FOR UP TO 3 DAYS.

QUICK TOMATO DIP

UNEXPECTED GUESTS AT THE DOOR? WHIP UP THIS
TANGY DIP. THE CHIVES AND PINE NUTS MAKE AN
ATTRACTIVE FINISHING TOUCH, BUT IF YOU DON'T
HAVE THEM ON HAND, JUST OMIT THEM.
SERVE WITH VEGETABLES, CHIPS OR CRACKERS.

1	LARGE TOMATO, SEEDED (SEE TIP, BELOW) AND FINELY CHOPPED, DIVIDED	1
1 CUP	LIGHT OR REGULAR SOUR CREAM	250 ML
1/4 CUP	FRESHLY GRATED PARMESAN CHEESE	60 ML
1/4 CUP	SUN-DRIED TOMATO PESTO (SEE TIP, PAGE 165)	60 ML
	SNIPPED FRESH CHIVES AND TOASTED PINE NUTS (OPTIONAL)	

IN A BOWL, COMBINE HALF THE TOMATO WITH SOUR
CREAM, PARMESAN AND PESTO. TRANSFER TO A SERVING
BOWL. GARNISH WITH THE REMAINING TOMATO AND
CHIVES AND PINE NUTS (IF USING). MAKES ABOUT $1\frac{1}{2}$ CUPS
(375 ML).

TIP: TO REMOVE THE SEEDS FROM A TOMATO, CUT THE
TOMATO IN HALF HORIZONTALLY. HOLDING A TOMATO
HALF OVER A BOWL, GENTLY SQUEEZE OUT THE SEEDS
AND SURROUNDING GEL. USE YOUR FINGER OR THE TIP
OF A KNIFE TO COAX OUT ANY LINGERING SEEDS. REPEAT
WITH OTHER HALF.

VARIATION: FOR A CREAMIER FLAVOR, REPLACE HALF THE
SOUR CREAM WITH MAYONNAISE.

WARM BACON, ARTICHOKE AND SPINACH DIP

THIS YUMMY DIP IS A BIG HIT AT TAILGATE PARTIES OR IN FRONT OF THE TV. SERVE WITH PITA CHIPS AND CRACKERS.

9	SLICES BACON	9
1 TBSP	VEGETABLE OIL	15 ML
1/2 CUP	FINELY CHOPPED ONION	125 ML
3	CLOVES GARLIC, MINCED	3
1/2 TSP	SWEET SMOKED OR REGULAR PAPRIKA (SEE TIP, PAGE 37)	2 ML
1	JAR (6 OZ/170 G) MARINATED ARTICHOKE HEARTS, DRAINED AND CHOPPED	1
2 CUPS	PACKED BABY SPINACH, CHOPPED	500 ML
3/4 CUP	FRESHLY GRATED PARMESAN OR ASIAGO CHEESE, DIVIDED	175 ML
1/2 CUP	LIGHT SOUR CREAM	125 ML
1/2 CUP	LIGHT MAYONNAISE	125 ML
1 TBSP	FRESHLY SQUEEZED LEMON JUICE	15 ML

PREHEAT OVEN TO 350°F (180°C). GREASE A SHALLOW 3-CUP (750 ML) BAKING DISH. IN A LARGE NONSTICK SKILLET, COOK BACON OVER MEDIUM-HIGH HEAT UNTIL CRISPY. TRANSFER TO A PLATE LINED WITH PAPER TOWELS. LET COOL, THEN FINELY CHOP. DRAIN FAT FROM SKILLET AND WIPE CLEAN. ADD OIL TO SKILLET AND HEAT OVER MEDIUM HEAT. SAUTÉ ONION FOR ABOUT 5 MINUTES OR UNTIL TRANSLUCENT. ADD GARLIC AND PAPRIKA; SAUTÉ FOR 15 SECONDS OR UNTIL FRAGRANT. REMOVE FROM HEAT AND LET COOL SLIGHTLY. RETURN BACON TO PAN. STIR IN ARTICHOKES, SPINACH, 1/2 CUP (125 ML) OF THE

PARMESAN, SOUR CREAM, MAYONNAISE AND LEMON JUICE. TRANSFER TO PREPARED BAKING DISH. SPRINKLE WITH THE REMAINING PARMESAN AND A LIGHT DUSTING OF PAPRIKA. BAKE FOR ABOUT 20 MINUTES OR UNTIL BUBBLING AND LIGHTLY BROWNED ON TOP. SERVE IMMEDIATELY. MAKES ABOUT 3 CUPS (750 ML).

TIP: FOR CRISPY BACON, CHOOSE REGULAR BACON RATHER THAN THE THICK-SLICED VARIETY. STORE UNCOOKED BACON IN AN AIRTIGHT CONTAINER FOR UP TO 1 WEEK OR IN THE FREEZER FOR UP TO 2 MONTHS.

MAKE AHEAD: ASSEMBLE DIP AND LET COOL COMPLETELY. COVER AND REFRIGERATE FOR UP TO 1 DAY. FREEZING IS NOT RECOMMENDED. BAKE AS INSTRUCTED ABOVE.

SO FAR, THIS IS THE OLDEST I'VE EVER BEEN.

ROASTED RED PEPPER
YOGURT DIP

USE A THICK AND CREAMY GREEK- OR BALKAN-STYLE YOGURT FOR THIS REFRESHING, BLUSH-COLORED DIP (OR, IF YOU MUST, USE LOW-FAT YOGURT). SERVE AS AN APPETIZER WITH A COLORFUL SELECTION OF VEGGIES AND CRACKERS. YOU COULD TUCK A SMALL CONTAINER OF THIS DIP INTO KIDS' LUNCH BAGS, ALONG WITH SOME BABY CARROTS AND SNOW PEAS.

1	CLOVE GARLIC, MINCED (OPTIONAL)	1
1/3 CUP	FINELY CHOPPED DRAINED ROASTED RED BELL PEPPERS (SEE TIP, BELOW)	75 ML
1 CUP	PLAIN YOGURT	250 ML
2 TO 3 TBSP	FRESHLY SQUEEZED LEMON JUICE	30 TO 45 ML
1/2 TSP	ASIAN CHILI PASTE (SEE TIP, PAGE 207) OR HOT PEPPER SAUCE	2 ML
	SALT AND FRESHLY GROUND BLACK PEPPER	

IN A BOWL, COMBINE GARLIC (IF USING), ROASTED PEPPERS, YOGURT, 2 TBSP (30 ML) LEMON JUICE AND CHILI PASTE. SEASON TO TASTE WITH SALT AND PEPPER. TASTE AND ADJUST SEASONING WITH LEMON JUICE, IF DESIRED. COVER AND REFRIGERATE FOR AT LEAST 4 HOURS OR FOR UP TO 1 DAY. MAKES ABOUT 1 CUP (250 ML).

TIP: ROASTED RED BELL PEPPERS ARE SOLD IN JARS OR IN THE DELI SECTION OF THE SUPERMARKET. BUT IT IS EASY TO ROAST YOUR OWN. PREHEAT OVEN TO 425°F (220°C). BRUSH WHOLE PEPPERS GENEROUSLY WITH OLIVE OIL. PLACE ON A BAKING SHEET LINED WITH PARCHMENT PAPER OR FOIL. ROAST FOR ABOUT 30 MINUTES, TURNING OCCASIONALLY, UNTIL SKINS ARE BLACKENED AND PUFFED.

TRANSFER PEPPERS TO A BOWL, COVER AND LET STAND FOR 15 MINUTES TO STEAM. PEEL OFF SKINS AND REMOVE CORE, RIBS AND SEEDS. STORE IN AN AIRTIGHT CONTAINER IN THE REFRIGERATOR FOR UP TO 5 DAYS. OR CUT INTO STRIPS, SPREAD IN A SINGLE LAYER ON A BAKING SHEET AND FREEZE. PACK FROZEN PEPPER PIECES INTO FREEZER BAGS AND STORE FOR UP TO 3 MONTHS.

CAMBOZOLA PÂTÉ WITH PORT AND CRANBERRIES

SERVE THIS PÂTÉ WITH YOUR FAVORITE CRACKERS OR POP SOME INTO A PRETTY RAMEKIN FOR A LOVELY HOSTESS GIFT.

8 OZ	CAMBOZOLA OR BRIE CHEESE, SOFTENED	250 G
4 OZ	CREAM CHEESE, SOFTENED	125 G
2 TBSP	PORT, DRY SHERRY OR CRANBERRY JUICE	30 ML
2 TBSP	CHOPPED DRIED CRANBERRIES	30 ML

IN A FOOD PROCESSOR, PROCESS CAMBOZOLA, CREAM CHEESE AND PORT UNTIL SMOOTH. TRANSFER TO A SMALL BOWL AND STIR IN CRANBERRIES. COVER AND REFRIGERATE FOR AT LEAST 1 HOUR OR FOR UP TO 3 DAYS. MAKES ABOUT 1½ CUPS (375 ML).

DATE PECAN TOPPER

TOP YOUR FAVORITE CRACKERS WITH SLICES OF REALLY GOOD CHEESE AND DOLLOPS OF THIS EXCELLENT NO-COOK CHUTNEY. YOU COULD ALSO PLACE THE TOPPER IN AN ATTRACTIVE BOWL IN THE CENTER OF A CHEESE PLATTER AND LET GUESTS HELP THEMSELVES. FOR A QUICK DESSERT, SPOON ABOUT 2 TBSP (30 ML) DATE PECAN TOPPER ON TOP OF INDIVIDUAL BOWLS OF SLICED STRAWBERRIES SPRINKLED WITH A LITTLE SUGAR AND ORANGE ZEST.

1/2 CUP	CHOPPED PITTED SOFT FRESH (MEDJOOL) DATES (ABOUT 6)	125 ML
1/2 CUP	CHOPPED TOASTED PECANS (SEE TIP, PAGE 127)	125 ML
I TBSP	PURE MAPLE SYRUP OR LIQUID HONEY	15 ML
I TBSP	BALSAMIC VINEGAR	15 ML
PINCH	CAYENNE PEPPER	PINCH

IN A SMALL BOWL, COMBINE DATES, PECANS, MAPLE SYRUP, VINEGAR AND CAYENNE. COVER AND REFRIGERATE FOR AT LEAST I HOUR OR FOR UP TO I DAY. MAKES ABOUT I CUP (250 ML).

TIP: SOFT FRESH DATES, SOMETIMES LABELED "MEDJOOL DATES," ARE NOW GROWN IN THE SOUTHERN UNITED STATES AS WELL AS THE MIDDLE EAST AND ARE BECOMING MORE WIDELY AVAILABLE IN SUPERMARKETS. THEY ARE DELICIOUS CHOPPED IN SALADS, SPRINKLED ON TOP OF PIZZAS AND FLATBREADS AND IN CAKES AND SQUARES.

SALADS AND DRESSINGS

MINT, MANGO AND
AVOCADO SALAD

FRESH AND FRUITY WITH FLARE, THIS SALAD GOES
PARTICULARLY WELL WITH SLIGHTLY SPICY DISHES,
SUCH AS INDIAN SPICED CHICKEN DRUMSTICKS
(PAGE 168) OR CHEESY BEAN QUESADILLAS (PAGE 112).

DRESSING

1	CLOVE GARLIC, MINCED	1
1/4 CUP	GRANULATED SUGAR	60 ML
1/4 CUP	VEGETABLE OIL	60 ML
1/4 CUP	CIDER OR WHITE VINEGAR	60 ML
2 TBSP	CHOPPED FRESH MINT	30 ML

SALAD

1	GREEN ONION, FINELY CHOPPED	1
1	MANGO, CHOPPED (SEE TIP, OPPOSITE)	1
1	RIPE AVOCADO, CHOPPED (SEE TIP, PAGE 129)	1
1	RED BELL PEPPER, CHOPPED	1
6 CUPS	MIXED SALAD GREENS	1.5 L
2 TBSP	CHOPPED FRESH MINT	30 ML
1/2 CUP	TOASTED SLIVERED OR SLICED ALMONDS (SEE TIP, PAGE 127)	125 ML
2 TBSP	SHREDDED ASIAGO OR FRESHLY GRATED PARMESAN CHEESE (OPTIONAL)	30 ML

DRESSING: IN A BOWL, WHISK TOGETHER GARLIC, SUGAR, OIL
AND VINEGAR UNTIL SUGAR IS DISSOLVED. STIR IN MINT.

SALAD: IN A LARGE, SHALLOW SALAD BOWL, COMBINE
GREEN ONION, MANGO, AVOCADO, RED PEPPER, SALAD
GREENS AND MINT. ADD ENOUGH DRESSING TO LIGHTLY
COAT THE INGREDIENTS AND TOSS TO COAT. SPRINKLE

WITH ALMONDS AND CHEESE. SERVE IMMEDIATELY.
SERVES 4 TO 6.

TIP: WHEN SELECTING A MANGO, PAY LESS ATTENTION
TO THE WAY IT LOOKS AND FOCUS ON HOW IT FEELS.
SQUEEZE IT GENTLY — IF IT'S RIPE, IT WILL BE SLIGHTLY
SOFT. IF YOU DON'T PLAN TO EAT THE MANGO FOR A
FEW DAYS, BUY ONE THAT IS FIRMER AND KEEP IT AT
ROOM TEMPERATURE. ONCE IT'S RIPE, MOVE IT TO THE
REFRIGERATOR TO SLOW FURTHER RIPENING. THERE
ARE SEVERAL WAYS TO PEEL AND SLICE A MANGO. THE
EASIEST WAY IS TO STAND THE MANGO, STEM END
DOWN, ON A CUTTING BOARD. WITH A SHARP KNIFE, CUT
AWAY THE PEEL, WORKING FROM TOP TO BOTTOM. THEN
CUT A THICK SLICE OFF EACH SIDE OF THE PIT (THESE ARE
KNOWN AS "CHEEKS"). SLICE OFF ANY REMAINING FLESH
AND CHOP ALL THE PIECES AS DESIRED.

MAKE AHEAD: THE DRESSING CAN BE STORED IN AN
AIRTIGHT CONTAINER IN THE REFRIGERATOR FOR UP
TO 1 DAY.

A PUN AT MATURITY IS FULL GROAN.

RAINBOW COLESLAW

A LIGHT MUSTARD VINAIGRETTE MAKES THIS PRETTY COLESLAW THE PERFECT SIDE DISH FOR BUFFETS, BARBECUES AND PICNICS. IT'S THE IDEAL SIDEKICK FOR STICKY ASIAN PORK BURGERS (PAGE 132).

SALAD

2	CARROTS, COARSELY SHREDDED	2
4 CUPS	SHREDDED RED CABBAGE (SEE TIP, OPPOSITE)	1 L
4 CUPS	SHREDDED GREEN CABBAGE	1 L
	ICE WATER	
1/2	RED ONION, THINLY SLICED (OPTIONAL)	1/2

DRESSING

2 TBSP	GRANULATED SUGAR	30 ML
1 TSP	CELERY SALT	5 ML
1/2 CUP	VEGETABLE OIL	125 ML
1/4 CUP	CIDER VINEGAR	60 ML
2 TSP	WHOLE-GRAIN DIJON MUSTARD	10 ML

SALAD: IN A LARGE BOWL, COMBINE CARROTS, RED CABBAGE AND GREEN CABBAGE; COVER WITH ICE WATER AND LET SOAK FOR 30 MINUTES (THIS WILL HELP MAKE IT REALLY CRUNCHY). DRAIN AND DRY IN A SALAD SPINNER (OR WRAP IN A CLEAN DISH TOWEL AND GENTLY PRESS TO REMOVE EXCESS WATER). PLACE VEGETABLES IN A LARGE SALAD BOWL. ADD RED ONION (IF USING).

DRESSING: IN A SMALL SAUCEPAN, COMBINE SUGAR, CELERY SALT, OIL, VINEGAR AND MUSTARD; BRING TO A BOIL OVER HIGH HEAT. BOIL, WITHOUT STIRRING, FOR

1 MINUTE. THE DRESSING WILL LOOK SLIGHTLY SYRUPY. REMOVE FROM HEAT AND IMMEDIATELY TOSS WITH VEGETABLES TO COAT EVENLY. REFRIGERATE FOR AT LEAST 30 MINUTES OR FOR UP TO 1 HOUR BEFORE SERVING. SERVES 6.

TIP: TO SHRED CABBAGE, FIRST CUT THE HEAD INTO QUARTERS. CUT OUT AND DISCARD THE THICK CORE. PLACE THE CABBAGE WITH ONE FLAT SIDE ON A CUTTING BOARD. USING A SHARP KNIFE, AND STARTING AT ONE EDGE, CUT $1/4$-INCH (0.5 CM) SLICES. THE LAYERS OF THE CABBAGE WILL NATURALLY FALL INTO SHREDS AS YOU CUT.

VARIATION

QUICK COLESLAW: IF YOU'RE IN A HURRY, REPLACE THE CARROTS, CABBAGE AND ONION WITH A 12-OZ (340 G) BAG OF YOUR FAVORITE COLESLAW MIX FROM THE PRODUCE AISLE. SOAK THE READY-CUT COLESLAW MIX IN ICE WATER FOR AT LEAST 5 MINUTES TO PERK IT UP A BIT BEFORE DRAINING, DRYING AND PROCEEDING WITH THE RECIPE.

MEN ARE LIKE A FINE WINE. THEY START OUT LIKE GRAPES. IT'S OUR JOB TO STAMP ON THEM UNTIL THEY MATURE INTO SOMETHING YOU WOULD HAVE DINNER WITH.

THE BEST BEET SALAD

MAKE THIS DEEP RED-COLORED SALAD A DAY AHEAD TO LET THE FLAVORS DEVELOP. IT'S ESPECIALLY GOOD WITH GRILLED SALMON. YOU CAN USE REGULAR RED BEETS OR THE PRETTY YELLOW ONES, BUT DON'T MIX THE TWO COLORS, BECAUSE THE SALAD WILL TAKE ON AN UNAPPEALING HUE!

DRESSING

2 TBSP	RED WINE VINEGAR	30 ML
2 TBSP	OLIVE OIL	30 ML
2 TBSP	FRESHLY SQUEEZED ORANGE JUICE	30 ML
I TSP	DIJON MUSTARD	5 ML
1/4 TSP	SALT	I ML
	FRESHLY GROUND BLACK PEPPER	

SALAD

I CUP	REDUCED-SODIUM CHICKEN BROTH, HOMEMADE VEGETABLE STOCK (SEE RECIPE, PAGE 90) OR WATER (SEE TIP, OPPOSITE)	250 ML
1/2 TSP	FINELY GRATED ORANGE ZEST	2 ML
I CUP	COUSCOUS	250 ML
6	COOKED SMALL BEETS, PEELED AND FINELY DICED (ABOUT 2 CUPS/500 ML)	6
1/3 CUP	DRIED CRANBERRIES OR CHOPPED DRIED APRICOTS	75 ML
1/4 CUP	CRUMBLED GOAT CHEESE (SEE TIP, OPPOSITE)	60 ML
1/4 CUP	TOASTED GREEN PUMPKIN SEEDS OR SLIVERED OR SLICED ALMONDS (SEE TIP, PAGE 127)	60 ML
2 CUPS	PACKED BABY SPINACH	500 ML

DRESSING: IN A SMALL BOWL, WHISK TOGETHER VINEGAR, OIL, ORANGE JUICE, MUSTARD, SALT AND PEPPER TO TASTE.

SALAD: IN A SAUCEPAN, BRING BROTH AND ORANGE ZEST TO A BOIL. STIR IN COUSCOUS AND IMMEDIATELY REMOVE FROM HEAT. COVER AND LET STAND FOR ABOUT 5 MINUTES OR UNTIL BROTH IS ABSORBED. FLUFF WITH A FORK AND TRANSFER TO A LARGE BOWL. ADD BEETS, CRANBERRIES, GOAT CHEESE AND PUMPKIN SEEDS. DRIZZLE DRESSING OVER TOP AND GENTLY STIR TO COMBINE. THE COUSCOUS WILL IMMEDIATELY START TO TURN A MARBLED DARK RED COLOR FROM THE BEET JUICES. DON'T OVER-STIR, OR THE SALAD WILL BECOME GLUEY. COVER AND REFRIGERATE FOR AT LEAST 1 HOUR AND PREFERABLY UP TO 24 HOURS TO LET THE FLAVORS DEVELOP. JUST BEFORE SERVING, STIR IN SPINACH. SERVES 4 TO 6.

TIP: IF YOU ARE USING HOMEMADE VEGETABLE STOCK, OTHER UNSALTED STOCK OR WATER, ADD $\frac{1}{4}$ TSP (1 ML) SALT OR MORE TO TASTE TO THE LIQUID BEFORE ADDING THE COUSCOUS.

TIP: GOAT CHEESE IS ALSO KNOWN AS CHÈVRE. WHITE, CREAMY AND SOMETIMES A BIT CRUMBLY, THE CHEESE HAS A FLAVOR THAT RANGES FROM MILD TO SLIGHTLY TART, DEPENDING ON ITS AGE. IT IS QUITE SALTY, SO SEASON THE SALAD CAUTIOUSLY.

MAKE AHEAD: THE DRESSING CAN BE STORED IN AN AIRTIGHT CONTAINER IN THE REFRIGERATOR FOR UP TO 1 DAY. AFTER ASSEMBLING THE SALAD, BUT BEFORE ADDING THE SPINACH, TRANSFER TO AN AIRTIGHT CONTAINER AND REFRIGERATE FOR UP TO 2 DAYS.

ROASTED BEET AND SPINACH SALAD WITH POMEGRANATE DRESSING

THIS SALAD LOOKS STUNNING AND TASTES EXOTIC.

POMEGRANATE DRESSING

3 TBSP	GRANULATED SUGAR	45 ML
I CUP	100% POMEGRANATE JUICE	250 ML
5 TBSP	FRESHLY SQUEEZED LEMON JUICE, DIVIDED	75 ML
	SALT AND FRESHLY GROUND BLACK PEPPER	
1/4 CUP	OLIVE OIL	60 ML

SALAD

I LB	BEETS, PREFERABLY SMALL, TRIMMED	500 G
6 CUPS	BABY SPINACH LEAVES	1.5 L
3 TBSP	CHOPPED FRESH DILL	45 ML
1/2 CUP	CRUMBLED GOAT OR FETA CHEESE (OPTIONAL)	125 ML
1/4 CUP	TOASTED GREEN PUMPKIN SEEDS (SEE TIP, PAGE 127)	60 ML
	SEEDS FROM 1/2 POMEGRANATE (SEE TIP, OPPOSITE)	

DRESSING: IN A SMALL SAUCEPAN, WHISK TOGETHER SUGAR, POMEGRANATE JUICE AND 3 TBSP (45 ML) OF THE LEMON JUICE; BRING TO A BOIL OVER MEDIUM-HIGH HEAT. REDUCE HEAT TO LOW AND SIMMER FOR 25 MINUTES OR UNTIL JUICE IS REDUCED BY ABOUT TWO-THIRDS, IS SYRUPY AND LIGHTLY COATS THE BACK OF A SPOON. LET COOL COMPLETELY. (THIS CAN BE DONE AHEAD. REFRIGERATE SYRUP IN A CLEAN JAR WITH A SCREW-TOP LID FOR UP TO 2 WEEKS. IF THE SYRUP BECOMES TOO THICK TO POUR, WARM IT IN THE MICROWAVE FOR

ABOUT 15 SECONDS TO LOOSEN IT BEFORE PROCEEDING.)

IN A SMALL BOWL, WHISK TOGETHER 2 TBSP (30 ML) OF THE POMEGRANATE SYRUP AND THE REMAINING LEMON JUICE. SEASON TO TASTE WITH SALT AND PEPPER. GRADUALLY WHISK IN OIL.

SALAD: PREHEAT OVEN TO 350°F (180°C). WRAP BEETS IN FOIL AND PLACE ON A LARGE BAKING SHEET. ROAST FOR ABOUT 1 HOUR OR UNTIL FORK-TENDER. UNWRAP BEETS AND LET COOL. PEEL BEETS AND CUT INTO BITE-SIZED CHUNKS. (IF BEETS ARE SMALL, YOU MIGHT ONLY NEED TO HALVE THEM.) IN A LARGE BOWL, TOSS BEETS WITH HALF THE DRESSING. IN A LARGE, SHALLOW SERVING BOWL, GENTLY TOSS SPINACH WITH THE REMAINING DRESSING. CAREFULLY SPOON BEETS INTO THE CENTER OF THE SPINACH. SPRINKLE DILL OVER BEETS. SPRINKLE GOAT CHEESE (IF USING), PUMPKIN SEEDS AND POMEGRANATE SEEDS OVER BEETS AND SPINACH. SERVES 4.

TIP: REMOVING POMEGRANATE SEEDS IS EASY. SUBMERGE THE POMEGRANATE IN A LARGE BOWL OF COLD WATER AND REMOVE THE SKIN AND WHITE PITH. THE SEEDS WILL SINK TO THE BOTTOM AND THE PITH WILL FLOAT TO THE TOP. THIS METHOD PREVENTS THE JUICE FROM SQUIRTING ALL OVER YOU.

TIP: FOR AN EASY APPETIZER, SPOON 2 TBSP (30 ML) POMEGRANATE SYRUP OVER A BLOCK OF CREAM CHEESE AND SERVE WITH CRACKERS. THE SYRUP IS ALSO DELICIOUS LIGHTLY DRIZZLED OVER GRILLED CHICKEN, PORK OR SALMON. AND IT MAKES A SENSATIONAL TOPPING FOR VANILLA BEAN ICE CREAM.

PANZANELLA

THIS IS AN INCREDIBLE VARIATION OF THE TRADITIONAL ITALIAN BREAD SALAD AND WAS CREATED BY CORPORATE CHEF SONNY SUNG, OF SORRENTINO'S RESTAURANT GROUP IN EDMONTON. THE SALAD TAKES A LITTLE BIT OF TIME, BUT THE RESULT IS OUTSTANDING. IT'S AMPLE, SO SERVE IT WITH A SIMPLY PREPARED MEAT, SUCH AS GRILLED STEAK OR LAMB CHOPS.

4 CUPS	CUBED CRUSTY BREAD	1 L
1/2 CUP	OLIVE OIL, DIVIDED	125 ML
2	SMALL ZUCCHINI, DICED	2
1/4 CUP	FINELY CHOPPED RED ONION	60 ML
1/4 CUP	SHREDDED FRESH BASIL (SEE TIP, OPPOSITE)	60 ML
6	OIL-PACKED SUN-DRIED TOMATOES, DRAINED AND CHOPPED	6
4	ANCHOVY FILLETS	4
2	CLOVES GARLIC, MINCED	2
1/3 CUP	PACKED FRESH CILANTRO LEAVES, CHOPPED	75 ML
3 TBSP	BALSAMIC VINEGAR	45 ML
1/2 CUP	CRUMBLED FETA CHEESE (SEE TIP, PAGE 199)	125 ML
6 CUPS	CHOPPED ROMAINE LETTUCE OR OTHER SALAD GREENS	1.5 L

PREHEAT OVEN TO 400°F (200°C). LINE A LARGE BAKING SHEET WITH PARCHMENT PAPER. SPREAD BREAD CUBES IN A SINGLE LAYER ON PREPARED BAKING SHEET. BAKE FOR 10 TO 12 MINUTES OR UNTIL GOLDEN BROWN AND CRISPY. TRANSFER TO A LARGE BOWL AND LET COOL WHILE YOU PREPARE THE REMAINING INGREDIENTS.

IN A LARGE SKILLET, HEAT 1 TBSP (15 ML) OF THE OIL OVER MEDIUM-HIGH HEAT. SAUTÉ ZUCCHINI, RED ONION AND BASIL FOR ABOUT 2 MINUTES OR UNTIL SOFTENED AND FRAGRANT. ADD TO THE BOWL AND TOSS WITH THE TOASTED BREAD CUBES. IN A BLENDER OR FOOD PROCESSOR, COMBINE SUN-DRIED TOMATOES, ANCHOVIES, GARLIC, CILANTRO, THE REMAINING OIL AND VINEGAR; PROCESS UNTIL SMOOTH. POUR OVER BREAD MIXTURE. ADD CHEESE AND TOSS TO COMBINE. LET STAND AT ROOM TEMPERATURE FOR 15 MINUTES TO LET FLAVORS DEVELOP.

PLACE ROMAINE LETTUCE IN A LARGE SALAD BOWL, ADD BREAD MIXTURE AND TOSS TO COMBINE. SERVES 4 TO 6.

TIP: FRESH BASIL IS A DELICATE HERB THAT BRUISES AND BECOMES AN UNAPPETIZING SHADE OF GREENISH-BLACK IF NOT HANDLED CAREFULLY. TO SHRED OR THINLY SLICE FRESH BASIL, FIRST REMOVE THE LEAVES FROM THE STALK. STACK THE LEAVES, A FEW AT A TIME, AND GENTLY ROLL THEM INTO A TIGHT CIGAR SHAPE. USING A SHARP KNIFE, SLICE THE ROLL VERY THINLY. YOU'LL HAVE PRETTY RIBBONS OF BASIL. THE CHEF'S TERM FOR THIS IS "CHIFFONADE."

THE BEST REMEDY FOR A SHORT TEMPER IS A LONG WALK.
– JACQUELINE SCHIFF

GOLFERS' FAVORITE STEAK SALAD

THIS HEARTY DINNER SALAD IS GUARANTEED TO
SATISFY BIG APPETITES AT THE END OF
A DAY ON THE LINKS.

BALSAMIC DRESSING

1	CLOVE GARLIC, MINCED	1
1/2 TSP	DRIED OREGANO	2 ML
1/4 TSP	GRANULATED SUGAR	1 ML
1/2 CUP	OLIVE OIL	125 ML
2 TBSP	BALSAMIC VINEGAR	30 ML
2 TBSP	RED WINE VINEGAR	30 ML
	SALT AND FRESHLY GROUND BLACK PEPPER	
2 TBSP	COLD WATER (IF NEEDED)	30 ML

SALAD

1 1/4 LBS	THICK BONELESS BEEF STRIP LOIN OR OTHER GRILLING STEAK	625 G
	SALT AND FRESHLY GROUND BLACK PEPPER	
2 TBSP	OLIVE OIL, DIVIDED (APPROX.)	30 ML
2	PORTOBELLO MUSHROOMS, STEMS AND GILLS REMOVED (SEE TIP, OPPOSITE), THICKLY SLICED	2
2	RED BELL PEPPERS, CUT INTO THICK WEDGES	2
1	RED ONION, CUT INTO THICK SLICES	1
6 CUPS	MIXED SALAD GREENS	1.5 L
1/2 CUP	FRESHLY GRATED PARMESAN CHEESE	125 ML

DRESSING: IN A BOWL, WHISK TOGETHER GARLIC,
OREGANO, SUGAR, OIL, BALSAMIC VINEGAR AND RED WINE
VINEGAR. SEASON TO TASTE WITH SALT AND PEPPER.
IF DRESSING IS TOO THICK TO POUR, ADD COLD WATER,

1 TSP (5 ML) AT A TIME, UNTIL DRESSING REACHES THE CONSISTENCY OF MAPLE SYRUP.

SALAD: SEASON STEAK WITH SALT AND PEPPER AND BRUSH WITH 1 TBSP (15 ML) OF THE OIL. SET ASIDE. IN A LARGE BOWL, TOSS MUSHROOMS, RED PEPPERS AND RED ONION WITH THE REMAINING OIL AND SALT AND PEPPER TO TASTE. SET ASIDE. PREHEAT BARBECUE GRILL TO MEDIUM-HIGH. GRILL STEAK FOR ABOUT 5 MINUTES PER SIDE FOR MEDIUM-RARE OR UNTIL DESIRED DONENESS. TRANSFER TO A CUTTING BOARD, COVER LOOSELY WITH FOIL AND LET STAND FOR 5 MINUTES.

MEANWHILE, GRILL MUSHROOMS, RED PEPPERS AND RED ONION FOR ABOUT 5 MINUTES, TURNING OCCASIONALLY, UNTIL LIGHTLY BROWNED. TRANSFER TO A PLATE. THINLY SLICE STEAK ACROSS THE GRAIN. DIVIDE SALAD GREENS AMONG INDIVIDUAL PLATES OR PLACE ON A SERVING PLATTER. ARRANGE STEAK AND VEGETABLES ON TOP. DRIZZLE WITH DRESSING AND SPRINKLE WITH PARMESAN. SERVES 3 TO 4.

TIP: THE IMPORTANT STEP WITH PORTOBELLO MUSHROOMS IS TO REMOVE THE STEMS AND THE DARK BROWN GILLS ON THE UNDERSIDE. USE THE EDGE OF A SPOON TO SCRAPE THEM AWAY.

MAKE AHEAD: THE DRESSING CAN BE STORED IN AN AIRTIGHT CONTAINER IN THE REFRIGERATOR FOR UP TO 1 DAY.

VARIATION: WHOLE ASPARAGUS SPEARS, TOMATO HALVES AND THICKLY SLICED ZUCCHINI ARE ALSO EXCELLENT GRILLED AND SERVED WITH THIS SALAD.

WARM MUSHROOM AND BACON SALAD

TRIED, TESTED, TERRIFIC. THAT WAS THE VERDICT
OF SHOPPERS AT EDMONTON'S CALLINGWOOD
FARMERS' MARKET, WHERE WE FEATURED THIS
CROWD-PLEASING SALAD IN A SUMMER COOKING
DEMONSTRATION. IT'S SUBSTANTIAL ENOUGH TO
SERVE AS AN ENTRÉE, OR YOU COULD SERVE IT
ALONGSIDE GRILLED CHICKEN OR STEAK.

4	SLICES BACON, CHOPPED	4
I TBSP	BUTTER	15 ML
I	SMALL ONION, FINELY CHOPPED	I
3 CUPS	SLICED EXOTIC MUSHROOMS, SUCH AS CREMINI, OYSTER OR SHIITAKE, OR A COMBINATION (SEE TIP, OPPOSITE)	750 ML
2	CLOVES GARLIC, MINCED	2
2 TBSP	CHOPPED FRESH PARSLEY	30 ML
I TBSP	CHOPPED FRESH THYME	15 ML
	SALT AND FRESHLY GROUND BLACK PEPPER	
2 TBSP	BRANDY, DRY SHERRY OR UNSWEETENED APPLE JUICE	30 ML
2 TBSP	SOUR CREAM	30 ML
I TSP	DIJON MUSTARD	5 ML
4 CUPS	PACKED ARUGULA OR BABY SPINACH LEAVES	I L
$1/4$ CUP	FRESHLY GRATED PARMESAN CHEESE	60 ML

IN A LARGE NONSTICK SKILLET, OVER MEDIUM-HIGH HEAT,
SAUTÉ BACON UNTIL CRISPY. TRANSFER TO A PLATE
LINED WITH PAPER TOWELS. DRAIN OFF FAT AND WIPE OUT
SKILLET WITH A PAPER TOWEL. IN SKILLET, MELT BUTTER

OVER MEDIUM HEAT. SAUTÉ ONION FOR ABOUT 3 MINUTES OR UNTIL SOFTENED. ADD MUSHROOMS AND SAUTÉ FOR ABOUT 5 MINUTES OR UNTIL BROWNED. STIR IN GARLIC, PARSLEY, THYME, $\frac{1}{2}$ TSP (2 ML) SALT AND PEPPER TO TASTE; SAUTÉ FOR 15 SECONDS OR UNTIL FRAGRANT. ADD BRANDY AND SIMMER UNTIL ALMOST EVAPORATED. STIR IN SOUR CREAM AND MUSTARD; COOK, STIRRING, UNTIL JUST WARMED THROUGH. (DO NOT LET BOIL.) TASTE AND ADJUST SEASONING WITH SALT AND PEPPER, IF DESIRED.

PLACE ARUGULA IN A LARGE BOWL AND TOSS WITH MUSHROOM MIXTURE, RESERVED BACON AND PARMESAN. SERVE IMMEDIATELY. SERVES 4 AS AN APPETIZER OR 2 AS A MAIN COURSE.

TIP: EXOTIC MUSHROOMS, SUCH AS CREMINI, PORTOBELLO, OYSTER AND SHIITAKE, ARE MORE FLAVORFUL THAN REGULAR WHITE (BUTTON) MUSHROOMS AND ARE AVAILABLE IN MOST SUPERMARKETS. THEY CAN BE USED INTERCHANGEABLY IN MANY RECIPES. ALTHOUGH SOMETIMES CALLED "WILD" MUSHROOMS, THE EXOTIC MUSHROOMS YOU FIND IN THE PRODUCE AISLE ARE GENERALLY CULTIVATED. SPECIALTY FOOD STORES AND FARMERS' MARKETS ARE GOOD SOURCES OF TRUE WILD MUSHROOMS THAT HAVE BEEN PLUCKED FROM FIELD AND FOREST.

SIGN ON FENCE: SALESMEN WELCOME!
DOG FOOD IS EXPENSIVE!

WARM POTATO, CHORIZO AND CORN SALAD

PAPRIKA-SPICED CHORIZO SAUSAGE ADDS A TINGLE OF HEAT TO THIS COLORFUL SALAD. IT'S PERFECT FOR PERKING UP GRILLED STEAK OR PAN-SEARED RED SNAPPER, COD OR HALIBUT.

DRESSING

1	CLOVE GARLIC, MINCED	1
1/2 TSP	DRIED OREGANO	2 ML
1/4 TSP	SALT	1 ML
PINCH	GRANULATED SUGAR	PINCH
1/4 CUP	OLIVE OR WALNUT OIL	60 ML
1 1/2 TBSP	RED WINE VINEGAR OR SHERRY VINEGAR	22 ML
1 1/2 TSP	FRESHLY SQUEEZED LEMON JUICE	7 ML
	FRESHLY GROUND BLACK PEPPER	

SALAD

1 LB	BABY NEW POTATOES (UNPEELED)	500 G
2 TBSP	FRESHLY SQUEEZED LEMON JUICE	30 ML
4	FRESH CHORIZO OR HOT ITALIAN SAUSAGES, CASINGS REMOVED, CRUMBLED (SEE TIP, BELOW)	4
1	RED BELL PEPPER, CHOPPED	1
1 CUP	FROZEN CORN KERNELS (NO NEED TO THAW)	250 ML
4	GREEN ONIONS, CHOPPED	4
1/3 CUP	FRESHLY GRATED PARMESAN CHEESE OR CRUMBLED BLUE CHEESE	75 ML

DRESSING: IN A BOWL, WHISK TOGETHER GARLIC, OREGANO, SALT, SUGAR, OIL, VINEGAR AND LEMON JUICE. SEASON TO TASTE WITH PEPPER.

SALAD: IF NECESSARY, CUT POTATOES INTO 1½-INCH (4 CM) CHUNKS. PLACE IN A LARGE SAUCEPAN AND COVER WITH COLD SALTED WATER. BRING TO A BOIL OVER HIGH HEAT. REDUCE HEAT TO MEDIUM AND BOIL FOR 10 TO 12 MINUTES OR UNTIL TENDER. DRAIN, PLACE IN A LARGE SALAD BOWL AND TOSS GENTLY WITH LEMON JUICE. SET ASIDE TO COOL SLIGHTLY.

MEANWHILE, IN A LARGE NONSTICK SKILLET, OVER MEDIUM-HIGH HEAT, SAUTÉ CHORIZO FOR 6 TO 8 MINUTES OR UNTIL WELL BROWNED. (THEY SHOULD RELEASE ENOUGH FAT THAT YOU WON'T NEED TO ADD OIL TO THE PAN.) USING A SLOTTED SPOON, TRANSFER CHORIZO TO A PLATE LINED WITH PAPER TOWELS. DRAIN ALL BUT 1 TBSP (15 ML) OF THE FAT FROM THE PAN. SAUTÉ RED PEPPER AND CORN FOR ABOUT 5 MINUTES OR UNTIL SOFTENED AND BROWNED. ADD TO POTATOES. ADD THE RESERVED CHORIZO, GREEN ONIONS AND DRESSING. TOSS GENTLY TO COAT. SPRINKLE WITH PARMESAN. SERVE IMMEDIATELY. SERVES 4.

TIP: CHORIZO IS A SPICY PORK SAUSAGE SEASONED WITH PAPRIKA THAT'S USED IN A LOT OF PORTUGUESE, MEXICAN AND SPANISH RECIPES. IT IS WIDELY AVAILABLE IN SUPERMARKETS. FOR THIS RECIPE, USE THE FRESH CHORIZO, RATHER THAN THE CURED PORK VERSION THAT LOOKS LIKE SALAMI. HOT ITALIAN SAUSAGE IS A GOOD SUBSTITUTE FOR CHORIZO.

MAKE AHEAD: THE DRESSING CAN BE STORED IN AN AIRTIGHT CONTAINER IN THE REFRIGERATOR FOR UP TO 1 DAY.

COCONUT CHICKEN AND PEACH SALAD

COLORFUL AND EASY, AN AMAZING SUMMER ENTRÉE.

DRESSING

1	PEACH, PEELED (SEE TIP, PAGE 321) AND CHOPPED	1
2 TBSP	FRESHLY SQUEEZED LIME JUICE (APPROX.)	30 ML
2 TBSP	CIDER VINEGAR	30 ML
1 TBSP	LIQUID HONEY (APPROX.)	15 ML
1/2 TSP	DIJON MUSTARD	2 ML
1/2 TSP	SALT	2 ML
	FRESHLY GROUND BLACK PEPPER	
1/4 CUP	OLIVE OIL	60 ML

SALAD

3	BONELESS SKINLESS CHICKEN BREASTS (ABOUT 1 1/4 LBS/625 G)	3
1	EGG WHITE	1
1 TBSP	COLD WATER	15 ML
1 TSP	SALT	5 ML
1/2 TSP	DIJON MUSTARD	2 ML
1/4 TSP	FRESHLY GROUND BLACK PEPPER	1 ML
3/4 CUP	PANKO (SEE TIP, PAGE 319) OR DRY BREAD CRUMBS	175 ML
3/4 CUP	FLAKED SWEETENED COCONUT	175 ML
1/4 CUP	OLIVE OIL (APPROX.)	60 ML
6 CUPS	MIXED SALAD GREENS	1.5 L
2	PEACHES, PEELED AND CHOPPED	2
1 CUP	BLUEBERRIES	250 ML
1/4 CUP	TOASTED GREEN PUMPKIN SEEDS OR SLIVERED OR SLICED ALMONDS (SEE TIP, PAGE 127)	60 ML

DRESSING: IN A BLENDER OR FOOD PROCESSOR, COMBINE PEACH, LIME JUICE, VINEGAR, HONEY, MUSTARD, SALT AND PEPPER TO TASTE; PURÉE UNTIL SMOOTH. WITH THE MOTOR RUNNING, THROUGH THE FEED TUBE, GRADUALLY ADD OIL; BLEND UNTIL THICK AND CREAMY-LOOKING. TASTE AND ADD MORE HONEY OR LIME JUICE IF NEEDED FOR THE DESIRED TANGINESS (IT WILL DEPEND ON THE SWEETNESS OF THE PEACH).

SALAD: PLACE CHICKEN BETWEEN TWO PIECES OF PLASTIC WRAP AND POUND LIGHTLY WITH A ROLLING PIN OR THE BOTTOM OF A SKILLET TO FLATTEN. CUT LENGTHWISE INTO 1-INCH (2.5 CM) WIDE STRIPS (YOU'LL GET 3 OR 4 FROM EACH BREAST). IN A SHALLOW DISH, WHISK TOGETHER EGG WHITE, COLD WATER, SALT, MUSTARD AND PEPPER. IN ANOTHER SHALLOW DISH, COMBINE PANKO AND COCONUT. DIP CHICKEN STRIPS IN EGG WHITE MIXTURE, ALLOWING EXCESS TO DRIP OFF, THEN ROLL IN PANKO MIXTURE, SHAKING OFF EXCESS. DISCARD EXCESS EGG WHITE MIXTURE AND PANKO MIXTURE. IN A LARGE SKILLET, HEAT HALF THE OIL OVER MEDIUM-HIGH HEAT. FRY CHICKEN, IN BATCHES, FOR 3 TO 4 MINUTES PER SIDE OR UNTIL GOLDEN AND NO LONGER PINK INSIDE, ADDING MORE OIL AS NEEDED BETWEEN BATCHES. USING A SLOTTED SPOON, TRANSFER CHICKEN TO A PLATE.

MEANWHILE, IN A LARGE BOWL, TOSS SALAD GREENS WITH HALF THE DRESSING. DIVIDE AMONG 4 PLATES. SPRINKLE WITH PEACHES AND BLUEBERRIES. TOP WITH CHICKEN STRIPS, DRIZZLE WITH THE REMAINING DRESSING AND SPRINKLE WITH PUMPKIN SEEDS. SERVES 4.

KILLER QUINOA SALAD

QUINOA (PRONOUNCED KEEN-WAH) IS THE MOST
NUTRITIOUS GRAIN THERE IS. SOMETHING SO GOOD FOR
YOU SHOULDN'T TASTE SO GOOD, BUT IT DOES. SERVE
THIS NUTTY-TEXTURED SALAD ALONE OR WITH GRILLED
CHICKEN OR PORK. THIS IS AN EXCELLENT BUFFET
SALAD THAT WILL HOLD FOR ABOUT AN HOUR.

DRESSING

	FINELY GRATED ZEST AND JUICE OF 1 LEMON	
3 TBSP	OLIVE OR VEGETABLE OIL	45 ML
1/2 TSP	GROUND CORIANDER	2 ML
1/2 TSP	GROUND CUMIN	2 ML
1/2 TSP	PAPRIKA	2 ML
	SALT AND FRESHLY GROUND BLACK PEPPER	

SALAD

1 CUP	RED OR WHITE QUINOA, RINSED WELL (SEE TIP, OPPOSITE)	250 ML
1/2 TSP	SALT	2 ML
2 CUPS	COLD WATER	500 ML
1 CUP	DRIED CRANBERRIES	250 ML
1/4 CUP	FINELY DICED DRIED APRICOTS	60 ML
	WARM WATER	
2	RIPE AVOCADOS (SEE TIP, PAGE 129)	2
2	GREEN ONIONS, SLICED DIAGONALLY	2
1/4 CUP	TOASTED SLIVERED OR SLICED ALMONDS (SEE TIP, PAGE 127)	60 ML

DRESSING: IN A BOWL, WHISK TOGETHER LEMON ZEST,
LEMON JUICE, OIL, CORIANDER, CUMIN AND PAPRIKA.
SEASON TO TASTE WITH SALT AND PEPPER.

SALAD: IN A SAUCEPAN, COMBINE QUINOA, SALT AND COLD WATER; BRING TO A BOIL OVER MEDIUM-HIGH HEAT. STIR, REDUCE HEAT TO LOW, COVER AND SIMMER FOR ABOUT 15 MINUTES OR UNTIL WATER IS ABSORBED AND QUINOA IS TENDER. FLUFF WITH A FORK, SPREAD ON A LARGE BAKING SHEET AND LET COOL COMPLETELY.

MEANWHILE, PLACE CRANBERRIES AND APRICOTS IN A SMALL BOWL. COVER WITH WARM WATER AND LET STAND FOR ABOUT 5 MINUTES OR UNTIL PLUMP. DRAIN AND SET ASIDE.

PEEL AVOCADOS AND CUT INTO BITE-SIZED CHUNKS. PLACE IN A BOWL AND TOSS WITH 1 TBSP (15 ML) OF THE DRESSING TO PREVENT DISCOLORATION. PLACE COOLED QUINOA IN A LARGE SALAD BOWL. ADD CRANBERRY MIXTURE, AVOCADOS, GREEN ONIONS AND ALMONDS. ADD THE REMAINING DRESSING AND TOSS TO COMBINE. SERVES 6.

TIP: FIRST CULTIVATED BY THE INCAS, QUINOA IS AN ANCIENT GRAIN THAT IS GROWING IN POPULARITY. AVAILABLE IN RED AND WHITE VARIETIES, IT HAS A MILD, NUTTY FLAVOR AND EXPANDS FOUR TO FIVE TIMES WHEN COOKED. IT'S IMPORTANT TO RINSE IT THOROUGHLY UNDER COLD RUNNING WATER BEFORE COOKING TO REMOVE THE SLIGHTLY BITTER COATING ON THE GRAINS. REFRIGERATE RAW QUINOA TO PREVENT IT FROM BECOMING RANCID.

MAKE AHEAD: THE DRESSING CAN BE STORED IN AN AIRTIGHT CONTAINER IN THE REFRIGERATOR FOR UP TO 1 DAY. THE QUINOA CAN BE COOKED UP TO 1 DAY IN ADVANCE; AFTER COOLING, TRANSFER TO AN AIRTIGHT CONTAINER AND REFRIGERATE.

QUINOA SALAD À LA GREQUE

QUINOA, THE NEW SUPER-GRAIN, IS AVAILABLE AT MOST SUPERMARKETS. IF YOU CAN'T FIND IT ON A SHELF, CHECK THE BULK BINS OR HEAD TO YOUR LOCAL HEALTH FOOD STORE. THIS SALAD HAS FIRST-CLASS FLAVOR AND WILL HOLD IN THE FRIDGE FOR UP TO 24 HOURS. IT'S GREAT FOR BUFFETS.

1 CUP	RED OR WHITE QUINOA, RINSED WELL (SEE TIP, PAGE 77)	250 ML
1/2 TSP	SALT	2 ML
2 CUPS	COLD WATER	500 ML
1 TSP	DRIED OREGANO	5 ML
1/2 TSP	GROUND CUMIN	2 ML
1/2 TSP	SALT	2 ML
1/4 TSP	FRESHLY GROUND BLACK PEPPER	1 ML
3 TBSP	EXTRA VIRGIN OR VIRGIN OLIVE OIL	45 ML
3 TBSP	FRESHLY SQUEEZED LEMON JUICE	45 ML
1/2	ENGLISH CUCUMBER, QUARTERED LENGTHWISE AND SLICED	1/2
1 1/2 CUPS	CHERRY TOMATOES, HALVED (OR WHOLE GRAPE TOMATOES)	375 ML
1 CUP	FRESH OR FROZEN CORN KERNELS (SEE TIP, OPPOSITE), COOKED	250 ML
3/4 CUP	CHOPPED TOASTED PECANS OR WALNUTS (SEE TIP, PAGE 127)	175 ML
1/2 CUP	CRUMBLED FETA CHEESE (SEE TIP, PAGE 199)	125 ML
1/3 CUP	CHOPPED PITTED KALAMATA OLIVES (NOT FROM A CAN)	75 ML
1/4 CUP	CHOPPED FRESH PARSLEY	60 ML

IN A SAUCEPAN, COMBINE QUINOA, SALT AND COLD WATER; BRING TO A BOIL OVER MEDIUM-HIGH HEAT. STIR,

REDUCE HEAT TO LOW, COVER AND SIMMER FOR ABOUT
15 MINUTES OR UNTIL WATER IS ABSORBED AND QUINOA IS
TENDER. FLUFF WITH A FORK, SPREAD ON A LARGE BAKING
SHEET AND LET COOL COMPLETELY.

IN A LARGE SERVING BOWL, WHISK TOGETHER OREGANO,
CUMIN, SALT, PEPPER, OIL AND LEMON JUICE. STIR IN
COOLED QUINOA, CUCUMBER, TOMATOES, CORN, PECANS,
FETA, OLIVES AND PARSLEY. COVER AND REFRIGERATE
FOR AT LEAST 4 HOURS OR UP TO 24 HOURS TO LET THE
FLAVORS DEVELOP. SERVES 6 TO 8.

TIP: TO REMOVE FRESH CORN KERNELS FROM THE COB,
IF NECESSARY, FIRST REMOVE THE HUSKS AND SILK BITS
BY PULLING THEM DOWN. SNAP OFF THE STEM. PLACE
THE COB, STEM END DOWN, ON THE COUNTER OR IN A
SHALLOW DISH. HOLD THE TOP FIRMLY AND, WITH A SHARP
KNIFE, CUT STRAIGHT DOWN TO REMOVE THE KERNELS.
TURN THE COB TWO OR THREE TIMES UNTIL ALL THE
KERNELS ARE REMOVED.

MAKE AHEAD: THE QUINOA CAN BE COOKED UP TO 1 DAY
IN ADVANCE; AFTER COOLING, TRANSFER TO AN AIRTIGHT
CONTAINER AND REFRIGERATE.

PERFECTION IS OVERRATED.

MEDITERRANEAN COUSCOUS SALAD

THIS VIBRANT-TASTING SALAD IS WONDERFUL
FOR LUNCH OR A LIGHT SUPPER. IT TRAVELS WELL,
SO TOTE SOME TO WORK. OR DOUBLE THE RECIPE
FOR A BUFFET. IT GOES PARTICULARLY WELL WITH
TURKEY BURGERS IN PITA POCKETS (PAGE 130).

DRESSING

3 TBSP	WHITE WINE VINEGAR	45 ML
3 TBSP	OLIVE OIL	45 ML
	FRESHLY GROUND BLACK PEPPER	
	SALT (OPTIONAL)	

SALAD

1 CUP	REDUCED-SODIUM CHICKEN BROTH, HOMEMADE VEGETABLE STOCK (SEE RECIPE, PAGE 90) OR WATER	250 ML
1 CUP	COUSCOUS	250 ML
16	PITTED KALAMATA OLIVES (NOT FROM A CAN)	16
6	MARINATED ARTICHOKE HEARTS, DRAINED AND HALVED	6
6	GREEN ONIONS, FINELY CHOPPED	6
1/2 CUP	CHOPPED DRAINED ROASTED RED BELL PEPPERS (SEE TIP, PAGE 54)	125 ML
1/2 CUP	CRUMBLED FETA CHEESE (SEE TIP, PAGE 199)	125 ML
1/4 CUP	FINELY CHOPPED FRESH PARSLEY	60 ML
1 TBSP	CHOPPED FRESH THYME, MINT OR DILL	15 ML

DRESSING: IN A SMALL BOWL, WHISK TOGETHER VINEGAR,
OIL, AND PEPPER TO TASTE. IF DESIRED, SEASON WITH
SALT TO TASTE. (THE FETA CHEESE IN THE SALAD IS
QUITE SALTY, SO SEASON THE DRESSING CAUTIOUSLY.)

SALAD: IN A SAUCEPAN, OVER MEDIUM-HIGH HEAT, BRING BROTH TO A BOIL. STIR IN COUSCOUS AND IMMEDIATELY REMOVE FROM HEAT. COVER AND LET STAND UNTIL BROTH IS ABSORBED, ABOUT 5 MINUTES. FLUFF COUSCOUS WITH A FORK AND TRANSFER TO A LARGE BOWL. ADD OLIVES, ARTICHOKES, GREEN ONIONS, ROASTED PEPPERS, FETA, PARSLEY AND THYME. POUR DRESSING OVER COUSCOUS MIXTURE AND TOSS TO COMBINE. COVER AND REFRIGERATE FOR AT LEAST 4 HOURS TO LET THE FLAVORS DEVELOP. BEFORE SERVING, TASTE AND ADJUST SEASONING WITH SALT, PEPPER AND ADDITIONAL VINEGAR, IF DESIRED. SERVES 4.

TIP: LEFTOVER PARSLEY CAN BE FROZEN. REMOVE THE STALKS, DISCARDING THEM OR FREEZING THEM WHOLE TO USE IN STOCKS. IN A FOOD PROCESSOR, FINELY CHOP THE LEAVES. SPREAD THE CHOPPED PARSLEY ON A LARGE BAKING SHEET AND FREEZE, UNCOVERED, FOR 1 HOUR. TRANSFER FROZEN PARSLEY TO A FREEZER BAG OR AIRTIGHT CONTAINER. THE FROZEN CHOPPED PARSLEY CAN BE ADDED DIRECTLY TO SOUPS, STEWS AND HOT SAUCES. IT IS NOT RECOMMENDED FOR USE IN SALADS.

MAKE AHEAD: THE DRESSING CAN BE STORED IN AN AIRTIGHT CONTAINER IN THE REFRIGERATOR FOR UP TO 5 DAYS. TRANSFER SALAD TO AN AIRTIGHT CONTAINER AND REFRIGERATE FOR UP TO 2 DAYS.

IT'S BEEN MONDAY ALL WEEK.

CHICKPEA AND FETA SALAD

*THIS IS A GREAT BUFFET SALAD —
LEMONY AND, OF COURSE, HEALTHY!*

DRESSING

2	CLOVES GARLIC, MINCED	2
1/3 CUP	EXTRA VIRGIN OR REGULAR OLIVE OIL	75 ML
	FINELY GRATED ZEST AND JUICE OF 1 LARGE LEMON	
	FRESHLY GROUND BLACK PEPPER	

SALAD

2	CANS (19 OZ/ 540 ML) CHICKPEAS, DRAINED AND RINSED	2
1/4 CUP	PACKED FRESH MINT, CHOPPED	60 ML
3 TBSP	FINELY CHOPPED RED ONION	45 ML
2 TBSP	CHOPPED FRESH PARSLEY	30 ML
3/4 CUP	CRUMBLED FETA CHEESE (SEE TIP, PAGE 199)	175 ML
	SALT (OPTIONAL, SEE TIP, BELOW)	

DRESSING: IN A SMALL BOWL, WHISK TOGETHER GARLIC, OIL, LEMON ZEST, LEMON JUICE AND PEPPER TO TASTE.

SALAD: IN A LARGE SALAD BOWL, GENTLY COMBINE CHICKPEAS, MINT, RED ONION AND PARSLEY. POUR DRESSING OVER CHICKPEA MIXTURE, SPRINKLE FETA OVER TOP AND TOSS TO COMBINE. TASTE AND SEASON WITH SALT AND ADDITIONAL PEPPER, IF DESIRED. SERVES 4 TO 6.

TIP: THE FETA CHEESE IS QUITE SALTY, SO WE GENERALLY DON'T ADD SALT TO THIS SALAD, BUT TASTE IT AND DECIDE FOR YOURSELF.

MAKE AHEAD: THE DRESSING CAN BE STORED IN AN AIRTIGHT CONTAINER IN THE REFRIGERATOR FOR UP TO 1 DAY.

SUN-DRIED TOMATO VINAIGRETTE

MAKING YOUR OWN SALAD DRESSING IS EASY AND FUN, PLUS YOU CAN MAKE SMALL QUANTITIES. (AND YOU WON'T HAVE TO FACE A REFRIGERATOR FULL OF HALF-USED, OUT-OF-DATE BOTTLES.) THIS ONE IS EXCELLENT TOSSED WITH SALAD GREENS, DRIZZLED OVER STEAMED VEGETABLES OR SERVED WITH PAN-FRIED FISH.

2	CLOVES GARLIC, MINCED	2
2 TBSP	FINELY CHOPPED DRAINED OIL-PACKED SUN-DRIED TOMATOES	30 ML
	SALT AND FRESHLY GROUND BLACK PEPPER	
I TBSP	SUN-DRIED TOMATO PESTO	15 ML
I TBSP	BALSAMIC VINEGAR	15 ML
I TBSP	RED WINE VINEGAR	15 ML
4 TO 6 TBSP	COLD WATER	60 TO 90 ML
1/4 CUP	OLIVE OIL	60 ML

IN A BLENDER OR FOOD PROCESSOR, COMBINE GARLIC, SUN-DRIED TOMATOES, 1/2 TSP (2 ML) SALT, 1/8 TSP (0.5 ML) PEPPER, PESTO, BALSAMIC VINEGAR, RED WINE VINEGAR AND 4 TBSP (60 ML) COLD WATER; PROCESS UNTIL WELL INCORPORATED (THE MIXTURE WON'T BE COMPLETELY SMOOTH). WITH THE MOTOR RUNNING, THROUGH THE FEED TUBE, GRADUALLY ADD OIL; PROCESS UNTIL WELL INCORPORATED. STIR IN ADDITIONAL COLD WATER, IF NEEDED, TO REACH DESIRED CONSISTENCY. TASTE AND ADJUST SEASONING WITH SALT AND PEPPER, IF DESIRED. MAKES ABOUT 3/4 CUP (175 ML).

MAKE AHEAD: STORE IN AN AIRTIGHT CONTAINER IN THE REFRIGERATOR FOR UP TO 5 DAYS.

CRANBERRY VINAIGRETTE

THIS DRESSING IS EXCELLENT TOSSED WITH SPINACH. GOOD ADDITIONS ARE CHOPPED COOKED TURKEY OR CHICKEN, CRUMBLED COOKED BACON, DRIED CRANBERRIES AND CHOPPED PECANS. CHOPPED KIWI AND HALVED RED GRAPES ALSO WORK WELL.

1/4 TSP	DRIED OREGANO	1 ML
3 TBSP	RED WINE VINEGAR	45 ML
2 TBSP	FROZEN CRANBERRY COCKTAIL, THAWED	30 ML
1 TBSP	DIJON MUSTARD	15 ML
1 TO 2 TSP	LIQUID HONEY OR GRANULATED SUGAR	5 TO 10 ML
3 TBSP	OLIVE OIL	45 ML
	SALT AND FRESHLY GROUND BLACK PEPPER	

IN A BOWL, WHISK TOGETHER OREGANO, VINEGAR, CRANBERRY COCKTAIL, MUSTARD AND 1 TSP (5 ML) HONEY. GRADUALLY WHISK IN OIL. SEASON TO TASTE WITH SALT AND PEPPER. TASTE AND WHISK IN ADDITIONAL HONEY IF YOU PREFER A SWEETER DRESSING. MAKES ABOUT 1/2 CUP (125 ML).

MAKE AHEAD: STORE IN AN AIRTIGHT CONTAINER IN THE REFRIGERATOR FOR UP TO 1 WEEK.

MANDARIN GINGER VINAIGRETTE

HERE'S A GREAT DRESSING TO SPICE UP A SPINACH SALAD. TOP WITH MANDARIN OR ORANGE SEGMENTS, FRESH BEAN SPROUTS, TOASTED ALMONDS OR SESAME SEEDS AND CHOPPED FRESH CILANTRO.

2 TBSP	FINELY CHOPPED SHALLOT OR RED ONION	30 ML
2 TSP	GRATED GINGERROOT	10 ML
1/3 CUP	FRESHLY SQUEEZED MANDARIN ORANGE JUICE OR ORANGE JUICE	75 ML
2 1/2 TBSP	SEASONED RICE VINEGAR	37 ML
1 TBSP	VEGETABLE OIL	15 ML
1/2 TSP	SESAME OIL	2 ML
	SALT AND FRESHLY GROUND BLACK PEPPER	

IN A BOWL, WHISK TOGETHER SHALLOT, GINGER, ORANGE JUICE, VINEGAR, VEGETABLE OIL AND SESAME OIL. SEASON TO TASTE WITH SALT AND PEPPER. MAKES ABOUT 2/3 CUP (150 ML).

MAKE AHEAD: STORE IN AN AIRTIGHT CONTAINER IN THE REFRIGERATOR FOR UP TO 1 WEEK.

MANY PEOPLE HAVE EATEN MY COOKING AND GONE ON TO LEAD NORMAL LIVES.

CITRUS POPPY SEED
YOGURT DRESSING

MAKE THIS DRESSING WITH LIMES OR ORANGES, OR A COMBINATION OF THE TWO — IT'S UP TO YOU. TOSS WITH MIXED GREENS AND TOP WITH SLICED STRAWBERRIES, RED ONIONS AND TOASTED ALMONDS.

1/2 CUP	PLAIN YOGURT	125 ML
1 TSP	FINELY GRATED LIME OR ORANGE ZEST	5 ML
2 TBSP	FRESHLY SQUEEZED LIME OR ORANGE JUICE	30 ML
1 TO 2 TSP	LIQUID HONEY	5 TO 10 ML
1/2 TSP	DIJON MUSTARD	2 ML
	SALT AND FRESHLY GROUND BLACK PEPPER	
2 TSP	POPPY SEEDS	10 ML

IN A BOWL, WHISK TOGETHER YOGURT, LIME ZEST, LIME JUICE, HONEY AND MUSTARD. SEASON TO TASTE WITH SALT AND PEPPER. STIR IN POPPY SEEDS. MAKES ABOUT 2/3 CUP (150 ML).

MAKE AHEAD: STORE IN AN AIRTIGHT CONTAINER IN THE REFRIGERATOR FOR UP TO 5 DAYS.

IT IS EASY TO BE BRAVE FROM A SAFE DISTANCE.

CREAMY HORSERADISH DRESSING

TOSS THIS TANGY DRESSING WITH TORN ROMAINE AND SHREDDED RADICCHIO TO SERVE ALONGSIDE GRILLED STEAK. IT ALSO WORKS WELL WITH FRESH BEETS.

2 TBSP	CHOPPED FRESH PARSLEY	30 ML
2 TBSP	LIGHT MAYONNAISE	30 ML
2 TBSP	LIGHT SOUR CREAM	30 ML
2 TBSP	FRESHLY SQUEEZED LEMON JUICE	30 ML
1 TBSP	PREPARED HORSERADISH	15 ML
	SALT AND FRESHLY GROUND BLACK PEPPER	

IN A BOWL, WHISK TOGETHER PARSLEY, MAYONNAISE, SOUR CREAM, LEMON JUICE AND HORSERADISH. SEASON TO TASTE WITH SALT AND PEPPER. MAKES ABOUT $\frac{1}{2}$ CUP (125 ML).

MAKE AHEAD: STORE IN AN AIRTIGHT CONTAINER IN THE REFRIGERATOR FOR UP TO 5 DAYS.

STRENGTH IS THE CAPACITY TO BREAK A
CHOCOLATE BAR INTO FOUR PIECES WITH YOUR
BARE HANDS – AND THEN EAT JUST ONE OF THE PIECES.
– JUDITH VIORST

ROASTED GARLIC
CAESAR DRESSING

HERE'S A RICH, CREAMY AND LOWER-FAT VERSION OF EVERYONE'S FAVORITE SALAD DRESSING. THE SECRET? IT'S MADE WITH FLAVORFUL ROASTED GARLIC INSTEAD OF RAW EGGS OR MAYONNAISE.

1	HEAD GARLIC	1
	SALT AND FRESHLY GROUND BLACK PEPPER	
2 TBSP	CIDER VINEGAR	30 ML
1 TBSP	COLD WATER (APPROX.)	15 ML
1 TBSP	FRESHLY SQUEEZED LEMON JUICE	15 ML
1 TSP	DIJON MUSTARD	5 ML
1/2 TSP	WORCESTERSHIRE SAUCE	2 ML
1/4 CUP	OLIVE OIL	60 ML
2 TBSP	FRESHLY GRATED PARMESAN CHEESE	30 ML

PREHEAT OVEN TO 350°F (180°C). CUT A THIN SLICE OFF THE TOP OF THE GARLIC HEAD, EXPOSING THE CLOVES. WRAP IN FOIL, PLACE IN A SMALL BAKING DISH AND ROAST FOR 30 TO 40 MINUTES OR UNTIL GARLIC IS VERY TENDER. LET COOL SLIGHTLY. SQUEEZE THE INDIVIDUAL CLOVES OUT OF THEIR PAPERY SKIN AND PLACE IN A FOOD PROCESSOR. ADD 1/2 TSP (2 ML) SALT, 1/8 TSP (0.5 ML) PEPPER, VINEGAR, COLD WATER, LEMON JUICE, MUSTARD AND WORCESTERSHIRE SAUCE; PULSE A FEW TIMES, UNTIL MIXTURE IS SMOOTH. ADD OIL AND PULSE UNTIL CREAMY. TRANSFER TO A BOWL AND STIR IN PARMESAN. TASTE AND ADJUST SEASONING WITH SALT AND PEPPER, IF DESIRED. WHISK IN 1 TO 2 TSP (5 TO 10 ML) MORE COLD WATER IF YOU DESIRE A LOOSER CONSISTENCY. MAKES ABOUT 2/3 CUP (150 ML).

SOUPS

HOMEMADE VEGETABLE STOCK

HOMEMADE STOCK REALLY MAKES A DIFFERENCE —
PARTICULARLY IN SOUPS AND STEWS. VEGETABLE
STOCK CAN BE USED INTERCHANGEABLY WITH
CHICKEN AND BEEF STOCK OR BROTH IN MANY
RECIPES. IT'S FAST AND IT'S CHEAP. AND BECAUSE
IT CONTAINS NO SALT OR ADDITIVES, IT'S HEALTHY.
MAKE ONE OR TWO BATCHES AND FREEZE IT IN 1- AND
4-CUP (250 ML AND 1 L) PORTIONS SO THAT YOU HAVE
STOCK ON HAND FOR A VARIETY OF RECIPES.

6	MUSHROOMS, QUARTERED (OR 1 CUP/250 ML MUSHROOM STEMS)	6
2	STALKS CELERY, THICKLY SLICED	2
1	LEEK, THICKLY SLICED	1
1	CARROT, THICKLY SLICED	1
1	ONION, THICKLY SLICED	1
1	TOMATO, QUARTERED	1
6	WHOLE BLACK PEPPERCORNS	6
2	PARSLEY STEMS	2
2	BAY LEAVES	2
1/8 TSP	DRIED THYME	0.5 ML

IN A LARGE SAUCEPAN OR DUTCH OVEN, COMBINE
MUSHROOMS, CELERY, LEEK, CARROT, ONION, TOMATO,
PEPPERCORNS, PARSLEY STEMS, BAY LEAVES, THYME AND
7 CUPS (1.75 L) WATER. BRING TO A BOIL OVER HIGH HEAT.
IF ANY SCUM RISES TO THE TOP, SKIM IT OFF WITH A
LARGE SPOON. REDUCE HEAT TO LOW, COVER, LEAVING
LID AJAR, AND SIMMER FOR 45 MINUTES. THE STOCK
WILL HAVE REDUCED CONSIDERABLY. STRAIN THROUGH A
FINE-MESH SIEVE, DISCARDING SOLIDS. LET COOL. MAKES
ABOUT 4 CUPS (1 L).

CONTINUED ON PAGE 91...

Mint, Mango and Avocado Salad (page 58)

Killer Quinoa Salad (page 76)

Golden Cauliflower Cashew Soup (page 108)

Our New Favorite Flatbread (page 126)

TIP: HOMEMADE STOCK TASTES ONLY AS GOOD AS THE INGREDIENTS YOU PUT IN IT. DON'T DUMP SPOILED VEGETABLES OR PEELINGS INTO THE POT. HOWEVER, YOU CAN INCLUDE PARSLEY STEMS, SLIGHTLY WILTED MUSHROOMS AND TOMATOES THAT HAVE BECOME TOO SOFT FOR SALADS.

TIP: TO VARY THE FLAVOR OF THE STOCK, ADD A FEW FRESH OR ROASTED GARLIC CLOVES, A HANDFUL OF FENNEL STALKS OR THE TRIMMINGS OF 1 OR 2 BELL PEPPERS.

TIP: AVOID INGREDIENTS THAT WILL MAKE YOUR STOCK BITTER OR OVERWHELM THE FLAVOR. THESE INCLUDE CABBAGE, BRUSSELS SPROUTS, BROCCOLI, CAULIFLOWER, BEETS (UNLESS YOU'RE MAKING BORSCHT!), ASPARAGUS AND TURNIPS.

MAKE AHEAD: LET COOL FOR 30 MINUTES, THEN REFRIGERATE, UNCOVERED, IN A SHALLOW CONTAINER UNTIL COLD. COVER TIGHTLY AND KEEP REFRIGERATED FOR UP TO 2 DAYS OR FREEZE FOR UP TO 2 MONTHS.

VARIATION: FOR A MORE DEEPLY FLAVORED STOCK, SAUTÉ THE CELERY, LEEK, CARROT AND ONION IN 1 TBSP (15 ML) OLIVE OIL FOR 5 TO 7 MINUTES OR UNTIL THE ONION IS SOFTENED BEFORE ADDING THE REMAINING INGREDIENTS. ALTERNATIVELY, YOU COULD TOSS THE CELERY, LEEK, CARROT AND ONION WITH 1 TBSP (15 ML) OIL, SPREAD ON A LARGE RIMMED BAKING SHEET AND ROAST IN A PREHEATED 400°F (200°C) OVEN FOR 30 TO 45 MINUTES OR UNTIL BROWNED.

QUICK CHICKEN AND CORN CHOWDER

WHEN WE ASKED THEM TO TRY THIS CHOWDER, OUR STUDENT TASTE-TESTERS POLISHED OFF THE ENTIRE POT IN MINUTES, THEN GAVE IT TOP MARKS. DON'T SNIFF AT THE EVAPORATED MILK — IT'S THE SECRET TO THE SOUP'S CREAMY RICHNESS. SERVE IT WITH LAZY DAYS BUTTERMILK BISCUITS (PAGE 22).

4	SLICES BACON, CHOPPED	4
1 TO 2 TSP	VEGETABLE OIL (IF NEEDED)	5 TO 10 ML
10	READY-PEELED BABY CARROTS, CUT INTO THIRDS (SEE TIP, OPPOSITE)	10
3/4 CUP	FINELY CHOPPED ONION	175 ML
1	BONELESS SKINLESS CHICKEN BREAST, CUT INTO SMALL PIECES	1
2 CUPS	FROZEN CORN KERNELS (NO NEED TO THAW)	500 ML
1 1/2 CUPS	FROZEN DICED HASH BROWN POTATOES (NO NEED TO THAW)	375 ML
	SALT AND FRESHLY GROUND BLACK PEPPER	
4 CUPS	REDUCED-SODIUM CHICKEN BROTH	1 L
2 TSP	CORNSTARCH	10 ML
2 TSP	COLD WATER	10 ML
1	CAN (370 ML) EVAPORATED MILK	1
2 TBSP	CHOPPED FRESH PARSLEY OR CHIVES	30 ML

IN A LARGE SAUCEPAN, SAUTÉ BACON OVER MEDIUM-HIGH HEAT UNTIL CRISPY. USING A SLOTTED SPOON, TRANSFER TO A PLATE LINED WITH PAPER TOWELS. DRAIN OFF ALL BUT 1 TBSP (15 ML) OF THE FAT FROM THE PAN. IF THERE IS LESS THAN 1 TBSP (15 ML) FAT, ADD OIL AS

NEEDED. REDUCE HEAT TO MEDIUM AND SAUTÉ CARROTS AND ONION, SCRAPING UP ANY BROWN BITS FROM THE BOTTOM OF THE PAN, FOR ABOUT 5 MINUTES OR UNTIL ONION IS SOFTENED. ADD RESERVED BACON, CHICKEN, CORN, HASH BROWNS, $\frac{1}{2}$ TSP (2 ML) SALT, PEPPER TO TASTE AND BROTH; BRING TO A BOIL. REDUCE HEAT TO LOW, COVER, LEAVING LID AJAR, AND SIMMER FOR 15 MINUTES OR UNTIL CHICKEN IS NO LONGER PINK INSIDE. IN A SMALL BOWL, WHISK TOGETHER CORNSTARCH AND COLD WATER UNTIL SMOOTH. STIR INTO SOUP, ALONG WITH EVAPORATED MILK AND PARSLEY; SIMMER, STIRRING, UNTIL STEAMING AND SLIGHTLY THICKENED. TASTE AND ADJUST SEASONING WITH SALT AND PEPPER, IF DESIRED. SERVES 6.

TIP: READY-PEELED BABY CARROTS ARE GREAT TIME SAVERS IN THE KITCHEN. ADD THEM WHOLE, HALVED OR COARSELY CHOPPED TO SOUPS, STEWS AND STIR-FRIES.

MAKE AHEAD: LET COOL FOR 30 MINUTES, THEN REFRIGERATE, UNCOVERED, IN A SHALLOW CONTAINER UNTIL COLD. COVER TIGHTLY AND KEEP REFRIGERATED FOR UP TO 1 DAY. REHEAT SLOWLY. WE DON'T RECOMMEND FREEZING THIS SOUP.

IF YOU PUT A CROUTON ON YOUR SUNDAE INSTEAD OF A CHERRY, IT COUNTS AS A SALAD.

CASABLANCA CHICKEN SOUP

THIS FRAGRANT SOUP TASTES EVEN BETTER THE NEXT DAY.

1½ TBSP	OLIVE OR VEGETABLE OIL	22 ML
1	ONION, CHOPPED	1
2	CLOVES GARLIC, MINCED	2
2 TSP	PACKED BROWN SUGAR	10 ML
1 TSP	PAPRIKA	5 ML
1 TSP	GROUND CUMIN	5 ML
	SALT AND FRESHLY GROUND BLACK PEPPER	
½ TSP	ASIAN CHILI PASTE (SEE TIP, PAGE 207)	2 ML
1	CAN (28 OZ/796 ML) NO-SALT-ADDED WHOLE TOMATOES, WITH JUICE (SEE TIP, PAGE 171)	1
1	SKINLESS BONE-IN CHICKEN BREAST	1
1½ CUPS	REDUCED-SODIUM CHICKEN BROTH	375 ML
1	CAN (19 OZ/540 ML) CHICKPEAS, DRAINED AND RINSED	1
2 TBSP	CHOPPED FRESH CILANTRO	30 ML
	FINELY GRATED ZEST AND JUICE OF ½ LEMON	

IN A LARGE SAUCEPAN OR DUTCH OVEN, HEAT OIL OVER MEDIUM HEAT. SAUTÉ ONION FOR ABOUT 5 MINUTES OR UNTIL SOFTENED. ADD GARLIC, BROWN SUGAR, PAPRIKA, CUMIN, ½ TSP (2 ML) SALT, PEPPER TO TASTE AND CHILI PASTE; SAUTÉ FOR ABOUT 15 SECONDS OR UNTIL FRAGRANT. ADD TOMATOES WITH JUICE, BREAKING THEM UP WITH A SPOON. ADD CHICKEN AND BROTH; BRING TO A BOIL. REDUCE HEAT TO LOW, COVER, LEAVING LID AJAR, AND SIMMER, STIRRING OCCASIONALLY, FOR ABOUT 25 MINUTES OR UNTIL CHICKEN IS NO LONGER PINK

INSIDE. REMOVE FROM HEAT. USING TONGS, TRANSFER CHICKEN TO A PLATE AND LET COOL FOR ABOUT 5 MINUTES OR UNTIL COOL ENOUGH TO HANDLE. (IF A SMOOTH SOUP IS DESIRED, USE AN IMMERSION BLENDER, FOOD PROCESSOR OR BLENDER TO PURÉE SOUP TO DESIRED CONSISTENCY. RETURN TO POT, IF NECESSARY.) SHRED CHICKEN, DISCARDING BONE, AND RETURN TO SOUP. STIR IN CHICKPEAS AND BRING TO A BOIL OVER MEDIUM-HIGH HEAT. REDUCE HEAT AND SIMMER, UNCOVERED, STIRRING OFTEN, FOR 5 MINUTES. STIR IN CILANTRO, LEMON ZEST AND LEMON JUICE. TASTE AND ADJUST SEASONING WITH SALT AND PEPPER, IF DESIRED. SERVES 4 TO 6.

TIP: IN PLACE OF THE ASIAN CHILI PASTE, YOU COULD USE A PINCH OF HOT PEPPER FLAKES.

TIP: BONE-IN CHICKEN BREASTS MAY BE SOLD WHOLE OR IN HALVES, GENERALLY WITH THE SKIN ON. EITHER SIZE WILL WORK IN THIS SOUP, DEPENDING ON HOW MUCH CHICKEN YOU WANT. TO REMOVE THE SKIN, USE A PIECE OF PAPER TOWEL TO GRAB THE SKIN AT ONE END. PULL FIRMLY. THE SKIN SHOULD PEEL RIGHT OFF. IF YOU BUY A WHOLE BONE-IN CHICKEN BREAST THAT'S LABELED "BACK ATTACHED," JUST USE THE WHOLE THING IN THE SOUP. IT'LL TASTE EVEN BETTER.

MAKE AHEAD: LET COOL FOR 30 MINUTES, THEN REFRIGERATE, UNCOVERED, IN A SHALLOW CONTAINER UNTIL COLD. COVER TIGHTLY AND KEEP REFRIGERATED FOR UP TO 2 DAYS OR FREEZE FOR UP TO 2 MONTHS. THAW AND REHEAT SLOWLY.

SOUL SOUP

THIS COMFORTING AND NOURISHING CHICKEN SOUP IS READY IN MUCH LESS TIME THAN GRANDMA'S USED TO TAKE!

I TBSP	OLIVE OR VEGETABLE OIL	15 ML
2	CARROTS, THINLY SLICED	2
2	STALKS CELERY, THINLY SLICED	2
I	ONION, CHOPPED	I
2	CLOVES GARLIC, MINCED	2
I TSP	MINCED GINGERROOT	5 ML
I	SKINLESS BONE-IN CHICKEN BREAST (SEE TIP, PAGE 95)	I
I	SPRIG FRESH PARSLEY	I
	SALT AND FRESHLY GROUND BLACK PEPPER	
4 TO 5 CUPS	REDUCED-SODIUM CHICKEN BROTH	I TO 1.25 L
I TBSP	TOMATO PASTE (SEE TIP, PAGE 275)	15 ML
I TBSP	REDUCED-SODIUM SOY SAUCE	15 ML
1/2 CUP	SOUP NOODLES OR BROKEN SPAGHETTINI (SEE TIP, OPPOSITE)	125 ML
1/2 CUP	QUARTERED TRIMMED SNOW PEAS OR FROZEN PEAS	125 ML

IN A LARGE SAUCEPAN OR DUTCH OVEN, HEAT OIL OVER MEDIUM HEAT. SAUTÉ CARROTS, CELERY AND ONION FOR 5 MINUTES OR UNTIL ONION IS SOFTENED. ADD GARLIC AND GINGER; SAUTÉ FOR ABOUT 15 SECONDS OR UNTIL FRAGRANT. STIR IN CHICKEN, PARSLEY, 1/2 TSP (2 ML) SALT, PEPPER TO TASTE, 4 CUPS (I L) BROTH, TOMATO PASTE AND SOY SAUCE; BRING TO A BOIL. REDUCE HEAT TO LOW, COVER, LEAVING LID AJAR, AND SIMMER,

STIRRING OCCASIONALLY, FOR ABOUT 25 MINUTES OR UNTIL CHICKEN IS NO LONGER PINK INSIDE. USING TONGS, TRANSFER CHICKEN TO A PLATE AND LET COOL FOR ABOUT 5 MINUTES OR UNTIL COOL ENOUGH TO HANDLE. DISCARD PARSLEY SPRIG. STIR NOODLES INTO SOUP AND BRING TO A BOIL OVER MEDIUM-HIGH HEAT. REDUCE HEAT AND SIMMER, UNCOVERED, STIRRING OCCASIONALLY, FOR 4 TO 5 MINUTES OR UNTIL NOODLES ARE TENDER. MEANWHILE, SHRED CHICKEN, DISCARDING BONE. WHEN NOODLES ARE COOKED, RETURN CHICKEN TO PAN. ADD SNOW PEAS. ADD MORE BROTH IF SOUP IS TOO THICK. TASTE AND ADJUST SEASONING WITH SALT AND PEPPER, IF DESIRED. SIMMER FOR ABOUT 1 MINUTE OR UNTIL CHICKEN IS THOROUGHLY REHEATED. SERVES 4.

TIP: FOR THIS SOUP, WE LIKE TO USE TINY PASTA SHAPES LABELED "SOUP NOODLES." THEY COME IN FUN SHAPES THAT APPEAL TO KIDS, SUCH AS MINI BOWS, SHELLS, WHEELS AND ALPHABET LETTERS. THEY CAN BE COOKED DIRECTLY IN THE SOUP. BROKEN SPAGHETTINI PIECES ALSO WORK WELL. IF YOU WANT TO ADD LARGE PASTA SHAPES, SUCH AS BROAD EGG NOODLES, TO THE SOUP, WE RECOMMEND COOKING THEM IN A SEPARATE POT OF BOILING SALTED WATER TO AVOID MAKING THE SOUP CLOUDY. DRAIN THE COOKED PASTA AND ADD IT TO THE SOUP JUST BEFORE SERVING. YOU CAN ALSO USE LEFTOVER COOKED NOODLES.

A NEW YEAR'S RESOLUTION IS SOMETHING THAT GOES IN ONE YEAR AND OUT THE OTHER.

CREAMY ROASTED ONION, GARLIC AND BACON SOUP

ROASTING ONIONS AND GARLIC CARAMELIZES THEIR NATURAL SUGARS, PRODUCING A SWEET AND MELLOW TASTE.

3	LARGE ONIONS, THINLY SLICED	3
1 TSP	GRANULATED SUGAR	5 ML
	SALT AND FRESHLY GROUND BLACK PEPPER	
4 TSP	OLIVE OIL, DIVIDED	20 ML
1	HEAD GARLIC	1
4	SLICES BACON, CHOPPED	4
1	LARGE RUSSET POTATO, PEELED AND DICED	1
1	BAY LEAF	1
1/2 TSP	DRIED THYME	2 ML
4 TO 5 CUPS	REDUCED-SODIUM CHICKEN BROTH OR HOMEMADE VEGETABLE STOCK (PAGE 90)	1 TO 1.25 L
1/2 CUP	HALF-AND-HALF (10%) CREAM OR WHOLE MILK, WARMED	125 ML
2 TBSP	DRY SHERRY (OPTIONAL)	30 ML
	CHOPPED FRESH CHIVES	

PREHEAT OVEN TO 375°F (190°C). LINE 2 LARGE RIMMED BAKING SHEETS WITH GREASED FOIL. IN A LARGE BOWL, TOSS ONIONS WITH SUGAR, 1/4 TSP (1 ML) SALT, PEPPER TO TASTE AND 3 TSP (15 ML) OF THE OIL. SPREAD IN A SINGLE LAYER ON PREPARED BAKING SHEETS. CUT A THIN SLICE OFF THE TOP OF THE GARLIC HEAD, EXPOSING THE CLOVES, AND DRIZZLE WITH THE REMAINING OIL. WRAP GARLIC HEAD IN FOIL. PUSH A FEW ONIONS ASIDE AND PLACE GARLIC ON ONE OF THE BAKING SHEETS. ROAST FOR ABOUT 25 MINUTES, STIRRING ONIONS AND ROTATING PANS HALFWAY THROUGH, UNTIL ONIONS ARE

TRANSLUCENT AND STARTING TO BROWN AND GARLIC IS TENDER. SQUEEZE GARLIC CLOVES OUT OF THEIR PAPERY SKIN. (AT THIS POINT, THE VEGETABLES CAN BE COOLED AND STORED IN AN AIRTIGHT CONTAINER IN THE REFRIGERATOR FOR UP TO 24 HOURS.)

IN A LARGE SAUCEPAN, SAUTÉ BACON OVER MEDIUM-HIGH HEAT UNTIL CRISPY. DRAIN OFF FAT AND SET ASIDE 2 TBSP (30 ML) BACON FOR GARNISH, LEAVING REMAINING BACON IN PAN. ADD ROASTED ONIONS AND GARLIC TO THE PAN. ADD POTATO, BAY LEAF, THYME AND 4 CUPS (1 L) BROTH; BRING TO A BOIL. REDUCE HEAT TO LOW, COVER, LEAVING LID AJAR, AND SIMMER FOR 15 MINUTES OR UNTIL POTATO IS TENDER. DISCARD BAY LEAF. USING AN IMMERSION BLENDER, OR IN A FOOD PROCESSOR OR BLENDER IN BATCHES, PURÉE SOUP UNTIL SMOOTH. RETURN TO PAN, IF NECESSARY. ADD MORE BROTH IF SOUP IS TOO THICK. STIR IN CREAM AND SHERRY, IF USING. REHEAT OVER MEDIUM HEAT, STIRRING OFTEN, UNTIL STEAMING. DO NOT LET BOIL OR CREAM MAY CURDLE. TASTE AND ADJUST SEASONING WITH SALT AND PEPPER, IF DESIRED. SERVE GARNISHED WITH RESERVED BACON AND CHIVES. SERVES 4.

TIP: IF YOU USE A SALT-FREE STOCK OR BROTH, YOU MAY WANT TO ADD MORE SALT TO THE SOUP.

TIP: WARMING THE CREAM BEFORE ADDING IT TO THE SOUP HELPS PREVENT IT FROM CURDLING.

MAKE AHEAD: LET COOL FOR 30 MINUTES, THEN REFRIGERATE, UNCOVERED, IN A SHALLOW CONTAINER UNTIL COLD. COVER TIGHTLY AND KEEP REFRIGERATED FOR UP TO 2 DAYS OR FREEZE FOR UP TO 2 MONTHS. THAW AND REHEAT SLOWLY.

HEARTY BEEF VEGETABLE AND NOODLE SOUP

WHEN THE FIRST SNOW FLIES, MAKE A POT
OF THIS SATISFYING SOUP TO KEEP AWAY THE
CHILLS. SERVE AS A MAIN COURSE WITH HUNKS
OF FRESH, CRISPY BREAD FOR DUNKING.

1 TBSP	VEGETABLE OIL	15 ML
2	ONIONS, CHOPPED	2
1/4 CUP	COLD WATER (APPROX.), DIVIDED	60 ML
2	CLOVES GARLIC, MINCED	2
1 1/2 TBSP	PAPRIKA	22 ML
1 TSP	DRIED MARJORAM OR BASIL	5 ML
1/2 TSP	SALT	2 ML
1/4 TSP	FRESHLY GROUND BLACK PEPPER	1 ML
PINCH	HOT PEPPER FLAKES	PINCH
2 TBSP	TOMATO PASTE (SEE TIP, PAGE 275)	30 ML
1 1/2 LBS	BONELESS BEEF CHUCK, CROSS RIB OR BLADE, CUT INTO 1/2-INCH (1 CM) CUBES	750 G
1	RED BELL PEPPER, CHOPPED	1
4 TO 5 CUPS	REDUCED-SODIUM BEEF OR CHICKEN BROTH	1 TO 1.25 L
1 1/2 CUPS	FROZEN MIXED VEGETABLES (NO NEED TO THAW)	375 ML
3 CUPS	MEDIUM EGG NOODLES	750 ML

IN A LARGE SAUCEPAN OR DUTCH OVEN, HEAT OIL OVER
MEDIUM HEAT. SAUTÉ ONIONS FOR 2 MINUTES OR
UNTIL THEY START TO SIZZLE. REDUCE HEAT TO LOW,
COVER AND COOK GENTLY, STIRRING OCCASIONALLY,
FOR 10 MINUTES. IF ONIONS START TO STICK, ADD 1 TO
2 TBSP (15 TO 30 ML) OF THE COLD WATER. IN A BOWL,
COMBINE GARLIC, PAPRIKA, MARJORAM, SALT, BLACK

PEPPER, HOT PEPPER FLAKES, TOMATO PASTE AND 2 TBSP (30 ML) COLD WATER. ADD TO PAN AND COOK, STIRRING, FOR 1 MINUTE. STIR IN BEEF AND RED PEPPER. ADD 4 CUPS (1 L) BROTH, INCREASE HEAT TO HIGH AND BRING TO A BOIL. REDUCE HEAT TO LOW, COVER AND SIMMER, STIRRING OCCASIONALLY, FOR $1\frac{1}{2}$ TO 2 HOURS OR UNTIL BEEF IS TENDER. MEANWHILE, COOK NOODLES ACCORDING TO PACKAGE INSTRUCTIONS. ADD FROZEN VEGETABLES TO THE SOUP AND RETURN TO A SIMMER; SIMMER FOR 2 MINUTES OR UNTIL HEATED THROUGH. DRAIN NOODLES AND ADD TO SOUP. ADD MORE BROTH IF SOUP IS TOO THICK; HEAT UNTIL STEAMING. SERVES 4.

TIP: ALTHOUGH CONVENTIONAL WISDOM SUGGESTS BROWNING MEAT AS YOU START MAKING A STEW OR SOUP, WE OFTEN SKIP THIS STEP AND DON'T TASTE THE DIFFERENCE. WE COAX EXTRA FLAVOR OUT OF THE ONIONS HERE BY SLOWLY "SWEATING" THEM AT THE START OF THE RECIPE.

MAKE AHEAD: PREPARE AND COOK SOUP, BUT DO NOT ADD FROZEN VEGETABLES OR NOODLES. LET COOL FOR 30 MINUTES, THEN REFRIGERATE, UNCOVERED, IN A SHALLOW CONTAINER UNTIL COLD. COVER TIGHTLY AND KEEP REFRIGERATED FOR UP TO 2 DAYS. REHEAT SLOWLY, ADDING FROZEN VEGETABLES AND NOODLES AS INSTRUCTED IN RECIPE ABOVE. WE DON'T RECOMMEND FREEZING THIS SOUP.

IF THE SHOE FITS, BUY IT IN EVERY COLOR!

SUNSET LENTIL SOUP

THE GLOW OF RED LENTILS AND COLORFUL
VEGETABLES IN THIS HEARTY SOUP REMIND US
OF A GLORIOUS SUNSET. IT'S READY IN AROUND
40 MINUTES — PERFECT FOR PUTTING TOGETHER
AT THE END OF A COLD WINTER'S DAY. SERVE WITH
LAZY DAYS BUTTERMILK BISCUITS (PAGE 22).

I TBSP	VEGETABLE OIL	15 ML
I	ONION, CHOPPED	I
I	CARROT, CHOPPED	I
3 CUPS	CHOPPED PEELED BUTTERNUT SQUASH (ABOUT $1/2$ SQUASH)	750 ML
$1\frac{1}{4}$ CUPS	ROASTED RED BELL PEPPERS (SEE TIP, PAGE 54), DRAINED AND CHOPPED	300 ML
I CUP	RED LENTILS, RINSED AND PICKED OVER (SEE TIP, OPPOSITE)	250 ML
$1/4$ TSP	DRIED ROSEMARY	I ML
$1/4$ TSP	DRIED THYME	I ML
	SALT AND FRESHLY GROUND BLACK PEPPER	
4 TO 5 CUPS	REDUCED-SODIUM CHICKEN BROTH OR HOMEMADE VEGETABLE STOCK (SEE RECIPE, PAGE 90)	I TO 1.25 L
2 TBSP	TOMATO PASTE	30 ML
2 TSP	CIDER VINEGAR	10 ML
	FINELY CHOPPED TOMATO (OPTIONAL)	

IN A LARGE SAUCEPAN OR DUTCH OVEN, HEAT OIL OVER
MEDIUM HEAT. SAUTÉ ONION, CARROT AND SQUASH FOR
ABOUT 5 MINUTES OR UNTIL ONION IS SOFTENED. ADD
ROASTED PEPPERS, LENTILS, ROSEMARY, THYME, $1/2$ TSP
(2 ML) SALT, PEPPER TO TASTE, 4 CUPS (I L) OF THE
BROTH AND TOMATO PASTE; INCREASE HEAT TO HIGH AND

BRING TO A BOIL. REDUCE HEAT TO LOW, COVER, LEAVING LID AJAR, AND SIMMER, STIRRING OCCASIONALLY, FOR 15 TO 20 MINUTES OR UNTIL VEGETABLES AND LENTILS ARE SOFT. USING AN IMMERSION BLENDER, OR IN A FOOD PROCESSOR OR BLENDER, PURÉE THE SOUP, LEAVING IT SOMEWHAT CHUNKY (PURÉE ABOUT HALF THE SOUP IF YOU'RE USING A FOOD PROCESSOR OR BLENDER). RETURN TO PAN, IF NECESSARY. ADD MORE BROTH IF SOUP IS TOO THICK. STIR IN VINEGAR. REHEAT OVER LOW HEAT, STIRRING OFTEN, UNTIL STEAMING. TASTE AND ADJUST SEASONING WITH SALT AND PEPPER, IF DESIRED. SERVE GARNISHED WITH CHOPPED TOMATO (IF USING). SERVES 6.

TIP: LENTILS DO NOT NEED TO BE SOAKED BEFORE COOKING. HOWEVER, YOU SHOULD RINSE THEM THOROUGHLY AND INSPECT THEM CAREFULLY, REMOVING ANY SMALL STONES OR BITS OF DEBRIS. THE EASIEST WAY TO DO THIS IS TO SPREAD THE LENTILS ON A CLEAN TEA TOWEL OR LARGE PLATE. COOKBOOKS OFTEN REFER TO THIS AS "SORTING" OR "PICKING OVER" LENTILS.

TIP: IF YOU USE A SALT-FREE STOCK OR BROTH, YOU MAY WANT TO ADD MORE SALT TO THE SOUP.

TIP: FOR A THICKER SOUP, PURÉE ALL OF THE SOUP. IF YOU PREFER CHUNKY SOUP, SKIP THE PURÉEING STEP.

MAKE AHEAD: LET COOL FOR 30 MINUTES, THEN REFRIGERATE, UNCOVERED, IN A SHALLOW CONTAINER UNTIL COLD. COVER TIGHTLY AND KEEP REFRIGERATED FOR UP TO 2 DAYS OR FREEZE FOR UP TO 2 MONTHS. THAW AND REHEAT TO SERVE.

TOMATO SOUP
WITH SMOKED PAPRIKA

*SPANISH SMOKED PAPRIKA PUTS A MELLOW, SMOKY
SPIN ON THIS FAMILIAR SOUP.*

4	SLICES BACON, CHOPPED	4
I TO 2 TSP	BUTTER OR OLIVE OIL (IF NEEDED)	5 TO 10 ML
I	ONION, CHOPPED	I
I	CARROT, CHOPPED	I
2	CLOVES GARLIC, MINCED	2
I TSP	SWEET SMOKED PAPRIKA (SEE TIP, PAGE 37)	5 ML
1/2 TSP	DRIED MARJORAM, ROSEMARY OR THYME	2 ML
	SALT AND FRESHLY GROUND BLACK PEPPER	
I	CAN (28 OZ/796 ML) NO-SALT-ADDED WHOLE TOMATOES, WITH JUICE (SEE TIP, PAGE 171)	I
2 TSP	GRANULATED SUGAR	10 ML
2 CUPS	REDUCED-SODIUM CHICKEN BROTH OR HOMEMADE VEGETABLE STOCK (SEE RECIPE, PAGE 90)	500 ML
I TBSP	FRESHLY SQUEEZED LEMON OR LIME JUICE	15 ML
	SOUR CREAM OR PLAIN YOGURT	

IN A LARGE SAUCEPAN OR DUTCH OVEN, SAUTÉ BACON
OVER MEDIUM-HIGH HEAT UNTIL CRISPY. USING A SLOTTED
SPOON, TRANSFER BACON TO A PLATE LINED WITH PAPER
TOWELS. DRAIN OFF ALL BUT I TBSP (15 ML) OF THE FAT
FROM THE PAN. IF THERE IS LESS THAN I TBSP (15 ML)
FAT, ADD BUTTER AS NEEDED. REDUCE HEAT TO MEDIUM.
ADD ONION AND CARROT; COOK , STIRRING OCCASIONALLY
AND SCRAPING UP BROWN BITS FROM BOTTOM OF PAN,

FOR ABOUT 5 MINUTES OR UNTIL ONION IS SOFTENED. ADD GARLIC, PAPRIKA, MARJORAM, $\frac{3}{4}$ TSP (3 ML) SALT AND $\frac{1}{4}$ TSP (I ML) PEPPER; SAUTÉ FOR 15 SECONDS OR UNTIL FRAGRANT. ADD TOMATOES WITH JUICE, BREAKING THEM UP WITH A SPOON. ADD HALF OF THE RESERVED BACON, SUGAR AND BROTH; INCREASE HEAT TO HIGH AND BRING TO A BOIL. REDUCE HEAT TO LOW, COVER, LEAVING LID AJAR, AND SIMMER FOR ABOUT 20 MINUTES OR UNTIL VEGETABLES ARE VERY SOFT. USING AN IMMERSION BLENDER, OR IN A FOOD PROCESSOR OR BLENDER IN BATCHES, PURÉE SOUP UNTIL SMOOTH. RETURN TO PAN, IF NECESSARY. STIR IN LEMON JUICE. REHEAT OVER LOW HEAT, STIRRING FREQUENTLY, UNTIL STEAMING. TASTE AND ADJUST SEASONING WITH SALT AND PEPPER, IF DESIRED. SERVE GARNISHED WITH A DOLLOP OF SOUR CREAM AND THE REMAINING RESERVED BACON. SERVES 6.

TIP: IF YOU USE A SALT-FREE STOCK OR BROTH, YOU MAY WANT TO ADD MORE SALT TO THE SOUP.

MAKE AHEAD: LET COOL FOR 30 MINUTES, THEN REFRIGERATE, UNCOVERED, IN A SHALLOW CONTAINER UNTIL COLD. COVER TIGHTLY AND KEEP REFRIGERATED FOR UP TO 2 DAYS OR FREEZE FOR UP TO 2 MONTHS. THAW AND REHEAT SLOWLY.

VARIATION: FOR A HEARTIER SOUP, ADD A CAN OF CHICKPEAS OR BLACK BEANS, DRAINED AND RINSED, AFTER PURÉEING THE SOUP. REHEAT OVER MEDIUM HEAT, STIRRING FREQUENTLY, UNTIL STEAMING.

CREAMY SWEET POTATO SOUP

PUT AWAY THE VEGETABLE PEELER. THIS QUICK
AND EASY SOUP USES A HANDY BAG OF FROZEN
PEELED SWEET POTATO CHUNKS, WHICH YOU CAN
FIND IN MOST SUPERMARKETS. CHECK OUT THE
VARIATION AND MAKE A MEAL OF IT.

1 TBSP	VEGETABLE OIL	15 ML
1	ONION, CHOPPED (SEE TIP, OPPOSITE)	1
2 TSP	MEDIUM INDIAN CURRY PASTE (SEE TIP, PAGE 109) OR CURRY POWDER	10 ML
1	PACKAGE (1 LB/500 G) FROZEN SWEET POTATO CHUNKS (NO NEED TO THAW)	1
2 CUPS	FROZEN CORN KERNELS (NO NEED TO THAW)	500 ML
2 TBSP	PACKED BROWN SUGAR	30 ML
	SALT AND FRESHLY GROUND BLACK PEPPER	
4 TO 5 CUPS	REDUCED-SODIUM CHICKEN BROTH OR HOMEMADE VEGETABLE STOCK (PAGE 90)	1 TO 1.25 L
1 CUP	COCONUT MILK (SEE TIP, PAGE 209)	250 ML
2 TBSP	CHOPPED FRESH CILANTRO (OPTIONAL)	30 ML
2 TBSP	FRESHLY SQUEEZED LIME JUICE	30 ML
	TOASTED SHREDDED COCONUT	

IN A LARGE SAUCEPAN OR DUTCH OVEN, HEAT OIL OVER
MEDIUM HEAT. SAUTÉ ONION FOR ABOUT 5 MINUTES OR
UNTIL SOFTENED. ADD CURRY PASTE AND COOK, STIRRING,
FOR 15 SECONDS OR UNTIL FRAGRANT. ADD SWEET POTATO,
CORN, BROWN SUGAR, $\frac{1}{2}$ TSP (2 ML) SALT, PEPPER TO
TASTE, 4 CUPS (1 L) BROTH AND COCONUT MILK; INCREASE
HEAT TO HIGH AND BRING TO A BOIL. REDUCE HEAT AND
SIMMER, STIRRING OCCASIONALLY, FOR ABOUT 15 MINUTES

OR UNTIL SWEET POTATO IS TENDER. USING AN IMMERSION BLENDER, OR IN A FOOD PROCESSOR OR BLENDER IN BATCHES, PURÉE SOUP UNTIL SMOOTH. (OR JUST PULSE A FEW TIMES, FOR A CHUNKIER SOUP.) RETURN TO PAN, IF NECESSARY. STIR IN CILANTRO (IF USING) AND LIME JUICE. ADD MORE BROTH IF SOUP IS TOO THICK. REHEAT OVER LOW HEAT, STIRRING OFTEN, UNTIL STEAMING. TASTE AND ADJUST SEASONING WITH SALT AND PEPPER, IF DESIRED. SERVE GARNISHED WITH COCONUT. SERVES 4 TO 6.

TIP: FREEZE CHOPPED FRESH ONIONS IN SEALABLE PLASTIC BAGS AND USE THEM IN SOUPS, STEWS, STIR-FRIES AND CASSEROLES. THERE'S NO NEED TO THAW THE ONIONS BEFORE COOKING THEM, BUT BE AWARE THAT THEY MIGHT SPATTER A BIT WHEN YOU START TO SAUTÉ THEM.

TIP: IF YOU CAN'T FIND FROZEN SWEET POTATO CHUNKS, USE 3 CUPS (750 ML) CHOPPED PEELED SWEET POTATOES.

TIP: IF YOU USE A SALT-FREE STOCK OR BROTH, YOU MAY WANT TO ADD MORE SALT TO THE SOUP.

MAKE AHEAD: LET COOL FOR 30 MINUTES, THEN REFRIGERATE, UNCOVERED, IN A SHALLOW CONTAINER UNTIL COLD. COVER TIGHTLY AND KEEP REFRIGERATED FOR UP TO 2 DAYS OR FREEZE FOR UP TO 2 MONTHS. THAW AND REHEAT SLOWLY.

VARIATION

CREAMY CHICKEN SWEET POTATO SOUP: FOR A HEARTIER SOUP, ADD SHREDDED COOKED CHICKEN AND/OR LEFTOVER STEAMED RICE AFTER PURÉEING THE SOUP.

GOLDEN CAULIFLOWER CASHEW SOUP

THIS SOUP COMBINES A MILD SPICINESS WITH THE NATURAL SWEETNESS OF CAULIFLOWER. FOR A MORE FIERY FLAVOR, USE HOT CURRY PASTE. SERVE WITH WARM BUTTERED NAAN.

1 TBSP	VEGETABLE OIL	15 ML
1	ONION, CHOPPED	1
1/2 CUP	ROASTED UNSALTED CASHEWS	125 ML
2 TBSP	MILD OR MEDIUM INDIAN CURRY PASTE (SEE TIP, OPPOSITE)	30 ML
1	LARGE RUSSET POTATO, PEELED AND DICED	1
4 CUPS	CAULIFLOWER FLORETS (ABOUT 1 LB/500 G)	1 L
	SALT AND FRESHLY GROUND BLACK PEPPER	
4 CUPS	REDUCED-SODIUM CHICKEN BROTH OR HOMEMADE VEGETABLE STOCK (SEE RECIPE, PAGE 90)	1 L
1 TBSP	LIQUID HONEY	15 ML
1/2 TO 1 CUP	2% OR WHOLE MILK, WARMED	125 TO 250 ML
1 TBSP	FRESHLY SQUEEZED LIME JUICE	15 ML
	CHOPPED TOASTED CASHEWS (SEE TIP, PAGE 127)	

IN A LARGE SAUCEPAN, HEAT OIL OVER MEDIUM HEAT. SAUTÉ ONION FOR ABOUT 5 MINUTES OR UNTIL SOFTENED. ADD CASHEWS AND CURRY PASTE; COOK, STIRRING, FOR 15 SECONDS OR UNTIL FRAGRANT. STIR IN POTATO, CAULIFLOWER, 1/2 TSP (2 ML) SALT, PEPPER TO TASTE, BROTH AND HONEY; INCREASE HEAT TO HIGH AND BRING TO A BOIL. REDUCE HEAT AND SIMMER FOR

ABOUT 15 MINUTES OR UNTIL VEGETABLES ARE TENDER. USING AN IMMERSION BLENDER, OR IN A FOOD PROCESSOR OR BLENDER IN BATCHES, PURÉE SOUP UNTIL SMOOTH. RETURN TO PAN, IF NECESSARY. GRADUALLY STIR IN ENOUGH OF THE WARMED MILK THAT THE SOUP IS JUST THICK ENOUGH TO COAT THE BACK OF A SPOON. REHEAT OVER LOW HEAT, STIRRING CONSTANTLY, UNTIL STEAMING. DO NOT LET BOIL OR MILK MAY CURDLE. JUST BEFORE SERVING, STIR IN LIME JUICE. TASTE AND ADJUST SEASONING WITH SALT AND PEPPER, IF DESIRED. SERVE GARNISHED WITH CHOPPED CASHEWS. SERVES 4 TO 6.

TIP: INDIAN CURRY PASTES ARE NOW WIDELY AVAILABLE AND CAN USUALLY BE FOUND IN THE ASIAN FOODS AISLE. WE PARTICULARLY LIKE THE PATAK'S BRAND OF PASTES, WHICH COME IN MILD, MEDIUM AND HOT. CURRY PASTE IS PREFERABLE TO CURRY POWDER BECAUSE THE SPICES ARE PRESERVED IN OIL AND HAVE A MORE AUTHENTIC, LESS HARSH TASTE. ONCE OPENED, JARS OF CURRY PASTE WILL KEEP IN THE REFRIGERATOR FOR UP TO 6 MONTHS.

TIP: IF YOU USE A SALT-FREE STOCK OR BROTH, YOU MAY WANT TO ADD MORE SALT TO THE SOUP.

TIP: WARMING THE MILK BEFORE ADDING IT TO THE SOUP HELPS PREVENT IT FROM CURDLING.

MAKE AHEAD: LET COOL FOR 30 MINUTES, THEN REFRIGERATE, UNCOVERED, IN A SHALLOW CONTAINER UNTIL COLD. COVER TIGHTLY AND KEEP REFRIGERATED FOR UP TO 2 DAYS. REHEAT SLOWLY. WE DON'T RECOMMEND FREEZING THIS SOUP.

BROCCOLI AND ALMOND SOUP

GROUND ALMONDS — WHICH ARE GOOD FOR YOU — ARE THE SECRET TO THIS RICH AND SILKY BROCCOLI SOUP.

1 TBSP	BUTTER OR OLIVE OIL	15 ML
1	ONION, CHOPPED	1
5 CUPS	BROCCOLI FLORETS AND PEELED, THINLY SLICED STEMS (ABOUT 1 LB/500 G)	1.25 L
½ CUP	GROUND ALMONDS	125 ML
	SALT AND FRESHLY GROUND BLACK PEPPER	
3 TO 3½ CUPS	HOMEMADE VEGETABLE STOCK (SEE RECIPE, PAGE 90) OR REDUCED-SODIUM CHICKEN BROTH	750 TO 875 ML
½ TSP	HOT PEPPER SAUCE	2 ML
1 CUP	2% OR WHOLE MILK	250 ML
½ TSP	DIJON MUSTARD	2 ML
2 TSP	FRESHLY SQUEEZED LEMON JUICE	10 ML
	TOASTED SLICED OR SLIVERED ALMONDS	

IN A LARGE SAUCEPAN, HEAT BUTTER OVER MEDIUM HEAT. SAUTÉ ONION FOR ABOUT 5 MINUTES OR UNTIL SOFTENED. STIR IN BROCCOLI, GROUND ALMONDS, ½ TSP (2 ML) SALT, PEPPER TO TASTE, STOCK AND HOT PEPPER SAUCE; BRING TO A BOIL. REDUCE HEAT AND SIMMER FOR 10 MINUTES OR UNTIL BROCCOLI IS JUST TENDER BUT NOT MUSHY. USING AN IMMERSION BLENDER, OR IN A FOOD PROCESSOR OR BLENDER IN BATCHES, PURÉE SOUP UNTIL SMOOTH. RETURN TO PAN, IF NECESSARY. STIR IN MILK AND MUSTARD; REHEAT OVER LOW HEAT, STIRRING OFTEN, UNTIL STEAMING. DO NOT LET BOIL OR MILK MAY CURDLE. JUST BEFORE SERVING, STIR IN LEMON JUICE. TASTE AND ADJUST SEASONING WITH SALT AND PEPPER, IF DESIRED. SERVE GARNISHED WITH TOASTED ALMONDS. SERVES 4.

SANDWICHES, WRAPS AND BURGERS

CHEESY BEAN QUESADILLAS

*THESE FULL-FLAVORED QUESADILLAS ARE SO
TASTY YOU WON'T EVEN MISS THE MEAT.
SERVE WITH A SPINACH SALAD WITH CITRUS
POPPY SEED YOGURT DRESSING (PAGE 86).*

1 TBSP	OLIVE OR VEGETABLE OIL	15 ML
1	GREEN OR RED BELL PEPPER, CHOPPED	1
3/4 CUP	FINELY CHOPPED ONION	175 ML
2	CLOVES GARLIC, MINCED	2
1 TSP	GROUND CUMIN	5 ML
1	CAN (19 OZ/ 540 ML) RED KIDNEY BEANS, DRAINED AND RINSED	1
1/2 TO 3/4 CUP	SALSA	125 TO 175 ML
1/2 TO 1 TSP	PURÉED CANNED CHIPOTLE PEPPERS (SEE TIP, OPPOSITE)	2 TO 5 ML
	SALT	
2 TBSP	CHOPPED FRESH CILANTRO	30 ML
4	9-INCH (23 CM) WHOLE WHEAT FLOUR TORTILLAS	4
1 1/2 CUPS	SHREDDED TEX-MEX CHEESE BLEND, JALAPEÑO JACK CHEESE OR JALAPEÑO HAVARTI CHEESE	375 ML
	SOUR CREAM AND ADDITIONAL SALSA	

IN A LARGE NONSTICK SKILLET, HEAT OIL OVER MEDIUM
HEAT. SAUTÉ GREEN PEPPER AND ONION FOR ABOUT
5 MINUTES OR UNTIL SOFTENED. ADD GARLIC AND CUMIN;
SAUTÉ FOR 15 SECONDS OR UNTIL FRAGRANT. STIR IN
BEANS AND LIGHTLY CRUSH THEM WITH A POTATO
MASHER. ADD 1/2 CUP (125 ML) OF THE SALSA, CHIPOTLE
PEPPERS TO TASTE AND 1/2 TSP (2 ML) SALT; COOK,

STIRRING, UNTIL HEATED THROUGH. STIR IN CILANTRO. ADJUST CONSISTENCY WITH MORE SALSA, IF DESIRED. TASTE AND ADJUST SEASONING WITH SALT, IF DESIRED. LAY 2 TORTILLAS ON A WORK SURFACE. SPREAD BEAN FILLING OVER BOTH TORTILLAS, THEN SPRINKLE WITH CHEESE. TOP WITH THE REMAINING TORTILLAS. HEAT A CLEAN NONSTICK SKILLET OVER MEDIUM-HIGH HEAT. COOK QUESADILLAS, ONE AT A TIME, PRESSING DOWN GENTLY WITH A SPATULA AND TURNING ONCE, FOR 3 TO 4 MINUTES PER SIDE OR UNTIL BROWNED ON BOTH SIDES AND CHEESE IS MELTED. TRANSFER TO A CUTTING BOARD AND CUT INTO LARGE WEDGES. SERVE WITH SOUR CREAM AND SALSA FOR DIPPING. SERVES 2 BIG APPETITES OR 4 SMALLER ONES.

TIP: CHIPOTLE PEPPERS ARE SMOKED JALAPEÑO PEPPERS, AND THEY'RE OFTEN SOLD PACKED IN MEXICAN ADOBO SAUCE. TYPICALLY, THE SMALL CANS CAN BE FOUND NEAR OTHER MEXICAN FOODS IN THE SUPERMARKET. LEFTOVER CHIPOTLES CAN BE PURÉED, TRANSFERRED TO AN AIRTIGHT CONTAINER AND REFRIGERATED FOR UP TO 4 WEEKS OR FROZEN FOR UP TO 6 MONTHS. YOU COULD USE AN EQUAL AMOUNT OF SMOKED OR SWEET PAPRIKA INSTEAD OF THE CHIPOTLES, BUT THE QUESADILLAS WILL TASTE DIFFERENT.

TIP: FEEL FREE TO SUBSTITUTE YOUR FAVORITE FLAVOR OF FLOUR TORTILLAS FOR THE WHOLE WHEAT.

MAKE AHEAD: THE BEAN FILLING CAN BE MADE AHEAD. LET COOL COMPLETELY AND REFRIGERATE IN AN AIRTIGHT CONTAINER FOR UP TO 2 DAYS OR FREEZE FOR UP TO 1 MONTH. THAW IN THE MICROWAVE OR OVERNIGHT IN THE REFRIGERATOR BEFORE ASSEMBLING QUESADILLAS.

PORTOBELLO MUSHROOM MELT

2 TBSP	SUN-DRIED TOMATO OR BASIL PESTO (SEE TIP, PAGE 165)	30 ML
2 TBSP	OLIVE OIL	30 ML
4	PORTOBELLO MUSHROOMS, STEMS AND GILLS REMOVED (SEE TIP, PAGE 69)	4
1 CUP	PACKED BABY SPINACH	250 ML
1	LARGE TOMATO, THINLY SLICED	1
	SALT AND FRESHLY GROUND BLACK PEPPER	
8	THIN SLICES PROVOLONE CHEESE (OR 1⅓ CUPS/325 ML SHREDDED MOZZARELLA CHEESE)	8
4	CIABATTA OR KAISER BUNS, SLICED IN HALF AND TOASTED	4
	MAYONNAISE	

PREHEAT BARBECUE GRILL TO MEDIUM-HIGH OR OVEN TO 400°F (200°C). IF USING THE OVEN, LINE A LARGE BAKING SHEET WITH PARCHMENT PAPER OR GREASED FOIL. IN A SMALL BOWL, COMBINE PESTO AND OIL. PLACE PORTOBELLOS CAP SIDE DOWN ON A WORK SURFACE. SPREAD PESTO MIXTURE OVER MUSHROOMS. DIVIDE SPINACH AMONG MUSHROOMS. TOP WITH TOMATO SLICES AND SPRINKLE WITH SALT AND PEPPER TO TASTE. TOP WITH PROVOLONE. IF USING THE BARBECUE, PLACE MUSHROOMS ON GREASED GRILL, CLOSE LID AND COOK FOR ABOUT 5 MINUTES OR UNTIL CHEESE IS MELTED. IF USING THE OVEN, PLACE MUSHROOMS ON PREPARED BAKING SHEET AND BAKE FOR 10 TO 12 MINUTES OR UNTIL CHEESE IS MELTED. SPREAD MAYONNAISE ON TOASTED BUNS AND MAKE SANDWICHES WITH GRILLED MUSHROOMS. SERVES 4.

MONTE CRISTO SANDWICHES

HERE'S A WELCOME — AND VERY RETRO — CHANGE FROM THE UBIQUITOUS GRILLED CHEESE! SERVE WITH YOUR FAVORITE MANGO CHUTNEY OR KETCHUP.

4	EGGS	4
2/3 CUP	MILK	150 ML
1/2 TSP	DRY MUSTARD	2 ML
1/2 TSP	PAPRIKA	2 ML
1/4 TSP	SALT	1 ML
	FRESHLY GROUND BLACK PEPPER	
8	SLICES WHITE OR WHOLE WHEAT BREAD	8
	BUTTER, SOFTENED	
1 1/3 CUPS	SHREDDED SHARP (OLD) CHEDDAR CHEESE OR SWISS CHEESE	325 ML
4 OZ	DELI HAM, THINLY SLICED	125 G
4 OZ	DELI TURKEY, THINLY SLICED	125 G
1 TBSP	BUTTER	15 ML

IN A LARGE, SHALLOW DISH, WHISK TOGETHER EGGS, MILK, MUSTARD, PAPRIKA, SALT AND PEPPER TO TASTE. LAY BREAD ON A WORK SURFACE AND SPREAD SOFTENED BUTTER ON ONE SIDE OF EACH SLICE. LAYER CHEESE, HAM AND TURKEY ON THE BUTTERED SIDE OF 4 SLICES. TOP WITH THE REMAINING 4 SLICES, BUTTERED SIDE DOWN. DIP SANDWICHES IN EGG MIXTURE, TURNING TO COAT UNTIL THE LIQUID HAS PARTIALLY SOAKED INTO THE BREAD. IN A LARGE NONSTICK SKILLET, MELT 1 TBSP (15 ML) BUTTER OVER MEDIUM HEAT. COOK SANDWICHES, TURNING ONCE, FOR ABOUT 5 MINUTES OR UNTIL BROWNED ON BOTH SIDES AND CHEESE IS MELTED. SERVES 4.

POWER PLAY PIZZA LOAF

YOU'LL SCORE SHORT-HANDED WHEN YOU SERVE THIS SUPER-SIZED, CUSTOMIZED, HOT AND CRISPY SANDWICH TO YOUR GANG ON HOCKEY NIGHT.

I	LOAF (ABOUT I LB/500 G) FRENCH BREAD (UNSLICED)	I
¼ CUP	OLIVE OIL	60 ML
¼ TO ⅓ CUP	SUN-DRIED TOMATO PESTO (SEE TIP, PAGE 165)	60 TO 75 ML
½ TSP	DRIED OREGANO	2 ML
	SALT AND FRESHLY GROUND BLACK PEPPER	
8 OZ	PROVOLONE OR MOZZARELLA CHEESE, THINLY SLICED OR SHREDDED	250 G
8 OZ	THINLY SLICED GOOD-QUALITY DELI HAM (WE LIKE TUSCAN-STYLE)	250 G
3	ROASTED RED BELL PEPPERS (SEE TIP, PAGE 54), DRAINED AND SLICED	3
I	TUB (7 OZ/200 G) BOCCONCINI CHEESE, DRAINED AND SLICED	I

PREHEAT OVEN TO 350°F (180°C). SLICE FRENCH LOAF IN HALF HORIZONTALLY AND PLACE CUT SIDE UP ON A WORK SURFACE. PULL AWAY SOME OF THE SOFT BREAD INSIDE (USE TO MAKE BREAD CRUMBS OR FEED TO THE BIRDS). BRUSH OLIVE OIL OVER INSIDE OF BOTH HALVES. SPREAD PESTO OVER BOTH HALVES AND SPRINKLE WITH OREGANO AND SALT AND PEPPER TO TASTE. LAYER PROVOLONE ON THE BOTTOM HALF, OVERLAPPING SLICES. LAYER HAM ON TOP, FOLLOWED BY ROASTED PEPPERS. TOP WITH BOCCONCINI. REPLACE THE TOP HALF OF THE LOAF AND PRESS DOWN TO FLATTEN SLIGHTLY. WRAP TIGHTLY IN FOIL. BAKE FOR ABOUT 40 MINUTES OR UNTIL CHEESES ARE MELTED AND OUTSIDE OF LOAF IS VERY CRISPY. CUT INTO 8 THICK SLICES. SERVES 4.

THE PERFECT LAST-MINUTE SOLUTION FOR A QUICK AND NUTRITIOUS DINNER. IF YOUR FAMILY TAKES TURNS ON DINNER DUTY, THEY'LL LIKE THIS ONE.

4	9-INCH (23 CM) FLOUR TORTILLAS, PREFERABLY WHOLE WHEAT	4
4 OZ	LIGHT CREAM CHEESE, SOFTENED	125 G
	SALT AND FRESHLY GROUND BLACK PEPPER	
1/2 CUP	SALSA	125 ML
2	GREEN ONIONS, THINLY SLICED	2
1/2 CUP	FROZEN CORN KERNELS, THAWED (SEE TIP, BELOW)	125 ML
8	THIN SLICES DELI HAM (ABOUT 6 OZ/175 G)	8
1 CUP	SHREDDED TEX-MEX CHEESE BLEND, JALAPEÑO JACK CHEESE OR CHEDDAR CHEESE	250 ML

PREHEAT OVEN TO 400°F (200°C). LAY TORTILLAS ON A WORK SURFACE. SPREAD CREAM CHEESE OVER TORTILLAS. SEASON TO TASTE WITH SALT AND PEPPER. TOP WITH SALSA, GREEN ONIONS, CORN, HAM AND CHEESE. ROLL UP TIGHTLY. PLACE SEAM SIDE DOWN ON A LARGE BAKING SHEET. BAKE FOR 10 TO 12 MINUTES OR UNTIL ENDS ARE BROWNED AND CHEESE HAS MELTED. CUT EACH ROLL IN HALF. SERVES 4.

TIP: THERE IS NO NEED TO COOK FROZEN CORN, AS IT HAS ALREADY BEEN BLANCHED. TO THAW IT, PLACE IT IN A BOWL OF HOT WATER AND LET STAND FOR 5 MINUTES. DRAIN AND BLOT ON PAPER TOWELS.

MAKE AHEAD: ASSEMBLE THE ROLLS, BUT DO NOT BAKE. WRAP INDIVIDUALLY IN PLASTIC WRAP AND REFRIGERATE FOR UP TO 1 DAY. UNWRAP BEFORE BAKING.

MAPLE MUSTARD SAUSAGE HEROES

THESE SUBMARINE SANDWICHES ARE A SUREFIRE HIT AT ANY TIME. GOOD-QUALITY PORK SAUSAGES WORK BEST, BUT YOU COULD USE TURKEY SAUSAGES, IF YOU PREFER.

8	GOOD-QUALITY PORK SAUSAGES (SEE TIP, OPPOSITE)	8
2 TBSP	PURE MAPLE SYRUP	30 ML
1/2 TSP	PACKED BROWN SUGAR	2 ML
1 TBSP	DIJON MUSTARD	15 ML
1 TBSP	CIDER VINEGAR	15 ML
2 TBSP	VEGETABLE OIL	30 ML
2	LARGE ONIONS, THINLY SLICED	2
1 TBSP	MUSTARD SEEDS	15 ML
1/2 TSP	SALT	2 ML
1 TO 2 TBSP	COLD WATER (IF NEEDED)	15 TO 30 ML
4	PANINI BUNS	4
	ADDITIONAL DIJON MUSTARD (OPTIONAL)	

PREHEAT OVEN TO 400°C (200°C). LINE A RIMMED BAKING SHEET WITH GREASED FOIL. PLACE SAUSAGES ON PREPARED BAKING SHEET. BAKE, TURNING ONCE, FOR 20 MINUTES. REMOVE SAUSAGES FROM OVEN AND BRUSH WITH MAPLE SYRUP. RETURN TO OVEN AND BAKE FOR 6 TO 8 MINUTES OR UNTIL WELL BROWNED AND NO LONGER PINK INSIDE.

MEANWHILE, IN A SMALL BOWL, COMBINE BROWN SUGAR, MUSTARD AND VINEGAR; SET ASIDE. IN A LARGE NONSTICK SKILLET, HEAT OIL OVER MEDIUM HEAT. ADD ONIONS, MUSTARD SEEDS AND SALT; REDUCE HEAT TO LOW AND

COOK, STIRRING FREQUENTLY, FOR 12 TO 15 MINUTES OR UNTIL ONIONS ARE VERY SOFT AND GOLDEN. IF ONIONS START TO STICK OR BROWN TOO QUICKLY, ADD COLD WATER AS NEEDED. STIR IN BROWN SUGAR MIXTURE. REMOVE FROM HEAT.

REMOVE SAUSAGES FROM OVEN, COVER LOOSELY WITH FOIL AND SET ASIDE. PLACE BUNS ON A BAKING SHEET AND BAKE FOR 5 MINUTES OR UNTIL HEATED THROUGH AND CRISPY. REHEAT ONIONS, IF DESIRED. CUT BUNS ALONG THE TOP, BUT NOT QUITE ALL THE WAY THROUGH, AND SPREAD WITH MUSTARD, IF DESIRED. PLACE 2 SAUSAGES IN EACH BUN AND TOP WITH ONIONS. SERVES 4.

TIP: DO NOT PRICK SAUSAGES BEFORE COOKING THEM AND, IF USING A SKILLET, ALWAYS COOK THEM ON MEDIUM HEAT TO ENSURE THAT THE SKINS DON'T BURST. THAT WAY, THE SAUSAGES WILL RETAIN THEIR JUICES. TO AVOID ACCIDENTALLY PIERCING THEM, USE KITCHEN TONGS, RATHER THAN A FORK, TO TURN THEM WHILE THEY'RE COOKING.

VARIATION: YOU CAN USE A BAGUETTE (FRENCH STICK) INSTEAD OF THE PANINI BUNS, IF YOU PREFER. CUT IT CROSSWISE INTO 4 EQUAL PIECES. WARM AS DIRECTED. SLICE EACH PIECE HORIZONTALLY, BUT NOT QUITE ALL THE WAY THROUGH. FILL WITH SAUSAGES AND ONIONS.

SIGN ON PLUMBER'S TRUCK: WE REPAIR WHAT YOUR HUSBAND FIXED

MEXICAN GRILLED
CHICKEN SANDWICH

IT'S MIDWEEK AND YOU'RE STARING DOWN AT A PACK OF BONELESS SKINLESS CHICKEN BREASTS. WHAT TO MAKE FOR SUPPER? HERE'S YOUR ANSWER. SERVE WITH SPICY SWEET POTATO AND PARSNIP "FRIES" (PAGE 260).

CHIPOTLE LIME MAYONNAISE

1	CLOVE GARLIC, MINCED	1
2 TBSP	CHOPPED FRESH CILANTRO	30 ML
1/4 CUP	LIGHT MAYONNAISE	60 ML
1/4 CUP	LIGHT SOUR CREAM	60 ML
2 TBSP	FRESHLY SQUEEZED LIME JUICE	30 ML
1 TSP	PURÉED CANNED CHIPOTLE PEPPER	5 ML
	SALT AND FRESHLY GROUND BLACK PEPPER	

CHIPOTLE PASTE

1 1/2 TSP	PACKED BROWN OR GRANULATED SUGAR	7 ML
1 TSP	PURÉED CANNED CHIPOTLE PEPPER	5 ML
1 TSP	DRIED OREGANO	5 ML
1 TSP	GROUND CUMIN	5 ML
1 TSP	FINELY GRATED LIME ZEST	5 ML
1 TSP	SALT	5 ML
	FRESHLY GROUND BLACK PEPPER	
2 TBSP	OLIVE OR VEGETABLE OIL	30 ML
4	BONELESS SKINLESS CHICKEN BREASTS (ABOUT 1 1/2 LBS/750 G)	4
1/4 CUP	FRESHLY SQUEEZED LIME JUICE	60 ML
4	LARGE WHITE OR MULTIGRAIN BUNS, SLICED IN HALF AND TOASTED	4
	TORN ICEBERG LETTUCE	
1	AVOCADO, PITTED, PEELED AND SLICED (SEE TIP, PAGE 129)	1
1	TOMATO, THINLY SLICED	1

CHIPOTLE LIME MAYONNAISE: IN A SMALL BOWL, COMBINE GARLIC, CILANTRO, MAYONNAISE, SOUR CREAM, LIME JUICE AND CHIPOTLE. SEASON TO TASTE WITH SALT AND PEPPER. USE IMMEDIATELY OR COVER AND REFRIGERATE FOR UP TO 2 DAYS.

CHIPOTLE PASTE: IN A SMALL BOWL, WHISK TOGETHER BROWN SUGAR, CHIPOTLE, OREGANO, CUMIN, LIME ZEST, SALT, PEPPER TO TASTE AND OIL UNTIL THE MIXTURE RESEMBLES A PASTE.

PLACE CHICKEN BETWEEN TWO SHEETS OF PLASTIC WRAP AND POUND LIGHTLY WITH A ROLLING PIN OR THE BOTTOM OF A SKILLET TO A UNIFORM THICKNESS. BRUSH CHICKEN WITH CHIPOTLE PASTE, COVER AND REFRIGERATE FOR 15 MINUTES.

MEANWHILE, PREHEAT BARBECUE GRILL TO MEDIUM. PLACE CHICKEN ON GREASED GRILL AND COOK FOR 5 TO 7 MINUTES PER SIDE OR UNTIL NO LONGER PINK INSIDE. TRANSFER TO A PLATE AND SPRINKLE WITH LIME JUICE. SLICE EACH BREAST INTO 3 OR 4 STRIPS. SPREAD CHIPOTLE LIME MAYONNAISE ON TOASTED BUNS AND MAKE SANDWICHES WITH LETTUCE, CHICKEN, AVOCADO AND TOMATO. SERVES 4.

TIP: IF YOU'RE IN A RUSH, YOU CAN COOK THE CHICKEN IMMEDIATELY INSTEAD OF MARINATING IT FOR 15 MINUTES. IT CAN ALSO BE COOKED IN A GRILL PAN ON THE STOVETOP FOR 5 TO 7 MINUTES PER SIDE.

VARIATION: WHEN MAKING THE CHIPOTLE LIME MAYONNAISE, YOU CAN OMIT THE SOUR CREAM AND USE DOUBLE THE AMOUNT OF MAYONNAISE, IF YOU PREFER.

GRILLED PESTO
CHICKEN SANDWICH

HERE'S A SUPER SUMMER SANDWICH. YOU CAN USE ROASTED RED BELL PEPPERS FROM A JAR IF YOU DON'T WANT TO GRILL YOUR OWN.

PESTO MAYONNAISE

1/3 CUP	LIGHT MAYONNAISE	75 ML
2 TBSP	SUN-DRIED TOMATO PESTO OR BASIL PESTO (SEE TIP, OPPOSITE)	30 ML
2 TSP	FRESHLY SQUEEZED LEMON JUICE	10 ML
	SALT AND FRESHLY GROUND BLACK PEPPER	
4	BONELESS SKINLESS CHICKEN BREASTS (ABOUT 1 1/2 LBS/750 G)	4
1 TSP	DRIED ITALIAN SEASONING OR DRIED OREGANO	5 ML
1 TSP	PAPRIKA	5 ML
1 TSP	SALT	5 ML
1/4 TSP	FRESHLY GROUND BLACK PEPPER	1 ML
2 TBSP	OLIVE OR VEGETABLE OIL, DIVIDED	30 ML
1	LARGE RED OR YELLOW BELL PEPPER, QUARTERED	1
4	CIABATTA OR KAISER BUNS, SLICED IN HALF AND TOASTED	4
1 CUP	PACKED BABY SPINACH OR MIXED BABY GREENS	250 ML
1/2 CUP	DRAINED MARINATED ARTICHOKE HEARTS, SLICED	125 ML

PESTO MAYONNAISE: IN A SMALL BOWL, COMBINE MAYONNAISE, PESTO AND LEMON JUICE. SEASON TO TASTE WITH SALT AND PEPPER. USE IMMEDIATELY OR COVER AND REFRIGERATE FOR UP TO 2 DAYS.

PREHEAT BARBECUE GRILL TO MEDIUM. PLACE CHICKEN BETWEEN TWO SHEETS OF PLASTIC WRAP AND POUND LIGHTLY WITH A ROLLING PIN OR THE BOTTOM OF A SKILLET TO A UNIFORM THICKNESS. IN A SMALL BOWL, COMBINE ITALIAN SEASONING, PAPRIKA, SALT AND PEPPER AND 1 TBSP (15 ML) OF THE OIL. BRUSH OVER BOTH SIDES OF CHICKEN. IN ANOTHER BOWL, TOSS RED PEPPERS WITH THE REMAINING OIL. PLACE CHICKEN AND RED PEPPERS ON GREASED GRILL AND COOK FOR 5 TO 7 MINUTES PER SIDE OR UNTIL CHICKEN IS NO LONGER PINK INSIDE AND SKIN OF PEPPERS IS STARTING TO BLACKEN. SLICE EACH CHICKEN BREAST INTO 3 OR 4 STRIPS. SPREAD PESTO MAYONNAISE ON TOASTED BUNS AND MAKE SANDWICHES WITH SPINACH, GRILLED PEPPERS, CHICKEN AND ARTICHOKES. SERVES 4.

TIP: TO USE UP OPEN JARS OF PESTO, STIR A SPOONFUL OR TWO INTO SOUP, TOSS IT WITH HOT PASTA, ADD IT TO A POTATO SALAD DRESSING, SPREAD IT ON A PIZZA BASE OR USE IT AS A TOPPING FOR GRILLED FISH OR CHICKEN.

VARIATION: THE CHICKEN CAN ALSO BE COOKED IN A GRILL PAN ON THE STOVETOP FOR 5 TO 7 MINUTES PER SIDE, IF YOU PREFER. FOR CONVENIENCE, USE ROASTED RED PEPPERS FROM A JAR OR THE DELI; DRAIN AND BLOT THEM ON PAPER TOWELS BEFORE ADDING THEM TO YOUR SANDWICH.

SIGN AT OPTOMETRIST'S OFFICE: IF YOU DON'T SEE WHAT YOU'RE LOOKING FOR, YOU'VE COME TO THE RIGHT PLACE.

CALIFORNIA TUNA SANDWICH

THIS SANDWICH IS TOO GOOD TO BE TUNA!
SERVE IT ON SLICES OF YOUR FAVORITE SPECIALTY
BREAD, SUCH AS CIABATTA OR FOCACCIA.
YOU CAN ALSO USE CRUSTY BUNS.

1	CAN (6 OZ/170 G) WATER-PACKED CHUNK TUNA, DRAINED	1
1/4 CUP	HUMMUS (SEE TIP, BELOW)	60 ML
3 TBSP	SUN-DRIED TOMATO PESTO (SEE TIP, PAGE 123)	45 ML
2 TO 3 TBSP	FRESHLY SQUEEZED LEMON JUICE	30 TO 45 ML
2 TBSP	DRAINED CAPERS	30 ML
1 TBSP	JUICE FROM CAPER JAR	15 ML
2 TSP	OLIVE OIL (OPTIONAL)	10 ML
1/2 TSP	GROUND CUMIN	2 ML
	SALT AND FRESHLY GROUND BLACK PEPPER	
8	SLICES CIABATTA BREAD	8
	SHREDDED ICEBERG LETTUCE	
1	TOMATO, SLICED	1

IN A MEDIUM BOWL, BREAK UP TUNA WITH A FORK. STIR IN HUMMUS, PESTO, LEMON JUICE TO TASTE, CAPERS, CAPER JUICE, OIL (IF USING) AND CUMIN. SEASON TO TASTE WITH SALT AND PEPPER. MAKE SANDWICHES WITH BREAD, TUNA MIXTURE, LETTUCE AND TOMATO SLICES. SERVES 4.

TIP: PREPARE A BATCH OF NO-FUSS HUMMUS (PAGE 50) TO MAKE THIS SANDWICH, THEN FREEZE THE EXTRA FOR ANOTHER DAY. ALTERNATIVELY, USE YOUR FAVORITE BRAND OF HUMMUS.

TIP: FOR EASY CANAPÉS, SPREAD THE TUNA FILLING ON WHOLE-GRAIN CRACKERS.

PO' BOY FISH SANDWICH

4	SKINLESS FIRM WHITE FISH FILLETS (EACH ABOUT 6 OZ/175 G)	4
1/4 CUP	MILK	60 ML
3 TBSP	ALL-PURPOSE FLOUR	45 ML
3 TBSP	CORNMEAL	45 ML
1 TBSP	CAJUN SEASONING	15 ML
1/2 TSP	SALT	2 ML
1/4 CUP	VEGETABLE OIL	60 ML
4	KAISER BUNS, SLICED IN HALF AND TOASTED	4
	TARTAR SAUCE (SEE RECIPE, PAGE 217)	
	SHREDDED LETTUCE	
	SLICED RED ONION (OPTIONAL)	
	SLICED TOMATO	

PREHEAT OVEN TO 425°F (220°C). LINE A BAKING SHEET WITH GREASED FOIL. RINSE FISH AND PAT DRY WITH PAPER TOWELS. (IF THE FISH HAS BEEN FROZEN, IT WILL BE QUITE WET, SO BE SURE TO DRY IT WELL.) PLACE MILK IN A SHALLOW DISH. IN ANOTHER SHALLOW DISH, WHISK TOGETHER FLOUR, CORNMEAL, CAJUN SEASONING AND SALT. DIP FISH IN MILK, ALLOWING EXCESS TO DRIP OFF. DIP IN FLOUR MIXTURE, PRESSING LIGHTLY TO MAKE IT ADHERE. DISCARD EXCESS MILK AND FLOUR MIXTURE. IN A LARGE NONSTICK SKILLET, HEAT OIL OVER MEDIUM HEAT. BROWN FISH FOR 1 MINUTE PER SIDE. TRANSFER TO PREPARED BAKING SHEET AND BAKE FOR ABOUT 5 MINUTES OR UNTIL FISH IS OPAQUE AND JUST STARTS TO FLAKE WHEN TESTED WITH A FORK. DO NOT OVERCOOK. SPREAD TARTAR SAUCE ON TOASTED BUNS AND MAKE SANDWICHES WITH FISH, LETTUCE, ONION AND TOMATO. SERVES 4.

OUR NEW FAVORITE FLATBREAD

THIS IS REALLY FUN TO MAKE ON FAMILY NIGHT. YES, THE SALAD GOES ON TOP — USE YOUR FINGERS!

4	MILD ITALIAN OR HERB-FLAVORED PORK SAUSAGES	4
3 TBSP	OLIVE OIL, DIVIDED	45 ML
4	6-INCH (15 CM) GREEK-STYLE PITAS (NO POCKETS), NAAN OR OTHER FLATBREAD	4
	SALT AND FRESHLY GROUND BLACK PEPPER	
2	RED-SKINNED APPLES, THINLY SLICED	2
4 OZ	MILD BLUE CHEESE, SUCH AS CAMBOZOLA, SLICED, OR STILTON, CRUMBLED (SEE TIP, OPPOSITE)	125 G
3 CUPS	PACKED ARUGULA OR BABY SPINACH	750 ML
1/4 CUP	CHOPPED TOASTED PECANS (SEE TIP, OPPOSITE)	60 ML
2 TO 3 TBSP	BOTTLED HONEY DIJON SALAD DRESSING	30 TO 45 ML

PREHEAT OVEN TO 375°F (190°C). REMOVE SAUSAGES FROM CASINGS AND CRUMBLE. IN A LARGE SKILLET, HEAT 1 TBSP (15 ML) OF THE OIL OVER MEDIUM HEAT. ADD SAUSAGE AND COOK, BREAKING IT UP WITH A SPOON, FOR 6 TO 8 MINUTES OR UNTIL WELL BROWNED. USING A SLOTTED SPOON, TRANSFER SAUSAGE TO A PLATE LINED WITH PAPER TOWELS. PLACE PITAS ON 2 LARGE BAKING SHEETS. BRUSH TOPS WITH THE REMAINING OIL. SEASON LIGHTLY WITH SALT AND PEPPER. ARRANGE APPLE SLICES ON PITAS, FOLLOWED BY A LAYER OF CHEESE. SCATTER SAUSAGE ON TOP. BAKE IN PREHEATED OVEN FOR ABOUT 15 MINUTES OR UNTIL CHEESE HAS MELTED AND EDGES OF PITAS ARE BROWNED.

MEANWHILE, IN A LARGE BOWL, TOSS ARUGULA AND PECANS WITH SALAD DRESSING. CUT EACH PITA INTO QUARTERS, THEN PLACE ON SERVING PLATES AND PUSH THE PIECES BACK TOGETHER. TOP EACH PITA WITH ARUGULA MIXTURE. SERVE IMMEDIATELY. SERVES 4.

TIP: TOASTING NUTS, SEEDS AND SHREDDED COCONUT HELPS TO BRING OUT THEIR FLAVOR. ALTHOUGH YOU CAN TOAST THEM IN THE OVEN, WE HAVE MORE SUCCESS – AND FEWER BURNT NUTS – ON THE STOVETOP. SPREAD NUTS, SEEDS OR COCONUT IN A DRY NONSTICK SKILLET AND COOK OVER MEDIUM HEAT, SHAKING OR STIRRING FREQUENTLY, FOR 4 TO 5 MINUTES OR UNTIL FRAGRANT AND LIGHTLY BROWNED. TIP NUTS ONTO A COLD PLATE TO STOP THE COOKING PROCESS AND LET COOL COMPLETELY.

VARIATION: FOR MORE KID APPEAL, REPLACE THE BLUE CHEESE WITH SHREDDED SHARP (OLD) CHEDDAR. YOU CAN ALSO SUBSTITUTE CANNED PEACH SLICES, THOROUGHLY DRAINED, FOR THE APPLES.

VARIATION: MANGO, TANGERINE, PEAR OR OTHER FRUIT-FLAVORED SALAD DRESSINGS ALSO WORK WELL WITH THIS RECIPE.

VARIATION

ORANGE DIJON DRESSING: IN A SMALL BOWL, WHISK TOGETHER 1 TBSP (15 ML) OLIVE OIL, 1 TBSP (15 ML) CIDER VINEGAR, 1 TBSP (15 ML) FRESHLY SQUEEZED ORANGE JUICE, 1 TSP (5 ML) GRANULATED SUGAR, $\frac{1}{2}$ TSP (2 ML) DIJON MUSTARD AND SALT AND FRESHLY GROUND BLACK PEPPER TO TASTE. TOSS WITH THE ARUGULA AND PECANS INSTEAD OF THE BOTTLED DRESSING.

SPICY SHRIMP WRAPS

THESE FIT THE MENU WHEN KITCHEN TIME IS FLEETING.

LIME CHILE MAYONNAISE

1	JALAPEÑO PEPPER, SEEDED AND FINELY CHOPPED (OR A PINCH OF CAYENNE PEPPER)	1
1/2 CUP	LIGHT OR REGULAR MAYONNAISE	125 ML
	GRATED ZEST OF 1 LIME	
3 TBSP	FRESHLY SQUEEZED LIME JUICE	45 ML
4	9-INCH (23 CM) FLOUR TORTILLAS	4
1 TSP	PAPRIKA OR SWEET SMOKED PAPRIKA (SEE TIP, PAGE 37)	5 ML
1 TSP	PACKED BROWN SUGAR	5 ML
1 TSP	SALT	5 ML
PINCH	CAYENNE PEPPER	PINCH
2 TBSP	OLIVE OR VEGETABLE OIL	30 ML
12 OZ	LARGE SHRIMP (SEE TIP, PAGE 151), THAWED IF FROZEN, PEELED AND DEVEINED	375 G
1	AVOCADO, PITTED, PEELED AND CHOPPED (SEE TIP, OPPOSITE)	1
	SHREDDED ICEBERG LETTUCE	
	DICED TOMATO	

LIME CHILE MAYONNAISE: IN A SMALL BOWL, COMBINE JALAPEÑO, MAYONNAISE, LIME ZEST AND LIME JUICE. USE IMMEDIATELY OR COVER AND REFRIGERATE FOR UP TO 2 DAYS.

PREHEAT OVEN TO 350°F (180°C). WRAP TORTILLAS IN FOIL AND WARM IN OVEN FOR 10 MINUTES. (OR HEAT IN THE MICROWAVE, ON A PLATE AND UNCOVERED, FOR ABOUT 20 SECONDS AFTER YOU'VE COOKED THE SHRIMP.)

MEANWHILE, IN A BOWL, COMBINE PAPRIKA, BROWN SUGAR, SALT, CAYENNE AND OIL. BLOT SHRIMP DRY AND ADD TO SPICE MIXTURE, STIRRING TO COAT. HEAT A LARGE NONSTICK SKILLET OVER MEDIUM HEAT. SAUTÉ SHRIMP FOR 3 TO 4 MINUTES OR UNTIL PINK AND OPAQUE. (IT MIGHT BE HARD TO TELL BECAUSE OF THE SPICE MIXTURE COATING. IF SO, REMOVE A SHRIMP FROM THE PAN AND GENTLY SCRAPE AWAY THE SPICES.)

LAY WARMED TORTILLAS ON A WORK SURFACE. SPREAD LIME CHILI MAYONNAISE GENEROUSLY OVER TORTILLAS. ALONG THE BOTTOM THIRD OF EACH TORTILLA, LAYER AVOCADO, LETTUCE, TOMATO AND SHRIMP. ROLL UP TIGHTLY. SERVES 4.

TIP: REMOVE THE PIT BEFORE PEELING AN AVOCADO. USE A SHARP KNIFE TO SCORE LENGTHWISE AROUND THE MIDDLE OF THE AVOCADO DOWN TO THE PIT. HOLDING THE AVOCADO IN BOTH HANDS, TWIST THE TWO SIDES IN OPPOSITE DIRECTIONS. IF THE AVOCADO IS RIPE, IT SHOULD COME APART EASILY. HOLD THE HALF CONTAINING THE EXPOSED PIT IN ONE HAND. FIRMLY STRIKE THE PIT WITH THE EDGE OF THE KNIFE, EMBEDDING IT IN THE PIT, AND TWIST THE KNIFE TO LOOSEN AND REMOVE THE PIT. PROCEED WITH PEELING AND SLICING OR CHOPPING THE AVOCADO HALVES OR SIMPLY SCOOP OUT THE FLESH WITH A SPOON.

VARIATION: FOR A MORE AUTHENTIC MEXICAN TASTE, USE CORN TORTILLAS. THESE ARE GENERALLY SMALLER THAN FLOUR TORTILLAS, SO ALLOW 2 CORN TORTILLAS PER SERVING.

TURKEY BURGERS IN PITA POCKETS

THESE BURGERS ARE MOIST AND FULL OF FLAVOR.
MEDITERRANEAN COUSCOUS SALAD (PAGE 80)
IS A GOOD ACCOMPANIMENT.

ROASTED RED PEPPER MAYO

1/2 CUP	LIGHT MAYONNAISE	125 ML
2 TBSP	FINELY CHOPPED DRAINED ROASTED RED BELL PEPPER (SEE TIP, PAGE 54)	30 ML
1 TBSP	FRESHLY SQUEEZED LEMON JUICE	15 ML
	SALT AND FRESHLY GROUND BLACK PEPPER	

BURGERS

1/4 CUP	DRY BREAD CRUMBS OR CRACKER CRUMBS	60 ML
1	EGG, LIGHTLY BEATEN	1
2	CLOVES GARLIC, MINCED	2
2 TBSP	FINELY CHOPPED DRAINED OIL-PACKED SUN-DRIED TOMATOES	30 ML
2 TBSP	FINELY CHOPPED FRESH PARSLEY	30 ML
1/2 TSP	DRIED THYME OR ROSEMARY	2 ML
1/2 TSP	SALT	2 ML
1/4 TSP	FRESHLY GROUND BLACK PEPPER	1 ML
1/4 TSP	CAYENNE PEPPER	1 ML
1 LB	LEAN GROUND TURKEY	500 G
2 TBSP	OLIVE OR VEGETABLE OIL	30 ML
3 TBSP	HOT RED PEPPER JELLY, WARMED TO LOOSEN SLIGHTLY	45 ML
2	6- TO 7-INCH (15 TO 18 CM) PITA BREADS, CUT IN HALF AND WARMED (SEE TIP, OPPOSITE)	2
	SLICED TOMATO	
	SHREDDED ICEBERG LETTUCE	

ROASTED RED PEPPER MAYO: IN A BOWL, COMBINE MAYONNAISE, ROASTED PEPPER AND LEMON JUICE. SEASON TO TASTE WITH SALT AND PEPPER. USE IMMEDIATELY OR COVER AND REFRIGERATE FOR UP TO 2 DAYS.

BURGERS: IN A LARGE BOWL, COMBINE BREAD CRUMBS AND EGG; LET SOAK FOR 5 MINUTES. STIR IN GARLIC, SUN-DRIED TOMATOES, PARSLEY, THYME, SALT, BLACK PEPPER AND CAYENNE. ADD TURKEY AND STIR OR USE CLEAN HANDS TO MIX THOROUGHLY. SHAPE INTO 4 PATTIES, ABOUT $1/2$ INCH (1 CM) THICK (OR MORE IF YOU LIKE SMALLER BURGERS). PLACE ON A PLATE, COVER AND REFRIGERATE FOR AT LEAST 30 MINUTES OR UP TO 4 HOURS.

MEANWHILE, PREHEAT BARBECUE GRILL TO MEDIUM. BRUSH BOTH SIDES OF PATTIES WITH OIL. PLACE ON GREASED GRILL AND COOK FOR 5 TO 6 MINUTES PER SIDE OR UNTIL NO LONGER PINK INSIDE. REMOVE FROM HEAT AND BRUSH WITH HOT RED PEPPER JELLY. GENTLY PRY OPEN PITA HALVES AND SPREAD ROASTED RED PEPPER MAYO INSIDE. FILL EACH WITH A BURGER, TOMATO AND LETTUCE. SERVES 4.

TIP: TO WARM PITAS, WRAP LOOSELY IN PAPER TOWELS AND MICROWAVE ON HIGH FOR 30 SECONDS. OR WRAP IN FOIL AND WARM IN A 350°F (180°C) OVEN FOR 10 MINUTES.

TIP: YOU CAN ALSO COOK THE PATTIES IN A LARGE NONSTICK SKILLET OR GRILL PAN ON THE STOVETOP OVER MEDIUM HEAT.

DON'T MAKE ME USE MY OPERA VOICE.

STICKY ASIAN PORK BURGERS

1/4 CUP	DRY BREAD CRUMBS OR CRACKER CRUMBS	60 ML
1/4 CUP	MILK	60 ML
1 LB	LEAN GROUND PORK	500 G
1	CLOVE GARLIC, MINCED	1
2 TO 3 TSP	MINCED GINGERROOT	10 TO 15 ML
2 TBSP	HOISIN SAUCE	30 ML
1 TSP	ASIAN CHILI PASTE (SEE TIP, PAGE 207)	5 ML
	SALT AND FRESHLY GROUND BLACK PEPPER	
2 TBSP	SWEET CHILI DIPPING SAUCE	30 ML
4	KAISER BUNS, HALVED AND TOASTED	4
	SWEET CHILI AÏOLI (SEE RECIPE, PAGE 261) OR MAYONNAISE	
	SHREDDED LETTUCE (OPTIONAL)	

IN A LARGE BOWL, COMBINE BREAD CRUMBS AND MILK; LET SOAK FOR 5 MINUTES. ADD PORK, GARLIC, GINGER, HOISIN SAUCE AND CHILI PASTE. SEASON WITH SALT AND PEPPER. STIR OR USE CLEAN HANDS TO MIX THOROUGHLY. SHAPE INTO 4 PATTIES, ABOUT 1/2 INCH (1 CM) THICK (OR MORE IF YOU LIKE SMALLER BURGERS). PLACE ON A PLATE, COVER AND REFRIGERATE FOR AT LEAST 30 MINUTES OR FOR UP TO 4 HOURS.

MEANWHILE, PREHEAT BARBECUE GRILL TO MEDIUM. PLACE PATTIES ON GREASED GRILL AND COOK FOR ABOUT 5 MINUTES PER SIDE OR UNTIL NO LONGER PINK INSIDE. JUST BEFORE THE END OF COOKING, BRUSH BOTH SIDES OF BURGERS WITH CHILI SAUCE. SPREAD SWEET CHILI AÏOLI OVER TOASTED BUNS AND MAKE SANDWICHES WITH BURGERS AND LETTUCE. SERVES 4.

FAST FAMILY FAVORITES

SWEET-AND-SOUR CHICKEN WITH VEGETABLES

SAUCE

1 TBSP	FINELY GRATED GINGERROOT	15 ML
½ TSP	CORNSTARCH	2 ML
½ CUP	PINEAPPLE OR APRICOT JAM	125 ML
¼ CUP	CIDER VINEGAR	60 ML
2 TBSP	REDUCED-SODIUM SOY SAUCE	30 ML
½ TSP	ASIAN CHILI PASTE (SEE TIP, PAGE 207)	2 ML
1 LB	BONELESS SKINLESS CHICKEN BREASTS (2 OR 3 BREASTS)	500 G
¼ CUP	COLD WATER	60 ML
1 CUP	CRACKER CRUMBS (SEE TIP, OPPOSITE)	250 ML
½ TSP	GARLIC POWDER	2 ML
⅛ TSP	FRESHLY GROUND BLACK PEPPER	0.5 ML
4 TBSP	OLIVE OR VEGETABLE OIL, DIVIDED	60 ML
4	STALKS CELERY, THINLY SLICED	4
2	LARGE CARROTS, THINLY SLICED	2
24	SNOW PEAS	24
4	GREEN ONIONS, FINELY CHOPPED	4
2 TBSP	TOASTED SESAME SEEDS	30 ML

SAUCE: IN A BOWL, WHISK TOGETHER GINGER, CORNSTARCH, PINEAPPLE JAM, VINEGAR, SOY SAUCE AND CHILI PASTE. SET ASIDE.

PREHEAT OVEN TO 250°F (120°C). PLACE CHICKEN BREASTS BETWEEN TWO SHEETS OF PLASTIC WRAP AND POUND LIGHTLY WITH A ROLLING PIN OR THE BOTTOM OF A SKILLET TO A UNIFORM THICKNESS. CUT CHICKEN LENGTHWISE INTO 1-INCH (2.5 CM) WIDE STRIPS. CUT STRIPS IN HALF CROSSWISE. PLACE COLD WATER IN A

SHALLOW BOWL. IN ANOTHER BOWL, COMBINE CRACKER CRUMBS, GARLIC POWDER AND PEPPER. DIP CHICKEN PIECES IN WATER, SHAKING OFF EXCESS, THEN ROLL IN CRUMB MIXTURE. DISCARD EXCESS WATER AND CRUMB MIXTURE. IN A LARGE SKILLET, HEAT 3 TBSP (45 ML) OF THE OIL OVER MEDIUM-HIGH HEAT. FRY CHICKEN, IN BATCHES IF NECESSARY, UNTIL GOLDEN ON BOTH SIDES AND NO LONGER PINK INSIDE. TRANSFER TO A PLATE LINED WITH PAPER TOWELS TO DRAIN EXCESS OIL, THEN PLACE IN AN OVENPROOF DISH AND KEEP WARM, UNCOVERED, IN OVEN. WIPE OUT SKILLET AND HEAT THE REMAINING OIL OVER MEDIUM-HIGH HEAT. STIR-FRY CELERY AND CARROTS FOR 2 MINUTES OR UNTIL TENDER-CRISP. ADD SNOW PEAS AND STIR-FRY FOR I MINUTE. ADD SAUCE AND BRING TO A BOIL, STIRRING. IMMEDIATELY REMOVE FROM HEAT, ADD RESERVED CHICKEN AND GREEN ONIONS AND GENTLY STIR TO COAT WITH SAUCE. SERVE SPRINKLED WITH SESAME SEEDS. SERVES 4.

TIP: IN PLACE OF THE ASIAN CHILI PASTE, YOU COULD USE $1/4$ TSP (I ML) HOT PEPPER FLAKES.

TIP: PRACTICALLY ANY SAVORY CRACKER WILL DO (WE LIKE RITZ), BUT TRY TO AVOID ANYTHING WITH CHUNKY BITS OF WHOLE GRAINS.

VARIATION: ADD A CHOPPED RED OR GREEN BELL PEPPER WHEN STIR-FRYING THE CELERY AND CARROTS. OR ADD A CAN OF DRAINED RINSED SLICED WATER CHESTNUTS AND/ OR BABY SWEET CORN WITH THE SAUCE. TRY REPLACING THE SESAME SEEDS WITH CHOPPED ROASTED UNSALTED PEANUTS OR CASHEWS.

STOVETOP CHICKEN POT PIE

HERE'S A SPEEDIER VERSION OF A FAMILY FAVORITE.

2	LARGE BONELESS SKINLESS CHICKEN BREASTS (ABOUT I LB/500 G), CUT INTO BITE-SIZE PIECES	2
	SALT AND FRESHLY GROUND BLACK PEPPER	
2	SLICES BACON, CHOPPED	2
I TO 2 TSP	OLIVE OIL (IF NEEDED)	5 TO 10 ML
I TBSP	BUTTER	15 ML
I	SMALL ONION, FINELY CHOPPED	I
I	STALK CELERY, FINELY CHOPPED	I
2 TBSP	ALL-PURPOSE FLOUR	30 ML
1/4 TSP	DRIED THYME	I ML
I1/4 TO 11/2 CUPS	REDUCED-SODIUM CHICKEN BROTH	300 TO 375 ML
2 TBSP	DRY SHERRY OR UNSWEETENED APPLE JUICE	30 ML
I CUP	FROZEN MIXED VEGETABLES (NO NEED TO THAW)	250 ML
1/4 CUP	HEAVY OR WHIPPING (35%) CREAM, WARMED	60 ML
1/2	PACKAGE (14 OZ/398 G) FROZEN PUFF PASTRY, THAWED	1/2
I	EGG, LIGHTLY BEATEN	I

IN A LARGE BOWL, TOSS CHICKEN WITH 1/2 TSP (2 ML) SALT AND 1/8 TSP (0.5 ML) PEPPER. IN A LARGE, DEEP NONSTICK SKILLET, SAUTÉ BACON OVER MEDIUM-HIGH HEAT UNTIL CRISPY. USING A SLOTTED SPOON, TRANSFER BACON TO A PLATE LINED WITH PAPER TOWELS. DRAIN OFF ALL BUT I TBSP (15 ML) OF THE FAT FROM PAN. IF THERE IS LESS THAN I TBSP (15 ML) FAT, ADD OIL AS NEEDED.

REDUCE HEAT TO MEDIUM. ADD CHICKEN AND SAUTÉ FOR ABOUT 5 MINUTES OR UNTIL BROWNED AND NO LONGER PINK INSIDE. TRANSFER TO A PLATE. REDUCE HEAT TO LOW AND ADD BUTTER TO PAN. ADD ONION AND CELERY; COVER AND COOK, STIRRING OCCASIONALLY, FOR 6 TO 8 MINUTES OR UNTIL VEGETABLES ARE SOFTENED BUT NOT BROWNED. (THIS TECHNIQUE IS CALLED "SWEATING.") ADD FLOUR AND THYME; COOK, STIRRING, FOR 30 SECONDS. GRADUALLY WHISK IN $1\frac{1}{4}$ CUPS (300 ML) OF THE BROTH AND SHERRY; INCREASE HEAT TO HIGH AND BRING TO A BOIL, STIRRING. REDUCE HEAT AND SIMMER FOR 5 MINUTES OR UNTIL SAUCE IS THICK ENOUGH TO LIGHTLY COAT THE BACK OF A SPOON. ADD MORE BROTH IF SAUCE IS TOO THICK. RETURN BACON AND CHICKEN TO PAN AND STIR IN FROZEN VEGETABLES; RETURN TO A SIMMER. SIMMER FOR 5 MINUTES OR UNTIL VEGETABLES ARE TENDER. STIR IN CREAM. TASTE AND ADJUST SEASONING WITH SALT AND PEPPER, IF DESIRED.

MEANWHILE, PREHEAT OVEN TO 425°F (220°C). LINE A LARGE BAKING SHEET WITH PARCHMENT PAPER. ON A LIGHTLY FLOURED SURFACE, ROLL OUT PASTRY INTO A 10-INCH (25 CM) SQUARE. CUT INTO FOUR 5-INCH (12.5 CM) SQUARES. WITH THE TIP OF A SHARP KNIFE, LIGHTLY SCORE A BORDER ABOUT $\frac{1}{4}$ INCH (0.5 CM) INSIDE EACH SQUARE. PLACE ON PREPARED BAKING SHEET. BRUSH WITH BEATEN EGG. BAKE FOR 12 TO 15 MINUTES OR UNTIL PUFFY AND GOLDEN.

IF NECESSARY, REHEAT CHICKEN MIXTURE, STIRRING OFTEN, OVER LOW HEAT. SERVE EACH PORTION TOPPED WITH A PASTRY SQUARE. SERVES 4.

PRONTO ITALIAN CHICKEN

ITALIANS CALL THIS DISH SALTIMBOCCA, WHICH MEANS "JUMP IN THE MOUTH," BECAUSE IT'S SO QUICK TO MAKE. OUR FAMILY-FRIENDLY VERSION USES CHICKEN AND FRESH BASIL, ALTHOUGH TRADITIONALLY IT'S MADE WITH VEAL AND SAGE. SERVE WITH TOMATO ORZO PILAF (PAGE 274) AND STEAMED GREEN BEANS DRESSED WITH A SQUEEZE OF FRESH LEMON JUICE.

4	BONELESS SKINLESS CHICKEN BREASTS	4
8	LARGE FRESH BASIL LEAVES	8
8	SLICES PROSCIUTTO (SEE TIP, OPPOSITE)	8
1/4 CUP	ALL-PURPOSE FLOUR	60 ML
1/4 CUP	OLIVE OIL	60 ML
1/2 CUP	DRY WHITE WINE	125 ML
1/2 CUP	REDUCED-SODIUM CHICKEN BROTH	125 ML
2 TBSP	UNSALTED BUTTER	30 ML

CUT EACH CHICKEN BREAST IN HALF CROSSWISE. PLACE BETWEEN TWO SHEETS OF PLASTIC WRAP AND POUND LIGHTLY WITH A ROLLING PIN OR THE BOTTOM OF A SKILLET TO A UNIFORM THICKNESS. PLACE CHICKEN ON A WORK SURFACE. PLACE A BASIL LEAF ON TOP OF ONE PIECE OF CHICKEN. PLACE ONE SLICE OF PROSCIUTTO OVER THE BASIL AND WRAP IT AROUND AND UNDER THE CHICKEN, MAKING SURE THE BASIL IS COVERED AND GENTLY PRESSING THE PROSCIUTTO TO MAKE ITS ENDS HOLD TOGETHER. (DON'T WORRY IF THE PROSCIUTTO TEARS; JUST PATCH IT TOGETHER.) REPEAT WITH REMAINING CHICKEN, BASIL AND PROSCIUTTO. PLACE FLOUR ON A PLATE. DIP BOTH SIDES OF THE PROSCIUTTO-WRAPPED CHICKEN PIECES IN FLOUR TO LIGHTLY COAT. DISCARD

EXCESS FLOUR. IN A LARGE NONSTICK SKILLET, HEAT OIL OVER MEDIUM HEAT. SAUTÉ CHICKEN, 4 PIECES AT A TIME, FOR ABOUT 3 MINUTES PER SIDE OR UNTIL PROSCIUTTO IS CRISP AND CHICKEN IS NO LONGER PINK INSIDE. TRANSFER TO A PLATE AND KEEP WARM. ADD WINE AND BROTH TO THE PAN; INCREASE HEAT TO HIGH AND BRING TO A BOIL. BOIL UNTIL REDUCED TO ABOUT 2 TBSP (30 ML). REMOVE FROM HEAT, ADD BUTTER AND SWIRL PAN UNTIL IT MELTS, ABOUT 30 SECONDS. SERVE CHICKEN IMMEDIATELY, WITH SAUCE SPOONED OVER TOP. SERVES 4 TO 6.

TIP: PROSCIUTTO IS AN ITALIAN HAM THAT IS SALT-CURED AND AIR-DRIED. IT IS NOT SMOKED. PROSCIUTTO IS AVAILABLE IN MOST DELI SECTIONS. ASK FOR IT TO BE THINLY SLICED. IF THEY DON'T HAVE IT AT THE DELI COUNTER, LOOK FOR IT IN VACUUM-SEALED PACKAGES.

I COOK WITH A FLAIR FOR THE DRAMATIC AND DEPRAVED INDIFFERENCE TO CALORIES.

WEEKNIGHT CHICKEN CACCIATORE

YOU CAN MAKE YOUR GANG A "PROPER" DINNER ON
A BUSY WEEKNIGHT. A JAR OF PASTA SAUCE HELPS
TO SPEED UP THE COOKING TIME OF THIS POPULAR
ITALIAN-STYLE STEW. SERVE OVER A CHUNKY PASTA,
SUCH AS PENNE, OR WITH LIGHT CHIVE MASHED
POTATOES (PAGE 266).

I TBSP	OLIVE OR VEGETABLE OIL	15 ML
2	CARROTS, CHOPPED	I
2	STALKS CELERY, CHOPPED	2
I	ONION, CHOPPED	I
2 CUPS	SLICED MUSHROOMS	500 ML
2	CLOVES GARLIC, MINCED	2
I TSP	DRIED ITALIAN SEASONING, BASIL OR OREGANO	5 ML
8	BONELESS SKINLESS CHICKEN THIGHS, CUT INTO BITE-SIZE PIECES	8
I	JAR (24 OZ/700 ML) TOMATO PASTA SAUCE	I
½ CUP	DRY RED WINE, REDUCED-SODIUM CHICKEN BROTH, HOMEMADE VEGETABLE STOCK (SEE RECIPE, PAGE 90) OR WATER	125 ML
	SALT AND FRESHLY GROUND BLACK PEPPER	
¼ CUP	CHOPPED FRESH PARSLEY	60 ML
I TBSP	BALSAMIC, RED WINE OR CIDER VINEGAR (SEE TIP, OPPOSITE)	15 ML
⅓ CUP	FRESHLY GRATED PARMESAN CHEESE (OPTIONAL)	75 ML

IN A LARGE SAUCEPAN OR DUTCH OVEN, HEAT OIL OVER
MEDIUM HEAT. SAUTÉ CARROTS, CELERY AND ONION
FOR 5 MINUTES OR UNTIL ONION IS SOFTENED. ADD
MUSHROOMS AND SAUTÉ FOR ABOUT 5 MINUTES OR

UNTIL SOFTENED. ADD GARLIC AND ITALIAN SEASONING; SAUTÉ FOR 15 SECONDS OR UNTIL FRAGRANT. STIR IN CHICKEN, PASTA SAUCE, WINE, $\frac{1}{2}$ TSP (2 ML) SALT AND PEPPER TO TASTE; BRING TO A BOIL. REDUCE HEAT TO LOW, COVER AND SIMMER, STIRRING OCCASIONALLY, FOR ABOUT 30 MINUTES OR UNTIL CHICKEN IS NO LONGER PINK INSIDE, VEGETABLES ARE TENDER AND SAUCE IS THICK ENOUGH TO HEAP ON A SPOON. STIR IN PARSLEY AND VINEGAR. TASTE AND ADJUST SEASONING WITH SALT AND PEPPER, IF DESIRED. SERVE SPRINKLED WITH PARMESAN, IF DESIRED. SERVES 4.

TIP: IF YOU USE WATER OR A SALT-FREE STOCK OR BROTH, YOU MAY WANT TO ADD MORE SALT. SALT IS, IN ANY RECIPE, A MATTER OF PERSONAL PREFERENCE, SO FEEL FREE TO INCREASE OR REDUCE THE QUANTITIES WE SUGGEST. BEFORE ADDING MORE SALT AT THE END OF THE COOKING TIME, BE SURE TO TASTE THE DISH FIRST.

TIP: WHEN A SPLASH OF VINEGAR OR CITRUS JUICE IS ADDED TO A STEW OR SAUCE JUST BEFORE SERVING, IT HELPS TO BRIGHTEN AND HEIGHTEN THE FLAVORS.

MAKE AHEAD: LET COOL FOR 30 MINUTES, THEN REFRIGERATE, UNCOVERED, IN A SHALLOW CONTAINER UNTIL COLD. COVER TIGHTLY AND KEEP REFRIGERATED FOR UP TO 2 DAYS. REHEAT SLOWLY.

VARIATION: SUBSTITUTE 8 SKINLESS CHICKEN DRUMSTICKS FOR THE THIGHS. SIMMER FOR 40 TO 50 MINUTES OR UNTIL CHICKEN IS FALLING OFF THE BONE.

HANDY CHICKEN BURRITOS

THESE ZESTY WRAPS ARE A BIG HIT WITH KIDS
OF ALL AGES. IF YOU HAVE A DAUGHTER SERVING
HER OBLIGATORY TIME AS A TEEN VEGETARIAN,
REPLACE THE CHICKEN WITH TOFU. IT'S GOOD!

3 TBSP	VEGETABLE OIL, DIVIDED	45 ML
8 OZ	BONELESS SKINLESS CHICKEN BREAST (ABOUT 1 LARGE), CUT INTO BITE-SIZE PIECES	250 G
1	SMALL ONION, CHOPPED	1
1	GREEN OR RED BELL PEPPER, CHOPPED	1
1	CLOVE GARLIC, MINCED	1
1/2 TSP	GROUND CUMIN	2 ML
1/2 TSP	GROUND CORIANDER	2 ML
1/2 TSP	CHILI POWDER	2 ML
1/4 TO 1/2 TSP	SALT	1 TO 2 ML
	FRESHLY GROUND BLACK PEPPER	
1 CUP	DRAINED CANNED TOMATOES	250 ML
1 CUP	FROZEN CORN KERNELS (NO NEED TO THAW)	250 ML
1 TBSP	CHOPPED FRESH CILANTRO (OPTIONAL)	15 ML
4	9-INCH (23 CM) FLOUR TORTILLAS	4
1 CUP	SHREDDED TEX-MEX CHEESE BLEND, JALAPEÑO JACK CHEESE OR SHARP (OLD) CHEDDAR CHEESE	250 ML
	SALSA AND SOUR CREAM (OPTIONAL)	

PREHEAT OVEN TO 400°F (200°C). GREASE A LARGE BAKING
SHEET. IN A LARGE NONSTICK SKILLET, HEAT 1 TBSP
(15 ML) OF THE OIL OVER MEDIUM HEAT. SAUTÉ CHICKEN
FOR 3 MINUTES OR UNTIL LIGHTLY BROWNED ON ALL
SIDES. USING A SLOTTED SPOON, TRANSFER CHICKEN TO
A PLATE. ADD 1 TBSP (15 ML) OIL TO THE PAN. SAUTÉ ONION

AND GREEN PEPPER FOR 5 MINUTES OR UNTIL SOFTENED. ADD GARLIC, CUMIN, CORIANDER, CHILI POWDER AND SALT AND PEPPER TO TASTE; SAUTÉ FOR 15 SECONDS OR UNTIL FRAGRANT. RETURN CHICKEN AND ACCUMULATED JUICES TO PAN. ADD TOMATOES, CORN AND CILANTRO (IF USING), BREAKING TOMATOES UP WITH A SPOON; BRING TO A BOIL. REDUCE HEAT AND SIMMER FOR 4 TO 5 MINUTES OR UNTIL MIXTURE IS SLIGHTLY THICKENED AND HEAPS ON A SPOON. REMOVE FROM HEAT AND LET COOL FOR 5 MINUTES. PLACE TORTILLAS ON A WORK SURFACE. SPOON A QUARTER OF THE CHICKEN MIXTURE ALONG AND JUST BELOW THE CENTER OF EACH TORTILLA. SPRINKLE WITH CHEESE, DIVIDING EVENLY. FOLD UP BOTTOM EDGE OF TORTILLA, FOLD IN SIDES, THEN ROLL UP. PLACE SEAM SIDE DOWN ON PREPARED BAKING SHEET AND BRUSH WITH THE REMAINING OIL. BAKE FOR 15 TO 20 MINUTES OR UNTIL GOLDEN. (DON'T WORRY IF SOME SAUCE OOZES OUT DURING COOKING.) TO SERVE, CUT IN HALF DIAGONALLY. SERVE WITH SALSA AND SOUR CREAM, IF DESIRED. SERVES 4.

TIP: USE SUN-DRIED TOMATO, SPINACH OR CHEESE-FLAVORED FLOUR TORTILLAS TO ADD COLOR AND KID-APPEAL.

MAKE AHEAD: LET COOKED BURRITOS COOL COMPLETELY, THEN WRAP EACH BURRITO TIGHTLY IN PLASTIC WRAP. PLACE IN AN AIRTIGHT CONTAINER AND FREEZE FOR UP TO 2 WEEKS. REHEAT FROM FROZEN IN THE MICROWAVE ON HIGH FOR 5 MINUTES.

VARIATION

HANDY CHICKEN BEAN BURRITOS: SUBSTITUTE 1 CUP (250 ML) DRAINED RINSED CANNED BLACK BEANS FOR THE CORN. OR USE A COMBINATION.

CASHEW BEEF AND BROCCOLI STIR-FRY

WHY ORDER CHINESE TAKEOUT WHEN YOU CAN MAKE THIS POPULAR STIR-FRY DISH SO EASILY IN YOUR OWN KITCHEN? SERVE IT WITH STEAMED RICE OR NOODLES.

1 TBSP	GRANULATED SUGAR	15 ML
1/3 CUP	WATER	75 ML
1/4 CUP	OYSTER SAUCE	60 ML
2 TBSP	REDUCED-SODIUM SOY SAUCE	30 ML
1 TBSP	RICE WINE (SAKE) OR DRY SHERRY (OPTIONAL)	15 ML
1/2 TSP	ASIAN CHILI PASTE (SEE TIP, PAGE 207)	2 ML
2 TBSP	VEGETABLE OIL, DIVIDED	30 ML
1 LB	BONELESS BEEF TOP SIRLOIN GRILLING STEAK, CUT ACROSS THE GRAIN INTO 1/8-INCH (3 MM) THICK STRIPS (SEE TIP, OPPOSITE)	500 G
1	ONION, THINLY SLICED	1
2	CLOVES GARLIC, MINCED	2
1	LARGE CARROT, THINLY SLICED	1
4 CUPS	BROCCOLI FLORETS	1 L
1 TBSP	MINCED GINGERROOT	15 ML
2 TBSP	WATER	30 ML
1/2 CUP	ROASTED UNSALTED CASHEWS	125 ML

IN A BOWL, WHISK TOGETHER SUGAR, 1/3 CUP (75 ML) WATER, OYSTER SAUCE, SOY SAUCE, RICE WINE AND CHILI PASTE; SET ASIDE. IN A LARGE NONSTICK SKILLET, HEAT 1 TBSP (15 ML) OF THE OIL OVER MEDIUM-HIGH HEAT. STIR-FRY STEAK UNTIL WELL BROWNED BUT STILL SLIGHTLY PINK INSIDE. (DON'T CROWD THE PAN; YOU WANT TO KEEP THE MEAT IN A SINGLE LAYER. IF NECESSARY COOK THE

CONTINUED ON PAGE 145...

Sticky Asian Pork Burgers (page 132) and Rainbow Coleslaw (page 60)

Shrimp Hurry Curry (page 150)

Upside-Down Pizza Pie (page 160)

Chicken Med (page 174)

STEAK IN TWO BATCHES.) USING A SLOTTED SPOON, TRANSFER STEAK TO A PLATE. REDUCE HEAT TO MEDIUM. ADD THE REMAINING OIL TO THE PAN. STIR-FRY ONION FOR 3 MINUTES OR UNTIL JUST STARTING TO SOFTEN. ADD GARLIC, CARROT, BROCCOLI, GINGER AND 2 TBSP (30 ML) WATER; STIR-FRY FOR 30 SECONDS OR UNTIL FRAGRANT. STIR IN OYSTER SAUCE MIXTURE AND BRING TO BOIL. REDUCE HEAT TO LOW, COVER AND SIMMER FOR ABOUT 3 MINUTES OR UNTIL BROCCOLI IS TENDER-CRISP. RETURN STEAK AND ANY ACCUMULATED JUICES TO THE PAN. STIR IN CASHEWS, INCREASE HEAT TO MEDIUM AND BRING TO A BOIL. REDUCE HEAT AND SIMMER, UNCOVERED, FOR 1 MINUTE OR UNTIL HEATED THROUGH. SERVES 4.

TIP: RICE WINE — A.K.A. SAKE — IS A JAPANESE ALCOHOLIC DRINK THAT'S OFTEN FEATURED IN ASIAN COOKING. MOST LIQUOR STORES CARRY IT, AND AT THE TIME OF WRITING, IT COST AROUND $10 FOR A BIG BOTTLE. INVEST IN A BOTTLE (IT KEEPS FOR AGES) AND ENJOY THE THRILL WHEN EVERYONE TELLS YOU HOW AUTHENTIC YOUR STIR-FRIES TASTE! DRY SHERRY IS A GOOD SUBSTITUTE FOR RICE WINE, OR YOU CAN SIMPLY OMIT IT FROM THE RECIPE. BUT THAT WOULD BE A SHAME.

TIP: IN PLACE OF THE ASIAN CHILI PASTE, YOU COULD USE A PINCH OF HOT PEPPER FLAKES.

TIP: TO MAKE THE STEAK EASIER TO SLICE THINLY, PLACE IT IN THE FREEZER IT FOR 30 MINUTES.

YOU KNOW YOU ARE OLD WHEN YOU'VE LOST ALL YOUR MARVEL.
— MERRY BROWNE

EMPANADA MUFFINS

EMPANADAS ARE LITTLE LATIN AMERICAN PIES WITH A VARIETY OF FILLINGS. THIS IS A KID-FRIENDLY SAVORY VERSION MADE IN A MUFFIN PAN THAT CAN BE SERVED WITH A PLATE OF VEGGIES AND DIP AS A QUICK DINNER. (EMPANADAS ALSO GO DOWN WELL WITH A BEER FOR THE BIG BOYS.) WE USED REFRIGERATED BISCUIT DOUGH — IT'S FAST.

12 OZ	LEAN GROUND BEEF	375 G
2	CLOVES GARLIC, MINCED	2
1	SMALL ONION, CHOPPED	1
1	GREEN OR RED BELL PEPPER, CHOPPED	1
1 CUP	SLICED MUSHROOMS	250 ML
1 TSP	GROUND CUMIN	5 ML
1/2 TSP	DRIED OREGANO	2 ML
1/2 TSP	SALT	2 ML
1/4 TSP	CAYENNE PEPPER (OR TO TASTE)	1 ML
3/4 CUP	TOMATO-BASED CHILI SAUCE	175 ML
1/2 CUP	FROZEN CORN KERNELS (NO NEED TO THAW)	125 ML
2 TO 3 TBSP	COLD WATER (IF NEEDED)	30 TO 45 ML
2	PACKAGES (EACH 12 OZ/340 G) REFRIGERATED BISCUIT DOUGH	2
1 1/4 CUPS	SHREDDED TEX-MEX CHEESE BLEND, CHEDDAR CHEESE OR MOZZARELLA CHEESE	300 ML
	SALSA AND SOUR CREAM	

SET OUT TWO 12-CUP NONSTICK MUFFIN PANS. IN A LARGE NONSTICK SKILLET, OVER MEDIUM-HIGH HEAT, COOK BEEF, GARLIC, ONION, GREEN PEPPER AND MUSHROOMS, BREAKING BEEF UP WITH A SPOON, FOR 6 TO 8 MINUTES

OR UNTIL BEEF IS NO LONGER PINK. DRAIN OFF EXCESS FAT. ADD CUMIN, OREGANO, SALT AND CAYENNE; COOK, STIRRING OFTEN, FOR I MINUTE. ADD CHILI SAUCE AND CORN; BRING TO A BOIL. REDUCE HEAT AND SIMMER, STIRRING OCCASIONALLY, FOR 15 MINUTES OR UNTIL SAUCE IS REDUCED AND THE MIXTURE IS THICK ENOUGH TO HEAP ON A SPOON. IF IT GETS TOO DRY DURING THAT TIME, ADD COLD WATER I TBSP (15 ML) AT A TIME AS NEEDED TO PREVENT BURNING. LET COOL COMPLETELY (OR IT WILL MAKE THE PASTRY SOGGY).

PREHEAT OVEN TO 400°F (200°C). ON A CUTTING BOARD, LAY OUT THE BISCUIT DOUGH (20 PIECES). ROLL OUT TO ABOUT 4-INCH (10 CM) CIRCLES. FIT INTO UNGREASED MUFFIN PANS. DIVIDE MEAT MIXTURE AMONG MUFFIN CUPS. TOP WITH CHEESE. BAKE FOR 13 TO 15 MINUTES OR UNTIL BROWNED AND SET. SERVE IMMEDIATELY, WITH SALSA AND SOUR CREAM. MAKES 20 EMPANADAS.

TIP: FOR BEST RESULTS, USE A GOOD-QUALITY NONSTICK MUFFIN PAN.

MAKE AHEAD: LET THE COOKED MEAT FILLING COOL FOR 30 MINUTES, THEN REFRIGERATE, UNCOVERED, IN A SHALLOW CONTAINER UNTIL COLD. COVER TIGHTLY AND KEEP REFRIGERATED FOR UP TO 2 DAYS OR FREEZE FOR UP TO 2 MONTHS. THAW AND PROCEED WITH THE RECIPE.

THERE IS NO SNOOZE BUTTON ON A CAT
WHO WANTS BREAKFAST.

STIR-FRIED PORK
AND NAPA CABBAGE

NAPA CABBAGE, SOMETIMES CALLED CHINESE
CABBAGE, HAS AN ELONGATED SHAPE AND PALE GREEN
RUFFLED LEAVES. IT'S EXCELLENT COOKED IN
STIR-FRIES OR RAW IN SALADS. ITS COUSIN, BOK CHOY,
CAN ALSO BE USED IN THIS RECIPE, WHICH HAS
A FLAVORFUL, BROTH-LIKE SAUCE.

1 LB	BONELESS PORK SIRLOIN CHOPS, CUT INTO 1/4-INCH (0.5 CM) THICK SLICES (SEE TIP, OPPOSITE)	500 G
2 1/2 TBSP	REDUCED-SODIUM SOY SAUCE, DIVIDED	32 ML
3 TBSP	HOISIN SAUCE	45 ML
1 TBSP	CIDER OR RICE VINEGAR	15 ML
1 TSP	ASIAN CHILI PASTE (OPTIONAL)	5 ML
1	LARGE CLOVE GARLIC, MINCED	1
1 TSP	FINELY GRATED GINGERROOT	5 ML
1 TBSP	COLD WATER	15 ML
3 TBSP	VEGETABLE OIL, DIVIDED	45 ML
1	RED OR YELLOW BELL PEPPER, THINLY SLICED	1
6 CUPS	CHOPPED NAPA CABBAGE	1.5 L
4	GREEN ONIONS, THINLY SLICED	4

IN A BOWL, TOSS PORK WITH 1 1/2 TSP (7 ML) OF THE SOY
SAUCE; SET ASIDE. IN A SMALL BOWL, WHISK TOGETHER
THE REMAINING SOY SAUCE, HOISIN SAUCE, VINEGAR
AND CHILI PASTE (IF USING). IN ANOTHER SMALL BOWL,
COMBINE GARLIC, GINGER AND COLD WATER. (THE WATER
WILL HELP PREVENT THE GARLIC FROM SCORCHING WHEN
IT GOES INTO THE PAN.) IN A LARGE, DEEP NONSTICK
SKILLET, HEAT 1 TBSP (15 ML) OF THE OIL OVER

MEDIUM-HIGH HEAT. STIR-FRY HALF THE PORK UNTIL BROWNED AND NO LONGER PINK INSIDE. USING A SLOTTED SPOON, TRANSFER TO A PLATE. ADD ANOTHER 1 TBSP (15 ML) OIL TO THE PAN, IF NECESSARY, AND REPEAT WITH THE REMAINING PORK. ADD THE REMAINING OIL TO THE PAN. ADD GARLIC MIXTURE (IT WILL IMMEDIATELY START TO SIZZLE). ADD RED PEPPER AND CABBAGE, STIRRING THOROUGHLY TO COMBINE WITH GARLIC MIXTURE. THE PAN WILL LOOK QUITE FULL. STIR-FRY FOR 2 TO 3 MINUTES OR UNTIL CABBAGE STARTS TO WILT. ADD SOY SAUCE MIXTURE AND RETURN PORK AND ANY ACCUMULATED JUICES TO THE PAN; REDUCE HEAT AND SIMMER, STIRRING, FOR 1 TO 2 MINUTES OR UNTIL THE WHITE STEM PARTS OF THE CABBAGE ARE TENDER-CRISP AND EVERYTHING IS HOT. SPRINKLE WITH GREEN ONIONS AND STIR AGAIN. SERVE IN BOWLS WITH STEAMED RICE. SERVES 4.

TIP: BONELESS PORK SIRLOIN CHOPS, SOMETIMES LABELED "STEAKS," ARE IDEAL FOR SLICING AND COOKING IN STIR-FRIES AND ARE GENERALLY CHEAPER THAN PORK TENDERLOIN (ALTHOUGH PORK TENDERLOIN ALSO WORKS WELL IN THIS RECIPE). MOST PORK CUTS ARE VERY LEAN AND WILL BE DRY IF OVERCOOKED.

TIP: IN PLACE OF THE ASIAN CHILI PASTE, YOU COULD USE A PINCH OF HOT PEPPER FLAKES.

A WOMAN SHOULD HAVE A SET OF SCREWDRIVERS, A CORDLESS DRILL AND A BLACK LACE BRA.
— MAYA ANGELOU

SHRIMP HURRY CURRY

SERVE THIS SPEEDY MEAL WITH STEAMED BASMATI RICE, MANGO CHUTNEY AND WARM NAAN. TO BOOST THE VEGGIE QUOTA, STIR IN A COUPLE OF HANDFULS OF BABY SPINACH JUST BEFORE SERVING.

I TBSP	VEGETABLE OIL	15 ML
I	ONION, CHOPPED	I
I	RED BELL PEPPER, CHOPPED	I
I	SMALL ZUCCHINI, CHOPPED (OPTIONAL)	I
1/4 CUP	MILD OR MEDIUM INDIAN CURRY PASTE (SEE TIP, PAGE 109)	60 ML
2	LARGE RIPE TOMATOES, COARSELY CHOPPED (OR 2 CUPS/500 ML CANNED DICED TOMATOES, WITH JUICE)	2
3/4 TO I CUP	REDUCED-SODIUM CHICKEN BROTH, HOMEMADE VEGETABLE STOCK (SEE RECIPE, PAGE 90) OR WATER	175 TO 250 ML
I LB	MEDIUM OR LARGE SHRIMP (SEE TIP, OPPOSITE), PEELED AND DEVEINED, THAWED IF FROZEN	500 G
I CUP	FROZEN BABY PEAS (NO NEED TO THAW)	250 ML
2 TBSP	CHOPPED FRESH CILANTRO	30 ML
1/3 CUP	HEAVY OR WHIPPING (35%) CREAM, WARMED (SEE TIP, PAGE 99)	75 ML

IN A LARGE NONSTICK SKILLET, HEAT OIL OVER MEDIUM HEAT. SAUTÉ ONION AND RED PEPPER FOR 5 MINUTES OR UNTIL SOFTENED. ADD ZUCCHINI AND CURRY PASTE; COOK , STIRRING, FOR ABOUT I MINUTE OR UNTIL VERY FRAGRANT. STIR IN TOMATOES AND 3/4 CUP (175 ML) OF THE BROTH; BRING TO A BOIL. REDUCE HEAT AND SIMMER, STIRRING OCCASIONALLY, FOR ABOUT 5 MINUTES OR UNTIL TOMATOES ARE SOFTENED AND ZUCCHINI IS TENDER BUT

NOT MUSHY. STIR IN SHRIMP AND PEAS. ADD MORE BROTH IF SAUCE IS TOO THICK (IT WILL DEPEND ON THE JUICINESS OF THE TOMATOES). INCREASE HEAT AND RETURN TO A BOIL, STIRRING. REDUCE HEAT AND SIMMER FOR 3 TO 4 MINUTES OR UNTIL SHRIMP ARE PINK AND OPAQUE. (DON'T OVERCOOK THE SHRIMP OR THEY WILL BE TOUGH.) STIR IN CILANTRO AND CREAM. SERVE IMMEDIATELY. SERVES 4.

TIP: IF YOU USE WATER OR A SALT-FREE STOCK OR BROTH, YOU MAY WANT TO ADD $\frac{1}{4}$ TO $\frac{1}{2}$ TSP (1 TO 2 ML) SALT AT THE END OF COOKING. BUT TASTE FIRST, BECAUSE THE CURRY PASTE YOU USE COULD BE QUITE SALTY.

TIP: SHRIMP ARE SOLD BY THE COUNT, WHICH MEANS THE APPROXIMATE NUMBER OF SHRIMP YOU GET TO THE POUND (500 G). FOR THIS RECIPE, YOU CAN USE EITHER LARGE SHRIMP (26 TO 30 COUNT OR 31 TO 40 COUNT) OR MEDIUM SHRIMP (41 TO 50 COUNT).

MAKE AHEAD: MAKE THE SAUCE, BUT DON'T ADD THE SHRIMP, PEAS, CILANTRO OR CREAM. LET COOL COMPLETELY, THEN TRANSFER TO AN AIRTIGHT CONTAINER AND REFRIGERATE FOR UP TO 2 DAYS. TO FINISH THE CURRY, PLACE SAUCE IN A LARGE SKILLET AND HEAT THROUGH OVER LOW HEAT, THEN PROCEED WITH THE RECIPE.

VARIATION

CHICKEN HURRY CURRY: SUBSTITUTE 3 BONELESS SKINLESS CHICKEN BREASTS (ABOUT 1 LB/500 G), CHOPPED INTO BITE-SIZE PIECES, FOR THE SHRIMP. SIMMER FOR 8 TO 10 MINUTES OR UNTIL CHICKEN IS NO LONGER PINK INSIDE.

SUPER SHRIMP PASTA SUPPER

*VERY LAST MINUTE — YOU'LL HAVE DINNER ON THE
TABLE IN THE TIME IT TAKES TO BOIL THE PASTA.*

12 OZ	BOW-TIE, PENNE OR FUSILLI PASTA (ABOUT 4 CUPS/1 L)	375 G
1 CUP	FROZEN BABY PEAS (NO NEED TO THAW)	250 ML
12 OZ	COOKED SMALL SHRIMP, THAWED IF FROZEN (SEE TIP, BELOW)	375 G
1	TUB (8 OZ/250 G) TZATZIKI OR SPICY TZATZIKI DIP	1
1/4 CUP	CHOPPED FRESH PARSLEY OR CHIVES (OPTIONAL)	60 ML
1/2 CUP	FRESHLY GRATED PARMESAN CHEESE	125 ML

IN A LARGE POT OF BOILING SALTED WATER, COOK PASTA
ACCORDING TO PACKAGE DIRECTIONS. TWO MINUTES
BEFORE PASTA IS READY, ADD PEAS AND COOK FOR
2 MINUTES. PLACE SHRIMP IN A COLANDER OVER THE SINK.
DRAIN PASTA AND PEAS INTO COLANDER. THE HOT WATER
WILL HEAT THE SHRIMP. RETURN TO POT. ADD TZATZIKI
AND PARSLEY (IF USING); TOSS TO COMBINE. SERVE
SPRINKLED WITH PARMESAN. SERVES 4.

TIP: TO QUICKLY THAW FROZEN SHRIMP, TAKE IT OUT OF
ITS PACKAGE AND PLACE IT IN A BOWL OF COLD WATER
SET IN THE KITCHEN SINK. LET A TRICKLE OF COLD
WATER FROM THE TAP RUN INTO THE BOWL, WITH THE
OVERFLOW GOING DOWN THE DRAIN. THE SHRIMP WILL
BE THAWED IN 10 TO 15 MINUTES, DEPENDING ON SIZE
AND QUANTITY.

CAREFUL OR YOU'LL END UP IN MY NEW NOVEL.

BAKED PESTO COD

FAST AND FOOLPROOF, THIS RECIPE IS IDEAL
FOR THOSE WHO CLAIM THEY DON'T KNOW HOW TO
COOK FISH. A JAR OF STORE-BOUGHT PESTO PERKS
UP THE FLAVOR, WHILE A FIERCELY HOT OVEN COOKS
THE COD TO PERFECTION IN MINUTES. SERVE WITH
STEAMED RICE AND SAUTÉED CHERRY TOMATOES
AND CORN (PAGE 257).

1/4 CUP	FRESHLY GRATED PARMESAN CHEESE	60 ML
1/4 CUP	GROUND ALMONDS	60 ML
1/4 CUP	SUN-DRIED TOMATO OR BASIL PESTO (SEE TIP, PAGE 165)	60 ML
2 TBSP	FRESHLY SQUEEZED LEMON JUICE	30 ML
1/4 CUP	CRACKER CRUMBS (SEE TIP, PAGE 135) OR DRY BREAD CRUMBS	60 ML
2 TSP	OLIVE OR VEGETABLE OIL	10 ML
4	SKINLESS COD FILLETS (EACH ABOUT 6 OZ/175 G)	4

PREHEAT OVEN TO 450°F (230°F). LINE A LARGE BAKING
SHEET WITH GREASED FOIL. IN A SMALL BOWL, COMBINE
PARMESAN, ALMONDS, PESTO AND LEMON JUICE. IN
ANOTHER BOWL, COMBINE CRACKER CRUMBS AND OIL.
RINSE COD AND PAT DRY WITH PAPER TOWELS. (IF THE
FISH HAS BEEN FROZEN AND THAWED, IT WILL BE QUITE
WET, SO BE SURE TO DRY IT WELL.) PLACE COD ON
PREPARED BAKING SHEET. SPREAD PESTO MIXTURE ON
TOP OF FISH, PRESSING IT IN PLACE. SPRINKLE CRUMB
MIXTURE ON TOP OF PESTO. BAKE FOR 6 TO 8 MINUTES
OR UNTIL TOPPING IS BROWNED AND CRISP AND FISH IS
BARELY OPAQUE AND IS JUST STARTING TO FLAKE WHEN
TESTED WITH A FORK. DO NOT OVERCOOK. SERVES 4.

TUNA PASTA FOR TWO

FAST, FRESH AND CHEAP, THIS IS A MAD-RUSH
MEAL FOR STUDENTS AND EMPTY NESTERS ALIKE.
WE LIKE LOTS OF PARMESAN ON TOP OF THIS DISH,
BUT USE LESS IF YOU PREFER.

6 OZ	SPAGHETTINI OR ANGEL HAIR PASTA (PREFERABLY WHOLE WHEAT)	175 G
I TBSP	OLIVE OR VEGETABLE OIL	15 ML
1/2 CUP	CHOPPED YELLOW, ORANGE OR RED BELL PEPPER	125 ML
1/4 CUP	FINELY CHOPPED ONION	60 ML
2	CLOVES GARLIC, MINCED	2
3 CUPS	ROUGHLY CHOPPED RIPE TOMATOES (ABOUT 3 LARGE)	750 ML
I	CAN (6 OZ/170 G) WATER-PACKED CHUNK TUNA, DRAINED AND FLAKED	I
3 CUPS	PACKED BABY SPINACH	750 ML
I TBSP	DRAINED CAPERS	15 ML
	FINELY GRATED ZEST AND JUICE OF 1/2 LEMON	
	FRESHLY GROUND BLACK PEPPER	
	SALT (OPTIONAL)	
1/3 TO 1/2 CUP	FRESHLY GRATED PARMESAN CHEESE	75 TO 125 ML

IN A LARGE POT OF BOILING SALTED WATER, COOK PASTA
ACCORDING TO PACKAGE DIRECTIONS. DRAIN, RESERVING
1/3 CUP (75 ML) COOKING WATER.

MEANWHILE, IN A LARGE NONSTICK SKILLET, HEAT OIL
OVER MEDIUM HEAT. SAUTÉ YELLOW PEPPER AND ONION
FOR ABOUT 5 MINUTES OR UNTIL SOFTENED. ADD GARLIC
AND SAUTÉ FOR 15 SECONDS OR UNTIL FRAGRANT. ADD

TOMATOES AND COOK, STIRRING OCCASIONALLY, FOR ABOUT 4 MINUTES OR UNTIL THEY START TO SOFTEN AND RELEASE THEIR JUICES. STIR IN TUNA, SPINACH, CAPERS, LEMON ZEST, LEMON JUICE AND PEPPER TO TASTE. COOK, STIRRING, FOR 1 MINUTE OR UNTIL SPINACH STARTS TO WILT AND SAUCE IS HEATED THROUGH. REMOVE FROM HEAT. TASTE AND SEASON WITH SALT, IF DESIRED. ADD PASTA AND RESERVED COOKING WATER, TOSSING TO COAT. SERVE SPRINKLED WITH PARMESAN TO TASTE. SERVES 2.

TIP: THIS IS A GREAT WAY TO USE UP THOSE OVERLY RIPE TOMATOES SITTING ON THE COUNTER. DON'T SUBSTITUTE UNDER-RIPE OR CANNED TOMATOES FOR THIS RECIPE — IT SIMPLY WON'T WORK.

I'M SEARCHING FOR THE MEANING OF LIFE, BUT WILL SETTLE FOR MY CAR KEYS.

SKILLET LASAGNA

YOU WANT LASAGNA, BUT CAN'T FACE THE WORK?
HERE'S THE SOLUTION. YOU'LL NEED A SKILLET THAT'S
DEEP AND AT LEAST 12 INCHES (30 CM) WIDE.

I LB	LEAN GROUND BEEF	500 G
I	ONION, CHOPPED	I
I	RED OR GREEN BELL PEPPER, CHOPPED	I
2 CUPS	SLICED BUTTON OR CREMINI MUSHROOMS (OPTIONAL)	500 ML
2	CLOVES GARLIC, MINCED	2
I TSP	DRIED BASIL	5 ML
$1/2$ TSP	DRIED OREGANO	2 ML
I	JAR (24 OZ/700 ML) TOMATO PASTA SAUCE	I
2 TO 3 CUPS	REDUCED-SODIUM BEEF BROTH, HOMEMADE VEGETABLE STOCK (SEE RECIPE, PAGE 90) OR WATER (APPROX.)	500 TO 750 ML
	SALT AND FRESHLY GROUND BLACK PEPPER	
4 CUPS	BROAD EGG NOODLES (SEE TIP, OPPOSITE)	I L
I CUP	LOW-FAT COTTAGE OR RICOTTA CHEESE	250 ML
$1/4$ CUP	FRESHLY GRATED PARMESAN CHEESE	60 ML
I CUP	SHREDDED MOZZARELLA CHEESE	250 ML

IN A LARGE SKILLET, OVER MEDIUM-HIGH HEAT, START TO
BROWN BEEF, BREAKING IT UP WITH A SPOON. AS SOON
AS IT STARTS TO SIZZLE AND RELEASE SOME JUICES,
REDUCE HEAT TO MEDIUM AND ADD ONION, RED PEPPER
AND MUSHROOMS. COOK, STIRRING OCCASIONALLY, FOR
5 MINUTES OR UNTIL BEEF IS BROWNED AND VEGETABLES
ARE SOFTENED. ADD GARLIC, BASIL AND OREGANO; SAUTÉ

FOR 15 SECONDS OR UNTIL FRAGRANT. DRAIN OFF EXCESS FAT. STIR IN PASTA SAUCE, 2 CUPS (500 ML) BROTH, $1/2$ TSP (2 ML) SALT AND PEPPER TO TASTE; BRING TO A BOIL, STIRRING. ADD NOODLES AND RETURN TO A BOIL. REDUCE HEAT TO LOW, COVER AND SIMMER, STIRRING OCCASIONALLY, FOR 10 TO 12 MINUTES OR UNTIL LIQUID IS ABSORBED AND NOODLES ARE TENDER. IF THE MIXTURE BECOMES TOO DRY BEFORE THE NOODLES ARE COOKED, ADD MORE BROTH, $1/4$ CUP (60 ML) AT A TIME. TASTE AND ADJUST SEASONING WITH SALT AND PEPPER, IF DESIRED (BUT REMEMBER THAT THE CHEESES WILL ADD SALT).

MEANWHILE, PREHEAT BROILER, WITH RACK SET 6 INCHES (15 CM) BELOW THE HEAT SOURCE. IN A MEDIUM BOWL, COMBINE COTTAGE CHEESE AND PARMESAN. REMOVE BEEF MIXTURE FROM HEAT AND WRAP A DOUBLE LAYER OF FOIL AROUND SKILLET HANDLE (YOU CAN SKIP THE FOIL IF THE HANDLE IS OVENPROOF). DROP DOLLOPS OF COTTAGE CHEESE MIXTURE OVER BEEF MIXTURE. SPRINKLE MOZZARELLA OVER TOP. BROIL UNTIL CHEESE IS MELTED, BUBBLING AND BROWNED. SERVE IMMEDIATELY. SERVES 4 TO 6.

TIP: IF YOU USE WATER OR A SALT-FREE STOCK OR BROTH, YOU MAY WANT TO ADD MORE SALT.

TIP: A QUALITY BRAND OF EGG-ENRICHED NOODLES WORKS BEST IN THIS RECIPE. LESS EXPENSIVE NOODLES SOMETIMES TURN GLUEY.

LIBRARIANS IMPROVE CIRCULATION.

SPAGHETTI AMATRICIANA

THIS CLASSIC ITALIAN SAUCE IS TYPICALLY MADE WITH PANCETTA. WE SUBSTITUTED REGULAR BACON BECAUSE THAT'S WHAT WE HAD IN THE REFRIGERATOR. THE KIDS LOVED IT.

10	SLICES BACON, CHOPPED	10
1	ONION, FINELY CHOPPED	1
2 TO 3	CLOVES GARLIC, MINCED	2 TO 3
1/2 TSP	DRIED BASIL OR ITALIAN SEASONING	2 ML
1/4 TSP	HOT PEPPER FLAKES (OR TO TASTE)	1 ML
1	CAN (28 OZ/796 ML) NO-SALT-ADDED WHOLE TOMATOES, WITH JUICE (SEE TIP, PAGE 171)	1
1/2 TO 1 TSP	SALT	2 TO 5 ML
1/4 TSP	FRESHLY GROUND BLACK PEPPER	1 ML
3/4 TO 1 CUP	FRESHLY GRATED PARMESAN CHEESE, DIVIDED	175 TO 250 ML
1/4 CUP	CHOPPED FRESH PARSLEY	60 ML
2 TSP	BALSAMIC VINEGAR	10 ML
12 OZ	SPAGHETTI (PREFERABLY WHOLE WHEAT)	375 G

IN A LARGE SAUCEPAN, SAUTÉ BACON OVER MEDIUM-HIGH HEAT UNTIL CRISPY. USING A SLOTTED SPOON, TRANSFER BACON TO A PLATE LINED WITH PAPER TOWELS. DRAIN OFF ALL BUT 1 TBSP (15 ML) OF THE FAT FROM PAN. REDUCE HEAT TO MEDIUM AND SAUTÉ ONION FOR ABOUT 3 MINUTES OR UNTIL SOFTENED. ADD GARLIC TO TASTE, BASIL AND HOT PEPPER FLAKES; SAUTÉ FOR 15 SECONDS OR UNTIL FRAGRANT. STIR IN TOMATOES WITH JUICE, BREAKING THEM UP WITH A SPOON AND SCRAPING UP BROWN BITS

FROM BOTTOM OF PAN. RETURN THREE-QUARTERS OF THE BACON TO THE PAN. ADD $\frac{1}{2}$ TSP (2 ML) SALT AND PEPPER; BRING TO A BOIL. REDUCE HEAT AND SIMMER, STIRRING OCCASIONALLY, FOR 10 MINUTES OR UNTIL SAUCE IS SLIGHTLY THICKENED. STIR IN $\frac{1}{2}$ CUP (125 ML) OF THE PARMESAN, PARSLEY AND VINEGAR. TASTE AND ADJUST SEASONING WITH SALT, IF DESIRED.

MEANWHILE, IN A LARGE POT OF BOILING SALTED WATER, COOK SPAGHETTI ACCORDING TO PACKAGE DIRECTIONS. DRAIN, RESERVING $\frac{1}{2}$ CUP (125 ML) OF THE COOKING WATER. TOSS SAUCE WITH SPAGHETTI AND AS MUCH OF THE RESERVED COOKING WATER AS NEEDED TO GET THE DESIRED CONSISTENCY. SERVE SPRINKLED WITH THE REMAINING BACON AND PARMESAN TO TASTE. SERVES 4.

TIP: IN THIS RECIPE, IT'S ESPECIALLY IMPORTANT TO SEASON ACCORDING TO TASTE AND AS YOU GO. THE RESULTS ARE AFFECTED BY THE TYPE OF BACON AND THE SALTINESS OF THE PARMESAN YOU USE AND WHETHER OR NOT YOU USE NO-SALT-ADDED CANNED TOMATOES, AS WE SUGGEST. (WE KNOW IT IS SOMETIMES EASIER TO USE WHATEVER YOU HAVE ON HAND.)

MAKE AHEAD: LET SAUCE COOL FOR 30 MINUTES, THEN REFRIGERATE, UNCOVERED, IN A SHALLOW CONTAINER UNTIL COLD. COVER TIGHTLY AND KEEP REFRIGERATED FOR UP TO 2 DAYS OR FREEZE FOR UP TO 2 MONTHS. THAW IN THE REFRIGERATOR AND REHEAT SLOWLY. COOK THE SPAGHETTI JUST BEFORE SERVING.

UPSIDE-DOWN PIZZA PIE

HERE'S A FAMILY FAVORITE. THE MEAT SAUCE CAN BE MADE AHEAD. ADD CHOPPED MUSHROOMS, BELL PEPPERS, SHREDDED ZUCCHINI OR OTHER VEGETABLES, IF YOU LIKE.

MEAT SAUCE

I LB	LEAN GROUND BEEF	500 G
I	SMALL CARROT, FINELY CHOPPED	I
I	STALK CELERY, FINELY CHOPPED	I
I	CLOVE GARLIC, MINCED	I
1/2 CUP	FINELY CHOPPED ONION	125 ML
1/2 TSP	DRIED OREGANO, BASIL OR ITALIAN SEASONING	2 ML
2 CUPS	TOMATO PASTA SAUCE	500 ML
1/3 CUP	REDUCED-SODIUM BEEF OR CHICKEN BROTH	75 ML
	SALT AND FRESHLY GROUND BLACK PEPPER	
1 1/2 CUPS	SHREDDED MOZZARELLA CHEESE	375 ML

TOPPING

I CUP	ALL-PURPOSE FLOUR	250 ML
1/2 CUP	CORNMEAL	125 ML
3/4 TSP	BAKING POWDER	3 ML
1/4 TSP	BAKING SODA	I ML
1/2 TSP	SALT	2 ML
I	EGG	I
3/4 CUP	BUTTERMILK	175 ML
3 TBSP	UNSALTED BUTTER, MELTED AND SLIGHTLY COOLED	45 ML

MEAT SAUCE: IN A LARGE SAUCEPAN OR NONSTICK SKILLET, OVER MEDIUM-HIGH HEAT, START TO BROWN BEEF, BREAKING IT UP WITH A SPOON. WHEN IT STARTS

TO SIZZLE AND RELEASE SOME JUICES, REDUCE HEAT TO MEDIUM AND ADD CARROT, CELERY, GARLIC, ONION AND OREGANO. COOK, STIRRING OCCASIONALLY, FOR 5 MINUTES OR UNTIL BEEF IS BROWNED AND ONION IS SOFTENED. DRAIN OFF EXCESS FAT. ADD PASTA SAUCE, BROTH AND SALT AND PEPPER TO TASTE; BRING TO A BOIL. REDUCE HEAT TO LOW, COVER, LEAVING LID AJAR, AND SIMMER, STIRRING OCCASIONALLY, FOR 15 MINUTES OR UNTIL VEGETABLES ARE TENDER AND SAUCE IS SLIGHTLY THICKENED. TRANSFER TO A 9-INCH (23 CM) PIE PLATE AND LET COOL FOR 15 MINUTES. SPRINKLE WITH CHEESE.

TOPPING: PREHEAT OVEN TO 450°F (230°C). IN A BOWL, WHISK TOGETHER FLOUR, CORNMEAL, BAKING POWDER, BAKING SODA AND SALT. IN ANOTHER BOWL, WHISK TOGETHER EGG, BUTTERMILK AND BUTTER. STIR BUTTERMILK MIXTURE INTO FLOUR MIXTURE. DROP SPOONFULS OF TOPPING OVER MEAT MIXTURE, THEN USE A FORK TO SPREAD TOPPING EVENLY OVER MEAT MIXTURE. BAKE FOR 15 TO 20 MINUTES OR UNTIL TOPPING IS BROWNED AND A TESTER INSERTED IN THE CENTER OF THE TOPPING COMES OUT CLEAN. CUT INTO WEDGES IN THE PAN. SERVES 4 TO 6.

TIP: JARS OF TOMATO PASTA SAUCE ARE AVAILABLE IN SEVERAL VARIETIES. WE LIKE THE SPICY ROASTED RED BELL PEPPER VERSION MADE BY A COUPLE OF MAJOR BRANDS, BUT YOU CAN USE YOUR FAVORITE FLAVOR.

MAKE AHEAD: AFTER COOKING THE MEAT SAUCE, LET COOL COMPLETELY. TRANSFER TO AN AIRTIGHT CONTAINER AND REFRIGERATE FOR UP TO 2 DAYS OR FREEZE FOR UP TO 1 MONTH. THAW IN THE REFRIGERATOR.

BILL'S QUICK GARLIC BREAD

HERE'S A DELICIOUS TIME SAVER FROM EDMONTON'S BILL GARRIOCK. THE OWNER OF GARLIC'S PURITY PLUS MAKES AN AWESOME ALL-NATURAL CAESAR DRESSING. USE OTHER READY-MADE CAESAR DRESSINGS FROM THE REFRIGERATED SECTION OF THE SUPERMARKET, BUT NOT THE BOTTLED STUFF FROM THE SHELF.

| 4 | GREEK-STYLE PITAS (NO POCKETS) | 4 |
| 1/4 CUP | PREPARED REFRIGERATED CAESAR SALAD DRESSING | 60 ML |

PREHEAT OVEN TO 200°F (100°C). PLACE PITAS ON A WORK SURFACE AND SPREAD 1 TBSP (15 ML) DRESSING OVER THE TOP OF EACH. HEAT A LARGE NONSTICK SKILLET OVER MEDIUM HEAT. PLACE ONE PITA, DRESSING SIDE DOWN, INTO THE HOT SKILLET. COOK FOR 1 TO 2 MINUTES OR UNTIL THE UNDERSIDE IS GOLDEN BROWN. FLIP PITA OVER AND BROWN THE OTHER SIDE, ABOUT 2 MINUTES. TRANSFER TO A BAKING SHEET AND PLACE IN OVEN TO KEEP WARM. REPEAT WITH THE REMAINING PITAS. CUT EACH PITA INTO QUARTERS. SERVE IMMEDIATELY. SERVES 4 TO 6.

VARIATION: KIDS LOVE IT IF YOU MAKE THE GARLIC BREAD WITH HOT DOG BUNS. SLICE THE BUNS IN HALF HORIZONTALLY AND BRUSH THE CUT SIDES WITH CAESAR DRESSING. BROWN THE BUNS, CUT SIDES DOWN, OVER MEDIUM HEAT, PRESSING DOWN GENTLY WITH A SPATULA. DO NOT FLIP THEM. THIS IS AN EXCELLENT WAY TO USE UP LEFTOVER HOT DOG BUNS.

POULTRY, BEEF AND PORK

CHICKEN MUSHROOM FLORENTINE

THIS DISH HAS DEFINITE DINNER PARTY APPEAL.
IT CAN BE ASSEMBLED AHEAD OF TIME AND PLACED
IN THE OVEN WHEN YOUR GUESTS ARRIVE.
SERVE WITH TOMATO ORZO PILAF (PAGE 274).

1 TBSP	OLIVE OR VEGETABLE OIL	15 ML
1/2 CUP	FINELY CHOPPED ONION	125 ML
2 CUPS	SLICED MUSHROOMS	500 ML
2	CLOVES GARLIC, MINCED	2
1/4 TSP	DRIED OREGANO	1 ML
	SALT AND FRESHLY GROUND BLACK PEPPER	
1 TBSP	COLD WATER	15 ML
1/2 CUP	FRESHLY GRATED PARMESAN CHEESE	125 ML
4	BONELESS SKINLESS CHICKEN BREASTS (ABOUT 1 1/2 LBS/750 G)	4
1/4 CUP	PREPARED BASIL PESTO OR SUN-DRIED TOMATO PESTO (SEE TIP, OPPOSITE)	60 ML
1 CUP	PACKED BABY SPINACH	250 ML
1 1/3 CUPS	SHREDDED PROVOLONE OR MOZZARELLA CHEESE	325 ML
2 TBSP	CHOPPED FRESH PARSLEY	30 ML

PREHEAT OVEN TO 350°F (180°C). LIGHTLY GREASE A
SHALLOW 13- BY 9-INCH (33 BY 23 CM) BAKING DISH. IN
A NONSTICK SKILLET, HEAT OIL OVER MEDIUM HEAT.
SAUTÉ ONION FOR 3 MINUTES OR UNTIL SOFTENED.
ADD MUSHROOMS AND SAUTÉ FOR 5 MINUTES OR UNTIL
LIGHTLY BROWNED. ADD GARLIC, OREGANO, 1/4 TSP (1 ML)
SALT, 1/8 TSP (0.5 ML) PEPPER AND WATER; SAUTÉ FOR
15 SECONDS OR UNTIL FRAGRANT. STIR IN PARMESAN
AND SET ASIDE. PLACE CHICKEN BETWEEN TWO SHEETS

OF PLASTIC WRAP AND POUND LIGHTLY WITH A ROLLING PIN OR THE BOTTOM OF A SKILLET TO A UNIFORM THICKNESS. SEASON CHICKEN ON BOTH SIDES WITH SALT AND PEPPER. PLACE IN SINGLE LAYER IN PREPARED BAKING DISH. SPREAD PESTO OVER TOP OF CHICKEN. TOP WITH A LAYER OF SPINACH, THEN ONION MIXTURE. BAKE FOR ABOUT 30 MINUTES OR UNTIL CHICKEN IS NO LONGER PINK INSIDE. TOP WITH PROVOLONE. BAKE FOR 5 MINUTES OR UNTIL CHEESE IS MELTED. SPRINKLE WITH PARSLEY. SERVES 4.

TIP: JARS OF PREPARED SUN-DRIED TOMATO PESTO, AS WELL AS TRADITIONAL BASIL PESTO, ARE READILY AVAILABLE IN GROCERY STORES. KEEP A JAR IN THE REFRIGERATOR AND SPREAD PESTO ON PIZZA AND SANDWICHES OR STIR IT INTO SOUPS AND PASTA SAUCES.

MAKE AHEAD: ASSEMBLE CHICKEN MUSHROOM FLORENTINE, COVER AND REFRIGERATE FOR UP TO 6 HOURS BEFORE BAKING. ADD 5 TO 10 MINUTES TO THE BAKING TIME BEFORE ADDING THE CHEESE.

ALWAYS MAKE NEW MISTAKES.

THE NEW CLASSY CHICKEN

OUR GROWN-UP KIDS AGREE: IT'S THE SAME
GREAT TASTE AS THE ORIGINAL CLASSY CHICKEN
THAT YOU ALL LOVE SO MUCH — BUT IT'S HEALTHIER!
SERVE OVER RICE, WITH SPINACH SALAD TOSSED
WITH ORANGE SEGMENTS AND MANDARIN GINGER
VINAIGRETTE (PAGE 85) ON THE SIDE.

1 1/4 LBS	BONELESS SKINLESS CHICKEN BREASTS (ABOUT 3), CUT INTO BITE-SIZE PIECES	625 G
	SALT AND FRESHLY GROUND BLACK PEPPER	
2 TBSP	OLIVE OR VEGETABLE OIL	30 ML
3 CUPS	BROCCOLI FLORETS	750 ML
1/2 CUP	SHREDDED SHARP (OLD) CHEDDAR CHEESE (OPTIONAL)	125 ML
1/2 CUP	DRY BREAD CRUMBS	125 ML
2 TSP	BUTTER, MELTED	10 ML

SAUCE

1/4 CUP	ALL-PURPOSE FLOUR	60 ML
2 TSP	MADRAS CURRY POWDER	10 ML
1 CUP	REDUCED-SODIUM CHICKEN BROTH	250 ML
1/2 CUP	SKIM OR 2% MILK	125 ML
1/2 CUP	PLAIN YOGURT	125 ML
1/2 CUP	LIGHT MAYONNAISE	125 ML

PREHEAT OVEN TO 350°F (180°C). GREASE A SHALLOW
BAKING DISH LARGE ENOUGH TO HOLD THE CHICKEN IN A
SINGLE LAYER. PLACE CHICKEN ON A PLATE AND SEASON
WITH SALT AND PEPPER. IN A LARGE SKILLET, HEAT OIL
OVER MEDIUM HEAT. SAUTÉ CHICKEN FOR 5 TO 7 MINUTES
OR UNTIL BROWNED AND NO LONGER PINK INSIDE.
TRANSFER TO PREPARED BAKING DISH.

MEANWHILE, IN A LARGE POT OF BOILING SALTED WATER, BLANCH BROCCOLI FOR 1 MINUTE. DRAIN AND SPOON OVER CHICKEN.

SAUCE: IN A LARGE BOWL, WHISK TOGETHER FLOUR, CURRY POWDER, BROTH, MILK, YOGURT AND MAYONNAISE. (THAT'S RIGHT — THERE'S NO BUTTER!) POUR OVER CHICKEN MIXTURE.

SPRINKLE CHICKEN MIXTURE WITH CHEDDAR CHEESE (IF USING). TOSS BREAD CRUMBS WITH BUTTER AND SPRINKLE OVER TOP. BAKE FOR 30 MINUTES OR UNTIL BUBBLING AND TOP IS GOLDEN BROWN. SERVES 4 TO 6.

TIP: YOU CAN USE 4 CUPS (1 L) LEFTOVER CHOPPED COOKED CHICKEN OR TURKEY INSTEAD OF COOKING THE CHICKEN BREASTS.

THERE ARE TWO THINGS WE SHOULD GIVE OUR CHILDREN.
ONE IS ROOTS AND THE OTHER IS WINGS.
— HODDING CARTER

INDIAN SPICED CHICKEN DRUMSTICKS

THERE'S NO SAUCE WITH THESE MOIST, SUCCULENT DRUMSTICKS, SO IT'S FUN TO PICK THEM UP WITH YOUR FINGERS. FOR AN INDIAN-THEMED BUFFET, DOUBLE THE RECIPE AND SERVE WITH BEJEWELED COUSCOUS (PAGE 278), MINT, MANGO AND AVOCADO SALAD (PAGE 58) AND SWEET POTATO SAMOSAS (PAGE 42).

8	SKINLESS CHICKEN DRUMSTICKS	8
I TSP	GROUND CORIANDER	5 ML
I TSP	GROUND TURMERIC	5 ML
I TSP	GROUND CUMIN	5 ML
I TSP	PAPRIKA	5 ML
1/2 TSP	SALT	2 ML
1/4 TSP	HOT PEPPER FLAKES	I ML
1/4 TSP	FRESHLY GROUND BLACK PEPPER	I ML
I TBSP	VEGETABLE OR OLIVE OIL	15 ML
3 TBSP	WHITE WINE VINEGAR OR CIDER VINEGAR	45 ML
1/4 CUP	REDUCED-SODIUM CHICKEN BROTH OR HOMEMADE VEGETABLE STOCK (SEE RECIPE, PAGE 90)	60 ML

USING A SHARP KNIFE, SCORE EACH DRUMSTICK TWO OR THREE TIMES. IN A BOWL, COMBINE CORIANDER, TURMERIC, CUMIN, PAPRIKA, SALT, HOT PEPPER FLAKES AND BLACK PEPPER. STIR IN OIL AND VINEGAR TO MAKE A RUNNY PASTE. USING PLASTIC SANDWICH OR FREEZER BAGS AS GLOVES (BECAUSE THE MIXTURE WILL STAIN YOUR HANDS), RUB THE SPICE MIXTURE ALL OVER THE DRUMSTICKS. PLACE IN A SHALLOW DISH, COVER AND REFRIGERATE FOR AT LEAST 4 HOURS OR FOR UP TO 24 HOURS.

PREHEAT OVEN TO 400°F (200°C). LINE A ROASTING PAN OR A LARGE METAL BAKING PAN WITH GREASED FOIL. ARRANGE DRUMSTICKS IN A SINGLE LAYER IN PREPARED PAN. DRIZZLE BROTH OVER CHICKEN, COVER PAN TIGHTLY WITH FOIL AND BAKE FOR 25 MINUTES. SPOON PAN JUICES OVER CHICKEN AND BAKE, UNCOVERED, FOR 25 TO 35 MINUTES OR UNTIL JUICES RUN CLEAR WHEN CHICKEN IS PIERCED AND CHICKEN IS SHRINKING AWAY FROM THE BONE AND IS NICELY BROWNED. SPOON PAN JUICES OVER CHICKEN AGAIN. LET REST FOR 5 MINUTES BEFORE SERVING. SERVES 4.

TIP: IF YOU USE A SALT-FREE STOCK OR BROTH, YOU MAY WANT TO ADD MORE SALT. SALT IS, IN ANY RECIPE, A MATTER OF PERSONAL PREFERENCE, SO FEEL FREE TO INCREASE OR REDUCE THE QUANTITIES WE SUGGEST.

THERE HAS NEVER BEEN A STATUE ERECTED TO THE MEMORY OF SOMEONE WHO LET WELL ENOUGH ALONE.
— JULES ELLINGER

CHICKEN WITH
TOMATOES AND HONEY

THIS AROMATIC STEW HAS A HINT OF MIDDLE EASTERN FLAVORS. SERVE WITH LIGHT CHIVE MASHED POTATOES (PAGE 266) OR STEAMED COUSCOUS.

2 TBSP	BUTTER OR OLIVE OIL	30 ML
1	ONION, FINELY CHOPPED	1
1 TSP	GROUND CINNAMON	5 ML
1/8 TSP	SAFFRON THREADS (SEE TIP, OPPOSITE)	0.5 ML
	SALT AND FRESHLY GROUND BLACK PEPPER	
1	CAN (28 OZ/796 ML) NO-SALT-ADDED WHOLE TOMATOES, WITH JUICE (SEE TIP, OPPOSITE)	1
2 TBSP	LIQUID HONEY	30 ML
8	SKINLESS CHICKEN DRUMSTICKS OR SKINLESS BONE-IN CHICKEN THIGHS	8
2 TBSP	CHOPPED FRESH PARSLEY	30 ML
1 TBSP	FRESHLY SQUEEZED LEMON JUICE OR CIDER VINEGAR	15 ML
2 TBSP	TOASTED SLIVERED OR SLICED ALMONDS	30 ML
1 TBSP	TOASTED SESAME SEEDS	15 ML

IN A LARGE DUTCH OVEN, MELT BUTTER OVER LOW HEAT. ADD ONION AND COOK GENTLY, STIRRING OCCASIONALLY, FOR 10 MINUTES OR UNTIL SOFTENED AND LIGHT GOLDEN BROWN. ADD CINNAMON, SAFFRON, 1 TSP (5 ML) SALT AND PEPPER TO TASTE; COOK, STIRRING, FOR 15 SECONDS OR UNTIL FRAGRANT. STIR IN TOMATOES WITH JUICE, BREAKING THEM UP WITH A SPOON. STIR IN HONEY, INCREASE HEAT TO HIGH AND BRING TO A BOIL, STIRRING. REDUCE HEAT TO LOW AND NESTLE DRUMSTICKS IN

SAUCE. COVER, LEAVING LID AJAR, AND SIMMER, STIRRING OCCASIONALLY, FOR 20 MINUTES. UNCOVER AND SIMMER FOR 20 MINUTES OR UNTIL JUICES RUN CLEAR WHEN CHICKEN IS PIERCED AND CHICKEN IS FALLING OFF THE BONE. STIR IN PARSLEY AND LEMON JUICE. TASTE AND ADJUST SEASONING WITH SALT AND PEPPER, IF DESIRED. SPRINKLE WITH ALMONDS AND SESAME SEEDS JUST BEFORE SERVING. SERVES 4.

TIP: SAFFRON IS A VIVID YELLOW-ORANGE SPICE THAT'S MADE FROM THE DRIED STIGMA OF A CROCUS FLOWER. COMMON IN MIDDLE EASTERN COOKING, SAFFRON HAS A UNIQUE, SLIGHTLY BITTER FLAVOR. OMIT IT IF YOU DON'T HAVE IT, BUT DON'T SUBSTITUTE TURMERIC. ALTHOUGH SIMILAR IN COLOR, TURMERIC TASTES QUITE DIFFERENT.

TIP: WHEN MAKING A SAUCE WITH CANNED TOMATOES, WE PREFER TO USE WHOLE TOMATOES PACKED IN JUICE, WITH NO ADDED SALT OR SEASONINGS. THESE ARE THE CLOSEST TO FRESH TOMATOES IN TASTE AND TEXTURE, AND WE CAN CONTROL THE LEVELS OF SALT AND OTHER SEASONINGS IN THE RECIPE. DICED, CRUSHED OR STEWED TOMATOES MAY HAVE ADDITIVES THAT CAN AFFECT THE OUTCOME OF A RECIPE.

MAKE AHEAD: AFTER COOKING BUT BEFORE ADDING THE PARSLEY AND LEMON JUICE, LET COOL, TRANSFER TO AN AIRTIGHT CONTAINER AND REFRIGERATE FOR UP TO 1 DAY OR FREEZE FOR UP TO 1 MONTH. THAW, REHEAT IN A LARGE SAUCEPAN OVER LOW HEAT, STIRRING FREQUENTLY, AND PROCEED WITH THE RECIPE.

SATURDAY CHICKEN STEW WITH SWEET POTATOES

WHEN IT'S COLD OUTSIDE, STAY IN AND COOK. THE KIDS CAN DO THE PREP, AND YOU CAN BE THE SOUS CHEF. (THAT MEANS YOU'RE ON CLEAN-UP DUTY.) SERVE WITH LAZY DAYS BUTTERMILK BISCUITS (PAGE 22) OR A CRISPY BAGUETTE.

1 TBSP	OLIVE OR VEGETABLE OIL	15 ML
2	CARROTS, CHOPPED	2
2	STALKS CELERY, CHOPPED	2
1	ONION, CHOPPED	1
2	CLOVES GARLIC, MINCED	2
2 TBSP	ALL-PURPOSE FLOUR	30 ML
2 CUPS	REDUCED-SODIUM CHICKEN BROTH	500 ML
3/4 CUP	UNSWEETENED APPLE JUICE	175 ML
4	SPRIGS FRESH PARSLEY	4
1	BAY LEAF	1
1/4 TSP	DRIED THYME OR OREGANO	1 ML
	SALT AND FRESHLY GROUND BLACK PEPPER	
8	SKINLESS BONE-IN CHICKEN THIGHS	8
1 LB	SWEET POTATO, PEELED AND CUT INTO 1-INCH (2.5 CM) CHUNKS (ABOUT 2 1/2 CUPS/625 ML)	500 G
1 CUP	FROZEN PEAS (NO NEED TO THAW)	250 ML
1 TBSP	CIDER VINEGAR	15 ML

IN A LARGE SAUCEPAN OR DUTCH OVEN, HEAT OIL OVER MEDIUM HEAT. SAUTÉ CARROTS, CELERY AND ONION FOR ABOUT 5 MINUTES OR UNTIL ONION IS SOFTENED. ADD GARLIC AND SAUTÉ FOR 15 SECONDS OR UNTIL FRAGRANT. SPRINKLE WITH FLOUR AND COOK, STIRRING, FOR 1 MINUTE. GRADUALLY STIR IN BROTH AND APPLE JUICE. ADD PARSLEY,

BAY LEAF, THYME, 1/2 TSP (2 ML) SALT AND 1/4 TSP (1 ML) PEPPER; BRING TO A BOIL, STIRRING OCCASIONALLY. ADD CHICKEN (THAT'S RIGHT, YOU DON'T HAVE TO BROWN IT) AND SWEET POTATOES; BRING TO A BOIL. REDUCE HEAT TO LOW, COVER AND SIMMER, STIRRING OCCASIONALLY, FOR 40 MINUTES OR UNTIL JUICES RUN CLEAR WHEN CHICKEN IS PIERCED. STIR IN PEAS AND VINEGAR; RETURN TO A SIMMER. SIMMER FOR ABOUT 2 MINUTES OR UNTIL PEAS ARE HEATED THROUGH. TASTE AND ADJUST SEASONING WITH SALT AND PEPPER, IF DESIRED. DISCARD PARSLEY SPRIGS AND BAY LEAF. SERVES 4 TO 6.

TIP: THE SWEET POTATOES BECOME QUITE SOFT IN THIS RECIPE, WHICH HELPS TO THICKEN THE GRAVY. IF YOU PREFER THEM TO BE TENDER BUT STILL HOLD THEIR SHAPE, ADD THEM HALFWAY THROUGH THE COOKING TIME.

MAKE AHEAD: LET COOL FOR 30 MINUTES, THEN REFRIGERATE, UNCOVERED, IN A SHALLOW CONTAINER UNTIL COLD. COVER TIGHTLY AND KEEP REFRIGERATED FOR UP TO 2 DAYS. REHEAT IN A LARGE SAUCEPAN OVER LOW HEAT, STIRRING FREQUENTLY.

A GRANDMOTHER PRETENDS SHE DOESN'T KNOW WHO YOU ARE ON HALLOWEEN.
— ERMA BOMBECK

CHICKEN MED

FRESH FENNEL, WITH ITS BIG FEATHERY STALK, CAN LOOK A BIT SCARY ON THE SUPERMARKET SHELF (WHERE IT IS SOMETIMES LABELED "ANISE"). BUT TRY IT IN THIS ONE-POT DISH, AND WE THINK YOU'LL LIKE THE WAY ITS MILD ANISEED FLAVOR MELLOWS, PRODUCING A RICH-TASTING MEAL. SERVE WITH CRUSTY BREAD — THERE'S LOTS OF SAUCE.

2 TBSP	ALL-PURPOSE FLOUR	30 ML
	SALT AND FRESHLY GROUND BLACK PEPPER	
2 TBSP	OLIVE OR VEGETABLE OIL, DIVIDED	30 ML
8	BONELESS SKINLESS CHICKEN THIGHS, CUT INTO BITE-SIZE PIECES	8
1	FENNEL BULB, THINLY SLICED (SEE TIP, OPPOSITE)	1
1	SMALL ONION, THINLY SLICED	1
1	RED BELL PEPPER, THINLY SLICED	1
2	CLOVES GARLIC, MINCED	2
2 TSP	CHOPPED FRESH ROSEMARY (OR $\frac{1}{2}$ TSP/2 ML DRIED)	10 ML
1	CAN (14 OZ/398 ML) NO-SALT-ADDED WHOLE TOMATOES, WITH JUICE (SEE TIP, PAGE 171)	1
1 LB	BABY NEW POTATOES, CUT IN HALF OR INTO QUARTERS	500 G
$\frac{2}{3}$ CUP	REDUCED-SODIUM CHICKEN BROTH OR HOMEMADE VEGETABLE STOCK (SEE RECIPE, PAGE 90)	150 ML
1 CUP	FROZEN BABY PEAS (NO NEED TO THAW)	250 ML
2 TBSP	CHOPPED FRESH PARSLEY	30 ML

IN A LARGE BOWL, COMBINE FLOUR, $\frac{1}{2}$ TSP (2 ML) SALT AND $\frac{1}{4}$ TSP (1 ML) PEPPER. ADD CHICKEN AND TOSS TO COAT. IN A LARGE, DEEP NONSTICK SKILLET, HEAT 1 TBSP

(15 ML) OIL OVER MEDIUM-HIGH HEAT. SAUTÉ CHICKEN FOR ABOUT 5 MINUTES OR UNTIL LIGHTLY BROWNED ON ALL SIDES. USING A SLOTTED SPOON, TRANSFER CHICKEN TO A PLATE. REDUCE HEAT TO MEDIUM. ADD THE REMAINING OIL TO THE PAN. SAUTÉ FENNEL, ONION AND RED PEPPER FOR 5 TO 7 MINUTES OR UNTIL SOFTENED. ADD GARLIC AND ROSEMARY; SAUTÉ FOR 15 SECONDS OR UNTIL FRAGRANT. STIR IN TOMATOES WITH JUICE, POTATOES AND BROTH, BREAKING TOMATOES UP WITH A SPOON; BRING TO A BOIL. REDUCE HEAT TO LOW, COVER AND SIMMER, STIRRING OCCASIONALLY, FOR 10 MINUTES. RETURN CHICKEN AND ACCUMULATED JUICES TO THE PAN, COVER AND SIMMER FOR 30 MINUTES OR UNTIL POTATOES AND CHICKEN ARE FORK-TENDER. STIR IN PEAS AND PARSLEY; RETURN TO A SIMMER. SIMMER FOR ABOUT 2 MINUTES OR UNTIL PEAS ARE HEATED THROUGH. TASTE AND ADJUST SEASONING WITH SALT AND PEPPER, IF DESIRED. SERVES 4.

TIP: IF THE FENNEL BULB HAS FEATHERY STALKS ATTACHED, TRIM THEM OFF ABOUT 1 INCH (2.5 CM) ABOVE THE BULB. CUT THE BULB IN HALF VERTICALLY AND REMOVE THE WOODY CORE FROM EACH HALF. CUT EACH HALF CROSSWISE INTO VERY THIN SLICES.

TIP: IF YOU USE A SALT-FREE STOCK OR BROTH, YOU MAY WANT TO ADD MORE SALT.

MAKE AHEAD: LET COOL, TRANSFER TO AN AIRTIGHT CONTAINER AND REFRIGERATE FOR UP TO 2 DAYS. REHEAT IN A LARGE SAUCEPAN OVER LOW HEAT, STIRRING FREQUENTLY. FREEZING IS NOT RECOMMENDED.

TURKEY MEATBALL KORMA

GROUND TURKEY IS A WINNER WHEN TURNED
INTO THESE TASTY MEATBALLS, COOKED IN A MILDLY
SPICED, CREAMY COCONUT SAUCE. SERVE
WITH STEAMED WHITE OR BROWN BASMATI RICE
AND SWEET POTATO SAMOSAS (PAGE 42),
WITH HOT PEPPER JELLY ON THE SIDE.

1/4 CUP	DRY BREAD CRUMBS OR CRACKER CRUMBS	60 ML
3 TBSP	CHOPPED FRESH CILANTRO, DIVIDED	45 ML
1/4 TSP	GRATED GINGERROOT (SEE TIP, PAGE 252)	1 ML
	SALT	
1	EGG, LIGHTLY BEATEN	1
2 TO 3 TBSP	MILD OR MEDIUM INDIAN CURRY PASTE (SEE TIP, PAGE 109), DIVIDED	30 TO 45 ML
1 LB	LEAN OR EXTRA-LEAN GROUND TURKEY	500 G
1 TBSP	VEGETABLE OIL	15 ML
1 CUP	FINELY CHOPPED ONION	250 ML
	COLD WATER	
1 CUP	COCONUT MILK (SEE TIP, PAGE 209)	250 ML
1/2 TO 1 CUP	REDUCED-SODIUM CHICKEN BROTH OR HOMEMADE VEGETABLE STOCK (SEE RECIPE, PAGE 90)	125 TO 250 ML
1/2 TSP	GRANULATED SUGAR	2 ML
16	SUGAR SNAP PEAS, TRIMMED AND CUT IN HALF DIAGONALLY	16
12	CHERRY TOMATOES, CUT IN HALF	12
	TOASTED ALMONDS AND/OR TOASTED UNSWEETENED SHREDDED COCONUT	

IN A LARGE BOWL, COMBINE BREAD CRUMBS, 1 TBSP (15 ML)
OF THE CILANTRO, GINGER, 1/4 TSP (1 ML) SALT, EGG AND
1 TBSP (15 ML) OF THE CURRY PASTE; LET STAND FOR

5 MINUTES. ADD GROUND TURKEY AND, USING CLEAN HANDS, MIX THOROUGHLY. SCOOP TABLESPOONFULS (15 ML) OF MEAT MIXTURE AND SHAPE INTO ABOUT 20 MEATBALLS. IN A LARGE NONSTICK SKILLET, HEAT OIL OVER MEDIUM-HIGH HEAT. COOK MEATBALLS, IN TWO BATCHES IF NECESSARY, TURNING FREQUENTLY, FOR 5 TO 7 MINUTES OR UNTIL BROWNED ALL OVER BUT STILL SLIGHTLY PINK INSIDE. (THEY WILL FINISH COOKING IN THE SAUCE.) TRANSFER MEATBALLS TO A PLATE. REDUCE HEAT TO MEDIUM. ADD ONION TO PAN AND SAUTÉ FOR ABOUT 5 MINUTES OR UNTIL SOFTENED. IF ONION STARTS TO STICK, ADD 1 TO 2 TBSP (15 TO 30 ML) COLD WATER. ADD THE REMAINING CURRY PASTE TO TASTE AND 1 TBSP (15 ML) COLD WATER; COOK, STIRRING, FOR 1 MINUTE. WHISK IN COCONUT MILK, $1/2$ CUP (125 ML) BROTH AND SUGAR UNTIL CURRY PASTE HAS DISSOLVED. RETURN MEATBALLS TO THE PAN AND BRING TO A BOIL. REDUCE HEAT AND SIMMER, TURNING MEATBALLS OCCASIONALLY, FOR ABOUT 10 MINUTES OR UNTIL MEATBALLS ARE NO LONGER PINK INSIDE AND SAUCE IS SLIGHTLY THICKENED. IF DESIRED, ADD MORE BROTH. (IF YOU REMOVE THE SKILLET FROM THE HEAT TO ANSWER THE PHONE, THE MEATBALLS WILL ABSORB QUITE A BIT OF THE SAUCE WHILE YOU'RE GONE!) TASTE AND ADJUST SEASONING WITH SALT, IF DESIRED. ADD PEAS, TOMATOES AND THE REMAINING CILANTRO; SIMMER FOR 2 MINUTES. SERVE GARNISHED WITH ALMONDS AND/OR COCONUT. SERVES 4.

TIP: IF YOU USE A SALT-FREE STOCK OR BROTH, YOU MAY WANT TO ADD MORE SALT.

SLOW COOKER ASIAN-STYLE BEEF

*CLASSIC BEEF CASSEROLE GETS A MAKEOVER WITH THE
SWEET AND SPICY FLAVORS OF GINGER, GARLIC AND
HOISIN SAUCE. IT'S DELICIOUS SERVED WITH BUTTERY
NOODLES, MASHED SWEET POTATO OR STEAMED RICE.*

3 LB	BONELESS BEEF CROSS RIB OR BLADE ROAST, CUT INTO 1-INCH (2.5 CM) CUBES	1.5 KG
2 TBSP	REDUCED-SODIUM SOY SAUCE	30 ML
2 TBSP	VEGETABLE OIL (APPROX.), DIVIDED	30 ML
3	LARGE CARROTS, THINLY SLICED	3
2	ONIONS, THINLY SLICED	2
2	STALKS CELERY, THINLY SLICED	2
3 TBSP	RICE WINE (SAKE) OR DRY SHERRY (SEE TIP, PAGE 145)	45 ML
4	CLOVES GARLIC, MINCED	4
2 TSP	GRATED GINGERROOT (SEE TIP, PAGE 252)	10 ML
1 TBSP	ALL-PURPOSE FLOUR	15 ML
1 1/2 CUPS	REDUCED-SODIUM BEEF BROTH	375 ML
1/3 CUP	HOISIN SAUCE	75 ML
1 TBSP	RICE VINEGAR OR CIDER VINEGAR	15 ML
1 TSP	ASIAN CHILI PASTE (SEE TIP, PAGE 207)	5 ML
8 OZ	SUGAR SNAP PEAS, TRIMMED AND CUT IN HALF DIAGONALLY	250 G

PREHEAT A LARGE (MINIMUM 5-QUART) SLOW COOKER.
IN A LARGE BOWL, TOSS BEEF WITH SOY SAUCE; SET
ASIDE. IN A LARGE SAUCEPAN OR DUTCH OVEN, HEAT
1 TBSP (15 ML) OIL OVER MEDIUM-HIGH HEAT. COOK BEEF,
IN TWO OR THREE BATCHES, UNTIL BROWNED ON ALL
SIDES, ADDING MORE OIL AS NEEDED. USING A SLOTTED

SPOON, TRANSFER BEEF TO A PLATE. REDUCE HEAT TO MEDIUM-LOW AND ADD I TBSP (I5 ML) OIL TO THE PAN. ADD CARROTS, ONIONS AND CELERY; COVER AND COOK, STIRRING OCCASIONALLY, FOR IO MINUTES OR UNTIL VEGETABLES ARE SOFTENED. ADD RICE WINE AND BOIL, SCRAPING UP BROWN BITS FROM BOTTOM OF PAN. ADD GARLIC AND GINGER; COOK, STIRRING, FOR I5 SECONDS OR UNTIL FRAGRANT. SPRINKLE WITH FLOUR AND COOK, STIRRING CONSTANTLY, FOR I MINUTE. GRADUALLY WHISK IN BROTH, HOISIN SAUCE, VINEGAR AND CHILI PASTE. RETURN BEEF AND ACCUMULATED JUICES TO THE PAN; INCREASE HEAT AND BRING TO A BOIL, STIRRING. TRANSFER TO SLOW COOKER. COVER AND COOK ON HIGH FOR 4 TO 5 HOURS OR ON LOW FOR 8 TO IO HOURS, UNTIL BEEF IS FORK-TENDER. STIR IN SUGAR SNAP PEAS, COVER AND COOK FOR ABOUT 5 MINUTES OR UNTIL TENDER-CRISP. SERVE IMMEDIATELY. SERVES 6.

TIP: IN PLACE OF THE ASIAN CHILI PASTE, YOU COULD USE $\frac{1}{4}$ TSP (I ML) HOT PEPPER FLAKES.

TIP: WHEN BROWNING THE BEEF, MAKE SURE NOT TO OVERCROWD THE PAN; OTHERWISE, THE MEAT WILL STEAM INSTEAD OF BROWNING.

MAKE AHEAD: AFTER SLOW COOKING BUT BEFORE ADDING THE PEAS, LET COOL, TRANSFER TO AN AIRTIGHT CONTAINER AND REFRIGERATE FOR UP TO 2 DAYS OR FREEZE FOR UP TO I MONTH. THAW OVERNIGHT IN THE REFRIGERATOR. REHEAT IN A LARGE SAUCEPAN OVER LOW HEAT, STIRRING FREQUENTLY, AND PROCEED WITH THE RECIPE.

SLOW COOKER BEEF DAUBE

TRÈS DELICIEUX! DAUBE *IS* FRENCH FOR "COVERED CASSEROLE," WHICH MAKES THIS THE PERFECT SLOW COOKER DINNER. THE RED WINE AND HERBS ARE THE KEYS TO ITS HEARTINESS, SO DON'T SKIP THEM. AND DON'T BE AFRAID OF ALL THE GARLIC — THE CLOVES ARE BRAISED WHOLE TO PRODUCE A RICH, MELLOW FLAVOR. SERVE WITH EASY BACON CORN RISOTTO (PAGE 276) OR LIGHT CHIVE MASHED POTATOES (PAGE 266).

I TBSP	OLIVE OR VEGETABLE OIL	15 ML
2	ONIONS, THINLY SLICED	2
3	LARGE CARROTS, THINLY SLICED	3
8	CLOVES GARLIC, LIGHTLY CRUSHED	8
I TBSP	ALL-PURPOSE FLOUR	15 ML
I TBSP	TOMATO PASTE (SEE TIP, PAGE 275)	15 ML
I 1/2 CUPS	DRY RED WINE	375 ML
1/2 CUP	REDUCED-SODIUM BEEF BROTH	125 ML
3 LB	BONELESS BEEF CROSS RIB OR BLADE ROAST, CUT INTO I-INCH (2.5 CM) CUBES	1.5 KG
2	2-INCH (5 CM) STRIPS ORANGE ZEST	2
I	BAY LEAF	I
I TSP	DRIED ROSEMARY	5 ML
1/2 TSP	DRIED THYME	2 ML
1/2 TSP	DRIED BASIL	2 ML
1/2 TSP	CRUSHED FENNEL SEEDS	2 ML
	SALT AND FRESHLY GROUND BLACK PEPPER	

PREHEAT A LARGE (MINIMUM 5-QUART) SLOW COOKER. IN A LARGE SAUCEPAN OR DUTCH OVEN, HEAT OIL OVER MEDIUM-HIGH HEAT. REDUCE HEAT TO LOW, ADD ONIONS, COVER AND COOK, STIRRING OCCASIONALLY,

FOR 5 MINUTES OR UNTIL SOFTENED. INCREASE HEAT TO MEDIUM, ADD CARROTS AND COOK, UNCOVERED AND STIRRING OCCASIONALLY, FOR 10 MINUTES OR UNTIL ONIONS ARE GOLDEN. ADD GARLIC, FLOUR AND TOMATO PASTE; COOK, STIRRING CONSTANTLY, FOR 1 MINUTE OR UNTIL FLOUR IS BROWN. GRADUALLY WHISK IN WINE AND BROTH. ADD BEEF, ORANGE ZEST, BAY LEAF, ROSEMARY, THYME, BASIL, FENNEL SEEDS, 1 TSP (5 ML) SALT AND 1/4 TSP (1 ML) PEPPER; BRING TO A BOIL, STIRRING OCCASIONALLY. TRANSFER TO SLOW COOKER. COVER AND COOK ON HIGH FOR 4 TO 5 HOURS OR ON LOW FOR 8 TO 10 HOURS, UNTIL BEEF IS FORK-TENDER. DISCARD ORANGE ZEST AND BAY LEAF. TASTE AND ADJUST SEASONING WITH SALT AND PEPPER, IF DESIRED. SERVES 6.

TIP: ALTHOUGH CONVENTIONAL WISDOM SUGGESTS BROWNING BEEF IN OIL WHEN MAKING A STEW OR CASSEROLE, WE OFTEN DON'T BOTHER, AND NO ONE TASTES THE DIFFERENCE.

MAKE AHEAD: AFTER SLOW COOKING, LET COOL, TRANSFER TO AN AIRTIGHT CONTAINER AND REFRIGERATE FOR UP TO 2 DAYS OR FREEZE FOR UP TO 1 MONTH. THAW OVERNIGHT IN THE REFRIGERATOR AND REHEAT IN A LARGE SAUCEPAN OVER LOW HEAT, STIRRING FREQUENTLY.

VARIATION: YOU CAN LEAVE OUT ONE OR TWO OF THE HERBS IF YOU PREFER — THE CASSEROLE WILL STILL TASTE DELICIOUS.

SIGN IN VET'S OFFICE: BACK IN 5 MINUTES. SIT. STAY.

STAY ABED STEW

DO ALL THE SLICING AND CHOPPING THE NIGHT BEFORE, THEN IN THE MORNING PROCEED WITH THE RECIPE. ONCE EVERYTHING IS IN THE SLOW COOKER, HEAD BACK TO BED OR OFF TO TENNIS — OR, IF YOU MUST, GO TO WORK! WHEN YOU GET HOME, SERVE THE AROMATIC STEW OVER MOUNDS OF FLUFFY MASHED POTATOES — HEAVEN! YOU ARE SUCH A GOOD COOK!

2 TBSP	OLIVE OR VEGETABLE OIL, DIVIDED	30 ML
2	ONIONS, THINLY SLICED	2
2	CLOVES GARLIC, MINCED	2
1 TSP	DRY MUSTARD	5 ML
1/2 TSP	DRIED THYME	2 ML
	SALT AND FRESHLY GROUND BLACK PEPPER	
3	LARGE CARROTS, THICKLY SLICED	3
3	STALKS CELERY, THINLY SLICED	3
1	LARGE PARSNIP (SEE TIP, PAGE 261), THICKLY SLICED	1
1 CUP	CUBED PEELED TURNIP	250 ML
2 TBSP	ALL-PURPOSE FLOUR	30 ML
1 1/2 CUPS	REDUCED-SODIUM BEEF BROTH	375 ML
1/2 CUP	TOMATO-BASED CHILI SAUCE	125 ML
3 LB	BONELESS BEEF CROSS RIB, BLADE OR ROUND ROAST, CUT INTO 1-INCH (2.5 CM) CUBES	1.5 KG
2	BAY LEAVES	2
1/4 CUP	CHOPPED FRESH PARSLEY	60 ML
1 TBSP	WORCESTERSHIRE SAUCE (SEE TIP, OPPOSITE)	15 ML

PREHEAT A LARGE (MINIMUM 5-QUART) SLOW COOKER. IN A LARGE SAUCEPAN OR DUTCH OVEN, HEAT 1 TBSP (15 ML) OIL OVER MEDIUM HEAT. SAUTÉ ONIONS FOR 5 MINUTES

OR UNTIL SOFTENED. ADD GARLIC, MUSTARD, THYME, 1 TSP (5 ML) SALT AND PEPPER TO TASTE; SAUTÉ FOR 15 SECONDS OR UNTIL FRAGRANT. TRANSFER TO SLOW COOKER. ADD THE REMAINING OIL TO THE SKILLET AND HEAT OVER MEDIUM HEAT. SAUTÉ CARROTS, CELERY, PARSNIP AND TURNIP FOR 5 TO 7 MINUTES OR UNTIL STARTING TO SOFTEN AND BROWN. SPRINKLE WITH FLOUR AND COOK, STIRRING, FOR 1 MINUTE. GRADUALLY WHISK IN BROTH. ADD CHILI SAUCE AND STIR UNTIL THICKENED. STIR IN BEEF (THAT'S RIGHT — YOU DON'T HAVE TO BROWN IT!), BAY LEAVES, PARSLEY AND WORCESTERSHIRE SAUCE; BRING TO A BOIL, STIRRING. TRANSFER TO SLOW COOKER. COVER AND COOK ON HIGH FOR 4 TO 5 HOURS OR ON LOW FOR 8 TO 10 HOURS, UNTIL BEEF IS FORK-TENDER. DISCARD BAY LEAVES. TASTE AND ADJUST SEASONING WITH SALT AND PEPPER, IF DESIRED. SERVES 6.

TIP: WORCESTERSHIRE SAUCE (PRONOUNCED WOOS-TER-SHEER) IS A DARK BROWN SAUCE WITH A PIQUANT, SPICY FLAVOR THAT WAS DEVELOPED FOR BRITISH COLONIALS IN INDIA. IT TAKES ITS NAME FROM WORCESTER, ENGLAND, WHERE IT WAS FIRST BOTTLED. THE SAUCE IS USED TO SEASON MEATS, SAUCES AND SOUPS AND IS AN ESSENTIAL INGREDIENT IN A BLOODY MARY COCKTAIL.

MAKE AHEAD: AFTER SLOW COOKING, LET COOL, TRANSFER TO AN AIRTIGHT CONTAINER AND REFRIGERATE FOR UP TO 2 DAYS. REHEAT IN A LARGE SAUCEPAN OVER LOW HEAT, STIRRING FREQUENTLY. WE DON'T RECOMMEND FREEZING THIS STEW, BECAUSE THE VEGETABLES BECOME MUSHY AFTER THAWING.

SHORTCUT BEEF AND MUSHROOM PIE

TENDER BEEF AND MUSHROOMS IN RICH GRAVY, TOPPED WITH A FLAKY PASTRY CRUST. THE SHORTCUT — FROZEN PUFF PASTRY ROLLED, CUT INTO INDIVIDUAL PORTIONS AND BAKED SEPARATELY FROM THE FILLING. MAKE THE FILLING AND PASTRY "HATS" ON SUNDAY AND YOU HAVE A FAST MIDWEEK DINNER FOR 4.

1 TBSP	OLIVE OR VEGETABLE OIL	15 ML
1 1/2 LB	BONELESS BEEF CROSS RIB OR BLADE ROAST, CUT INTO 1-INCH (2.5 CM) CUBES	750 G
1	LARGE ONION, CHOPPED	1
4 CUPS	QUARTERED MUSHROOMS	1 L
2	CLOVES GARLIC, MINCED	2
1/2 TSP	DRIED THYME	2 ML
1 1/2 TBSP	ALL-PURPOSE FLOUR	22 ML
1 1/2 CUPS	REDUCED-SODIUM BEEF BROTH OR HOMEMADE VEGETABLE STOCK (SEE RECIPE, PAGE 90)	375 ML
1 TBSP	BALSAMIC VINEGAR	15 ML
1 TBSP	TOMATO PASTE (SEE TIP, PAGE 275)	15 ML
	SALT AND FRESHLY GROUND BLACK PEPPER	
1/2	PACKAGE (14 OZ/398 G) FROZEN PUFF PASTRY, THAWED	1/2
1	EGG, LIGHTLY BEATEN	1

PREHEAT OVEN TO 325°F (160°C). IN A DUTCH OVEN OR FLAMEPROOF CASSEROLE DISH, HEAT OIL OVER MEDIUM-HIGH HEAT. SAUTÉ BEEF, IN BATCHES, FOR ABOUT 5 MINUTES OR UNTIL WELL BROWNED. USING A SLOTTED SPOON, TRANSFER BEEF TO A PLATE. REDUCE HEAT TO MEDIUM. ADD ONION AND MUSHROOMS TO JUICES IN PAN

AND SAUTÉ FOR 5 TO 7 MINUTES OR UNTIL BROWNED. ADD GARLIC AND THYME; SAUTÉ FOR 15 SECONDS OR UNTIL FRAGRANT. SPRINKLE WITH FLOUR AND COOK, STIRRING CONSTANTLY, FOR 1 MINUTE. RETURN MEAT AND ACCUMULATED JUICES TO THE PAN. GRADUALLY STIR IN BROTH, VINEGAR, TOMATO PASTE, $\frac{1}{2}$ TSP (2 ML) SALT AND $\frac{1}{4}$ TSP (1 ML) PEPPER; BRING TO A BOIL. COVER AND BAKE IN PREHEATED OVEN FOR ABOUT 2 HOURS OR UNTIL BEEF IS FORK-TENDER AND GRAVY IS THICK. REMOVE FROM OVEN, TASTE AND ADJUST SEASONINGS WITH SALT AND PEPPER, IF DESIRED. SET ASIDE, COVERED.

INCREASE OVEN TEMPERATURE TO 425°F (220°C). LINE A LARGE BAKING SHEET WITH PARCHMENT PAPER. ON A LIGHTLY FLOURED SURFACE, ROLL OUT PASTRY INTO A 10-INCH (25 CM) SQUARE. CUT INTO FOUR 5-INCH (12.5 CM) SQUARES. WITH THE TIP OF A SHARP KNIFE, LIGHTLY SCORE A BORDER ABOUT $\frac{1}{4}$ INCH (0.5 CM) INSIDE EACH SQUARE. PLACE ON PREPARED BAKING SHEET. BRUSH WITH BEATEN EGG. BAKE FOR 12 TO 15 MINUTES OR UNTIL PUFFY AND GOLDEN.

IF NECESSARY, REHEAT BEEF MIXTURE IN A LARGE SAUCEPAN, STIRRING OFTEN, OVER LOW HEAT. SERVE EACH PORTION TOPPED WITH A PASTRY SQUARE. SERVES 4.

TIP: IF YOU USE A SALT-FREE STOCK OR BROTH, YOU MAY WANT TO ADD MORE SALT. SALT IS, IN ANY RECIPE, A MATTER OF PERSONAL PREFERENCE, SO FEEL FREE TO INCREASE OR REDUCE THE QUANTITIES WE SUGGEST. BEFORE ADDING MORE SALT AT THE END OF THE COOKING TIME, BE SURE TO TASTE THE DISH FIRST.

SWEET POTATO SHEPHERD'S PIE

IN OUR NEW TAKE ON THIS CLASSIC COMFORT FOOD DISH, WE USE LEAN GROUND PORK, FOR A WELCOME CHANGE FROM GROUND BEEF. NUTRITIOUS SWEET POTATO MAKES A COLORFUL TOPPING.

2	SLICES BACON, CHOPPED	2
I TO 2 TSP	BUTTER OR OLIVE OIL (IF NEEDED)	5 TO IO ML
I LB	LEAN GROUND PORK	500 G
2	CLOVES GARLIC, MINCED	2
I	STALK CELERY, FINELY CHOPPED	I
1/2 CUP	FINELY CHOPPED ONION	125 ML
1/2 CUP	REDUCED-SODIUM CHICKEN BROTH	125 ML
1/2 CUP	UNSWEETENED APPLE JUICE	125 ML
I TBSP	KETCHUP	15 ML
I TBSP	REDUCED-SODIUM SOY SAUCE	15 ML
1/2 TSP	DRIED OREGANO	2 ML
	SALT AND FRESHLY GROUND BLACK PEPPER	
I CUP	FROZEN CORN KERNELS, FROZEN BABY PEAS OR A COMBINATION (NO NEED TO THAW)	250 ML
2 TBSP	CHOPPED FRESH PARSLEY	30 ML
I TBSP	CIDER VINEGAR	15 ML

SWEET POTATO TOPPING

I LB	SWEET POTATO (SEE TIP, PAGE 261), PEELED AND CUBED	500 G
I LB	YUKON GOLD POTATOES (SEE TIP, PAGE 259), PEELED AND CUBED	500 G
	SALT	
1/2 TO 3/4 CUP	MILK, WARMED	125 TO 175 ML
2 TBSP	BUTTER	30 ML
1/8 TSP	GROUND NUTMEG	0.5 ML

PREHEAT OVEN TO 350°F (180°C). GREASE AN 8-CUP (2 L) CASSEROLE DISH. IN A LARGE SAUCEPAN, SAUTÉ BACON OVER MEDIUM-HIGH HEAT UNTIL CRISPY. USING A SLOTTED SPOON, TRANSFER BACON TO A PLATE LINED WITH PAPER TOWELS. DRAIN OFF ALL BUT 1 TBSP (15 ML) FAT. IF THERE IS LESS THAN 1 TBSP (15 ML) FAT, ADD BUTTER AS NEEDED. REDUCE HEAT TO MEDIUM. ADD PORK, GARLIC, CELERY AND ONION; COOK, BREAKING PORK UP WITH A SPOON, FOR 5 TO 7 MINUTES OR UNTIL PORK IS NO LONGER PINK AND ONION IS SOFTENED. DRAIN OFF FAT. RETURN BACON TO THE PAN. ADD BROTH, APPLE JUICE, KETCHUP, SOY SAUCE, OREGANO, 1/2 TSP (2 ML) SALT AND 1/4 TSP (1 ML) PEPPER; BRING TO A BOIL. REDUCE HEAT AND SIMMER, STIRRING OCCASIONALLY, FOR 20 MINUTES OR UNTIL LIQUID HAS ALMOST EVAPORATED. ADD CORN, PARSLEY AND VINEGAR; COOK, STIRRING, FOR 1 MINUTE. TASTE AND ADJUST SEASONING WITH SALT AND PEPPER, IF DESIRED. TRANSFER TO PREPARED CASSEROLE DISH.

SWEET POTATO TOPPING: MEANWHILE, PLACE SWEET POTATO AND POTATOES IN A LARGE SAUCEPAN AND COVER WITH COLD WATER. ADD 1 TSP (5 ML) SALT. BRING TO A BOIL OVER HIGH HEAT. REDUCE HEAT, COVER AND SIMMER BRISKLY FOR 20 TO 25 MINUTES OR UNTIL TENDER. DRAIN WELL AND TRANSFER TO A LARGE BOWL. ADD 1/2 CUP (125 ML) WARM MILK, BUTTER, 1/2 TSP (5 ML) SALT AND NUTMEG. MASH WELL, ADDING MORE MILK IF DESIRED. TASTE AND ADJUST SEASONING WITH SALT, IF DESIRED.

SPREAD POTATO MIXTURE OVER MEAT MIXTURE. BAKE FOR 30 TO 40 MINUTES OR UNTIL BUBBLING AND STARTING TO BROWN AT THE EDGES. SERVES 4.

RUM- AND LIME-GLAZED PORK RIBS

A TASTE OF THE CARIBBEAN!

SPICE RUB

I TBSP	PAPRIKA	15 ML
I TBSP	GROUND CORIANDER	15 ML
I TBSP	GROUND CUMIN	15 ML
2 TSP	DRIED THYME	10 ML
2 TSP	SALT	10 ML
I TSP	GROUND CINNAMON	5 ML
2 LBS	COUNTRY-STYLE PORK RIBS, CUT INTO INDIVIDUAL RIBS (SEE TIP, OPPOSITE)	I KG
1/4 CUP	UNSWEETENED APPLE JUICE, CHICKEN BROTH OR WATER	60 ML

GLAZE

I CUP	PINEAPPLE OR APRICOT JAM	250 ML
1/4 CUP	DARK RUM	60 ML
1/4 CUP	FRESHLY SQUEEZED LIME JUICE	60 ML
2 TBSP	CIDER VINEGAR	30 ML

SPICE RUB: IN A BOWL, COMBINE PAPRIKA, CORIANDER, CUMIN, THYME, SALT AND CINNAMON.

PREHEAT OVEN TO 275°F (140°C). LINE A 13- BY 9-INCH (33 BY 23 CM) BAKING PAN OR A LARGE RIMMED BAKING SHEET WITH GREASED FOIL. RUB RIBS LIBERALLY WITH SPICE MIXTURE. PLACE IN A SINGLE LAYER IN PREPARED PAN. DRIZZLE APPLE JUICE OVER RIBS AND COVER TIGHTLY WITH FOIL. BAKE FOR ABOUT 2 HOURS OR UNTIL RIBS ARE FORK-TENDER AND THE MEAT IS STARTING TO FALL OFF THE BONE.

GLAZE: IN A SMALL SAUCEPAN, COMBINE JAM, RUM, LIME JUICE AND VINEGAR; BRING TO A BOIL OVER HIGH HEAT. REDUCE HEAT AND SIMMER FOR 1 MINUTE. REMOVE FROM HEAT AND KEEP WARM.

PREHEAT BARBECUE GRILL TO MEDIUM-HIGH AND LIGHTLY GREASE THE RACK. TRANSFER RIBS TO A LARGE PLATE AND BRUSH WITH GLAZE. GRILL FOR 5 TO 8 MINUTES, TURNING FREQUENTLY AND BRUSHING WITH GLAZE, UNTIL CRISPY. SERVES 4.

TIP: COUNTRY-STYLE RIBS ARE MEATIER THAN BABY BACK OR SPARERIBS. YOU CAN USE THOSE CUTS WITH THIS RECIPE, IF YOU PREFER. YOU'LL NEED 4 LBS (2 KG) FOR 4 SERVINGS.

HOLIDAY BLESSING: MAY YOUR FAMILY BE FUNCTIONAL AND YOUR BATTERIES BE INCLUDED.

PORK WITH CREAMY PECAN MUSHROOM SAUCE

A CONTEMPORARY TAKE ON AN OLD FAVORITE. GROUND TOASTED NUTS ARE A FLAVORFUL WAY TO THICKEN SAUCE WITHOUT DAIRY.

3/4 CUP	COARSELY CHOPPED TOASTED PECANS (SEE TIP, PAGE 127)	175 ML
	SALT	
3/4 TO 1 CUP	WATER	175 TO 250 ML
1 1/2 LBS	BONELESS FAST-FRY PORK SIRLOIN CHOPS	750 G
	FRESHLY GROUND BLACK PEPPER	
2 TBSP	OLIVE OR VEGETABLE OIL, DIVIDED	30 ML
1	ONION, FINELY CHOPPED	1
4 CUPS	SLICED MUSHROOMS	1 L
2	CLOVES GARLIC, MINCED	2
1/2 TSP	DRIED CRUMBLED SAGE OR OREGANO	2 ML
2 TBSP	DRY SHERRY OR UNSWEETENED APPLE JUICE	30 ML
1/4 TO 1/2 CUP	REDUCED-SODIUM CHICKEN BROTH, HOMEMADE VEGETABLE STOCK (SEE RECIPE, PAGE 90) OR WATER	60 TO 125 ML
1/4 CUP	CHOPPED FRESH PARSLEY	60 ML

IN A FOOD PROCESSOR OR BLENDER, PROCESS PECANS AND 1/2 TSP (2 ML) SALT FOR 1 MINUTE OR UNTIL A GRAINY PASTE FORMS. SCRAPE DOWN THE SIDES OF THE BOWL. WITH THE MOTOR RUNNING, THROUGH THE FEED TUBE, GRADUALLY ADD WATER UNTIL THE MIXTURE HAS THE CONSISTENCY OF HALF-AND-HALF CREAM. TRANSFER TO A BOWL AND SET ASIDE. SEASON PORK WITH SALT AND PEPPER. IN A LARGE NONSTICK SKILLET, HEAT 1 TBSP

(15 ML) OIL OVER MEDIUM-HIGH HEAT. COOK PORK CHOPS, IN TWO BATCHES IF NECESSARY, FOR 2 TO 3 MINUTES PER SIDE OR UNTIL BROWNED AND JUST A HINT OF PINK REMAINS INSIDE. TRANSFER PORK TO A PLATE AND KEEP WARM. REDUCE HEAT TO MEDIUM AND ADD THE REMAINING OIL TO THE PAN. SAUTÉ ONION AND MUSHROOMS FOR 5 TO 7 MINUTES OR UNTIL ONION IS SOFTENED AND MUSHROOMS ARE BROWNED. ADD GARLIC, SAGE AND SHERRY; COOK, STIRRING AND SCRAPING UP BROWN BITS FROM BOTTOM OF PAN, FOR 30 SECONDS OR UNTIL SHERRY IS EVAPORATED AND GARLIC IS FRAGRANT. RETURN PORK AND ACCUMULATED JUICES TO PAN, STIR IN PECAN MIXTURE AND BRING TO A BOIL. REDUCE HEAT AND SIMMER FOR 1 MINUTE, ADDING BROTH AS NEEDED TO ACHIEVE THE DESIRED CONSISTENCY. TASTE AND ADJUST SEASONING WITH SALT AND PEPPER, IF DESIRED. STIR IN PARSLEY. SERVES 4 TO 6.

TIP: YOU COULD ALSO USE 2 PORK TENDERLOINS (EACH ABOUT 12 OZ/375 G), THINLY SLICED.

VARIATION: REPLACE THE PORK WITH $1\frac{1}{2}$ LBS (750 G) BONELESS SKINLESS CHICKEN BREASTS (ABOUT 3 LARGE BREASTS), CUT INTO BITE-SIZE PIECES, AND COOK UNTIL NO LONGER PINK INSIDE.

I TOLD MY KIDS: "I NEVER WANT TO LIVE IN A VEGETATIVE STATE – NO LIFE-SUPPORT MACHINES, NO TUBES AND NO FLUIDS. IF IT EVER HAPPENS, JUST PULL THE PLUG." SO THEY UNPLUGGED MY COMPUTER AND THREW OUT MY WINE.

CHERRY BALSAMIC-GLAZED PORK TENDERLOIN

SERVE THIS TERRIFICALLY SWEET AND TANGY PORK WITH MASHED POTATOES AND PEAS (PAGE 267) AND ROASTED PAPRIKA CAULIFLOWER (PAGE 255). THE GLAZE IS ALSO EXCELLENT ON LAMB CHOPS AND CHICKEN.

CHERRY BALSAMIC GLAZE

I TBSP	OLIVE OIL	15 ML
1/4 CUP	FINELY CHOPPED SHALLOTS OR ONION	60 ML
I	CLOVE GARLIC, MINCED	I
1/4 CUP	RUBY PORT OR CRANBERRY JUICE	60 ML
I TBSP	CHOPPED FRESH ROSEMARY OR THYME (OR 1/2 TSP/2 ML DRIED)	15 ML
1/2 TSP	FINELY GRATED ORANGE ZEST	2 ML
1/4 TSP	SALT	I ML
1/8 TSP	FRESHLY GROUND BLACK PEPPER	0.5 ML
3/4 CUP	GOOD-QUALITY CHERRY PRESERVES (SEE TIP, PAGE 299)	175 ML
3 TBSP	BALSAMIC VINEGAR	45 ML
2	PORK TENDERLOINS (EACH ABOUT 12 OZ/375 G)	2
	SALT AND FRESHLY GROUND BLACK PEPPER	
2 TBSP	OLIVE OIL	30 ML

CHERRY BALSAMIC GLAZE: IN A SMALL SAUCEPAN, HEAT OIL OVER MEDIUM HEAT. ADD SHALLOTS, REDUCE HEAT TO LOW AND COOK GENTLY, STIRRING OCCASIONALLY, FOR ABOUT 5 MINUTES OR UNTIL SOFTENED. ADD GARLIC AND COOK, STIRRING, FOR 15 SECONDS OR UNTIL FRAGRANT. INCREASE HEAT TO MEDIUM, ADD PORT AND BRING TO A SIMMER; SIMMER UNTIL REDUCED TO I TBSP

(15 ML). STIR IN ROSEMARY, ORANGE ZEST, SALT, PEPPER, CHERRY PRESERVES AND VINEGAR; SIMMER, STIRRING OCCASIONALLY, FOR 15 MINUTES OR UNTIL SLIGHTLY REDUCED AND GLAZE LIGHTLY COATS THE BACK OF A SPOON. USING AN IMMERSION BLENDER, OR IN A FOOD PROCESSOR OR BLENDER, PURÉE GLAZE UNTIL SMOOTH. (OR OMIT THIS STEP AND LEAVE THE GLAZE CHUNKY.) SET ASIDE HALF THE GLAZE FOR SERVING. KEEP THE REMAINING GLAZE WARM FOR BRUSHING ON THE PORK.

MEANWHILE, PREHEAT BARBECUE GRILL TO HIGH AND LIGHTLY GREASE THE RACK. REMOVE ANY SILVERY SKIN FROM PORK. SEASON GENEROUSLY WITH SALT AND PEPPER AND BRUSH WITH OIL. PLACE ON GREASED GRILL AND SEAR ON ALL SIDES, ABOUT 3 MINUTES TOTAL. REDUCE HEAT TO MEDIUM, BRUSH PORK WITH WARM GLAZE, COVER AND GRILL FOR 20 TO 25 MINUTES, TURNING OCCASIONALLY AND BRUSHING WITH GLAZE, UNTIL A MEAT THERMOMETER INSERTED IN THE THICKEST PART REGISTERS 155°F (68°C) AND JUST A HINT OF PINK REMAINS INSIDE. TRANSFER PORK TO A CUTTING BOARD, COVER LOOSELY WITH FOIL AND LET REST FOR 10 MINUTES. (THE PORK WILL CONTINUE TO "COOK" IN ITS OWN HEAT, AND THE TEMPERATURE WILL RISE BY ABOUT ANOTHER 5°F/3°C.)

WARM THE RESERVED SAUCE (WHICH WILL HAVE THICKENED) IN A SMALL SAUCEPAN OVER LOW HEAT (OR IN THE MICROWAVE ON HIGH FOR ABOUT 20 SECONDS). DILUTE WITH 1 TO 2 TBSP (15 TO 30 ML) WATER, IF NECESSARY. THINLY SLICE PORK AND SERVE WITH SAUCE. SERVES 4 TO 6.

GINGER PEACH PORK TENDERLOIN

SPICE RUB

1 TSP	GROUND CORIANDER	5 ML
1 TSP	PAPRIKA	5 ML
1 TSP	DRIED OREGANO	5 ML
1 TSP	BROWN OR GRANULATED SUGAR	5 ML
1/2 TSP	CELERY SALT	2 ML
1/4 TSP	FRESHLY GROUND BLACK PEPPER	1 ML
2	PORK TENDERLOINS (EACH ABOUT 12 OZ/375 G)	2
2 TBSP	OLIVE OR VEGETABLE OIL	30 ML

GINGER PEACH CHUTNEY

1 TBSP	OLIVE OR VEGETABLE OIL	15 ML
1/2	RED BELL PEPPER, FINELY CHOPPED	1/2
1/4 CUP	FINELY CHOPPED ONION	60 ML
2	RIPE PEACHES, PEELED (SEE TIP, PAGE 321) AND CHOPPED	2
2 TSP	BROWN OR GRANULATED SUGAR	10 ML
1/2 TSP	MINCED GINGERROOT	2 ML
1/4 TSP	SALT	1 ML
	FRESHLY GROUND BLACK PEPPER	
2 TBSP	FRESHLY SQUEEZED LEMON JUICE	30 ML

SPICE RUB: IN A SMALL BOWL, COMBINE CORIANDER, PAPRIKA, OREGANO, BROWN SUGAR, CELERY SALT AND PEPPER.

REMOVE ANY SILVERY SKIN FROM PORK. RUB SPICE RUB LIBERALLY OVER BOTH TENDERLOINS. PLACE ON A PLATE, COVER AND REFRIGERATE FOR AT LEAST 15 MINUTES OR FOR UP TO 4 HOURS.

PREHEAT BARBECUE GRILL TO MEDIUM AND LIGHTLY GREASE THE RACK. BRUSH PORK WITH OIL. PLACE PORK ON GREASED GRILL, COVER AND GRILL FOR 25 TO 30 MINUTES, TURNING OCCASIONALLY, UNTIL A MEAT THERMOMETER INSERTED IN THE THICKEST PART REGISTERS 155°F (68°C) AND JUST A HINT OF PINK REMAINS INSIDE. TRANSFER PORK TO A CUTTING BOARD, COVER LOOSELY WITH FOIL AND LET REST FOR 10 MINUTES. (THE PORK WILL CONTINUE TO "COOK" IN ITS OWN HEAT, AND THE TEMPERATURE WILL RISE BY ABOUT ANOTHER 5°F/3°C.)

GINGER PEACH CHUTNEY: IN A SMALL SAUCEPAN, HEAT OIL OVER MEDIUM HEAT. SAUTÉ RED PEPPER AND ONION FOR ABOUT 5 MINUTES OR UNTIL SOFTENED. ADD PEACHES, BROWN SUGAR, GINGER, SALT, PEPPER TO TASTE AND LEMON JUICE; BRING TO A BOIL. REDUCE HEAT AND SIMMER, STIRRING OCCASIONALLY, FOR 15 TO 20 MINUTES OR UNTIL PEACHES ARE SOFTENED AND CHUTNEY IS THICK ENOUGH TO HEAP ON A SPOON. REMOVE FROM HEAT. IF YOU PREFER A SMOOTHER CONSISTENCY, MASH WITH A POTATO MASHER.

THINLY SLICE PORK AND SERVE WITH CHUTNEY. SERVES 4 TO 6.

VARIATION: TO COOK THIS PORK IN THE OVEN, PLACE ON THE RACK OF A ROASTING PAN AND BAKE IN A 375°F (190°C) OVEN FOR 30 TO 40 MINUTES OR UNTIL A MEAT THERMOMETER INSERTED IN THE THICKEST PART REGISTERS 155°F (68°C) AND JUST A HINT OF PINK REMAINS INSIDE.

GRILLED HERB PORK TENDERLOIN

THIS RECIPE IS PERFECT FOR CASUAL
SUMMER ENTERTAINING. SERVE WITH PATRAS
POTATOES (PAGE 263) AND GREEN BEANS WITH
LEMON THYME PESTO (PAGE 250).

2	CLOVES GARLIC, MINCED	2
6 TBSP	CHOPPED MIXED FRESH HERBS, SUCH AS ROSEMARY, THYME, PARSLEY, SAGE, BASIL OR CHIVES	90 ML
3 TBSP	OLIVE OIL	45 ML
2	PORK TENDERLOINS (EACH ABOUT 12 OZ/375 G)	2
	SALT AND FRESHLY GROUND BLACK PEPPER	

IN A SMALL BOWL, COMBINE GARLIC, HERBS AND OIL.
REMOVE ANY SILVERY SKIN FROM PORK. SEASON
GENEROUSLY WITH SALT AND PEPPER. RUB HERB MIXTURE
ALL OVER BOTH TENDERLOINS. PLACE ON A PLATE, COVER
AND REFRIGERATE FOR AT LEAST 1 HOUR OR UP TO
6 HOURS.

PREHEAT BARBECUE GRILL TO MEDIUM AND LIGHTLY
GREASE THE RACK. REMOVE PORK FROM MARINADE,
DISCARDING ANY EXCESS MARINADE. PLACE PORK ON
GREASED GRILL, COVER AND GRILL FOR 25 TO 30 MINUTES,
TURNING OCCASIONALLY, UNTIL A MEAT THERMOMETER
INSERTED IN THE THICKEST PART REGISTERS 155°F (68°C)
AND JUST A HINT OF PINK REMAINS INSIDE. TRANSFER
PORK TO A CUTTING BOARD, COVER LOOSELY WITH FOIL
AND LET REST FOR 10 MINUTES BEFORE SLICING AND
SERVING. (THE PORK WILL CONTINUE TO "COOK" IN ITS
OWN HEAT, AND THE TEMPERATURE WILL RISE BY ABOUT
ANOTHER 5°F/3°C.) SERVES 4 TO 6.

FISH AND SEAFOOD

TOMATO, SHRIMP AND FETA BAKE

SERVE THIS TASTY QUICK-FIX DINNER
WITH STEAMED RICE OR PASTA.

1 TBSP	OLIVE OR VEGETABLE OIL	15 ML
1	RED BELL PEPPER, CHOPPED	1
2 CUPS	SLICED MUSHROOMS	500 ML
2	CLOVES GARLIC, MINCED	2
2	TOMATOES, FINELY CHOPPED	2
2 CUPS	TOMATO PASTA SAUCE (SEE TIP, PAGE 161)	500 ML
1/2 CUP	HEAVY OR WHIPPING (35%) CREAM (OPTIONAL)	125 ML
1 LB	LARGE SHRIMP (SEE TIP, OPPOSITE), PEELED AND DEVEINED, THAWED IF FROZEN	500 G
1/2 CUP	CRUMBLED FETA CHEESE (SEE TIP, OPPOSITE)	125 ML
2 TBSP	CHOPPED FRESH PARSLEY	30 ML
	FINELY GRATED ZEST OF 1 LEMON	

PREHEAT OVEN TO 400°F (200°C). GREASE AN 8-CUP (2 L)
CASSEROLE DISH. IN A LARGE NONSTICK SKILLET, HEAT OIL
OVER MEDIUM HEAT. SAUTÉ RED PEPPER FOR 2 MINUTES
OR UNTIL SLIGHTLY SOFTENED. ADD MUSHROOMS AND
SAUTÉ FOR 3 TO 4 MINUTES OR UNTIL LIGHTLY BROWNED.
ADD GARLIC AND SAUTÉ FOR 15 SECONDS OR UNTIL
FRAGRANT. REMOVE FROM HEAT AND STIR IN TOMATOES,
PASTA SAUCE AND CREAM. TRANSFER SAUCE TO PREPARED
CASSEROLE DISH. NESTLE, BUT DON'T IMMERSE, SHRIMP
IN SAUCE. SPRINKLE FETA OVER TOP OF SHRIMP. COVER
AND BAKE FOR ABOUT 20 MINUTES OR UNTIL SAUCE IS
BUBBLING. UNCOVER AND BAKE FOR 10 TO 13 MINUTES OR

CONTINUED ON PAGE 199...

Turkey Meatball Korma (page 176)

Grilled Herb Pork Tenderloin (page 196),
Patras Potatoes (page 263) and Green Beans
with Lemon Thyme Pesto (page 250)

Halibut with Strawberry Basil Salsa (page 202)

Thai Poached Salmon and Noodles (page 208)

UNTIL SHRIMP ARE PINK AND OPAQUE AND CHEESE IS MELTED. IMMEDIATELY SPRINKLE PARSLEY AND LEMON ZEST OVER TOP. SERVE IMMEDIATELY. SERVES 4.

TIP: SHRIMP ARE SOLD BY THE COUNT, WHICH MEANS THE APPROXIMATE NUMBER OF SHRIMP YOU GET TO THE POUND (500 G). FOR THIS RECIPE, USE LARGE SHRIMP (26 TO 30 COUNT OR 31 TO 40 COUNT).

TIP: FETA IS A SALTY CHEESE OFTEN USED IN MEDITERRANEAN DISHES. IT'S TRADITIONALLY MADE FROM SHEEP'S OR GOAT'S MILK, ALTHOUGH SOME VERSIONS ARE MADE FROM COW'S MILK. WE RECOMMEND BUYING FETA THAT'S PACKED IN BRINE IN TUBS. NOT ONLY DOES IT HAVE A TANGIER FLAVOR THAN FETA SOLD DRY IN VACUUM PACKS, BUT IT ALSO STAYS MOISTER.

MAKE AHEAD: PREPARE THE SAUCE AND TRANSFER IT TO THE CASSEROLE DISH, BUT DO NOT ADD THE SHRIMP OR FETA. COVER AND REFRIGERATE FOR UP TO 24 HOURS. PROCEED WITH THE RECIPE, ADDING 5 TO 10 MINUTES TO THE BAKING TIME WHILE THE DISH IS COVERED.

ALWAYS END THE NAME OF YOUR CHILD WITH A VOWEL,
SO THAT WHEN YOU YELL, THE NAME WILL CARRY.
— BILL COSBY

YOU GOTTA HAVE COD!

A CREAMY SAUCE AND A CRUNCHY TOPPING TURN
COD INTO COMFORT FOOD. SERVE WITH MASHED
POTATOES AND PEAS (PAGE 267) OR WITH
STEAMED RICE AND GREEN BEANS.

4	SKINLESS COD FILLETS (EACH ABOUT 6 OZ/175 G)	4
1 TBSP	BUTTER, MELTED	15 ML
	SALT AND FRESHLY GROUND BLACK PEPPER	
2½ CUPS	WHOLE OR 2% MILK	625 ML
1	BAY LEAF	1
1 CUP	CRUSHED PLAIN OR CHEESE-FLAVORED POTATO CHIPS	250 ML
⅓ CUP	FRESHLY GRATED PARMESAN CHEESE	75 ML
	PAPRIKA	

SAUCE

2 TBSP	BUTTER	30 ML
3 TBSP	ALL-PURPOSE FLOUR	45 ML
1 TBSP	DIJON MUSTARD	15 ML
1 CUP	SHREDDED SHARP (OLD) CHEDDAR CHEESE	250 ML
⅛ TSP	GRATED NUTMEG	0.5 ML
	SALT AND FRESHLY GROUND BLACK PEPPER	

BUTTER A BAKING DISH LARGE ENOUGH TO HOLD THE FISH
IN A SINGLE LAYER AND SET ASIDE. RINSE COD AND PAT
DRY WITH PAPER TOWELS. (IF THE FISH HAS BEEN FROZEN
AND THAWED, IT WILL BE QUITE WET, SO BE SURE TO DRY
IT WELL.) BRUSH COD WITH MELTED BUTTER AND SEASON
WITH SALT AND PEPPER. PLACE COD IN A LARGE NONSTICK
SKILLET. ADD MILK AND BAY LEAF; GENTLY WARM MILK

OVER MEDIUM HEAT UNTIL ALMOST SIMMERING. DO NOT LET BOIL. REDUCE HEAT TO LOW, COVER AND POACH FISH FOR 5 TO 7 MINUTES OR UNTIL FISH IS BARELY OPAQUE AND IS JUST STARTING TO FLAKE WHEN TESTED WITH A FORK. USING A LARGE SPATULA, TRANSFER FISH TO PREPARED BAKING DISH, ARRANGING IT IN A SINGLE LAYER. RESERVE COOKING MILK, DISCARDING BAY LEAF.

SAUCE: IN A MEDIUM SAUCEPAN, MELT BUTTER OVER MEDIUM HEAT. ADD FLOUR AND COOK, STIRRING, FOR 2 MINUTES OR UNTIL IT LOOKS SANDY. GRADUALLY WHISK IN RESERVED MILK AND MUSTARD; BRING TO A BOIL, WHISKING CONSTANTLY. REDUCE HEAT AND SIMMER, STIRRING CONSTANTLY, FOR 5 TO 7 MINUTES OR UNTIL THICKENED. REMOVE FROM HEAT AND STIR IN CHEDDAR, NUTMEG AND SALT AND PEPPER TO TASTE.

MEANWHILE, PREHEAT BROILER TO HIGH. POUR CHEESE SAUCE OVER FISH. SPRINKLE WITH CRUSHED POTATO CHIPS, PARMESAN AND A LIGHT DUSTING OF PAPRIKA. BROIL FOR 3 TO 5 MINUTES OR UNTIL GOLDEN BROWN. SERVES 4.

A LOT OF MONEY IS TAINTED — T'AIN'T YOURS
AND T'AIN'T MINE.

HALIBUT WITH STRAWBERRY BASIL SALSA

THE SUMMERY FLAVOR OF STRAWBERRIES AND BASIL LEND A REFRESHING TANG TO TENDER HALIBUT. THIS SALSA IS ALSO GOOD WITH SALMON OR RED SNAPPER.

STRAWBERRY BASIL SALSA

1½ CUPS	CHOPPED FRESH STRAWBERRIES (ABOUT 8 OZ/250 G)	375 ML
½ CUP	DRAINED CANNED MANDARIN ORANGE SEGMENTS IN JUICE, CHOPPED (SEE TIP, OPPOSITE)	125 ML
1 TBSP	FINELY CHOPPED RED ONION	15 ML
1 TBSP	SHREDDED FRESH BASIL	15 ML
1 TO 2 TBSP	FRESHLY SQUEEZED LIME JUICE	15 TO 30 ML
⅛ TSP	SALT	0.5 ML
⅛ TSP	FRESHLY GROUND BLACK PEPPER	0.5 ML
4	SKIN-ON OR SKINLESS HALIBUT FILLETS (EACH ABOUT 6 OZ/175 G)	4
	SALT AND FRESHLY GROUND BLACK PEPPER	
2 TBSP	OLIVE OR VEGETABLE OIL	30 ML

STRAWBERRY BASIL SALSA: IN A BOWL, COMBINE STRAWBERRIES, MANDARIN ORANGES, ONION, BASIL, 1 TBSP (15 ML) LIME JUICE, SALT AND PEPPER. COVER AND REFRIGERATE FOR AT LEAST 30 MINUTES OR FOR UP TO 2 HOURS. TASTE AND ADD MORE LIME JUICE, IF DESIRED.

PREHEAT OVEN TO 425°F (220°C). LINE A RIMMED BAKING SHEET WITH PARCHMENT PAPER OR GREASED FOIL. RINSE HALIBUT AND PAT DRY WITH PAPER TOWELS. (IF THE FISH HAS BEEN FROZEN AND THAWED, IT WILL BE QUITE WET,

SO BE SURE TO DRY IT WELL.) SEASON WITH SALT AND PEPPER. IN A LARGE NONSTICK SKILLET, HEAT OIL OVER MEDIUM-HIGH HEAT. COOK HALIBUT, SKIN OR SKINNED SIDE UP, FOR ABOUT 2 MINUTES OR UNTIL BOTTOM IS NICELY BROWNED. TRANSFER TO PREPARED BAKING SHEET, BROWNED SIDE UP, AND BAKE FOR 5 TO 6 MINUTES OR UNTIL FISH IS BARELY OPAQUE AND IS JUST STARTING TO FLAKE WHEN TESTED WITH A FORK. DO NOT OVERCOOK. SERVE HALIBUT TOPPED WITH SALSA. SERVES 4.

TIP: YOU CAN USE 1 OR 2 FRESH MANDARIN ORANGES INSTEAD OF CANNED, IF YOU PREFER. PEEL THE MANDARINS AND SEPARATE INTO SEGMENTS. REMOVE ANY WHITE PITH AND SEEDS, THEN CHOP.

TEACHER: NAME THE FOUR SEASONS.
CHILD: SALT, PEPPER, MUSTARD AND VINEGAR

PICKEREL WITH CREAMY LEMON DILL SAUCE

AS CANADA'S FRESHWATER FISHING FRATERNITY WILL TELL YOU, PICKEREL IS WORTH PURSUING. AS WITH COOKING ANY FRESH FISH, THE KEY IS TO KEEP IT SIMPLE. THIS RECIPE ALSO WORKS WELL WITH TROUT OR PERCH. SERVE WITH STEAMED RICE AND GREEN BEANS WITH LEMON THYME PESTO (PAGE 250).

CREAMY LEMON DILL SAUCE

1	CLOVE GARLIC, LIGHTLY CRUSHED	1
PINCH	SALT	PINCH
1/2 CUP	HEAVY OR WHIPPING (35%) CREAM	125 ML
1 TBSP	FRESHLY SQUEEZED LEMON JUICE	15 ML
2 TBSP	CHOPPED FRESH DILL	30 ML
1/2 CUP	MILK	125 ML
1/3 CUP	ALL-PURPOSE FLOUR	75 ML
1 TSP	PAPRIKA	5 ML
1 TSP	SALT	5 ML
1/4 TSP	FRESHLY GROUND BLACK PEPPER	1 ML
1 1/4 LBS	PICKEREL FILLETS, PREFERABLY SKIN-ON (SEE TIP, OPPOSITE), CUT INTO 4 PIECES	625 G
1/4 CUP	OLIVE OIL	60 ML
4	LEMON WEDGES	4

CREAMY LEMON DILL SAUCE: IN A SMALL SAUCEPAN, COMBINE GARLIC, SALT, CREAM AND LEMON JUICE. BRING TO A BOIL OVER MEDIUM HEAT. REDUCE HEAT AND SIMMER FOR ABOUT 15 MINUTES OR UNTIL REDUCED BY ONE-THIRD. DISCARD GARLIC AND STIR IN DILL. KEEP WARM.

PLACE MILK IN A SHALLOW DISH. IN ANOTHER SHALLOW DISH, WHISK TOGETHER FLOUR, PAPRIKA, SALT AND PEPPER. RINSE PICKEREL AND PAT DRY WITH PAPER TOWELS. (IF THE FISH HAS BEEN FROZEN AND THAWED, IT WILL BE QUITE WET, SO BE SURE TO DRY IT WELL.) DIP PICKEREL IN MILK, LETTING EXCESS DRIP OFF. DIP FISH IN SEASONED FLOUR, SHAKING OFF EXCESS. DISCARD EXCESS MILK AND SEASONED FLOUR. IN A LARGE NONSTICK SKILLET, HEAT OIL OVER MEDIUM-HIGH HEAT. COOK PICKEREL, SKIN OR SKINNED SIDE UP, FOR 2 TO 3 MINUTES OR UNTIL GOLDEN BROWN. FLIP FISH OVER, REDUCE HEAT TO MEDIUM AND COOK FOR 1 TO 2 MINUTES OR UNTIL FISH IS BARELY OPAQUE AND IS JUST STARTING TO FLAKE WHEN TESTED WITH A FORK. SERVE IMMEDIATELY WITH A DRIZZLE OF SAUCE AND A LEMON WEDGE FOR GARNISH. SERVES 4.

TIP: DON'T WORRY IF YOU CAN ONLY GET SKINLESS PICKEREL FILLETS — THE COOKING TECHNIQUE AND TIMES ARE THE SAME.

SUCCESS CONSISTS OF GOING FROM FAILURE TO FAILURE WITHOUT LOSS OF ENTHUSIASM.

SALMON WITH
TOMATO CHILI RELISH

THIS TANGY, ASIAN-FLAVORED RELISH BALANCES THE SLIGHTLY OILY TASTE OF SALMON. YOU CAN USE SKIN-ON OR SKINLESS SALMON HERE. SERVE WITH STEAMED RICE AND SUGAR SNAP PEAS WITH LIME AND MINT (PAGE 256).

TOMATO CHILI RELISH

2	LARGE TOMATOES, PEELED (SEE TIP, PAGE 215), QUARTERED AND SEEDED	2
1	CLOVE GARLIC	1
3 TBSP	PACKED BROWN SUGAR	45 ML
1 TSP	MINCED GINGERROOT	5 ML
2 TBSP	RED WINE VINEGAR	30 ML
1/4 TSP	ASIAN CHILI PASTE (SEE TIP, OPPOSITE) OR HOT PEPPER FLAKES	1 ML
1 TBSP	CHOPPED FRESH CILANTRO	15 ML
4	SKIN-ON OR SKINLESS SALMON FILLETS (EACH 5 TO 6 OZ/150 TO 175 G), PREFERABLY CENTER-CUT	4
	SALT AND FRESHLY GROUND BLACK PEPPER	
1 TBSP	VEGETABLE OIL	15 ML

TOMATO CHILI RELISH: IN A FOOD PROCESSOR OR BLENDER, COMBINE TOMATOES, GARLIC, BROWN SUGAR, GINGER, VINEGAR AND CHILI PASTE; PURÉE UNTIL SMOOTH. POUR INTO A SMALL SAUCEPAN AND BRING TO A BOIL OVER HIGH HEAT. REDUCE HEAT AND SIMMER, STIRRING OCCASIONALLY, FOR ABOUT 10 MINUTES OR UNTIL SYRUPY. SKIM OFF ANY FOAM THAT RISES TO THE SURFACE. STIR IN CILANTRO. TRANSFER TO A BOWL AND LET COOL TO ROOM TEMPERATURE.

RINSE SALMON AND PAT DRY WITH PAPER TOWELS.

(IF THE FISH HAS BEEN FROZEN AND THAWED, IT WILL BE QUITE WET, SO BE SURE TO DRY IT WELL.) SEASON WITH SALT AND PEPPER. IN A LARGE NONSTICK SKILLET, HEAT OIL OVER MEDIUM-HIGH HEAT. COOK SALMON, SKIN OR SKINNED SIDE UP, FOR ABOUT 5 MINUTES OR UNTIL GOLDEN BROWN. FLIP SALMON OVER, REDUCE HEAT TO MEDIUM AND COOK FOR 3 MINUTES OR UNTIL FISH IS BARELY OPAQUE AND IS JUST STARTING TO FLAKE WHEN TESTED WITH A FORK. SERVE WITH RELISH SPOONED OVER TOP. SERVES 4.

TIP: ASIAN CHILI PASTE (NOT TO BE CONFUSED WITH SWEET CHILI DIPPING SAUCE) IS A MIX OF CHILE PEPPERS, VINEGAR, SUGAR AND SALT. IT'S A GREAT WAY TO ADD HEAT TO SOUPS, SAUCES AND STIR-FRIES. IT IS FIERY, SO USE IT CAUTIOUSLY. A POPULAR VERSION IS SAMBAL OELEK, USUALLY FOUND IN THE ASIAN FOODS AISLE OF THE SUPERMARKET. A GOOD SUBSTITUTE IS HOT PEPPER FLAKES, ADDED TO TASTE.

TIP: TOMATO CHILI RELISH IS ALSO DELICIOUS WITH CHEESE QUESADILLAS, GRILLED CHICKEN OR GRILLED SHRIMP.

MAKE AHEAD: THE COOLED RELISH CAN BE REFRIGERATED IN AN AIRTIGHT CONTAINER FOR UP TO 2 DAYS. BRING TO ROOM TEMPERATURE BEFORE SERVING.

GOOD MOTHERS LET THEIR CHILDREN LICK THE BEATERS. GREAT MOTHERS TURN THE MIXER OFF FIRST.

THAI POACHED SALMON AND NOODLES

POACHING IS A METHOD OF COOKING IN LIQUID AT VERY LOW HEAT. HERE, IT RESULTS IN MARVELOUSLY MOIST SALMON IN A FRAGRANT SAUCE. THE RECIPE CAN BE DOUBLED IF YOU HAVE COMPANY — JUST BE SURE YOUR GUESTS LIKE SPICY CUISINE.

2	SKINLESS SALMON FILLETS (EACH ABOUT 6 OZ/175 G), PREFERABLY CENTRE-CUT	2
2 TSP	RED THAI CURRY PASTE	10 ML
1 TSP	VEGETABLE OIL	5 ML
2/3 CUP	COCONUT MILK (SEE TIP, OPPOSITE)	150 ML
3/4 CUP	REDUCED-SODIUM CHICKEN BROTH OR HOMEMADE VEGETABLE STOCK (SEE RECIPE, PAGE 90)	175 ML
2 TBSP	FRESHLY SQUEEZED LIME JUICE	30 ML
1 TSP	REDUCED-SODIUM SOY SAUCE	5 ML
1/2 TSP	PACKED BROWN SUGAR	2 ML
1/2 TSP	SALT	2 ML
2 TBSP	CHOPPED FRESH BASIL	30 ML
3 CUPS	MEDIUM EGG NOODLES	750 ML
2	GREEN ONIONS, CHOPPED	2
1/2 CUP	SHREDDED CARROTS	125 ML
	CHOPPED PEANUTS OR TOASTED UNSWEETENED SHREDDED COCONUT	

RINSE SALMON AND PAT DRY WITH PAPER TOWELS. (IF THE FISH HAS BEEN FROZEN AND THAWED, IT WILL BE QUITE WET, SO BE SURE TO DRY IT WELL.) SET ASIDE. IN A NONSTICK SKILLET, HEAT CURRY PASTE AND OIL OVER MEDIUM-HIGH HEAT, STIRRING, FOR ABOUT 20 SECONDS OR UNTIL FRAGRANT. ADD COCONUT MILK, STIRRING TO

DISSOLVE CURRY PASTE. STIR IN BROTH, LIME JUICE, SOY SAUCE, BROWN SUGAR AND SALT; BRING TO A BOIL. REDUCE HEAT AND SIMMER FOR 5 MINUTES. PLACE SALMON IN PAN AND COOK, SPOONING SAUCE OVER TOP OF FISH FREQUENTLY, FOR 6 TO 8 MINUTES OR UNTIL FISH IS BARELY OPAQUE AND IS JUST STARTING TO FLAKE WHEN TESTED WITH A FORK. (MAKE SURE THE SAUCE IS BARELY BUBBLING WHILE THE SALMON COOKS.) PUSH SALMON TO THE SIDE OF THE PAN AND STIR BASIL INTO SAUCE.

MEANWHILE, IN A LARGE POT OF BOILING SALTED WATER, COOK NOODLES ACCORDING TO PACKAGE DIRECTIONS. DRAIN AND DIVIDE NOODLES BETWEEN 2 PLATES. TOP EACH WITH A SALMON FILLET AND SPOON SAUCE OVER TOP. GARNISH WITH GREEN ONIONS, CARROTS AND PEANUTS. SERVES 2.

TIP: COCONUT MILK CREATES A CREAMY SAUCE AND TAMES THE HEAT IN CURRIES. IT'S HIGH IN CALORIES, SO YOU MIGHT WANT TO USE THE REDUCED-FAT (LIGHT) VERSION IN THIS RECIPE. CANS OF COCONUT MILK CAN USUALLY BE FOUND IN EITHER THE ASIAN/ETHNIC FOODS AISLE OR NEAR BAKING INGREDIENTS. ALTHOUGH WE HAVE FROZEN LEFTOVER COCONUT MILK, WE FIND THAT IT SEPARATES DURING THAWING, SO WE DON'T RECOMMEND IT.

TIP: IF YOU USE A SALT-FREE STOCK OR BROTH, YOU MAY WANT TO ADD MORE SALT. SALT IS, IN ANY RECIPE, A MATTER OF PERSONAL PREFERENCE, SO FEEL FREE TO INCREASE OR REDUCE THE QUANTITIES WE SUGGEST.

INDIAN SALMON CAKES

FANTASTIC! THESE MILDLY SPICY FISH CAKES CAN BE EASILY MADE WITH INGREDIENTS IN YOUR PANTRY AND FREEZER. SERVE WITH A DOLLOP OF MANGO CHUTNEY OR PLAIN YOGURT AND MINT, MANGO AND AVOCADO SALAD (PAGE 58). FOR MORE CONSERVATIVE PALATES, TRY THE QUICK CANUCK SALMON CAKES (PAGE 212).

I	CAN (7 OZ/213 G) RED SALMON	I
2 CUPS	FROZEN SHREDDED HASH BROWN POTATOES (NO NEED TO THAW)	500 ML
1/4 CUP	FINELY CHOPPED ONION	60 ML
2 TBSP	ALL-PURPOSE FLOUR	30 ML
2 TBSP	CHOPPED FRESH CILANTRO	30 ML
I	EGG, LIGHTLY BEATEN	I
2 TBSP	MILD OR MEDIUM INDIAN CURRY PASTE (SEE TIP, OPPOSITE)	30 ML
2 TBSP	VEGETABLE OIL	30 ML

PREHEAT OVEN TO 375°F (190°C). LINE A LARGE BAKING SHEET WITH GREASED FOIL. DRAIN SALMON AND PLACE IN LARGE BOWL; REMOVE SKIN AND BONES AND FLAKE FISH WITH A FORK. ADD HASH BROWNS, ONION, FLOUR, CILANTRO, EGG AND CURRY PASTE; MIX THOROUGHLY. DIVIDE SALMON MIXTURE INTO 4 EQUAL PORTIONS AND FORM EACH PORTION INTO A 3/4-INCH (2 CM) THICK PATTY. PLACE ON A PLATE OR CLEAN CHOPPING BOARD. IN A LARGE NONSTICK SKILLET, HEAT OIL OVER MEDIUM-HIGH HEAT. USING A SPATULA, GENTLY LIFT PATTIES INTO THE PAN. FRY FOR ABOUT 3 MINUTES PER SIDE OR UNTIL GOLDEN BROWN. IF THE PATTIES START TO BREAK APART WHEN YOU FLIP THEM, USE THE SPATULA TO GENTLY NUDGE

THEM BACK TOGETHER; THEY'LL FIRM UP AS THEY COOK. IF THE PATTIES START TO BROWN TOO QUICKLY, REDUCE HEAT TO MEDIUM. TRANSFER PATTIES TO PREPARED BAKING SHEET AND BAKE FOR 10 TO 12 MINUTES OR UNTIL HEATED THROUGH. SERVE IMMEDIATELY. MAKES 4 PATTIES.

TIP: INDIAN CURRY PASTES ARE NOW WIDELY AVAILABLE AND CAN USUALLY BE FOUND IN THE ASIAN FOODS AISLE. WE PARTICULARLY LIKE THE PATAK'S BRAND OF PASTES, WHICH COME IN MILD, MEDIUM AND HOT. CURRY PASTE IS PREFERABLE TO CURRY POWDER BECAUSE THE SPICES ARE PRESERVED IN OIL AND HAVE A MORE AUTHENTIC, LESS HARSH TASTE. ONCE OPENED, JARS OF CURRY PASTE WILL KEEP IN THE REFRIGERATOR FOR UP TO 6 MONTHS.

TIP: FOR AN EASY WAY TO DIVIDE AND FORM THE SALMON MIXTURE INTO 4 EQUAL PORTIONS, SCOOP IT WITH A $1/2$-CUP (125 ML) DRY MEASURING CUP, PACKING AND LEVELING THE CUP. TURN THE FILLED CUP OVER YOUR OPEN HAND AND GENTLY SHAKE THE CUP TO RELEASE THE MEASURED MIXTURE. USE BOTH HANDS TO FINISH SHAPING THE CAKE.

MESSAGE IN CHINESE FORTUNE COOKIE:
IGNORE PREVIOUS COOKIE.

QUICK CANUCK SALMON CAKES

THESE TASTY FISH CAKES ARE FAST, FABULOUS AND INEXPENSIVE — IDEAL FOR A MIDWEEK MEAL. SERVE WITH SAUTÉED CHERRY TOMATOES AND CORN (PAGE 257). FOR MORE ADVENTUROUS EATERS, TRY THE INDIAN SALMON CAKES (PAGE 210).

1	CAN (7 OZ/213 G) RED SALMON	1
2 CUPS	FROZEN SHREDDED HASH BROWN POTATOES (NO NEED TO DEFROST)	500 ML
1/4 CUP	FINELY CHOPPED ONION	60 ML
2 TBSP	CHOPPED FRESH PARSLEY	30 ML
1 TBSP	ALL-PURPOSE FLOUR	15 ML
1	EGG, LIGHTLY BEATEN	1
	FINELY GRATED ZEST OF 1/2 LEMON	
2 TBSP	FRESHLY SQUEEZED LEMON JUICE	30 ML
1 TBSP	DIJON MUSTARD	15 ML
1/2 TSP	HOT PEPPER SAUCE	2 ML
2 TBSP	VEGETABLE OIL	30 ML

PREHEAT OVEN TO 375°F (190°C). LINE A LARGE BAKING SHEET WITH GREASED FOIL. DRAIN SALMON AND PLACE IN LARGE BOWL; REMOVE SKIN AND BONES AND FLAKE FISH WITH A FORK. ADD HASH BROWNS, ONION, PARSLEY, FLOUR, EGG, LEMON ZEST, LEMON JUICE, MUSTARD AND HOT PEPPER SAUCE; MIX THOROUGHLY. DIVIDE SALMON MIXTURE INTO 4 EQUAL PORTIONS AND FORM EACH PORTION INTO A 3/4-INCH (2 CM) THICK PATTY. PLACE ON A PLATE OR CLEAN CHOPPING BOARD. IN A LARGE NONSTICK SKILLET, HEAT OIL OVER MEDIUM-HIGH HEAT. USING A SPATULA, GENTLY LIFT PATTIES INTO THE PAN. FRY FOR ABOUT 3 MINUTES PER SIDE OR UNTIL GOLDEN BROWN.

IF THE PATTIES START TO BREAK APART WHEN YOU FLIP THEM, USE THE SPATULA TO GENTLY NUDGE THEM BACK TOGETHER; THEY'LL FIRM UP AS THEY COOK. IF THE PATTIES START TO BROWN TOO QUICKLY, REDUCE HEAT TO MEDIUM. TRANSFER PATTIES TO PREPARED BAKING SHEET AND BAKE FOR 10 TO 12 MINUTES OR UNTIL HEATED THROUGH. SERVE IMMEDIATELY. MAKES 4 PATTIES.

TIP: FOR AN EASY WAY TO DIVIDE AND FORM THE SALMON MIXTURE INTO 4 EQUAL PORTIONS, SCOOP IT WITH A $\frac{1}{2}$-CUP (125 ML) DRY MEASURING CUP, PACKING AND LEVELING THE CUP. TURN THE FILLED CUP OVER YOUR OPEN HAND AND GENTLY SHAKE THE CUP TO RELEASE THE MEASURED MIXTURE. USE BOTH HANDS TO FINISH SHAPING THE CAKE.

ASK NOT WHAT YOUR MOTHER CAN DO FOR YOU –
ASK WHAT YOU CAN DO FOR YOUR MOTHER.

RED SNAPPER WITH FRESH TOMATO BASIL SAUCE

THE FRESH-TASTING SAUCE THAT ACCOMPANIES THESE SNAPPER FILLETS ALSO WORKS WELL WITH COD AND HALIBUT. SERVE WITH LIGHT CHIVE MASHED POTATO (PAGE 266) AND ORANGE HERB CARROT RIBBONS (PAGE 254).

4	SKIN-ON OR SKINLESS RED SNAPPER FILLETS (EACH ABOUT 6 OZ/175 G)	4
	SALT AND FRESHLY GROUND BLACK PEPPER	
4	SLICES BACON, CHOPPED	4
2 TBSP	VEGETABLE OIL	30 ML
2	CLOVES GARLIC, MINCED	2
3/4 CUP	DRY WHITE WINE OR REDUCED-SODIUM CHICKEN BROTH	175 ML
3	TOMATOES, PEELED (SEE TIP, OPPOSITE), SEEDED AND ROUGHLY CHOPPED	3
1/4 CUP	CHOPPED FRESH BASIL OR PARSLEY	60 ML

RINSE SNAPPER AND PAT DRY WITH PAPER TOWELS. (IF THE FISH HAS BEEN FROZEN AND THAWED, IT WILL BE QUITE WET, SO DRY IT WELL.) SEASON WITH SALT AND PEPPER. SET ASIDE. IN A LARGE NONSTICK SKILLET, SAUTÉ BACON OVER MEDIUM-HIGH HEAT UNTIL CRISPY. USING A SLOTTED SPOON, TRANSFER BACON TO A PLATE LINED WITH PAPER TOWELS. DRAIN OFF AND RESERVE 1 TSP (5 ML) BACON FAT. WIPE OUT SKILLET WITH A PAPER TOWEL. ADD OIL TO SKILLET AND HEAT OVER MEDIUM-HIGH HEAT. ADD SNAPPER, SKIN OR SKINNED SIDE UP, AND COOK FOR ABOUT 5 MINUTES OR UNTIL GOLDEN BROWN. FLIP SNAPPER OVER, REDUCE HEAT TO MEDIUM AND COOK FOR 3 MINUTES OR UNTIL FISH IS BARELY OPAQUE AND

IS JUST STARTING TO FLAKE WHEN TESTED WITH A FORK. TRANSFER FISH TO A PLATE AND KEEP WARM. ADD RESERVED BACON FAT TO SKILLET AND SAUTÉ GARLIC FOR 15 SECONDS OR UNTIL FRAGRANT. ADD WINE AND BRING TO A BOIL; BOIL UNTIL REDUCED TO ABOUT 2 TBSP (30 ML). STIR IN TOMATOES AND RESERVED BACON; BRING TO A BOIL. REDUCE HEAT AND SIMMER FOR ABOUT 5 MINUTES OR UNTIL TOMATOES HAVE SOFTENED AND ARE JUICY AND HEATED THROUGH BUT NOT MUSHY. STIR IN BASIL. TASTE AND ADJUST SEASONING WITH SALT AND PEPPER, IF DESIRED (BUT REMEMBER THAT THE BACON ADDS QUITE A BIT OF SALTINESS). SPOON SAUCE ONTO EACH PLATE AND NESTLE A SNAPPER FILLET ON TOP OF EACH. SERVES 4.

TIP: TO PEEL FRESH TOMATOES, CUT AN X IN THE SKIN AT THE BOTTOM OF EACH TOMATO. PLUNGE INTO BOILING WATER FOR ABOUT 15 SECONDS. USING TONGS OR A SLOTTED SPOON, TRANSFER TOMATOES TO A BOWL OF ICE WATER TO STOP THE COOKING PROCESS. STARTING FROM THE X, PEEL OFF SKINS USING A PARING KNIFE.

IT'S GREAT TO HAVE GRAY HAIR.
ASK ANYONE WHO'S BALD.

— POTATO-CRUSTED TILAPIA —

OUR GOLDEN CRISPY COATING HAS A UNIQUE
INGREDIENT (MASHED POTATO FLAKES) THAT
MAKES FISH TASTE GREAT! IT ALSO WORKS WELL
WITH SOLE, PICKEREL OR YOUR FAVORITE MILD
WHITE FISH. SERVE WITH SAUTÉED CHERRY
TOMATOES AND CORN (PAGE 257).

3 TBSP	ALL-PURPOSE FLOUR	45 ML
I TSP	PAPRIKA	5 ML
I TSP	SALT	5 ML
$1/2$ TSP	GARLIC POWDER	2 ML
$1/4$ TSP	FRESHLY GROUND BLACK PEPPER	I ML
$1/2$ CUP	MILK	125 ML
I CUP	INSTANT (DRIED) MASHED POTATO FLAKES	250 ML
4	SKINLESS TILAPIA FILLETS (EACH ABOUT 6 OZ/175 G)	4
$1/4$ CUP	VEGETABLE OIL	60 ML
	LEMON WEDGES	
	TARTAR SAUCE (SEE RECIPE, OPPOSITE)	

IN A SHALLOW DISH, WHISK TOGETHER FLOUR, PAPRIKA,
SALT, GARLIC POWDER AND PEPPER. PLACE MILK IN
ANOTHER DISH. PLACE POTATO FLAKES IN A THIRD DISH.
RINSE TILAPIA AND PAT DRY WITH PAPER TOWELS. (IF
THE FISH HAS BEEN FROZEN AND THAWED, IT WILL BE
QUITE WET, SO BE SURE TO DRY IT WELL.) DIP TILAPIA IN
SEASONED FLOUR, SHAKING OFF EXCESS. DIP FISH IN MILK,
LETTING EXCESS DRIP OFF. THEN DIP FISH IN POTATO
FLAKES, PRESSING GENTLY SO THEY ADHERE TO BOTH
SIDES. DISCARD EXCESS SEASONED FLOUR, MILK AND
POTATO FLAKES. IN A LARGE NONSTICK SKILLET, HEAT

OIL OVER MEDIUM-HIGH HEAT. COOK TILAPIA FOR 2 TO
3 MINUTES OR UNTIL CRUST IS GOLDEN BROWN. FLIP FISH
OVER AND COOK FOR 1 TO 2 MINUTES OR UNTIL CRUST
IS GOLDEN BROWN AND FISH IS JUST STARTING TO
FLAKE WHEN TESTED WITH A FORK. SERVE IMMEDIATELY
WITH LEMON WEDGES AND TARTAR SAUCE ON THE SIDE.
SERVES 4.

TARTAR SAUCE

HOMEMADE TARTAR SAUCE IS REALLY EASY TO STIR
TOGETHER AND TASTES MUCH BETTER THAN THE
STUFF FROM A JAR. IF YOU ARE MAKING THE EFFORT
TO COOK FRESH FISH, IT'S WORTH TAKING A FEW EXTRA
MINUTES TO MAKE THIS ACCOMPANIMENT.

2 TBSP	FINELY CHOPPED DILL PICKLES	30 ML
2 TBSP	FINELY CHOPPED GREEN ONION	30 ML
1 TBSP	DRAINED CAPERS	15 ML
1/4 TSP	SALT	1 ML
	FRESHLY GROUND BLACK PEPPER	
1/2 CUP	MAYONNAISE	125 ML
2 TBSP	HEAVY OR WHIPPING (35%) CREAM	30 ML
2 TSP	JUICE FROM CAPER JAR	10 ML

IN A SMALL BOWL, WHISK TOGETHER PICKLES, GREEN
ONION, CAPERS, SALT, PEPPER TO TASTE, MAYONNAISE,
WHIPPING CREAM AND CAPER JUICE. COVER AND
REFRIGERATE FOR AT LEAST 30 MINUTES OR FOR UP TO
3 DAYS. MAKES ABOUT 1 CUP (250 ML).

LEMON NUT-CRUSTED TROUT

THIS RECIPE IS FAST ENOUGH FOR MIDWEEK, YET IMPRESSIVE ENOUGH FOR COMPANY. SERVE WITH STEAMED NEW POTATOES AND GREEN PEAS.

4	SKIN-ON RAINBOW TROUT FILLETS (EACH ABOUT 5 OZ/150 G)	4
	SALT AND FRESHLY GROUND BLACK PEPPER	
3/4 CUP	PANKO (SEE TIP, PAGE 319) OR DRY BREAD CRUMBS	175 ML
2 TBSP	CHOPPED FRESH PARSLEY	30 ML
2 TBSP	PINE NUTS OR SLICED OR SLIVERED ALMONDS	30 ML
	FINELY GRATED ZEST OF 1/2 LEMON	
2 TBSP	FRESHLY SQUEEZED LEMON JUICE	30 ML
2 TBSP	OLIVE OIL	30 ML
	LEMON WEDGES	

PREHEAT OVEN TO 475°F (240°C). LINE A LARGE BAKING SHEET WITH GREASED FOIL. RINSE TROUT AND PAT DRY WITH PAPER TOWELS. (IF THE FISH HAS BEEN FROZEN, IT WILL BE QUITE WET, SO BE SURE TO DRY IT WELL.) LAY TROUT, SKIN SIDE DOWN, ON PREPARED BAKING SHEET. SEASON WITH SALT AND PEPPER. IN A BOWL, COMBINE PANKO, PARSLEY, PINE NUTS, LEMON ZEST, LEMON JUICE AND OIL. (THE CRUMBS MIGHT CLUMP TOGETHER SLIGHTLY.) DIVIDE PANKO MIXTURE EVENLY OVER TROUT, PATTING DOWN GENTLY TO KEEP IT IN PLACE. BAKE FOR ABOUT 5 MINUTES OR UNTIL CRUST IS LIGHTLY BROWNED AND FISH IS JUST STARTING TO FLAKE WHEN TESTED WITH A FORK. SERVE IMMEDIATELY WITH LEMON WEDGES. SERVES 4.

PIZZA AND PASTA

MAKE-AHEAD EASY
WHOLE WHEAT PIZZA DOUGH

EFFORTLESS, LOW-COST AND DELICIOUS.

1 1/4 TO 1 1/2 CUPS	ALL-PURPOSE FLOUR	300 TO 375 ML
1 CUP	WHOLE WHEAT FLOUR	250 ML
2 1/4 TSP	QUICK-RISE INSTANT YEAST (ONE 1/4-OZ/8 G ENVELOPE))	11 ML
3/4 TSP	SALT	3 ML
1 CUP	VERY WARM WATER (SEE TIP, OPPOSITE)	250 ML
2 TBSP	OLIVE OIL	30 ML

IN A LARGE BOWL, WHISK TOGETHER 1 CUP (250 ML) ALL-PURPOSE FLOUR, WHOLE WHEAT FLOUR, YEAST AND SALT. USING CLEAN, DRY HANDS, MIX IN WARM WATER AND OIL. MIX IN ENOUGH OF THE REMAINING ALL-PURPOSE FLOUR TO MAKE THE DOUGH SOFT AND NO LONGER STICKY. (SOME OF THE DOUGH WILL STICK TO YOUR FINGERS; JUST PULL IT OFF WITH YOUR OTHER HAND AND ADD IT BACK INTO THE BOWL. THIS IS FUN!) TURN THE DOUGH OUT ONTO A LIGHTLY FLOURED WORK SURFACE AND KNEAD FOR 2 OR 3 MINUTES OR UNTIL SMOOTH. (TO KNEAD, USE ONE HAND TO GENTLY STRETCH THE EDGE OF THE DOUGH OUT A LITTLE WAY WITHOUT TEARING IT. USE YOUR OTHER HAND TO STEADY THE BALL OF DOUGH. FOLD AND PRESS THE STRETCHED AREA OF DOUGH BACK INTO THE BALL. REPEAT, TURNING THE DOUGH SLIGHTLY WITH EACH STRETCH.) COVER DOUGH WITH PLASTIC WRAP AND LET REST FOR 10 MINUTES BEFORE ROLLING. MAKES ENOUGH DOUGH FOR ONE 14-INCH (35 CM) THICK-CRUST PIZZA OR TWO 12-INCH (30 CM) THIN-CRUST PIZZAS.

FOR A THICK-CRUST PIZZA: PREHEAT OVEN TO 400°F (200°C). LIGHTLY OIL A 14-INCH (35 CM) PIZZA PAN. ON A LIGHTLY FLOURED WORK SURFACE, ROLL OUT THE FULL BATCH OF DOUGH TO FIT PAN. PLACE ON PREPARED PAN, COVER LOOSELY WITH PLASTIC WRAP TO PREVENT THE TOP FROM DRYING OUT AND LET RISE AT ROOM TEMPERATURE FOR 30 TO 45 MINUTES. BAKE FOR 10 MINUTES. REMOVE FROM OVEN AND ADD TOPPINGS. BAKE FOR 10 TO 20 MINUTES, DEPENDING ON TOPPINGS.

FOR TWO THIN-CRUST PIZZAS: PREHEAT OVEN TO 400°F (200°C). LIGHTLY OIL TWO 12-INCH (30 CM) PIZZA PANS. DIVIDE DOUGH IN HALF. ON A LIGHTLY FLOURED WORK SURFACE, ROLL OUT DOUGH TO FIT PANS. PLACE ON PREPARED PANS, ADD TOPPINGS AND BAKE FOR 10 TO 12 MINUTES, DEPENDING ON TOPPINGS.

TIP: TO ACTIVATE QUICK-RISE INSTANT YEAST, THE WATER NEEDS TO BE BETWEEN 120°F AND 130°F (49°C AND 54°C). TEMPERATURES VARY FOR OTHER TYPES OF YEAST. A THERMOMETER IS THE BEST WAY TO TEST THE TEMPERATURE. ALTERNATIVELY, USE VERY WARM TAP WATER — IF IT IS TOO HOT TO HOLD YOUR HAND UNDER, IT IS PROBABLY JUST RIGHT FOR THE QUICK-RISE YEAST.

MAKE AHEAD: PLACE DOUGH IN A LIGHTLY OILED AIRTIGHT CONTAINER AND REFRIGERATE FOR UP TO 24 HOURS. THE DOUGH WILL RISE TO ABOUT DOUBLE ITS BULK, SO MAKE SURE IT HAS ROOM TO GROW! OR FREEZE DOUGH IN A PLASTIC BAG FOR UP TO 1 MONTH; THAW IN THE REFRIGERATOR OVERNIGHT.

SWEET POTATO AND BACON PIZZA

SWEET POTATO ON A PIZZA? WITH BACON, SAGE AND CHEESE, IT'S A WINNER.

3	SLICES BACON, CHOPPED	3
1/2	LARGE RED ONION, THINLY SLICED	1/2
I CUP	THINLY SLICED SWEET POTATO (SEE TIP, OPPOSITE)	250 ML
	COLD WATER	
I TBSP	GRANULATED SUGAR	15 ML
I	CLOVE GARLIC, MINCED	I
2 TBSP	CHOPPED FRESH SAGE (OR 3/4 TSP/ 3 ML CRUMBLED DRIED SAGE)	30 ML
1/2 TSP	SALT	2 ML
	FRESHLY GROUND BLACK PEPPER	
I	UNBAKED 12- TO 14-INCH (30 TO 35 CM) PIZZA CRUST (STORE-BOUGHT OR SEE RECIPE, PAGE 220)	I
I TBSP	OLIVE OIL	15 ML
1/2 CUP	FRESHLY GRATED PARMESAN CHEESE	125 ML
1 1/4 CUPS	SHREDDED FONTINA, PROVOLONE OR MOZZARELLA CHEESE	300 ML

PREHEAT OVEN TO 400°F (200°C). LIGHTLY OIL A 12- OR 14-INCH (30 OR 35 CM) PIZZA PAN. IN A LARGE NONSTICK SKILLET, SAUTÉ BACON OVER MEDIUM-HIGH HEAT UNTIL CRISPY. USING A SLOTTED SPOON, TRANSFER BACON TO A PLATE LINED WITH PAPER TOWELS. DRAIN OFF ALL BUT I TBSP (15 ML) OF THE FAT. REDUCE HEAT TO LOW. ADD RED ONION AND SWEET POTATO, STIRRING TO COAT WITH FAT. ADD 1/4 CUP (60 ML) COLD WATER, COVER AND COOK, STIRRING FREQUENTLY, FOR 8 TO 10 MINUTES OR UNTIL VEGETABLES ARE SOFTENED. IF NECESSARY, ADD MORE

WATER, 1 TBSP (15 ML) AT A TIME, TO KEEP VEGETABLES FROM STICKING TO THE PAN. UNCOVER, SPRINKLE WITH SUGAR AND COOK, STIRRING FREQUENTLY, FOR 3 TO 5 MINUTES OR UNTIL SWEET POTATO STARTS TO BROWN AND LIQUID HAS EVAPORATED. STIR IN GARLIC, SAGE, SALT AND PEPPER TO TASTE; COOK FOR 15 SECONDS OR UNTIL FRAGRANT. TRANSFER VEGETABLES TO A PLATE AND LET COOL SLIGHTLY. PLACE PIZZA CRUST ON PREPARED PAN AND BRUSH WITH OIL. SPREAD SWEET POTATO MIXTURE EVENLY OVER CRUST. TOP WITH RESERVED BACON. SPRINKLE WITH PARMESAN AND FONTINA. BAKE FOR 10 TO 14 MINUTES OR UNTIL CRUST IS BROWNED AND SLIGHTLY PUFFED AND CHEESE IS BUBBLY. MAKES 8 SLICES.

TIP: TO SLICE THE SWEET POTATO INTO PIECES THAT ARE AN APPEALING SIZE FOR THE PIZZA, CUT THE PEELED SWEET POTATO INTO QUARTERS LENGTHWISE, THEN CUT EACH QUARTER INTO SLICES THE THICKNESS OF A $1 COIN.

MAKE AHEAD: STORE THE COOLED COOKED BACON AND THE COOLED COOKED SWEET POTATO MIXTURE IN SEPARATE AIRTIGHT CONTAINERS IN THE REFRIGERATOR FOR UP TO 2 DAYS.

VARIATION
SWEET POTATO, SPINACH AND BACON PIZZA: WHEN ASSEMBLING THE PIZZA, SPRINKLE 1 CUP (250 ML) PACKED BABY SPINACH OVER THE SWEET POTATOES BEFORE ADDING THE BACON AND CHEESES.

WHY DOES SOMEONE BELIEVE YOU WHEN YOU SAY THERE ARE 4 BILLION STARS, BUT CHECK WHEN YOU SAY THE PAINT IS WET?

CHICKEN FIESTA PIZZA

WITH ITS TEX-MEX FLAIR AND JUST A LITTLE BIT OF HEAT, THIS PIZZA DELIVERS FUN FOR FAMILY MOVIE NIGHT OR A KIDS' SLEEPOVER.

1	CLOVE GARLIC, MINCED	1
1/2 TSP	GROUND CUMIN	2 ML
1/2 TSP	SALT	2 ML
1/4 TSP	CAYENNE PEPPER	1 ML
2 TBSP	OLIVE OIL, DIVIDED	30 ML
1	RED BELL PEPPER, THINLY SLICED	1
1/2	LARGE RED ONION, THINLY SLICED	1/2
1 CUP	FROZEN CORN KERNELS (NO NEED TO THAW)	250 ML
1 TO 2 TBSP	COLD WATER (IF NEEDED)	15 TO 30 ML
1	LARGE BONELESS SKINLESS CHICKEN BREAST (ABOUT 8 OZ/250 G), THINLY SLICED	1
1	UNBAKED 12- TO 14-INCH (30 TO 35 CM) PIZZA CRUST (STORE-BOUGHT OR SEE RECIPE, PAGE 220)	1
1/2 CUP	SALSA	125 ML
1/2 CUP	DRAINED SLICED PICKLED JALAPEÑO PEPPERS (OPTIONAL)	125 ML
1 1/2 CUPS	SHREDDED TEX-MEX CHEESE BLEND, JALAPEÑO JACK CHEESE OR MOZZARELLA CHEESE	375 ML

PREHEAT OVEN TO 400°F (200°C). LIGHTLY OIL A 12- OR 14-INCH (30 OR 35 CM) PIZZA PAN. IN A SMALL BOWL, COMBINE GARLIC, CUMIN, SALT AND CAYENNE. SET ASIDE. IN A LARGE NONSTICK SKILLET, HEAT 1 TBSP (15 ML) OIL OVER MEDIUM HEAT. ADD RED PEPPER, RED ONION

AND CORN; COOK, STIRRING OCCASIONALLY, FOR 5 TO 7 MINUTES OR UNTIL VEGETABLES ARE SOFTENED AND LIGHTLY BROWNED. IF VEGETABLES START TO STICK, ADD COLD WATER AS NEEDED. TRANSFER TO A BOWL AND SET ASIDE. WIPE OUT SKILLET WITH PAPER TOWELS. ADD THE REMAINING OIL TO THE SKILLET AND HEAT OVER MEDIUM HEAT. SAUTÉ CHICKEN FOR ABOUT 5 MINUTES OR UNTIL BROWNED ON ALL SIDES AND NO LONGER PINK INSIDE. ADD GARLIC MIXTURE AND COOK, STIRRING, FOR ABOUT 30 SECONDS OR UNTIL CHICKEN IS COATED AND FRAGRANT. STIR CHICKEN INTO BOWL WITH VEGETABLES. LET COOL FOR 15 MINUTES. PLACE PIZZA CRUST ON PREPARED PAN. SPREAD SALSA EVENLY OVER CRUST. TOP WITH CHICKEN MIXTURE. SPRINKLE WITH JALAPEÑOS, IF USING. TOP WITH TEX-MEX CHEESE. BAKE FOR 12 TO 14 MINUTES OR UNTIL CRUST IS BROWNED AND SLIGHTLY PUFFED AND CHEESE IS BUBBLY. MAKES 8 SLICES.

TIP: THIS PIZZA HAS A LOT OF TOPPINGS, SO IT TAKES LONGER TO COOK THAN SOME.

MAKE AHEAD: AFTER COOKING AND COMBINING THE CHICKEN AND VEGETABLES, LET COOL, TRANSFER TO AN AIRTIGHT CONTAINER AND REFRIGERATE FOR UP TO 1 DAY.

A WOMAN HAS THE LAST WORD IN ANY ARGUMENT. ANYTHING A MAN SAYS AFTER THAT IS THE BEGINNING OF A NEW ARGUMENT.

ROASTED VEGETABLE CALZONES

*EVERYONE LOVES THESE POCKET-SHAPED
PIZZAS. THEY ARE PERFECT FOR A QUICK
SUPPER OR FOR LUNCH BOXES.*

1	RED ONION, CHOPPED	1
1	RED BELL PEPPER, CHOPPED	1
1	ZUCCHINI, CHOPPED	1
1 1/2 CUPS	SLICED MUSHROOMS	375 ML
1/2 TSP	DRIED OREGANO	2 ML
1/2 TSP	SALT	2 ML
PINCH	HOT PEPPER FLAKES (OPTIONAL)	PINCH
	FRESHLY GROUND BLACK PEPPER	
2 TBSP	OLIVE OIL	30 ML
2 TBSP	BALSAMIC VINEGAR	30 ML
1 CUP	SHREDDED MOZZARELLA CHEESE	250 ML
1/2 CUP	FRESHLY GRATED PARMESAN CHEESE	125 ML
	MAKE-AHEAD EASY WHOLE WHEAT PIZZA DOUGH (SEE RECIPE, PAGE 220) OR 2 LBS (1 KG) STORE-BOUGHT PIZZA DOUGH (THAWED IF FROZEN)	
	MILK	
2 TBSP	CORNMEAL	30 ML

PREHEAT OVEN TO 425°F (220°C). LIGHTLY OIL 2 LARGE
BAKING SHEETS. IN A LARGE BOWL, COMBINE RED ONION,
RED PEPPER, ZUCCHINI, MUSHROOMS, OREGANO, SALT, HOT
PEPPER FLAKES AND BLACK PEPPER TO TASTE. ADD OIL AND
TOSS TO COAT. SPREAD VEGETABLES IN A SINGLE LAYER ON
PREPARED BAKING SHEETS. ROAST, STIRRING OCCASIONALLY,
FOR 30 TO 35 MINUTES OR UNTIL VEGETABLES ARE
SOFTENED AND BROWNED. TRANSFER TO A BOWL
AND TOSS WITH VINEGAR. LET COOL FOR 15 MINUTES.

(THE VEGETABLES CAN PREPARED AHEAD UP TO THIS POINT. LET COOL COMPLETELY AND REFRIGERATE FOR UP TO 2 DAYS.) STIR IN MOZZARELLA AND PARMESAN.

MEANWHILE, DIVIDE DOUGH INTO 4 PIECES. ON A LIGHTLY FLOURED WORK SURFACE, ROLL OUT ONE PIECE OF DOUGH INTO AN 8- BY 5-INCH (20 BY 12.5 CM) OBLONG. SPREAD ONE-QUARTER OF THE ROASTED VEGETABLE MIXTURE OVER LOWER HALF OF DOUGH, LEAVING A $\frac{1}{2}$-INCH (1 CM) BORDER. FOLD TOP HALF OF DOUGH OVER FILLING AND PINCH EDGES TO SEAL. CUT 3 SLITS IN TOP OF CALZONE TO ALLOW STEAM TO ESCAPE. BRUSH LIGHTLY WITH MILK. REPEAT WITH THE REMAINING DOUGH AND FILLING. SPRINKLE CORNMEAL OVER AN UNGREASED LARGE BAKING SHEET. PLACE CALZONES ON BAKING SHEET. BAKE FOR 12 TO 15 MINUTES OR UNTIL BROWNED. SERVE IMMEDIATELY OR TRANSFER TO A WIRE RACK TO COOL COMPLETELY. MAKES 4 CALZONES.

MAKE AHEAD: LET BAKED CALZONES COOL, THEN WRAP INDIVIDUALLY IN PLASTIC WRAP AND PLACE IN AN AIRTIGHT CONTAINER. REFRIGERATE FOR UP TO 2 DAYS OR FREEZE FOR UP TO 1 MONTH.

VARIATION: THE ROASTED VEGETABLES ALSO WORK WELL AS A PIZZA TOPPING. AFTER COOKING THE VEGETABLES, ADD THE BALSAMIC VINEGAR AND PARMESAN CHEESE, BUT NOT THE MOZZARELLA. SPREAD THE VEGETABLE MIXTURE OVER AN UNBAKED 12-INCH (30 CM) PIZZA CRUST, SPRINKLE WITH THE MOZZARELLA AND BAKE IN A PREHEATED 400°F (200°C) OVEN FOR 10 TO 14 MINUTES OR UNTIL CRUST IS BROWNED AND SLIGHTLY PUFFED AND CHEESE IS BUBBLY.

A BOWLFUL OF DINNER

CONVENIENT AND KID-FRIENDLY ASIAN SOUP NOODLES GET A MAKEOVER IN THIS EASY RECIPE. DITCH THE SEASONING PACKETS AND COMBINE THE NOODLES WITH TASTY MARINATED BEEF AND NUTRITIOUS VEGGIES — DINNER IN A BOWL. WHAT A CLEVER PARENT YOU ARE!

MARINADE

1	CLOVE GARLIC, MINCED	1
1 TBSP	GRANULATED SUGAR	15 ML
$1/4$ TSP	MINCED GINGERROOT	1 ML
	GRATED ZEST OF 1 LEMON	
2 TBSP	REDUCED-SODIUM SOY SAUCE	30 ML
1 TBSP	VEGETABLE OIL	15 ML
1 LB	BONELESS BEEF TOP SIRLOIN GRILLING STEAK, CUT ACROSS THE GRAIN INTO $1/8$-INCH (3 MM) THICK SLICES (SEE TIP, OPPOSITE)	500 G
1 TBSP	VEGETABLE OIL	15 ML
3 CUPS	SLICED CREMINI MUSHROOMS (SEE TIP, OPPOSITE)	750 ML
2	CLOVES GARLIC, MINCED	2
1 TBSP	MINCED GINGERROOT	15 ML
1	CARROT, THINLY SLICED	1
4 CUPS	REDUCED-SODIUM BEEF OR CHICKEN BROTH	1 L
4	PACKAGES (EACH 3 OZ/85 G) INSTANT (RAMEN) SOUP NOODLES, SEASONING PACKETS DISCARDED	4
5 CUPS	CHOPPED BOK CHOY (ABOUT 1 LB/500 G)	1.25 L
2	GREEN ONIONS, CHOPPED	2

MARINADE: IN A BOWL, WHISK TOGETHER GARLIC, SUGAR, GINGER, LEMON ZEST, SOY SAUCE AND OIL. ADD BEEF TO

MARINADE AND STIR TO COAT EVENLY. SET ASIDE.

IN A LARGE SAUCEPAN, HEAT OIL OVER MEDIUM HEAT. SAUTÉ MUSHROOMS FOR 5 MINUTES OR UNTIL STARTING TO BROWN. ADD GARLIC AND GINGER; SAUTÉ FOR 15 SECONDS OR UNTIL FRAGRANT. ADD CARROT AND BROTH; BRING TO A BOIL. REDUCE HEAT AND SIMMER FOR 3 MINUTES OR UNTIL CARROT HAS SOFTENED SLIGHTLY. STIR IN NOODLES AND BOK CHOY; INCREASE HEAT TO HIGH AND BRING TO A BOIL. REDUCE HEAT TO LOW, COVER AND SIMMER FOR 2 TO 3 MINUTES OR UNTIL NOODLES AND BOK CHOY ARE TENDER BUT NOT MUSHY AND LIQUID IS ALMOST ABSORBED.

MEANWHILE, HEAT A LARGE NONSTICK SKILLET OVER MEDIUM-HIGH HEAT. ADD BEEF MIXTURE AND COOK, STIRRING FREQUENTLY, FOR 3 TO 4 MINUTES OR UNTIL BROWNED BUT STILL SLIGHTLY PINK INSIDE. SERVE NOODLES IN BOWLS, TOPPED WITH BEEF AND SPRINKLED WITH GREEN ONIONS. SERVES 4.

TIP: TO MAKE THE STEAK EASIER TO SLICE THINLY, PLACE IT IN THE FREEZER FOR 30 MINUTES.

TIP: CREMINI MUSHROOMS (SOMETIMES LABELED "BROWN MUSHROOMS") ARE ACTUALLY MINI PORTOBELLO MUSHROOMS, BUT ARE LESS EXPENSIVE. CREMINIS HAVE A DEEPER FLAVOR THAN REGULAR MUSHROOMS, BUT USE WHITE MUSHROOMS IF YOU PREFER.

VARIATION: USE 8 OZ (250 G) SUGAR SNAP PEAS, TRIMMED AND CUT IN HALF DIAGONALLY, IN PLACE OF THE BOK CHOY.

EASY BEEF AND SPINACH PASTA BAKE

THIS DISH CAN BE ASSEMBLED AHEAD OF TIME, AND IT FEEDS A GROUP.

I LB	LEAN GROUND BEEF	500 G
2	CLOVES GARLIC, MINCED	2
1/2 CUP	FINELY CHOPPED ONION	125 ML
2	JARS (EACH 24 OZ/700 ML) TOMATO PASTA SAUCE	2
I	JAR (12 OZ/340 ML) ROASTED RED BELL PEPPERS, DRAINED AND CHOPPED	I
I TO 1 1/2 CUPS	REDUCED-SODIUM BEEF OR CHICKEN BROTH, HOMEMADE VEGETABLE STOCK (SEE RECIPE, PAGE 90) OR WATER	250 TO 375 ML
I TSP	SALT	5 ML
1/2 TSP	DRIED OREGANO OR BASIL	2 ML
PINCH	HOT PEPPER FLAKES	PINCH
	FRESHLY GROUND BLACK PEPPER	
1/4 CUP	CHOPPED FRESH PARSLEY	60 ML
12 OZ	PENNE, FUSILLI OR SIMILAR PASTA (ABOUT 4 CUPS/I L)	375 G
I CUP	FRESHLY GRATED PARMESAN CHEESE	250 ML
2 CUPS	SHREDDED MOZZARELLA OR CHEDDAR CHEESE, OR A COMBINATION, DIVIDED	500 ML
4 CUPS	PACKED BABY SPINACH	I L

PREHEAT OVEN TO 375°F (190°C). GREASE A 13- BY 9-INCH (33 BY 23 CM) GLASS BAKING DISH. IN A LARGE SAUCEPAN, OVER MEDIUM-HIGH HEAT, COOK BEEF, BREAKING IT UP WITH A SPOON, FOR 2 TO 3 MINUTES OR UNTIL IT STARTS TO RELEASE JUICES. ADD GARLIC AND ONION; COOK, STIRRING, FOR 5 TO 7 MINUTES OR UNTIL ONION IS SOFTENED AND BEEF IS NO LONGER PINK. DRAIN OFF FAT. ADD PASTA SAUCE, ROASTED PEPPERS, I CUP (250 ML)

BROTH, SALT, OREGANO, HOT PEPPER FLAKES AND BLACK PEPPER TO TASTE; BRING TO A BOIL. REDUCE HEAT AND SIMMER, STIRRING OCCASIONALLY, FOR 20 MINUTES OR UNTIL SLIGHTLY THICKENED. STIR IN PARSLEY. TASTE AND ADJUST SEASONING WITH SALT AND BLACK PEPPER, IF DESIRED.

MEANWHILE, IN A LARGE POT OF BOILING SALTED WATER, COOK PASTA ACCORDING TO PACKAGE DIRECTIONS. DRAIN AND ADD TO MEAT SAUCE. STIR IN PARMESAN AND 1 CUP (250 ML) OF THE MOZZARELLA. CHECK THE CONSISTENCY OF THE PASTA MIXTURE; IF IT HEAPS ON A SPOON, IT IS TOO THICK (THE PASTA WILL ABSORB MORE OF THE SAUCE AS IT BAKES), SO ADD MORE BROTH TO LOOSEN THE CONSISTENCY. SPREAD HALF THE PASTA MIXTURE IN PREPARED BAKING DISH. ADD SPINACH IN AN EVEN LAYER, THEN TOP WITH THE REMAINING PASTA MIXTURE. SPRINKLE THE REMAINING MOZZARELLA OVER TOP. COVER TIGHTLY WITH FOIL AND BAKE FOR 30 MINUTES OR UNTIL BUBBLING AT THE EDGES. REMOVE FOIL AND BAKE FOR 10 MINUTES OR UNTIL CHEESE IS MELTED. LET STAND FOR 15 MINUTES BEFORE SERVING. SERVES 6 TO 8.

TIP: IF YOU USE WATER OR A SALT-FREE STOCK OR BROTH, YOU MAY WANT TO ADD MORE SALT.

MAKE AHEAD: AFTER ASSEMBLING BUT BEFORE BAKING, LET COOL FOR 30 MINUTES, THEN REFRIGERATE, UNCOVERED, UNTIL COLD. COVER TIGHTLY AND KEEP REFRIGERATED FOR UP TO 1 DAY. OR DOUBLE WRAP WITH FOIL AND FREEZE FOR UP TO 2 WEEKS. THAW IN THE REFRIGERATOR FOR 2 DAYS. BAKE, COVERED, FOR 40 TO 50 MINUTES; UNCOVER AND CONTINUE WITH RECIPE.

LIME HONEY PORK AND NOODLES

PICK UP THE INGREDIENTS FROM THE
SUPERMARKET ON THE WAY HOME, AND
DINNER WILL BE ON THE TABLE IN NO TIME.

	FINELY GRATED ZEST OF 1 LIME	
1/2 CUP	FRESHLY SQUEEZED LIME JUICE (SEE TIP, OPPOSITE)	125 ML
1/3 CUP	LIQUID HONEY	75 ML
1 1/2 TBSP	REDUCED-SODIUM SOY SAUCE	22 ML
1/2 TO 1 TSP	ASIAN CHILI PASTE (SEE TIP, PAGE 207) OR HOT PEPPER FLAKES	2 TO 5 ML
2	PORK TENDERLOINS (EACH ABOUT 12 OZ/375 G), THINLY SLICED	2
1 TSP	CORNSTARCH	5 ML
2 TBSP	VEGETABLE OIL	30 ML
4	GREEN ONIONS, CHOPPED	4
1	PACKAGE (12 OZ/340 G) BROCCOLI COLESLAW	1
1	PACKAGE (1 LB/500 G) STEAMED CHINESE NOODLES (SEE TIP, OPPOSITE)	1
1/4 CUP	TOASTED SESAME SEEDS OR SLICED OR SLIVERED ALMONDS (SEE TIP, PAGE 127)	60 ML

IN A SMALL BOWL, WHISK TOGETHER LIME ZEST, LIME
JUICE, HONEY, SOY SAUCE AND CHILI PASTE TO TASTE.
IN ANOTHER BOWL, COMBINE PORK AND 1/4 CUP (60 ML)
OF THE LIME MIXTURE. COVER AND REFRIGERATE FOR
AT LEAST 15 MINUTES OR FOR UP TO 1 HOUR. STIR
CORNSTARCH INTO THE REMAINING LIME MIXTURE AND
SET ASIDE. (THIS IS THE SAUCE.)

IN A LARGE NONSTICK SKILLET, HEAT 1 TBSP (15 ML) OIL
OVER MEDIUM-HIGH HEAT. USING A SLOTTED SPOON,

TRANSFER HALF THE PORK FROM THE MARINADE TO THE PAN, ALLOWING EXCESS LIQUID TO DRAIN BACK INTO THE BOWL. SAUTÉ PORK FOR 4 TO 5 MINUTES OR UNTIL GOLDEN BROWN AND JUST A HINT OF PINK REMAINS INSIDE. (IT WILL BROWN QUICKLY BECAUSE OF THE HONEY IN THE MARINADE.) TRANSFER TO A PLATE. WIPE OUT PAN WITH PAPER TOWELS. (BUT BE CAREFUL — IT'S HOT!) ADD THE REMAINING OIL AND REPEAT WITH THE REMAINING PORK, DISCARDING MARINADE AND LEAVING PORK IN THE PAN ONCE IT'S BROWNED. RETURN FIRST BATCH OF PORK TO THE PAN AND IMMEDIATELY ADD THE RESERVED SAUCE. ADD GREEN ONIONS AND BROCCOLI COLESLAW; TOSS TO COMBINE AND BRING TO A BOIL. REDUCE HEAT AND SIMMER FOR 1 MINUTE.

MEANWHILE, IN A LARGE POT OF BOILING SALTED WATER, COOK NOODLES FOR ABOUT 30 SECONDS. DRAIN AND DIVIDE AMONG 4 DEEP BOWLS OR PLATES. TOP WITH PORK MIXTURE. SPRINKLE WITH SESAME SEEDS AND SERVE IMMEDIATELY. (TELL YOUR FAMILY TO GENTLY MIX THE CONTENTS OF THEIR BOWL WITH THEIR FORKS.) SERVES 4.

TIP: LIMES VARY IN THE AMOUNT OF JUICE THEY YIELD. FOR THIS RECIPE, YOU'LL LIKELY NEED 3 TO 4 LIMES.

TIP: PACKAGES OF STEAMED CHINESE NOODLES ARE GENERALLY FOUND IN THE REFRIGERATED SECTION OF THE PRODUCE AISLE, NEAR TOFU AND SIMILAR PRODUCTS. YOU CAN MAKE THIS DISH WITH 12 OZ (375 G) SPAGHETTI OR SPAGHETTINI, IF YOU PREFER, COOKING ACCORDING TO PACKAGE DIRECTIONS.

FUSILLI WITH HAM, ASPARAGUS AND CORN

THE FLAVORS OF MINT AND LEMON REALLY BRIGHTEN THIS SUPER-QUICK PASTA DISH. YOU CAN USE CHOPPED ZUCCHINI IN PLACE OF THE ASPARAGUS, IF YOU PREFER.

3 TBSP	OLIVE OIL, DIVIDED	45 ML
I CUP	FINELY CHOPPED ONION	250 ML
1/2 TSP	SALT	2 ML
I TO 2 TBSP	COLD WATER (IF NEEDED)	15 TO 30 ML
12 OZ	ASPARAGUS, TRIMMED AND CUT INTO I-INCH (2.5 CM) LONG PIECES	375 G
1 1/2 CUPS	FRESH OR THAWED FROZEN CORN KERNELS	375 ML
8 OZ	THICK-CUT BLACK FOREST DELI HAM, CHOPPED	250 G
1 1/2 CUPS	FRESHLY GRATED PARMESAN CHEESE, DIVIDED	375 ML
3 TBSP	CHOPPED FRESH MINT	45 ML
	FRESHLY GROUND BLACK PEPPER	
12 OZ	FUSILLI OR PENNE PASTA, PREFERABLY WHOLE WHEAT (ABOUT 4 CUPS/I L)	375 G
2 TBSP	FRESHLY SQUEEZED LEMON JUICE (SEE TIP, OPPOSITE)	30 ML
1/2 TO 3/4 CUP	REDUCED-SODIUM CHICKEN BROTH OR HOMEMADE VEGETABLE STOCK (SEE RECIPE, PAGE 90)	125 TO 175 ML

IN A LARGE, DEEP NONSTICK SKILLET, HEAT I TBSP (15 ML) OIL OVER MEDIUM HEAT. ADD ONION AND SALT; COOK, STIRRING OCCASIONALLY, FOR 5 TO 6 MINUTES OR UNTIL ONION IS SOFTENED AND PALE GOLDEN. IF ONION STARTS TO STICK, ADD COLD WATER AS NEEDED. ADD

ASPARAGUS AND CORN; COOK FOR 5 TO 6 MINUTES OR
UNTIL ASPARAGUS IS TENDER. REMOVE FROM HEAT AND
STIR IN HAM, 1 CUP (250 ML) OF THE PARMESAN, MINT AND
PEPPER TO TASTE.

MEANWHILE, IN A LARGE POT OF BOILING SALTED WATER,
COOK PASTA ACCORDING TO PACKAGE DIRECTIONS. DRAIN,
RETURN PASTA TO POT, ADD HAM MIXTURE AND TOSS
TO COMBINE. RETURN POT TO MEDIUM HEAT AND STIR IN
LEMON JUICE AND THE REMAINING OIL. ADD ENOUGH OF
THE BROTH TO JUST MOISTEN THE PASTA AND COOK,
STIRRING, UNTIL HEATED THROUGH. SERVE SPRINKLED
WITH THE REMAINING PARMESAN. SERVES 4.

TIP: ADDING A LITTLE LEMON JUICE JUST BEFORE SERVING
HELPS TO BRIGHTEN THE FLAVOR OF MANY SOUPS AND
SAUCES. ALWAYS USE FRESHLY SQUEEZED LEMON JUICE,
NOT THE BOTTLED STUFF, WHICH HAS ADDITIVES. ONE
OR TWO TABLESPOONFULS (15 OR 30 ML) IS USUALLY
PLENTY — YOU DON'T WANT YOUR DISH TO TASTE LIKE
LEMONADE. TASTE THE DISH AS YOU GRADUALLY ADD THE
JUICE. CIDER VINEGAR OR SHERRY VINEGAR CAN ALSO
BE USED.

A SUCCESSFUL MAN IS ONE WHO CAN LAY A FIRM FOUNDATION
WITH THE BRICKS OTHERS HAVE THROWN AT HIM.
— DAVID BRINKLEY

PASTA WITH CAULIFLOWER, BACON AND PEAS

EASY, PEASY.

4 CUPS	CAULIFLOWER FLORETS, BROKEN OR CUT INTO BITE-SIZED PIECES	1 L
12 OZ	PENNE OR FUSILLI PASTA (ABOUT 4 CUPS/1 L)	375 G
1 CUP	FROZEN BABY PEAS (NO NEED TO THAW)	250 ML
4	SLICES BACON, CHOPPED	4
1 TO 2 TSP	BUTTER OR OLIVE OIL (IF NEEDED)	5 TO 10 ML
1/2 CUP	CHOPPED PECANS	125 ML
2	CLOVES GARLIC, MINCED	2
2 TBSP	CHOPPED FRESH PARSLEY (SEE TIP, OPPOSITE)	30 ML
1 TSP	PAPRIKA	5 ML
1/2 TSP	SALT	2 ML
	FRESHLY GROUND BLACK PEPPER	
1/3 CUP	REDUCED-SODIUM CHICKEN BROTH, DIVIDED	75 ML
1/2 CUP	FRESHLY GRATED PARMESAN CHEESE	125 ML

BRING A LARGE POT OF SALTED WATER TO A BOIL. ADD CAULIFLOWER, RETURN TO BOIL AND BLANCH FOR 1 MINUTE. USING A SLOTTED SPOON, TRANSFER TO A COLANDER AND SET ASIDE. ADD PASTA TO BOILING WATER AND COOK ACCORDING TO PACKAGE DIRECTIONS. TWO MINUTES BEFORE PASTA IS READY, ADD PEAS AND COOK FOR 2 MINUTES. DRAIN, RETURN TO POT AND SET ASIDE.

MEANWHILE, IN A LARGE NONSTICK SKILLET, SAUTÉ BACON OVER MEDIUM-HIGH HEAT UNTIL CRISPY. USING A SLOTTED SPOON, TRANSFER BACON TO A PLATE LINED WITH PAPER

TOWELS. DRAIN OFF ALL BUT I TBSP (I5 ML) OF THE FAT. IF THERE IS LESS THAN I TBSP (I5 ML) FAT, ADD BUTTER AS NEEDED. REDUCE HEAT TO MEDIUM. ADD PECANS AND COOK, STIRRING, FOR I MINUTE OR UNTIL LIGHTLY BROWNED. ADD GARLIC, PARSLEY, PAPRIKA, SALT, PEPPER TO TASTE AND 2 TBSP (30 ML) OF THE BROTH. COOK, STIRRING, FOR I5 SECONDS OR UNTIL FRAGRANT. STIR IN RESERVED CAULIFLOWER AND BACON. ADD CONTENTS OF SKILLET TO COOKED PASTA MIXTURE AND STIR IN THE REMAINING BROTH; COOK OVER MEDIUM HEAT, STIRRING, UNTIL HEATED THROUGH. SERVE SPRINKLED WITH PARMESAN. SERVES 4.

TIP: YOU CAN FREEZE FRESH PARSLEY FOR USE IN SOUPS, STEWS, PASTA AND SAUCES. (YOU'LL NEVER AGAIN HAVE TO THROW AWAY A HALF-USED BUNCH!) CUT OFF AND DISCARD THE STALKS AND WILTED LEAVES. (OR KEEP THE STALKS FOR WHEN YOU'RE MAKING STOCK.) FINELY CHOP THE PARSLEY LEAVES, EITHER WITH A KNIFE OR IN A FOOD PROCESSOR. SPREAD PARSLEY ON A LARGE RIMMED BAKING SHEET AND FREEZE, UNCOVERED, FOR ABOUT I HOUR OR UNTIL FIRM. TRANSFER TO AN AIRTIGHT CONTAINER OR FREEZER BAG AND STORE FOR UP TO 3 MONTHS. THIS METHOD ALSO WORKS FOR FREEZING FRESH CILANTRO.

I'M REALLY EASY TO GET ALONG WITH ONCE YOU LEARN TO WORSHIP ME.

PASTA WITH SPICY
SAUSAGE AND SQUASH

EASY AND VERY NUTRITIOUS, THIS PASTA DISH IS A GREAT WAY TO EAT YOUR VEGETABLES. IT IS DEFINITELY FOR SPICE LOVERS, BECAUSE IT'S NOT AS SUCCESSFUL WITH MILD SAUSAGE.

6	HOT ITALIAN SAUSAGES, CASINGS REMOVED, BROKEN INTO SMALL CHUNKS	6
1 CUP	THINLY SLICED RED ONION	250 ML
	VEGETABLE OIL (OPTIONAL)	
1 LB	BUTTERNUT SQUASH, PEELED AND CUT INTO $\frac{1}{2}$-INCH (1 CM) CUBES (ABOUT 3 CUPS/750 ML)	500 G
1 TBSP	PACKED BROWN SUGAR OR GRANULATED SUGAR	15 ML
2	CLOVES GARLIC, MINCED	2
2 TBSP	CHOPPED FRESH SAGE (OR $\frac{3}{4}$ TSP/ 3 ML CRUMBLED DRIED SAGE)	30 ML
	SALT AND FRESHLY GROUND BLACK PEPPER	
$1\frac{1}{4}$ TO $1\frac{3}{4}$ CUPS	REDUCED-SODIUM CHICKEN BROTH OR HOMEMADE VEGETABLE STOCK (SEE RECIPE, PAGE 90), DIVIDED	300 TO 425 ML
1 TBSP	BALSAMIC VINEGAR	15 ML
12 OZ	FUSILLI OR PENNE PASTA (ABOUT 4 CUPS/1 L)	375 G
$\frac{1}{4}$ CUP	CHOPPED FRESH PARSLEY	60 ML
	FRESHLY GRATED PARMESAN CHEESE	

HEAT A LARGE NONSTICK SKILLET OVER MEDIUM HEAT. FRY SAUSAGE, STIRRING FREQUENTLY, FOR 5 TO 7 MINUTES OR UNTIL VERY BROWNED AND NICELY CRUNCHY ON THE OUTSIDE. USING A SLOTTED SPOON,

TRANSFER SAUSAGE TO A PLATE LINED WITH PAPER TOWELS. POUR OFF AND RESERVE 2 TBSP (30 ML) OF THE SAUSAGE FAT. WIPE OUT PAN WITH PAPER TOWELS. RETURN 1 TBSP (15 ML) OF THE SAUSAGE FAT TO THE PAN AND SAUTÉ ONION FOR ABOUT 5 MINUTES OR UNTIL SOFTENED. TRANSFER ONION TO PLATE WITH SAUSAGE. ADD ANOTHER 1 TBSP (15 ML) SAUSAGE FAT TO THE PAN (OR USE VEGETABLE OIL). ADD SQUASH AND BROWN SUGAR; SAUTÉ FOR 4 OR 5 MINUTES OR UNTIL BROWNED. ADD GARLIC, SAGE, 1/2 TSP (2 ML) SALT, PEPPER TO TASTE AND 1 TBSP (15 ML) OF THE BROTH; SAUTÉ FOR 15 SECONDS OR UNTIL FRAGRANT. ADD 1 CUP (250 ML) BROTH AND BRING TO A BOIL. REDUCE HEAT TO LOW, COVER AND SIMMER, STIRRING OCCASIONALLY, FOR 7 TO 10 MINUTES OR UNTIL SQUASH IS TENDER. ADD MORE BROTH IF NECESSARY TO PREVENT SQUASH MIXTURE FROM BECOMING TOO DRY. RETURN SAUSAGE AND ONIONS TO THE PAN AND STIR IN ENOUGH BROTH TO MAKE THE MIXTURE LOOSE BUT NOT RUNNY; SIMMER UNTIL HEATED THROUGH. STIR IN VINEGAR. TASTE AND ADJUST SEASONING WITH SALT AND PEPPER, IF DESIRED (BUT BE CAUTIOUS, AS THE SAUSAGE IS HIGHLY SEASONED).

MEANWHILE, IN A LARGE POT OF BOILING SALTED WATER, COOK PASTA ACCORDING TO PACKAGE DIRECTIONS. DRAIN AND RETURN TO POT; TOSS WITH SAUSAGE MIXTURE AND PARSLEY. SERVE SPRINKLED GENEROUSLY WITH PARMESAN. SERVES 4.

TIP: IF YOU USE A SALT-FREE STOCK OR BROTH, YOU MAY WANT TO ADD MORE SALT.

REDUCED-GUILT
CHICKEN TOMATO ALFREDO

CHICKEN BROTH AND, YES, WATER LOWER THE CALORIES
WITHOUT SACRIFICING FLAVOR IN THIS EVER-POPULAR
PASTA DISH. HONESTLY, IT TASTES AMAZING.

1 LB	BONELESS SKINLESS CHICKEN BREASTS (ABOUT 2 LARGE), CUT INTO BITE-SIZE PIECES	500 G
1 TSP	SALT	5 ML
1/4 TSP	FRESHLY GROUND BLACK PEPPER	1 ML
2 TBSP	OLIVE OR VEGETABLE OIL (APPROX.), DIVIDED	30 ML
3/4 CUP	FINELY CHOPPED ONION (SEE TIP, OPPOSITE)	175 ML
2	CLOVES GARLIC, MINCED	2
1 CUP	WATER	250 ML
1 CUP	HEAVY OR WHIPPING (35%) CREAM	250 ML
1 CUP	REDUCED-SODIUM CHICKEN BROTH	250 ML
1/3 CUP	OIL-PACKED SUN-DRIED TOMATOES, DRAINED AND COARSELY CHOPPED	75 ML
1/8 TO 1/4 TSP	HOT PEPPER FLAKES	0.5 TO 1 ML
5 CUPS	PACKED BABY SPINACH	1.25 L
3 TBSP	FINELY CHOPPED FRESH BASIL	45 ML
12 OZ	PENNE PASTA (ABOUT 4 CUPS/1 L)	375 G
1/2 CUP	FRESHLY GRATED PARMESAN CHEESE	125 ML

SEASON CHICKEN WITH SALT AND BLACK PEPPER. IN A
LARGE NONSTICK SKILLET, HEAT 1 TBSP (15 ML) OIL OVER
MEDIUM-HIGH HEAT. SAUTÉ CHICKEN, IN BATCHES IF
NECESSARY, FOR ABOUT 5 MINUTES OR UNTIL BROWNED
ON ALL SIDES AND NO LONGER PINK INSIDE, ADDING MORE
OIL BETWEEN BATCHES AS NECESSARY. USING A SLOTTED

SPOON, TRANSFER CHICKEN TO A PLATE. ADD 1 TBSP (15 ML) OIL TO THE SKILLET. SAUTÉ ONION FOR 3 TO 4 MINUTES OR UNTIL SOFTENED. ADD GARLIC AND SAUTÉ FOR 15 SECONDS OR UNTIL FRAGRANT. STIR IN WATER, CREAM, BROTH, SUN-DRIED TOMATOES AND HOT PEPPER FLAKES; BRING TO A BOIL. REDUCE HEAT AND SIMMER BRISKLY FOR ABOUT 15 MINUTES OR UNTIL SAUCE IS SLIGHTLY REDUCED AND TOMATOES ARE PLUMPED. INCREASE HEAT TO MEDIUM AND RETURN CHICKEN AND ACCUMULATED JUICES TO THE PAN. ADD SPINACH AND BASIL; COOK, STIRRING OCCASIONALLY, FOR 2 MINUTES OR UNTIL CHICKEN IS HEATED THROUGH AND SPINACH IS JUST WILTED.

MEANWHILE, IN A LARGE POT OF BOILING SALTED WATER, COOK PASTA ACCORDING TO PACKAGE DIRECTIONS. DRAIN AND RETURN TO THE POT. ADD CHICKEN MIXTURE AND TOSS TO COMBINE. SERVE SPRINKLED WITH PARMESAN. SERVES 4.

TIP: YELLOW ONIONS VARY WIDELY IN SIZE. ONIONS FROM ONE BAG WE BOUGHT RANGED IN WEIGHT FROM 3 TO 10 OZ (90 TO 300 G) APIECE! WHILE THIS IS NOT GENERALLY A PROBLEM FOR CHUNKY SOUPS AND STEWS, IT CAN LEAD TO UNDESIRABLE RESULTS IN RECIPES SUCH AS CREAMY SAUCES, WHERE WE DON'T WANT TO OVERWHELM THE FLAVOR OR TEXTURE WITH ONION. FOR THIS REASON, WE OFTEN SPECIFY A VOLUME OF CHOPPED ONIONS RATHER THAN CALLING FOR "1 ONION, CHOPPED." DON'T WORRY IF THIS LEAVES YOU WITH PARTIALLY UNUSED ONION. SIMPLY CHOP THE WHOLE ONION, MEASURE OUT WHAT YOU NEED FOR THE RECIPE AND FREEZE THE REST IN AN AIRTIGHT CONTAINER FOR FUTURE USE.

CHICKEN AND BROCCOLI PASTA BAKE

THIS MARVELOUS MAKE-AHEAD NEEDS PLENTY OF SEASONING, SO DON'T BE SHY WITH THE SALT AND PEPPER.

12 OZ	BOW-TIE, FUSILLI, PENNE OR OTHER CHUNKY PASTA (ABOUT 4 CUPS/1 L)	375 G
4 CUPS	SMALL BROCCOLI FLORETS	1 L
1 LB	BONELESS SKINLESS CHICKEN BREASTS (ABOUT 2 LARGE), CUT INTO BITE-SIZE PIECES	500 G
1 TSP	SALT, DIVIDED	5 ML
1/4 TSP	FRESHLY GROUND BLACK PEPPER	1 ML
2 TBSP	OLIVE OR VEGETABLE OIL (APPROX.), DIVIDED	30 ML
2	CLOVES GARLIC, MINCED	2
2 CUPS	SLICED CREMINI MUSHROOMS	500 ML
1 CUP	FINELY CHOPPED ONION	250 ML
1/2 TSP	DRIED THYME OR OREGANO	2 ML
1/4 TSP	HOT PEPPER FLAKES (OPTIONAL)	1 ML
1 1/2 CUPS	REDUCED-SODIUM CHICKEN BROTH OR HOMEMADE VEGETABLE STOCK (SEE RECIPE, PAGE 90)	375 ML
1 CUP	HEAVY OR WHIPPING (35%) CREAM OR HALF-AND-HALF (10%) CREAM	250 ML
2 CUPS	SHREDDED JALAPEÑO JACK CHEESE (SEE TIP, PAGE 244)	500 ML
1/2 CUP	FRESHLY GRATED PARMESAN CHEESE	125 ML

TOPPING

1/2 CUP	DRY BREAD CRUMBS OR CRACKER CRUMBS	125 ML
1/4 CUP	FRESHLY GRATED PARMESAN CHEESE	60 ML
1/2 TSP	PAPRIKA	2 ML
1 TBSP	OLIVE OIL OR MELTED BUTTER	15 ML

PREHEAT OVEN TO 425°F (220°C). LIGHTLY GREASE A 13- BY 9-INCH (33 BY 23 CM) GLASS BAKING DISH. IN A LARGE POT OF BOILING SALTED WATER, COOK PASTA ACCORDING TO PACKAGE INSTRUCTIONS. TWO MINUTES BEFORE PASTA IS READY, ADD BROCCOLI AND COOK FOR 2 MINUTES. DRAIN, RETURN TO POT AND SET ASIDE.

MEANWHILE, SEASON CHICKEN WITH $\frac{1}{4}$ TSP (1 ML) OF THE SALT AND BLACK PEPPER. IN A LARGE NONSTICK SKILLET, HEAT 1 TBSP (15 ML) OIL OVER MEDIUM-HIGH HEAT. SAUTÉ CHICKEN, IN BATCHES IF NECESSARY, FOR ABOUT 5 MINUTES OR UNTIL BROWNED ON ALL SIDES AND NO LONGER PINK INSIDE, ADDING MORE OIL BETWEEN BATCHES AS NECESSARY. USING A SLOTTED SPOON, TRANSFER CHICKEN TO POT WITH PASTA MIXTURE. ADD 1 TBSP (15 ML) OIL TO THE SKILLET. SAUTÉ GARLIC, MUSHROOMS, ONION, THYME, HOT PEPPER FLAKES AND $\frac{1}{4}$ TSP (1 ML) SALT FOR 5 TO 7 MINUTES OR UNTIL ONIONS AND MUSHROOMS ARE SOFTENED. TRANSFER TO POT WITH PASTA MIXTURE. ADD BROTH, CREAM AND THE REMAINING SALT TO THE SKILLET; BRING TO A BOIL. REDUCE HEAT AND SIMMER, STIRRING OCCASIONALLY, FOR 10 MINUTES OR UNTIL SLIGHTLY THICKENED. POUR OVER PASTA MIXTURE. STIR IN JALAPEÑO JACK AND PARMESAN UNTIL THOROUGHLY COMBINED. SPREAD IN PREPARED BAKING DISH.

TOPPING: IN A BOWL, COMBINE BREAD CRUMBS, PARMESAN, PAPRIKA AND OIL. SPRINKLE EVENLY OVER PASTA.

CONTINUED ON NEXT PAGE...

BAKE FOR ABOUT 20 MINUTES OR UNTIL TOPPING IS GOLDEN BROWN AND PASTA IS BUBBLING. SERVES 4 TO 6.

TIP: JALAPEÑO JACK (AKA PEPPER JACK) CHEESE CONTAINS CHOPPED JALAPEÑO PEPPERS, SO IT ADDS A MILDLY SPICY TOUCH TO THIS DISH. SUBSTITUTE SHREDDED REGULAR MONTEREY JACK, HAVARTI OR CHEDDAR CHEESE, IF YOU PREFER.

TIP: IF YOU USE A SALT-FREE STOCK OR BROTH, YOU MAY WANT TO ADD MORE SALT. SALT IS, IN ANY RECIPE, A MATTER OF PERSONAL PREFERENCE, SO FEEL FREE TO INCREASE OR REDUCE THE QUANTITIES WE SUGGEST.

MAKE AHEAD: SPREAD PASTA MIXTURE IN THE PREPARED BAKING DISH, BUT DO NOT ADD TOPPING. LET COOL FOR 30 MINUTES, THEN REFRIGERATE, UNCOVERED, UNTIL COLD. COVER TIGHTLY AND KEEP REFRIGERATED FOR UP TO 2 DAYS. SPRINKLE WITH TOPPING AND PROCEED WITH THE RECIPE, ADDING MORE BROTH IF MIXTURE APPEARS TOO DRY. BAKE FOR ABOUT 30 MINUTES.

TYPICAL SYMPTOMS OF STRESS ARE EATING TOO MUCH, IMPULSE BUYING AND DRIVING TOO FAST. STRANGE, THAT'S MY IDEA OF A PERFECT DAY!

SIDE DISHES

ROASTED ASPARAGUS WITH CRUNCHY LEMON TOPPING

ROASTING IS A QUICK WAY TO COOK ASPARAGUS. A TOPPING OF TOASTED BREAD CRUMBS PROVIDES AN APPEALING CONTRAST IN TEXTURE.

1/4 CUP	FRESH BREAD CRUMBS (SEE TIP, OPPOSITE)	60 ML
2 TBSP	OLIVE OIL, DIVIDED	30 ML
I TSP	FINELY GRATED LEMON ZEST	5 ML
	SALT AND FRESHLY GROUND BLACK PEPPER	
I LB	SLENDER ASPARAGUS SPEARS, TRIMMED AND CUT INTO 1 1/2-INCH (4 CM) LONG PIECES	500 G
I TBSP	FRESHLY SQUEEZED LEMON JUICE	15 ML

PREHEAT OVEN TO 350°F (180°C). LINE A LARGE RIMMED BAKING SHEET WITH PARCHMENT PAPER OR GREASED FOIL. IN A BOWL, TOSS BREAD CRUMBS WITH I TBSP (15 ML) OIL, LEMON ZEST, A PINCH OF SALT AND PEPPER TO TASTE. SPREAD EVENLY ON PREPARED BAKING SHEET AND TOAST IN PREHEATED OVEN FOR 10 MINUTES, STIRRING OCCASIONALLY, UNTIL GOLDEN BROWN. LET COOL COMPLETELY AND TRANSFER TO A BOWL. (RESERVE THE LINED BAKING SHEET FOR THE ASPARAGUS.)

INCREASE OVEN TEMPERATURE TO 400°F (200°C). IN A BOWL, TOSS ASPARAGUS WITH THE REMAINING OIL, 1/4 TSP (1 ML) SALT AND PEPPER TO TASTE. SPREAD IN A SINGLE LAYER ON BAKING SHEET. ROAST FOR 10 TO 15 MINUTES, STIRRING ONCE, UNTIL LIGHTLY BROWNED AND TENDER-CRISP. TRANSFER TO A WARMED SERVING PLATTER AND SPRINKLE WITH LEMON JUICE AND TOASTED BREAD CRUMBS. SERVES 3 TO 4.

TIP: TO MAKE FRESH BREAD CRUMBS, IT IS BEST TO USE SLIGHTLY STALE BREAD. REMOVE THE CRUSTS, TEAR THE BREAD INTO PIECES AND PULSE IN A FOOD PROCESSOR. IF YOU DON'T HAVE A FOOD PROCESSOR, GRATE PIECES OF STALE BREAD ON A BOX GRATER. FRESH BREAD CRUMBS CAN BE FROZEN IN SEALABLE FOOD STORAGE BAGS.

MAKE AHEAD: COOL THE TOASTED BREAD CRUMBS AND STORE IN AN AIRTIGHT CONTAINER AT ROOM TEMPERATURE FOR UP TO 8 HOURS.

VARIATION
ROASTED ASPARAGUS WITH CRUNCHY CHEESE TOPPING: OMIT THE LEMON ZEST. JUST BEFORE SERVING, COMBINE THE TOASTED BREAD CRUMBS WITH 1/4 CUP (60 ML) FRESHLY GRATED PARMESAN CHEESE.

REMEMBER THAT NOT GETTING WHAT YOU WANT IS SOMETIMES A WONDERFUL STROKE OF LUCK.

STIR-FRIED BOK CHOY

THIS ASIAN CABBAGE IS BEST STIR-FRIED AND TOSSED WITH A SIMPLE SAUCE. CHOOSE BABY BOK CHOY WHEN IT'S AVAILABLE, BUT THE LARGE VERSION IS ALSO GOOD.

2 TBSP	OYSTER SAUCE	30 ML
2 TBSP	RICE WINE (SEE TIP, OPPOSITE), DRY SHERRY OR REDUCED-SODIUM CHICKEN OR VEGETABLE BROTH	30 ML
1 TSP	LIQUID HONEY OR GRANULATED SUGAR	5 ML
1/4 TSP	TOASTED SESAME OIL	1 ML
1 LB	BOK CHOY OR BABY BOK CHOY, RINSED WELL AND SHAKEN WELL TO REMOVE EXCESS WATER	500 G
1 TBSP	PEANUT OR VEGETABLE OIL	15 ML
2	CLOVES GARLIC, MINCED	2
1 TBSP	FINELY GRATED GINGERROOT (SEE TIP, PAGE 252)	15 ML
1 TBSP	COLD WATER	15 ML
2 TBSP	TOASTED SESAME SEEDS (SEE TIP, PAGE 127)	30 ML

IN A SMALL BOWL, COMBINE OYSTER SAUCE, RICE WINE, HONEY AND SESAME OIL; SET ASIDE. IF USING BABY BOK CHOY, CUT IN HALF LENGTHWISE. IF USING LARGE BOK CHOY, CUT STALKS ON THE DIAGONAL INTO 3/4-INCH (2 CM) PIECES. (SOME RECIPES SUGGEST SEPARATING THE LEAVES AND WHITE STEMS, BUT THAT'S NOT NECESSARY.) IN A LARGE, DEEP NONSTICK SKILLET, HEAT PEANUT OIL OVER MEDIUM-HIGH HEAT. STIR-FRY BOK CHOY, TURNING FREQUENTLY, FOR 2 TO 3 MINUTES OR UNTIL THE LEAVES ARE WILTED. USING A SPATULA, MAKE A WELL IN THE CENTER OF THE BOK CHOY AND ADD GARLIC,

GINGER AND COLD WATER; STIR-FRY FOR 15 SECONDS
OR UNTIL FRAGRANT. STIR IN OYSTER SAUCE MIXTURE,
INCREASE HEAT TO HIGH AND STIR-FRY FOR ABOUT
2 MINUTES OR UNTIL THE WHITE STEMS ARE TENDER-
CRISP. SPRINKLE WITH SESAME SEEDS AND SERVE
IMMEDIATELY. SERVES 4.

TIP: RICE WINE — A.K.A. SAKE — IS A JAPANESE ALCOHOLIC
DRINK THAT'S OFTEN FEATURED IN ASIAN COOKING. MOST
LIQUOR STORES CARRY IT, AND AT THE TIME OF WRITING,
IT COST AROUND $10 FOR A BIG BOTTLE. INVEST IN A
BOTTLE (IT KEEPS FOR AGES) AND ENJOY THE THRILL
WHEN EVERYONE TELLS YOU HOW AUTHENTIC YOUR
STIR-FRIES TASTE! DRY SHERRY IS A GOOD SUBSTITUTE
FOR RICE WINE, OR YOU CAN SIMPLY OMIT IT FROM THE
RECIPE. BUT THAT WOULD BE A SHAME.

THE REAL DIFFERENCE BETWEEN RICH AND REGULAR PEOPLE
IS THAT THE RICH SERVE SUCH MARVELOUS VEGETABLES.
— TRUMAN CAPOTE

GREEN BEANS WITH LEMON THYME PESTO

THIS PERKY PESTO ADDS ZING TO ALL KINDS OF VEGETABLES. HERE, WE TOSS IT WITH TENDER-CRISP GREEN BEANS, BUT IT'S ALSO DELICIOUS TOSSED WITH PEAS (SEE VARIATION, OPPOSITE), STEAMED BABY POTATOES, STEAMED BROCCOLI, GRILLED ZUCCHINI OR GRILLED MUSHROOMS. OR TRY SPREADING IT ON TOMATO HALVES AND BAKING THEM IN THE OVEN UNTIL HEATED THROUGH. YOU MUST USE FRESH THYME; THE DRIED STUFF WON'T DO IN THIS RECIPE.

LEMON THYME PESTO

2	CLOVES GARLIC	2
1/2 CUP	CHOPPED FRESH PARSLEY	125 ML
1/4 CUP	SKINNED PISTACHIOS (SEE TIP, PAGE 44), ALMONDS OR PINE NUTS	60 ML
2 TBSP	FRESH THYME LEAVES (SEE TIP, OPPOSITE)	30 ML
	FINELY GRATED ZEST OF 1/2 LEMON	
2 TBSP	FRESHLY SQUEEZED LEMON JUICE	30 ML
1/4 TSP	SALT	1 ML
	FRESHLY GROUND BLACK PEPPER	
1/2 CUP	OLIVE OIL	125 ML
12 OZ	GREEN BEANS (ABOUT 3 CUPS/ 750 ML), ENDS TRIMMED	375 G

LEMON THYME PESTO: IN A FOOD PROCESSOR, COMBINE GARLIC, PARSLEY, PISTACHIOS, THYME, LEMON ZEST, LEMON JUICE, SALT AND PEPPER TO TASTE; PROCESS UNTIL SMOOTH. SCRAPE DOWN THE SIDES. WITH THE MOTOR RUNNING, THROUGH THE FEED TUBE, GRADUALLY

ADD OIL UNTIL A RUNNY PASTE FORMS. YOU'LL HAVE ABOUT $\frac{1}{2}$ CUP (125 ML) PESTO.

IN A LARGE POT OF BOILING SALTED WATER, COOK BEANS FOR ABOUT 5 MINUTES OR UNTIL TENDER-CRISP. DRAIN AND RETURN TO POT. ADD 2 TO 3 TBSP (30 TO 45 ML) PESTO AND TOSS TO COAT. SERVES 4.

TIP: ALTHOUGH FRESH THYME IS READILY AVAILABLE IN MOST GROCERY STORES, CONSIDER GROWING YOUR OWN. IT IS ONE OF THE FEW CULINARY HERBS — ALONG WITH CHIVES AND MINT — THAT SURVIVES CANADIAN WINTERS.

MAKE AHEAD: STORE THE PESTO IN AN AIRTIGHT CONTAINER IN THE REFRIGERATOR FOR UP TO 2 DAYS. OR PORTION IT INTO AN ICE CUBE TRAY AND FREEZE UNTIL SOLID. TRANSFER CUBES TO A FREEZER BAG AND STORE IN THE FREEZER FOR UP TO 1 MONTH. EACH CUBE IS EQUIVALENT TO ABOUT 1 TBSP (15 ML) PESTO. TO THAW, PLACE PESTO CUBES IN A MICROWAVE-SAFE BOWL AND MICROWAVE ON HIGH IN 20-SECOND INTERVALS, STIRRING AFTER EACH.

VARIATION
LEMON THYME PESTO PEAS: FOR A SUPER-FAST SIDE DISH, MAKE THE PESTO AHEAD AND REFRIGERATE OR FREEZE. COOK FROZEN PEAS ACCORDING TO PACKAGE INSTRUCTIONS. DRAIN AND TOSS WITH 2 TO 3 TBSP (30 TO 45 ML) PESTO.

SIGN ON A MUFFLER SHOP: NO APPOINTMENT NECESSARY — WE HEAR YOU COMING.

SZECHUAN GREEN BEANS

A MILDLY SPICED SAUCE ADDS A TANTALIZING TINGLE TO ONE OF OUR FAVORITE VEGETABLES IN THIS EASY SIDE DISH. SERVE WITH GRILLED STEAK OR WITH GRILLED OR BAKED SALMON FILLETS.

I LB	GREEN BEANS (ABOUT 4 CUPS/I L), ENDS TRIMMED	500 G
I TBSP	VEGETABLE OIL	15 ML
2	GREEN ONIONS, THINLY SLICED	2
2	CLOVES GARLIC, MINCED	2
I TBSP	FINELY GRATED GINGERROOT (SEE TIP, BELOW)	15 ML
1/4 CUP	SWEET CHILI DIPPING SAUCE	60 ML
2 TBSP	HOMEMADE VEGETABLE STOCK (SEE RECIPE, PAGE 90), REDUCED-SODIUM CHICKEN OR VEGETABLE BROTH OR WATER	30 ML

IN A LARGE POT OF BOILING SALTED WATER, COOK BEANS FOR ABOUT 5 MINUTES OR UNTIL TENDER-CRISP. DRAIN AND RETURN TO POT.

MEANWHILE, IN A LARGE NONSTICK SKILLET, HEAT OIL OVER MEDIUM HEAT. SAUTÉ GREEN ONIONS, GARLIC AND GINGER FOR 30 SECONDS OR UNTIL FRAGRANT. ADD BEANS, CHILI SAUCE AND STOCK, STIRRING TO COAT BEANS. COOK, STIRRING, UNTIL SAUCE IS BUBBLING AND BEANS ARE HEATED THROUGH. SERVE IMMEDIATELY. SERVES 4 TO 6.

TIP: ASIAN COOKS OFTEN DON'T PEEL GINGERROOT BEFORE GRATING IT. SO WE DON'T EITHER!

Chicken Fiesta Pizza (page 224)

A Bowlful of Dinner (page 228)

Pasta with Spicy Sausage and Squash (page 238)

Easy Bacon Corn Risotto (page 276)

BRUSSELS SPROUTS
WITH GARLIC AND PINE NUTS

BRUSSELS SPROUT LOVERS — AND THERE SEEM TO BE MORE AND MORE OF YOU — REJOICE!

1 LB	BRUSSELS SPROUTS, TRIMMED AND HALVED LENGTHWISE	500 G
1 TBSP	OLIVE OIL	15 ML
1	CLOVE GARLIC, MINCED	1
1/4 TSP	SALT	1 ML
	FRESHLY GROUND BLACK PEPPER	
1/4 CUP	HOMEMADE VEGETABLE STOCK (SEE RECIPE, PAGE 90) OR REDUCED-SODIUM CHICKEN OR VEGETABLE BROTH	60 ML
1/4 CUP	PINE NUTS OR GREEN PUMPKIN SEEDS, TOASTED (SEE TIP, PAGE 127)	60 ML

IN A LARGE POT OF BOILING SALTED WATER, COOK BRUSSELS SPROUTS FOR 5 MINUTES OR UNTIL TENDER-CRISP. DRAIN AND TRANSFER TO A BOWL OF ICED WATER; LET COOL FOR 5 MINUTES. DRAIN AND DRY ON PAPER TOWELS. IN A LARGE NONSTICK SKILLET, HEAT OIL OVER MEDIUM HEAT. SAUTÉ BLANCHED BRUSSELS SPROUTS FOR 2 MINUTES. ADD GARLIC, SALT, PEPPER TO TASTE AND BROTH. COOK, STIRRING, FOR 3 TO 5 MINUTES OR UNTIL BRUSSELS SPROUTS ARE HEATED THROUGH. SPRINKLE WITH PINE NUTS. SERVE IMMEDIATELY. SERVES 4.

TIP: IF YOU USE A SALT-FREE STOCK OR BROTH, YOU MAY WANT TO ADD MORE SALT. SALT IS, IN ANY RECIPE, A MATTER OF PERSONAL PREFERENCE, SO FEEL FREE TO INCREASE OR REDUCE THE QUANTITIES WE SUGGEST.

ORANGE HERB CARROT RIBBONS

A VEGETABLE PEELER TRANSFORMS CARROTS INTO ATTRACTIVE FETTUCCINE SHAPES.

4	LARGE CARROTS, PEELED	4
I	CLOVE GARLIC, MINCED	I
I TSP	GRANULATED SUGAR	5 ML
3 TBSP	FRESHLY SQUEEZED ORANGE JUICE (SEE TIP, BELOW)	45 ML
I TBSP	BUTTER	15 ML
I TBSP	OLIVE OIL	15 ML
1/4 TSP	SALT	I ML
2 TBSP	CHOPPED FRESH PARSLEY	30 ML

RUN A VEGETABLE PEELER DOWN THE LENGTH OF EACH CARROT, PEELING OFF LONG RIBBONS. (YOU'LL END UP WITH SKINNY BITS YOU CAN'T SHAVE; DISCARD THEM OR KEEP THEM FOR WHEN YOU'RE MAKING STOCK.) IN A SMALL BOWL, COMBINE GARLIC, SUGAR AND ORANGE JUICE; SET ASIDE. IN A LARGE SKILLET, MELT BUTTER AND OIL OVER MEDIUM HEAT. ADD CARROT RIBBONS AND SALT. COOK, STIRRING FREQUENTLY, FOR 5 TO 7 MINUTES OR UNTIL CARROTS ARE TENDER-CRISP. USING A SPATULA, MAKE A WELL IN THE CENTER OF THE CARROTS AND POUR IN ORANGE JUICE MIXTURE; LET SIZZLE FOR 15 SECONDS OR UNTIL JUICE IS ALMOST EVAPORATED AND GARLIC IS FRAGRANT. REMOVE FROM HEAT, ADD PARSLEY AND TOSS TO COMBINE. SERVE IMMEDIATELY. SERVES 4.

TIP: IF YOU DON'T HAVE AN ORANGE TO JUICE, YOU CAN USE PREPARED UNSWEETENED ORANGE JUICE INSTEAD.

ROASTED PAPRIKA CAULIFLOWER

ROASTING CAULIFLOWER BRINGS OUT ITS
NATURAL SWEETNESS. IT'S PARTICULARLY GOOD
WITH GRILLED STEAK, LAMB OR PORK CHOPS.

I	LARGE HEAD CAULIFLOWER, CUT INTO FLORETS	I
3 TBSP	OLIVE OIL	45 ML
I TSP	SALT	5 ML
I TSP	PAPRIKA	5 ML
$\frac{1}{2}$ TSP	FRESHLY GROUND BLACK PEPPER	2 ML

PREHEAT OVEN TO 400°F (200°C). LINE A LARGE RIMMED
BAKING SHEET WITH PARCHMENT PAPER OR GREASED
FOIL. IN A LARGE BOWL, COMBINE OIL, SALT, PAPRIKA AND
PEPPER. ADD CAULIFLOWER AND TOSS TO COAT. SPREAD
OUT ON PREPARED BAKING SHEET. ROAST FOR ABOUT
30 MINUTES, FLIPPING FLORETS ONCE OR TWICE, UNTIL
CAULIFLOWER IS TENDER AND LIGHTLY BROWNED. SERVES
4 TO 6.

VARIATION

ROASTED CAULIFLOWER WITH ROMESCO SAUCE: FOR
A SPECIAL-OCCASION DINNER, SERVE THE ROASTED
CAULIFLOWER WITH SPAIN'S RAMBUNCTIOUS ROMESCO
SAUCE (PAGE 36).

SENIORS LAMENT: WE HAVE OFFICIALLY CROSSED OVER
INTO THE WORLD OF THE SKIRTED BATHING SUIT.

SUGAR SNAP PEAS WITH LIME AND MINT

TASTY STIR-FRIED VEGGIES IN A SNAP! YOU CAN USE FRESH BASIL IN PLACE OF THE MINT, IF YOU PREFER.

1 TBSP	BUTTER	15 ML
8 OZ	SUGAR SNAP PEAS, TRIMMED AND, IF DESIRED, CUT IN HALF DIAGONALLY	250 G
	SALT	
1/4 CUP	HOMEMADE VEGETABLE STOCK (SEE RECIPE, PAGE 90), REDUCED-SODIUM CHICKEN OR VEGETABLE BROTH OR WATER	60 ML
2 TBSP	FINELY CHOPPED FRESH MINT	30 ML
1/2 TSP	FINELY GRATED LIME ZEST	2 ML
1 TO 2 TBSP	FRESHLY SQUEEZED LIME JUICE	15 TO 30 ML
	FRESHLY GROUND BLACK PEPPER	

IN A LARGE NONSTICK SKILLET, MELT BUTTER OVER MEDIUM HEAT. ADD SUGAR SNAP PEAS AND 1/4 TSP (1 ML) SALT; TOSS TO COAT PEAS WITH BUTTER. ADD STOCK, COVER, LEAVING LID AJAR, AND COOK FOR 3 MINUTES OR UNTIL PEAS ARE TENDER-CRISP. STIR IN MINT, LIME ZEST, LIME JUICE TO TASTE AND PEPPER TO TASTE. TASTE AND ADJUST SEASONING WITH SALT, IF DESIRED. SERVE IMMEDIATELY. SERVES 2.

TIP: IF YOU USE A SALT-FREE STOCK OR BROTH, YOU MAY WANT TO ADD MORE SALT. SALT IS, IN ANY RECIPE, A MATTER OF PERSONAL PREFERENCE, SO FEEL FREE TO INCREASE OR REDUCE THE QUANTITIES WE SUGGEST. BEFORE ADDING MORE SALT AT THE END OF THE COOKING TIME, BE SURE TO TASTE THE DISH FIRST.

SAUTÉED CHERRY TOMATOES AND CORN

STIR-FRIED CHERRY TOMATOES WITH SWEET KERNELS OF CORN ARE FAST, FRESH AND EASY. THIS DISH IS PARTICULARLY TASTY WITH BAKED PESTO COD (PAGE 153) OR POTATO-CRUSTED TILAPIA (PAGE 216).

1 TBSP	OLIVE OIL	15 ML
1 CUP	FROZEN CORN KERNELS (NO NEED TO THAW)	250 ML
1 1/2 CUPS	CHERRY TOMATOES, HALVED	375 ML
1 TSP	GRANULATED SUGAR	5 ML
1/4 TSP	SALT	1 ML
1	CLOVE GARLIC, MINCED	1
1 TBSP	WATER	15 ML
2 TBSP	CHOPPED FRESH BASIL	30 ML
1 TSP	BALSAMIC VINEGAR	5 ML

IN A LARGE NONSTICK SKILLET, HEAT OIL OVER MEDIUM-HIGH HEAT. SAUTÉ CORN FOR 2 TO 3 MINUTES, STIRRING FREQUENTLY, UNTIL HEATED THROUGH AND STARTING TO BROWN. MEANWHILE, IN A BOWL, QUICKLY TOSS TOMATOES WITH SUGAR AND SALT. ADD TO THE PAN AND COOK, STIRRING FREQUENTLY, FOR 1 1/2 MINUTES OR UNTIL TOMATOES ARE WARM AND JUST SOFTENED BUT STILL HOLD THEIR SHAPE. REMOVE FROM HEAT AND, USING A SPATULA, MAKE A WELL IN THE CENTER OF THE TOMATO MIXTURE. IMMEDIATELY STIR IN GARLIC AND WATER; STIR FOR 15 SECONDS OR UNTIL WATER EVAPORATES AND GARLIC IS FRAGRANT. STIR IN BASIL AND VINEGAR. SERVE IMMEDIATELY. SERVES 4.

INDIAN CAULIFLOWER
AND POTATO CURRY

THIS IS AN AUTHENTIC AND EASY VEGETARIAN
STIR-FRY. MAKE THE CURRY INTO A SATISFYING
WRAP WITH WARMED NAAN AND A DOLLOP OF
MANGO CHUTNEY, OR SERVE OVER STEAMED
BASMATI RICE. IT ALSO GOES WELL WITH INDIAN
SPICED CHICKEN DRUMSTICKS (PAGE 168).

1 LB	POTATOES (SEE TIP, OPPOSITE), PEELED AND CUT INTO 1-INCH (2.5 CM) CHUNKS	500 G
2 TBSP	OLIVE OR VEGETABLE OIL	30 ML
1 TSP	CUMIN SEEDS	5 ML
1 TSP	GROUND CUMIN	5 ML
1 TSP	GROUND CORIANDER	5 ML
1 TSP	GROUND TURMERIC	5 ML
	SALT	
1/4 TSP	CAYENNE PEPPER	1 ML
1	SMALL HEAD CAULIFLOWER, CUT INTO SMALL FLORETS	1
3	TOMATOES, COARSELY CHOPPED	3
1/2 CUP	WATER	125 ML
1 CUP	FROZEN BABY PEAS (NO NEED TO THAW)	250 ML
2 TBSP	CHOPPED FRESH CILANTRO	30 ML
1 TO 2 TBSP	FRESHLY SQUEEZED LIME JUICE	15 TO 30 ML

IN A LARGE POT OF BOILING SALTED WATER, PARBOIL
POTATOES FOR 5 MINUTES. DRAIN AND SET ASIDE.
IN A LARGE, DEEP NONSTICK SKILLET, HEAT OIL OVER
MEDIUM-HIGH HEAT. ADD CUMIN SEEDS AND COOK,

STIRRING, FOR I MINUTE. (THE SEEDS WILL TURN DARKER BROWN, SMELL WONDERFUL AND MIGHT EVEN CRACKLE. THIS IS ALL GOOD.) ADD GROUND CUMIN, CORIANDER, TURMERIC, $\frac{1}{2}$ TSP (2 ML) SALT AND CAYENNE; COOK, STIRRING CONSTANTLY, FOR 30 SECONDS. QUICKLY ADD DRAINED POTATOES AND CAULIFLOWER; TOSS TO COAT WELL. ADD TOMATOES AND WATER; BRING TO A BOIL. REDUCE HEAT TO LOW, COVER AND SIMMER, STIRRING OCCASIONALLY, FOR ABOUT 15 MINUTES OR UNTIL VEGETABLES ARE TENDER. (CHECK UNDER THE LID A COUPLE OF TIMES AND ADD MORE WATER IF THE PAN IS GETTING TOO DRY.) STIR IN PEAS AND CILANTRO; RETURN TO A SIMMER, THEN SIMMER FOR I MINUTE. SPRINKLE WITH I TBSP (15 ML) LIME JUICE. TASTE AND ADJUST SEASONING WITH SALT AND LIME JUICE, IF DESIRED. SERVES 4.

TIP: THE BEST POTATOES FOR THIS RECIPE ARE YUKON GOLD OR ANOTHER YELLOW-FLESHED VARIETY, BUT YOU COULD ALSO USE RUSSETS. AND WHILE WE'RE TALKING ABOUT POTATOES, WHEN IT COMES TO MASHING THEM, DON'T BE TEMPTED TO USE A FOOD PROCESSOR OR AN ELECTRIC MIXER — THE POTATOES WILL TURN GLUEY. IF YOU WANT SMOOTHER MASHED POTATOES AND LIKE KITCHEN GADGETS, USE A POTATO RICER OR FOOD MILL.

TIP: USE I TO 2 TBSP (15 TO 30 ML) INDIAN CURRY PASTE IN PLACE OF THE INDIVIDUAL SPICES, IF YOU PREFER, BUT THE FLAVOR WILL BE SOMEWHAT DIFFERENT. CURRY PASTE IS WIDELY AVAILABLE IN SUPERMARKETS.

SPICY SWEET POTATO AND PARSNIP "FRIES"

ROASTED VEGETABLE "FRIES" ARE YUMMY AND HEALTHY. CUT THE VEGETABLES INTO THIN ROUNDS RATHER THAN STICKS — IT'S QUICKER AND THEY COOK MORE EVENLY. SERVE WITH DINNER OR AS AN APPETIZER. SWEET CHILI AÏOLI (SEE RECIPE, OPPOSITE) IS A GREAT DIPPING SAUCE.

2 TSP	GROUND CUMIN	10 ML
2 TSP	GROUND CORIANDER	10 ML
1 TSP	SALT	5 ML
1/2 TSP	CAYENNE PEPPER (OR TO TASTE)	2 ML
1/4 TSP	FRESHLY GROUND BLACK PEPPER	1 ML
3 TBSP	OLIVE OIL	45 ML
1 LB	PARSNIPS (SEE TIP, OPPOSITE), PEELED AND CUT INTO 1/4-INCH (0.5 CM) THICK ROUNDS	500 G
1 LB	SWEET POTATOES (SEE TIP, OPPOSITE), PEELED AND CUT INTO 1/4-INCH (0.5 CM) THICK ROUNDS	500 G

PREHEAT OVEN TO 400°F (200°C). LINE 2 LARGE RIMMED BAKING SHEETS WITH PARCHMENT PAPER OR GREASED FOIL. IN A LARGE BOWL, WHISK TOGETHER CUMIN, CORIANDER, SALT, CAYENNE, BLACK PEPPER AND OIL. ADD PARSNIPS AND SWEET POTATOES; TOSS TO COAT. SPREAD VEGETABLES IN A SINGLE LAYER ON PREPARED BAKING SHEETS. COVER LOOSELY WITH FOIL AND BAKE FOR 15 MINUTES. REMOVE FOIL, FLIP VEGETABLES, ROTATE PANS AND SWITCH PANS BETWEEN OVEN RACKS. BAKE, UNCOVERED, FOR 15 TO 20 MINUTES OR UNTIL VEGETABLES ARE TENDER AND BROWNED AT THE EDGES. SERVES 4 TO 6.

TIP: LOOK FOR FIRM PARSNIPS THAT ARE HEAVY FOR THEIR SIZE. AVOID PARSNIPS WITH WRINKLED SKIN OR LONG, SKINNY TAIL ENDS. PEEL WITH A VEGETABLE PEELER. SOME RECIPES SUGGEST REMOVING THE WOODY CORE, BUT WE DON'T BOTHER FOR THIS RECIPE, AS THE CORE SOFTENS DURING ROASTING. PARSNIPS ARE ALSO EXCELLENT SIMMERED AND MASHED WITH POTATOES.

TIP: SWEET POTATOES AND YAMS ARE NOT THE SAME THING, BUT THERE IS OFTEN CONFUSION OVER LABELING THESE TWO TUBERS IN SUPERMARKETS. NO MATTER WHAT YOUR GROCERY STORE CALLS THEM, YOU WANT THE ONES WITH ORANGE FLESH!

SWEET CHILI AÏOLI

THIS AÏOLI IS ALSO EXCELLENT SPREAD ON TOASTED BUNS AND SANDWICHED WITH STICKY ASIAN PORK BURGERS (SEE RECIPE, PAGE 132). OR TRY IT IN PLACE OF REGULAR MAYONNAISE IN YOUR FAVORITE TURKEY SALAD SANDWICH.

1/2 CUP	MAYONNAISE	125 ML
2 TBSP	SWEET CHILI DIPPING SAUCE	30 ML
1 TBSP	FRESHLY SQUEEZED LIME JUICE	15 ML

IN A BOWL, WHISK TOGETHER MAYONNAISE, CHILI SAUCE AND LIME JUICE. COVER AND REFRIGERATE FOR UP TO 2 DAYS. MAKES ABOUT 2/3 CUP (150 ML).

ONE NICE THING ABOUT EGOTISTS — THEY DON'T TALK ABOUT OTHER PEOPLE.

MAPLE-GLAZED PARSNIPS, SWEET POTATOES AND ONIONS

PERFECT WITH CHICKEN, TURKEY, PORK
OR HAM. ROASTING THE VEGETABLES INTENSIFIES
THEIR FLAVORS. SLICED CARROTS COULD ALSO
BE ADDED TO THIS RECIPE.

1 TSP	GROUND CORIANDER OR CINNAMON	5 ML
1 TSP	SALT	5 ML
	FRESHLY GROUND BLACK PEPPER	
3 TBSP	OLIVE OIL	45 ML
2 TBSP	PURE MAPLE SYRUP	30 ML
3	SMALL ONIONS, PEELED AND QUARTERED	3
1 LB	SWEET POTATOES (SEE TIP, PAGE 261), PEELED AND CUT INTO 1/4-INCH (0.5 CM) THICK ROUNDS	500 G
1 LB	PARSNIPS (SEE TIP, PAGE 261), PEELED AND CUT INTO 1/4-INCH (0.5 CM) THICK ROUNDS	500 G

PREHEAT OVEN TO 400°F (200°C). LINE 2 LARGE BAKING SHEETS WITH PARCHMENT PAPER OR GREASED FOIL. IN A LARGE BOWL, WHISK TOGETHER CORIANDER, SALT, PEPPER TO TASTE, OIL AND MAPLE SYRUP. ADD ONIONS, SWEET POTATOES AND PARSNIPS; TOSS TO COAT. SPREAD VEGETABLES IN A SINGLE LAYER ON PREPARED BAKING SHEETS. BAKE FOR ABOUT 25 MINUTES, FLIPPING VEGETABLES, ROTATING PANS AND SWITCHING PANS BETWEEN OVEN RACKS HALFWAY THROUGH, UNTIL VEGETABLES ARE TENDER AND BROWNED. SERVE IMMEDIATELY. SERVES 4 TO 6.

PATRAS POTATOES

ENJOY THE FLAVORS OF GREECE,
IN FUN FOIL-WRAPPED PACKETS.

3	CLOVES GARLIC, THINLY SLICED	3
1 TBSP	CHOPPED FRESH OREGANO (OR $3/4$ ML/3 ML DRIED)	15 ML
1 TSP	PAPRIKA	5 ML
1 TSP	SALT	5 ML
	FRESHLY GROUND BLACK PEPPER	
1/4 CUP	OLIVE OIL	60 ML
1 TSP	DIJON MUSTARD	5 ML
1 1/2 LBS	SMALL WAXY RED POTATOES (UNPEELED), CUT INTO 1/8-INCH (3 MM) SLICES	750 G
1	LEMON, CUT IN HALF	1
1/2 CUP	CRUMBLED FETA CHEESE	125 ML
1/4 CUP	CHOPPED FRESH CHIVES	60 ML

PREHEAT ONE SIDE OF THE BARBECUE GRILL TO HIGH. CUT 4 LENGTHS OF FOIL, EACH ABOUT 20 BY 12 INCHES (50 BY 30 CM). FOLD IN HALF CROSSWISE TO MAKE 12- BY 10-INCH (30 BY 25 CM) RECTANGLES. IN A LARGE BOWL, WHISK TOGETHER GARLIC, OREGANO, PAPRIKA, SALT, PEPPER TO TASTE, OIL AND MUSTARD. ADD POTATOES AND TOSS TO COAT. DIVIDE POTATO MIXTURE AMONG FOIL RECTANGLES, DRIZZLING MARINADE OVER TOP. FOLD UP THE SIDES OF THE PACKETS TO CLOSE THEM, SCRUNCHING THE EDGES TO SEAL. PLACE PACKETS ON UNLIT SIDE OF BARBECUE, COVER AND COOK FOR ABOUT 40 MINUTES OR UNTIL POTATOES ARE TENDER. USING TONGS, TRANSFER TO A LARGE SERVING PLATTER. OPEN PACKETS AND SQUEEZE LEMON JUICE OVER POTATOES. SPRINKLE WITH FETA CHEESE AND CHIVES. SERVES 4.

POTATOES BOULANGÈRE

THIS RECIPE EVOLVED FROM AN OLD CUSTOM IN
FRANCE. PEOPLE OFTEN DIDN'T HAVE OVENS, SO THEY
WOULD TAKE A PAN OF MEAT, POTATOES AND ONIONS
TO THE LOCAL BAKER — OR BOULANGÈRE — AND HAVE
HIM ROAST IT FOR THEM. THE MODERN VERSION IS
DELICIOUSLY SIMILAR TO LIGHT SCALLOPED POTATOES.

2 TBSP	BUTTER	30 ML
1	LARGE ONION, THINLY SLICED	1
2	CLOVES GARLIC, MINCED	2
2½ LBS	YUKON GOLD OR OTHER YELLOW-FLESHED POTATOES (SEE TIP, PAGE 259), PEELED AND THINLY SLICED	1.25 KG
2 TSP	CHOPPED FRESH ROSEMARY (OR ½ TSP/2 ML DRIED)	10 ML
2 TSP	CHOPPED FRESH THYME (OR ¼ TSP/1 ML DRIED)	10 ML
1 TSP	SALT	5 ML
	FRESHLY GROUND BLACK PEPPER	
2 TO 2½ CUPS	REDUCED-SODIUM CHICKEN BROTH (SEE TIP, OPPOSITE)	500 TO 625 ML
1 CUP	SHREDDED SHARP (OLD) CHEDDAR CHEESE	250 ML

PREHEAT OVEN TO 375°F (190°C). BUTTER A SHALLOW
12-CUP (3 L) CASSEROLE DISH. IN A LARGE SKILLET,
MELT BUTTER OVER MEDIUM HEAT. SAUTÉ ONION FOR
5 MINUTES OR UNTIL SOFTENED BUT NOT BROWNED.
ADD GARLIC AND SAUTÉ FOR 15 SECONDS OR UNTIL
FRAGRANT. ADD POTATOES, ROSEMARY, THYME, SALT,
PEPPER TO TASTE AND 2 CUPS (500 ML) BROTH; BRING TO
A BOIL. TRANSFER TO PREPARED CASSEROLE DISH, COVER

TIGHTLY AND BAKE FOR 40 MINUTES. UNCOVER AND USE A SPATULA TO LOOSEN POTATOES AROUND EDGES OF DISH, IF NECESSARY. BAKE, UNCOVERED, FOR 30 MINUTES OR UNTIL POTATOES ARE FORK-TENDER AND BROTH IS ALMOST ABSORBED BUT STILL VISIBLE AT EDGES OF DISH. (IF THE POTATOES BECOME TOO DRY BEFORE THEY ARE READY, ADD MORE BROTH.) SPRINKLE WITH CHEESE AND BAKE FOR 10 MINUTES OR UNTIL CHEESE IS MELTED. REMOVE FROM OVEN AND LET STAND FOR 15 MINUTES OR UNTIL LIQUID IS ALMOST ABSORBED. SERVES 6.

TIP: FOR THE BEST FLAVOR, WE PREFER TO USE CHICKEN BROTH IN THIS RECIPE. IF YOU LIKE, YOU CAN SUBSTITUTE HOMEMADE VEGETABLE STOCK (SEE RECIPE, PAGE 90) OR REDUCED-SODIUM VEGETABLE BROTH.

TIP: IF THE STEM OF YOUR FRESH THYME IS TENDER, YOU CAN CHOP IT IN WITH THE LEAVES. IF THE STEM IS WOODY, JUST USE THE LEAVES. TO QUICKLY STRIP THE LEAVES, PINCH THE STEM NEAR THE TOP WITH ONE HAND, THEN RUN THE THUMB AND FOREFINGER OF YOUR OTHER HAND STRAIGHT DOWN THE STEM. THE LEAVES WILL LAND ON THE CHOPPING BOARD, AND YOU CAN DISCARD THE BARE STEM. THIS TECHNIQUE ALSO WORKS WITH ROSEMARY AND OREGANO.

DON'T DRIVE FASTER THAN YOUR
GUARDIAN ANGEL CAN FLY.

LIGHT CHIVE MASHED POTATOES

THESE POTATOES ARE RICH, WITH A VERY CREAMY TASTE EVEN THOUGH THEY'RE MADE WITH LOW-FAT INGREDIENTS. THE DISTINCT TEXTURE AND TASTE OF RICOTTA CHEESE MAKES THE DIFFERENCE.

2 LBS	YUKON GOLD OR OTHER YELLOW-FLESHED POTATOES (SEE TIP, PAGE 259), PEELED AND CUT INTO UNIFORM CHUNKS	1 KG
1/2 CUP	SKIM MILK	125 ML
2 TBSP	LIGHT NON-HYDROGENATED MARGARINE	30 ML
1 CUP	LOW-FAT (5%) RICOTTA OR 2% COTTAGE CHEESE (SEE TIP, BELOW)	250 ML
1/2 CUP	CHOPPED FRESH CHIVES	125 ML
	SALT AND FRESHLY GROUND BLACK PEPPER	

PLACE POTATOES IN A LARGE POT OF COLD SALTED WATER. COVER AND BRING TO A BOIL OVER HIGH HEAT. REDUCE HEAT AND SIMMER FOR 15 TO 20 MINUTES OR UNTIL POTATOES ARE FORK-TENDER. DRAIN AND TRANSFER TO A LARGE BOWL OR RETURN TO THE POT. IN A SMALL MICROWAVE-SAFE BOWL OR MEASURING CUP, COMBINE MILK AND MARGARINE. MICROWAVE ON HIGH FOR 30 SECONDS OR UNTIL MILK IS WARM AND MARGARINE IS MELTED. ADD TO POTATOES AND MASH WITH A POTATO MASHER UNTIL SMOOTH. WITH A SPATULA, STIR IN RICOTTA AND CHIVES UNTIL THOROUGHLY COMBINED. SEASON TO TASTE WITH SALT AND PEPPER. SERVES 4 TO 6.

TIP: COTTAGE CHEESE IS LUMPIER THAN RICOTTA. IF YOU USE COTTAGE CHEESE, PURÉE IT IN A BLENDER OR MINI CHOPPER OR USING AN IMMERSION BLENDER BEFORE ADDING IT TO THE POTATOES.

MASHED POTATOES AND PEAS

RESTAURANTS OFTEN ENLIVEN MASHED POTATOES BY ADDING OTHER FLAVORFUL INGREDIENTS. THIS COMBINATION HAS GREAT TASTE AND COLOR. IT'S VERY GOOD SERVED WITH PRONTO ITALIAN CHICKEN (PAGE 138).

2 LBS	YUKON GOLD OR OTHER YELLOW-FLESHED POTATOES (SEE TIP, PAGE 259), PEELED AND CUT INTO UNIFORM CHUNKS	1 KG
6	CLOVES GARLIC, PEELED BUT LEFT WHOLE	6
2 CUPS	FROZEN BABY PEAS (NO NEED TO THAW)	500 ML
1 CUP	MILK	250 ML
2 TBSP	BUTTER	30 ML
1/2 TO 1 TSP	SALT	2 TO 5 ML
1/4 TSP	FRESHLY GROUND BLACK PEPPER	1 ML

PLACE POTATOES AND GARLIC IN A LARGE POT OF COLD SALTED WATER. COVER AND BRING TO A BOIL OVER HIGH HEAT. REDUCE HEAT AND SIMMER FOR 15 TO 20 MINUTES OR UNTIL POTATOES ARE FORK-TENDER. ADD PEAS AND RETURN TO A SIMMER; SIMMER FOR 1 MINUTE. DRAIN AND TRANSFER TO A LARGE BOWL OR RETURN TO THE POT. IN A MICROWAVE-SAFE BOWL OR MEASURING CUP, COMBINE MILK AND BUTTER. MICROWAVE ON HIGH FOR 30 SECONDS OR UNTIL MILK IS WARM AND BUTTER IS MELTED. ADD TO POTATO MIXTURE, ALONG WITH SALT TO TASTE AND PEPPER, AND MASH WITH A POTATO MASHER UNTIL POTATOES ARE SMOOTH. (THE PEAS WILL BE SOFT BUT STILL SOMEWHAT CHUNKY.) SERVES 4 TO 6.

HERBED BREAD STUFFING

HERE'S AN EXCELLENT ALL-PURPOSE STUFFING
TO ACCOMPANY ROAST TURKEY, CHICKEN OR PORK.
BAKING THE STUFFING IN A SEPARATE DISH IS
NOT ONLY MORE CONVENIENT, BUT ALSO REMOVES
THE FOOD SAFETY CONCERNS ASSOCIATED
WITH COOKING IT INSIDE THE BIRD.

1	LOAF (ABOUT 1 LB/500 G) FRENCH BREAD	1
1/4 CUP	BUTTER OR OLIVE OIL	60 ML
3	STALKS CELERY, FINELY CHOPPED	3
2	ONIONS, FINELY CHOPPED	2
1	LEEK (SEE TIP, OPPOSITE), THINLY SLICED	1
1/2 CUP	CHOPPED TOASTED PECANS (SEE TIP, PAGE 127)	125 ML
1/2 CUP	DRIED CRANBERRIES OR DRIED CHERRIES (OPTIONAL)	125 ML
1/2 CUP	CHOPPED FRESH PARSLEY	125 ML
3 TBSP	CHOPPED FRESH SAGE (OR 1 TBSP/ 15 ML CRUMBLED DRIED SAGE)	45 ML
1 TBSP	CHOPPED FRESH ROSEMARY OR THYME (OR 1 TSP/5 ML DRIED)	15 ML
1 TSP	SALT	5 ML
	FRESHLY GROUND BLACK PEPPER	
2 1/2 CUPS	REDUCED-SODIUM CHICKEN OR VEGETABLE BROTH OR HOMEMADE VEGETABLE STOCK (SEE RECIPE, PAGE 90)	625 ML
2	EGGS, LIGHTLY BEATEN	2

PREHEAT OVEN TO 275°F (140°C). CUT OR TEAR BREAD,
INCLUDING CRUST, INTO BITE-SIZE PIECES. SPREAD ON
2 LARGE BAKING SHEETS. BAKE FOR 20 TO 25 MINUTES,
STIRRING TWICE, UNTIL CRISP AND DRY. LET COOL FOR

10 MINUTES. TRANSFER TO A LARGE BOWL. INCREASE OVEN TEMPERATURE TO 375°F (190°C). BUTTER A 13- BY 9-INCH (33 BY 23 CM) GLASS BAKING DISH.

MEANWHILE, IN A LARGE NONSTICK SKILLET, MELT BUTTER OVER MEDIUM HEAT. SAUTÉ CELERY, ONIONS AND LEEK FOR ABOUT 6 MINUTES OR UNTIL SOFTENED BUT NOT BROWNED. TRANSFER TO BOWL WITH TOASTED BREAD CUBES. ADD PECANS, CRANBERRIES (IF USING), PARSLEY, SAGE, ROSEMARY, SALT AND PEPPER TO TASTE. ADD BROTH AND TOSS UNTIL LIQUID IS ABSORBED. STIR IN EGGS. SPREAD STUFFING IN PREPARED BAKING DISH AND COVER WITH FOIL. BAKE FOR 30 MINUTES OR UNTIL HEATED THROUGH. REMOVE FOIL AND BAKE FOR 15 TO 25 MINUTES OR UNTIL TOP IS BROWNED AND CRISP. SERVES UP TO 10.

TIP: RINSE LEEKS WELL, AS THEY OFTEN HAVE SOIL TRAPPED BETWEEN THEIR LAYERS. TO CLEAN THEM THOROUGHLY, SWIRL CHOPPED OR SLICED LEEKS IN A LARGE BOWL OF WATER. LET THE DIRT FALL TO THE BOTTOM AND REMOVE LEEKS WITH A SLOTTED SPOON. REPEAT IF NECESSARY. YOU CAN USE BOTH THE WHITE AND THE PALE TO MEDIUM GREEN PARTS OF THE LEEK. ONLY THE VERY DARK GREEN TOP 1 TO 2 INCHES (2.5 TO 5 CM) SHOULD BE DISCARDED.

TIP: IF YOU USE A SALT-FREE STOCK OR BROTH, YOU MAY WANT TO ADD MORE SALT. SALT IS, IN ANY RECIPE, A MATTER OF PERSONAL PREFERENCE, SO FEEL FREE TO INCREASE OR REDUCE THE QUANTITIES WE SUGGEST.

MAKE AHEAD: SPREAD STUFFING IN PREPARED BAKING DISH, COVER AND REFRIGERATE FOR UP TO 1 DAY. BAKE AS DIRECTED.

LITTLE SAVORY BREAD PUDDINGS

SERVE THESE AS A SIDE WITH ROAST
MEATS OR WITH A BOWL OF SOUP.

1 TBSP	OLIVE OR VEGETABLE OIL	15 ML
3/4 CUP	FINELY CHOPPED ONION	175 ML
2 TBSP	CHOPPED FRESH PARSLEY	30 ML
2 TBSP	CHOPPED FRESH SAGE (OR 3/4 TSP/ 3 ML CRUMBLED DRIED SAGE)	30 ML
1/2 TSP	DRIED THYME	2 ML
1/2 TSP	SALT	2 ML
	FRESHLY GROUND BLACK PEPPER	
6	EGGS	6
1 1/4 CUPS	HEAVY OR WHIPPING (35%) CREAM	300 ML
5 CUPS	CUBED WHITE SANDWICH BREAD (1/2-INCH/1 CM CUBES)	1.25 L
1 1/4 CUPS	SHREDDED SHARP (OLD) CHEDDAR OR SWISS CHEESE	300 ML

IN A NONSTICK SKILLET, HEAT OIL OVER MEDIUM HEAT.
SAUTÉ ONION FOR 3 MINUTES OR UNTIL SOFTENED.
TRANSFER TO A PLATE AND LET COOL SLIGHTLY. LINE
A 12-CUP NONSTICK MUFFIN PAN WITH PAPER LINERS
AND SPRAY THE INSIDE OF THE LINERS WITH NONSTICK
COOKING SPRAY. IN A BOWL, WHISK TOGETHER PARSLEY,
SAGE, THYME, SALT, PEPPER TO TASTE, EGGS AND
CREAM. DIVIDE HALF THE BREAD CUBES AMONG MUFFIN
CUPS. SPRINKLE WITH THE COOKED ONION AND HALF
THE CHEESE. REPEAT WITH THE REMAINING BREAD AND
CHEESE. POUR SOME OF THE EGG MIXTURE INTO EACH
CUP AND LET IT SOAK IN. TOP UP EACH MUFFIN CUP WITH
THE REMAINING EGG MIXTURE. POKE BREAD CUBES DOWN

WITH A SMALL SPOON TO ENSURE THEY ARE SUBMERGED. REFRIGERATE FOR AT LEAST 30 MINUTES OR FOR UP TO 4 HOURS.

PREHEAT OVEN TO 400°F (200°C). BAKE FOR ABOUT 20 MINUTES OR UNTIL PUDDINGS ARE PUFFY, BROWNED AND SET IN THE CENTER. LET COOL IN PAN ON A WIRE RACK FOR 15 MINUTES, THEN TRANSFER TO THE RACK TO COOL. MAKES 12 PUDDINGS.

TIP: FRESH SAGE IS WIDELY AVAILABLE IN SUPERMARKETS, SO MAKE THAT YOUR FIRST CHOICE. IF YOU SUBSTITUTE DRIED SAGE, LOOK FOR THE CRUMBLED VERSION. AVOID GROUND DRIED SAGE, WHICH RESEMBLES A BROWN-GRAY POWDER AND IS TOO POWERFUL.

MY CONGREGATION SUPPORTS ALL DENOMINATIONS, BUT OUR FAVORITES ARE TWENTIES AND FIFTIES.
– HENRY GIBSON

MUSHROOM AND QUINOA PILAF

COMBINING QUINOA WITH REGULAR LONG-GRAIN RICE IN THIS SIDE DISH IS A GREAT WAY TO INTRODUCE YOUR FAMILY TO THE HEALTHY SUPER-GRAIN. THIS PILAF GOES REALLY WELL WITH GRILLED STEAK OR PORK CHOPS. YOU COULD ALSO STIR CHOPPED TOASTED PECANS AND/OR BABY SPINACH INTO THE PILAF JUST BEFORE SERVING.

1 TBSP	OLIVE OIL OR BUTTER	15 ML
1 CUP	FINELY CHOPPED ONION	250 ML
4 CUPS	SLICED CREMINI OR WHITE MUSHROOMS (SEE TIP, PAGE 229)	1 L
1/2 TSP	SALT	2 ML
1/4 TSP	FRESHLY GROUND BLACK PEPPER	1 ML
1 TO 2 TBSP	COLD WATER (IF NEEDED)	15 TO 30 ML
2	CLOVES GARLIC, MINCED	2
2/3 CUP	RED OR WHITE QUINOA, RINSED WELL (SEE TIP, PAGE 77)	150 ML
2/3 CUP	LONG-GRAIN WHITE RICE	150 ML
1/2 TSP	DRIED OREGANO OR THYME	2 ML
2 2/3 TO 3 CUPS	HOT HOMEMADE VEGETABLE STOCK (SEE RECIPE, PAGE 90) OR REDUCED-SODIUM CHICKEN OR VEGETABLE BROTH	650 TO 750 ML
1/2 CUP	FRESHLY GRATED PARMESAN CHEESE	125 ML
1/4 CUP	CHOPPED FRESH PARSLEY	60 ML
1 TBSP	BALSAMIC VINEGAR (OPTIONAL)	15 ML

IN A LARGE SAUCEPAN, HEAT OIL OVER MEDIUM HEAT. SAUTÉ ONION FOR ABOUT 3 MINUTES OR UNTIL SOFTENED. ADD MUSHROOMS, SALT AND PEPPER; SAUTÉ FOR 5 TO 7 MINUTES OR UNTIL MUSHROOMS ARE

BROWNED. IF THE PAN GETS TOO DRY, ADD COLD WATER
AS NEEDED. ADD GARLIC, QUINOA, RICE AND OREGANO;
COOK, STIRRING, FOR 30 SECONDS OR UNTIL GRAINS
ARE COATED WITH OIL AND MIXTURE IS FRAGRANT.
ADD $2^2/_3$ CUPS (650 ML) HOT STOCK AND BRING TO A
BOIL. REDUCE HEAT TO LOW, COVER AND SIMMER FOR
15 MINUTES OR UNTIL LIQUID IS ABSORBED AND GRAINS
ARE TENDER. (IF LIQUID IS ABSORBED BEFORE GRAINS ARE
READY, ADD MORE STOCK AND CONTINUE TO SIMMER,
COVERED, UNTIL GRAINS ARE TENDER.) REMOVE FROM
HEAT AND STIR IN PARMESAN, PARSLEY AND VINEGAR
(IF USING). SERVE IMMEDIATELY. SERVES 6.

TIP: IF YOU USE A SALT-FREE STOCK OR BROTH, YOU
MAY WANT TO ADD MORE SALT. SALT IS, IN ANY RECIPE,
A MATTER OF PERSONAL PREFERENCE, SO FEEL FREE TO
INCREASE OR REDUCE THE QUANTITIES WE SUGGEST.

TIP: THIS PILAF CAN ALSO BE COOKED IN THE OVEN. AFTER
ADDING THE HOT STOCK, TRANSFER THE MIXTURE TO
A GLASS BAKING DISH, COVER TIGHTLY AND COOK IN A
PREHEATED 350°F (180°C) OVEN FOR 15 TO 20 MINUTES.

THE HEAVIER THE PACKAGE AND THE FARTHER YOU HAVE TO
CARRY IT, THE MORE YOUR NOSE WILL ITCH.

TOMATO ORZO PILAF

ORZO — THE RICE-SHAPED PASTA THAT'S OH SO GOOD. A COMFORTING SIDE DISH TO SERVE WITH PRONTO ITALIAN CHICKEN (PAGE 138), CHICKEN MUSHROOM FLORENTINE (PAGE 164) OR GRILLED MEAT OR FISH.

3 TBSP	BUTTER, DIVIDED	45 ML
1/3 CUP	FINELY CHOPPED ONION	75 ML
1	CLOVE GARLIC, MINCED	1
1 TSP	PAPRIKA	5 ML
	SALT AND FRESHLY GROUND BLACK PEPPER	
1 TBSP	TOMATO PASTE (SEE TIP, OPPOSITE)	15 ML
1 CUP	ORZO	250 ML
2 TO 2 1/2 CUPS	HOT HOMEMADE VEGETABLE STOCK (PAGE 90) OR REDUCED-SODIUM CHICKEN OR VEGETABLE BROTH	500 TO 625 ML
1/4 CUP	FRESHLY GRATED PARMESAN CHEESE	60 ML
2 TBSP	CHOPPED FRESH PARSLEY	30 ML

IN A MEDIUM SAUCEPAN, MELT 2 TBSP (30 ML) OF THE BUTTER OVER MEDIUM HEAT. ADD ONION, REDUCE HEAT TO LOW AND COOK GENTLY, STIRRING OCCASIONALLY, FOR ABOUT 5 MINUTES OR UNTIL SOFTENED BUT NOT BROWNED. INCREASE HEAT TO MEDIUM AND ADD GARLIC, PAPRIKA, 1/2 TSP (2 ML) SALT, 1/8 TSP (0.5 ML) PEPPER AND TOMATO PASTE; COOK, STIRRING, FOR 15 SECONDS OR UNTIL FRAGRANT. ADD ORZO, STIRRING TO COAT. ADD 2 CUPS (500 ML) HOT STOCK AND BRING TO A BOIL. REDUCE HEAT TO LOW, COVER AND SIMMER, STIRRING OCCASIONALLY, FOR ABOUT 15 MINUTES OR UNTIL LIQUID IS ABSORBED AND ORZO IS TENDER. (IF LIQUID IS ABSORBED BEFORE ORZO IS READY, ADD MORE STOCK AND CONTINUE TO SIMMER, COVERED,

UNTIL ORZO IS TENDER.) REMOVE FROM HEAT AND STIR IN PARMESAN, PARSLEY AND THE REMAINING BUTTER. TASTE AND ADJUST SEASONING WITH SALT AND PEPPER, IF DESIRED. SERVE IMMEDIATELY. SERVES 3 TO 4.

TIP: YOU CAN FREEZE THE UNUSED PORTION OF CANNED TOMATO PASTE. FREEZE IT IN ICE CUBE TRAYS UNTIL HARD, THEN TRANSFER THE CUBES TO A FREEZER BAG. EACH CUBE IS EQUIVALENT TO ABOUT 1 TBSP (15 ML). OR DOLLOP TABLESPOONFULS OF PASTE ONTO A BAKING SHEET, FREEZE UNTIL HARD, THEN TRANSFER TO FREEZER BAGS. EVEN BETTER, BUY TOMATO PASTE IN TUBES IF YOU CAN FIND THEM. TUBES OF TOMATO PASTE KEEP IN THE REFRIGERATOR FOR WEEKS. IF YOUR SUPERMARKET DOESN'T HAVE TUBES, CHECK OUT YOUR NEAREST ITALIAN DELI FOR IMPORTED BRANDS.

TIP: IF YOU USE A SALT-FREE STOCK OR BROTH, YOU MAY WANT TO ADD MORE SALT. SALT IS, IN ANY RECIPE, A MATTER OF PERSONAL PREFERENCE, SO FEEL FREE TO INCREASE OR REDUCE THE QUANTITIES WE SUGGEST. BEFORE ADDING MORE SALT AT THE END OF THE COOKING TIME, BE SURE TO TASTE THE DISH FIRST.

MAKE AHEAD: SPREAD PILAF ON A LARGE BAKING SHEET AND REFRIGERATE UNTIL THOROUGHLY COOLED. TRANSFER TO AN AIRTIGHT CONTAINER AND REFRIGERATE FOR UP TO 2 DAYS. REHEAT IN THE MICROWAVE, ADDING MORE STOCK IF THE PILAF SEEMS TOO DRY.

VARIATION
TOMATO RICE PILAF: SUBSTITUTE LONG-GRAIN WHITE RICE FOR THE ORZO.

EASY BACON CORN RISOTTO

COMFORTING, CREAMY RISOTTO DOESN'T HAVE TO TIE YOU TO THE STOVE. WE FOUND A WAY TO NIX ALL THAT TIME-CONSUMING STIRRING AND STILL GET FABULOUS RESULTS. THIS DISH IS SUPERB SERVED UNDER PAN-SEARED FISH, SUCH AS COD OR HALIBUT, OR WITH ROAST CHICKEN.

5 TO 5½ CUPS	REDUCED-SODIUM CHICKEN BROTH OR HOMEMADE VEGETABLE STOCK (SEE RECIPE, PAGE 90)	1.25 TO 1.375 L
6	SLICES BACON, CHOPPED	6
1 TBSP	BUTTER	15 ML
1	ONION, FINELY CHOPPED	1
1½ CUPS	FRESH OR THAWED FROZEN CORN KERNELS	375 ML
2	CLOVES GARLIC, MINCED	2
2 CUPS	SHORT-GRAIN WHITE RICE, SUCH AS ARBORIO (SEE TIP, OPPOSITE)	500 ML
	SALT AND FRESHLY GROUND BLACK PEPPER	
2 CUPS	CHERRY TOMATOES, HALVED	500 ML
1 CUP	FRESHLY GRATED PARMESAN CHEESE	250 ML

IN A LARGE SAUCEPAN, BRING BROTH TO A BOIL; REDUCE HEAT AND LET SIMMER. MEANWHILE, IN ANOTHER LARGE SAUCEPAN, SAUTÉ BACON OVER MEDIUM-HIGH HEAT UNTIL LIGHTLY BROWNED BUT NOT CRISPY. USING A SLOTTED SPOON, TRANSFER BACON TO A PLATE LINED WITH PAPER TOWELS. DRAIN OFF FAT AND WIPE OUT PAN WITH PAPER TOWELS. ADD BUTTER TO THE PAN AND MELT OVER MEDIUM HEAT. SAUTÉ ONION AND CORN FOR 5 MINUTES OR UNTIL TENDER. ADD GARLIC AND SAUTÉ FOR 15 SECONDS

OR UNTIL FRAGRANT. ADD RICE AND STIR TO COAT. RETURN BACON TO PAN AND ADD 4 CUPS (1 L) OF THE BROTH, $1/2$ TSP (2 ML) SALT AND $1/4$ TSP (1 ML) PEPPER. (REMOVE THE REMAINING BROTH FROM THE HEAT.) BRING RICE MIXTURE TO A BOIL; REDUCE HEAT TO LOW, COVER AND SIMMER FOR 10 MINUTES. UNCOVER, STIR THOROUGHLY, THEN STIR IN TOMATOES. IF LIQUID IS MOSTLY ABSORBED, ADD ANOTHER 1 CUP (250 ML) BROTH. COVER AND SIMMER, STIRRING OCCASIONALLY, FOR 10 MINUTES OR UNTIL LIQUID IS ALMOST ABSORBED AND RICE IS STILL SLIGHTLY FIRM TO THE BITE. REMOVE FROM HEAT AND STIR IN PARMESAN AND ENOUGH OF THE REMAINING BROTH TO MAKE IT CREAMY. TASTE AND ADJUST SEASONING WITH SALT AND PEPPER, IF DESIRED. COVER AND LET STAND FOR 10 MINUTES OR UNTIL RICE IS TENDER. SERVES 6 TO 8.

TIP: IF YOU USE A SALT-FREE STOCK OR BROTH, YOU MAY WANT TO ADD MORE SALT. SALT IS, IN ANY RECIPE, A MATTER OF PERSONAL PREFERENCE, SO FEEL FREE TO INCREASE OR REDUCE THE QUANTITIES WE SUGGEST. BEFORE ADDING MORE SALT AT THE END OF THE COOKING TIME, BE SURE TO TASTE THE DISH FIRST, AS THE BACON AND PARMESAN CONTRIBUTE QUITE A LOT OF SALT.

TIP: SHORT-GRAIN RICE IS ESSENTIAL TO A SMOOTH AND CREAMY RISOTTO. YOU WON'T GET THE SAME VELVETY FINISH IF YOU TRY TO MAKE RISOTTO WITH LONG-GRAIN RICE, SUCH AS BASMATI, CONVERTED OR JASMINE. SHORT-GRAIN RICE, SUCH AS ARBORIO OR CARNAROLI, IS SOMETIMES LABELED "RISOTTO RICE."

BEJEWELED COUSCOUS

EMERALD PISTACHIOS AND RUBY POMEGRANATE
SEEDS CREATE A PRETTY SIDE DISH THAT WILL
IMPRESS YOUR GUESTS. SERVE WITH INDIAN
SPICED CHICKEN DRUMSTICKS (PAGE 168) FOR
AN INFORMAL DINNER PARTY.

1	CHAI TEA BAG	1
1/2 CUP	WATER	125 ML
1 TBSP	LIQUID HONEY OR GRANULATED SUGAR	15 ML
1/4 TSP	SALT	1 ML
	GRATED ZEST OF 1/2 ORANGE	
3/4 CUP	ORANGE JUICE	175 ML
1 TBSP	BUTTER (OPTIONAL)	15 ML
1 CUP	COUSCOUS	250 ML
1/2 CUP	POMEGRANATE SEEDS (SEE TIP, PAGE 65)	125 ML
1/4 CUP	SKINNED UNSALTED PISTACHIOS (SEE TIP, PAGE 44), FINELY CHOPPED	60 ML
2 TBSP	CHOPPED FRESH MINT, CHIVES OR PARSLEY, OR A COMBINATION	30 ML

IN A MEDIUM SAUCEPAN, COMBINE TEA BAG, WATER,
HONEY, SALT AND ORANGE ZEST. BRING TO A BOIL OVER
HIGH HEAT, THEN IMMEDIATELY REMOVE FROM HEAT AND
LET STEEP FOR 10 MINUTES. DISCARD TEA BAG, SQUEEZING
GENTLY. ADD ORANGE JUICE AND BUTTER; BRING TO A
BOIL OVER HIGH HEAT. REMOVE FROM HEAT AND STIR
IN COUSCOUS; COVER AND LET STAND FOR ABOUT
5 MINUTES OR UNTIL LIQUID IS ABSORBED. FLUFF WITH
A FORK AND STIR IN POMEGRANATE SEEDS, PISTACHIOS
AND MINT. SERVE IMMEDIATELY OR LET COOL TO ROOM
TEMPERATURE. SERVES 3 TO 4.

COOKIES, SQUARES AND SWEETS

WHITE CHOCOLATE AND MACADAMIA NUT COOKIES

REMEMBER BEST CHOCOLATE CHIP COOKIES FROM OUR EARLIER BOOKS? THIS IS A SWANKY NEW VARIATION.

2 1/4 CUPS	ALL-PURPOSE FLOUR	550 ML
1/2 TSP	BAKING SODA	2 ML
1/2 TSP	SALT	2 ML
1 CUP	FIRMLY PACKED BROWN SUGAR	250 ML
1/2 CUP	GRANULATED SUGAR	125 ML
1 CUP	UNSALTED BUTTER, SOFTENED (SEE TIP, PAGE 285)	250 ML
2	EGGS, AT ROOM TEMPERATURE	2
2 TSP	VANILLA EXTRACT	10 ML
1 CUP	WHITE CHOCOLATE CHIPS	250 ML
1 CUP	CHOPPED MACADAMIA NUTS	250 ML

PREHEAT OVEN TO 350°F (180°C). LIGHTLY GREASE 2 LARGE BAKING SHEETS OR LINE WITH PARCHMENT PAPER. IN A BOWL, SIFT TOGETHER FLOUR, BAKING SODA AND SALT; SET ASIDE. IN A LARGE BOWL, CREAM BROWN SUGAR, GRANULATED SUGAR AND BUTTER UNTIL LIGHT AND FLUFFY. BEAT IN EGGS AND VANILLA UNTIL THOROUGHLY COMBINED. STIR IN FLOUR MIXTURE. STIR IN CHOCOLATE CHIPS AND MACADAMIA NUTS. DROP BY HEAPING TABLESPOONFULS (15 ML) ONTO PREPARED BAKING SHEET, SPACING THEM ABOUT 2 INCHES (5 CM) APART. BAKE, ONE SHEET AT A TIME, FOR 10 TO 12 MINUTES OR UNTIL GOLDEN BROWN. FOR EVEN BROWNING, ROTATE THE PAN HALFWAY THROUGH. LET COOL ON BAKING SHEET ON A WIRE RACK FOR 2 MINUTES, THEN TRANSFER TO RACK TO COOL COMPLETELY. MAKES ABOUT 30 COOKIES.

TIP: THE HIGH SUGAR CONTENT IN COOKIES MEANS THEY SOMETIMES GET OVERLY DARK ON THE BOTTOM. TO AVOID THIS, SET THE BAKING SHEET ON TOP OF A SECOND, UNGREASED BAKING SHEET. THIS IS CALLED DOUBLE PANNING.

TIP: MACADAMIA NUTS ARE EXPENSIVE, SO MAKE THESE COOKIES FOR THE PEOPLE YOU LOVE MOST. LOOK FOR MACADAMIA NUTS IN THE BULK BIN SECTION OF THE SUPERMARKET AND BUY ONLY AS MANY AS YOU NEED.

MAKE AHEAD: STORE IN AN AIRTIGHT CONTAINER AT ROOM TEMPERATURE FOR UP TO 5 DAYS, OR PLACE BETWEEN LAYERS OF WAXED PAPER IN AN AIRTIGHT CONTAINER AND FREEZE FOR UP TO 2 WEEKS.

ONCE YOU'VE SEEN A SHOPPING CENTER, YOU'VE SEEN A MALL.

CHOCOLATE SNOWCAPS

CHEWY AND CHEERFUL. PERFECT
FOR A COOKIE EXCHANGE.

4 OZ	SEMISWEET OR BITTERSWEET (DARK) CHOCOLATE, COARSELY CHOPPED	125 G
1/2 CUP	UNSALTED BUTTER	125 ML
2 CUPS	GRANULATED SUGAR	500 ML
2 TSP	BAKING POWDER	10 ML
2 TSP	VANILLA EXTRACT	10 ML
1/4 TSP	SALT	1 ML
3	EGGS, LIGHTLY BEATEN	3
2 CUPS	ALL-PURPOSE FLOUR	500 ML
1 CUP	CONFECTIONERS' (ICING) SUGAR	250 ML

IN A SMALL SAUCEPAN, MELT CHOCOLATE AND BUTTER
OVER LOW HEAT, STIRRING CONSTANTLY. REMOVE FROM
HEAT AND LET COOL TO ROOM TEMPERATURE (ABOUT
15 MINUTES).

IN A LARGE BOWL, WHISK TOGETHER SUGAR, BAKING
POWDER, VANILLA AND SALT. WHISK IN EGGS. STIR IN
COOLED CHOCOLATE MIXTURE. GRADUALLY ADD FLOUR,
STIRRING UNTIL COMBINED (THE MIXTURE WILL BE QUITE
STIFF). COVER AND REFRIGERATE FOR 2 HOURS OR
UNTIL FIRM.

PREHEAT OVEN TO 350°F (180°C). LIGHTLY GREASE 2 LARGE
BAKING SHEETS OR LINE WITH PARCHMENT PAPER. SCOOP
LEVEL TABLESPOONFULS (15 ML) OF DOUGH AND ROLL
INTO 1-INCH (2.5 CM) BALLS. ROLL IN CONFECTIONERS'
SUGAR. PLACE 2 INCHES (5 CM) APART ON PREPARED
BAKING SHEETS. BAKE, ONE SHEET AT A TIME, FOR 8 TO

10 MINUTES OR UNTIL EDGES ARE JUST SET. FOR EVEN BROWNING, ROTATE THE PAN HALFWAY THROUGH. LET COOL ON BAKING SHEETS ON WIRE RACKS FOR 5 MINUTES, THEN TRANSFER TO RACKS TO COOL COMPLETELY. MAKES ABOUT 5 DOZEN COOKIES.

TIP: USE GOOD-QUALITY NONSTICK BAKING SHEETS FOR THE BEST RESULTS WHEN BAKING COOKIES. IF YOUR BAKING SHEETS ARE OLDER, SCRATCHED AND/OR INCLINED TO STICK, LINE THEM WITH PARCHMENT PAPER BEFORE POSITIONING THE DOUGH.

MAKE AHEAD: STORE IN AN AIRTIGHT CONTAINER AT ROOM TEMPERATURE FOR UP TO 5 DAYS, OR PLACE BETWEEN LAYERS OF WAXED PAPER IN AN AIRTIGHT CONTAINER AND FREEZE FOR UP TO 2 WEEKS.

YES, MARRIAGE CAN BE FUN. TROUBLE IS, YOU'RE MARRIED **ALL** THE TIME.

CHOCOLATE SWIRL COOKIES

PRETTY PINWHEEL COOKIES —
AND NO NUTS, SO THEY CAN GO TO SCHOOL.

3/4 CUP	GRANULATED SUGAR	175 ML
1 CUP	UNSALTED BUTTER, SOFTENED (SEE TIP, OPPOSITE)	250 ML
1	EGG	1
2 TSP	VANILLA EXTRACT	10 ML
2 CUPS	ALL-PURPOSE FLOUR	500 ML
1/4 CUP	UNSWEETENED COCOA POWDER, SIFTED	60 ML

IN A LARGE BOWL, CREAM SUGAR AND BUTTER UNTIL LIGHT AND FLUFFY. BEAT IN EGG AND VANILLA. BEAT IN FLOUR. DIVIDE DOUGH IN HALF. USING YOUR HANDS OR AN ELECTRIC MIXER, MIX COCOA INTO ONE HALF OF THE DOUGH. SHAPE EACH PIECE OF DOUGH INTO A 7- BY 3-INCH (18 BY 7.5 CM) RECTANGLE. WRAP IN PLASTIC WRAP AND REFRIGERATE FOR 30 MINUTES.

ON A LIGHTLY FLOURED WORK SURFACE, ROLL OUT EACH PIECE OF DOUGH INTO A 12- BY 8-INCH (30 BY 20 CM) RECTANGLE. CAREFULLY PLACE CHOCOLATE DOUGH ON TOP OF VANILLA DOUGH. TRIM THE EDGES TO NEATEN, IF NECESSARY. STARTING WITH A LONG EDGE, ROLL UP DOUGH LIKE A JELLY ROLL. WRAP IN PLASTIC WRAP AND REFRIGERATE FOR AT LEAST 45 MINUTES OR FOR UP TO 2 DAYS.

PREHEAT OVEN TO 350°F (180°C). LIGHTLY GREASE 2 LARGE BAKING SHEETS OR LINE WITH PARCHMENT PAPER. USING A SHARP KNIFE, SLICE DOUGH INTO 1/8-INCH (3 MM) THICK ROUNDS. PLACE 2 INCHES (5 CM) APART ON PREPARED

BAKING SHEET. BAKE, ONE SHEET AT A TIME, FOR 6 TO 8 MINUTES OR UNTIL SET AND EDGES ARE LIGHTLY BROWNED. FOR EVEN BROWNING, ROTATE THE PAN HALFWAY THROUGH. TRANSFER COOKIES FROM BAKING SHEET TO A WIRE RACK AND LET COOL COMPLETELY. MAKES ABOUT 30 COOKIES.

TIP: FOR THE BEST RESULTS WHEN MAKING CAKES AND COOKIES, IT'S IMPORTANT FOR THE BUTTER AND EGGS TO BE AT ROOM TEMPERATURE, AROUND 70°F (21°C). IF THE INGREDIENTS ARE TOO COLD, THE FAT WILL NOT PROPERLY COMBINE WITH THE LIQUIDS IN THE MIXTURE. THIS WILL AFFECT THE TEXTURE OF THE FINISHED CAKE.

MAKE AHEAD: STORE IN AN AIRTIGHT CONTAINER AT ROOM TEMPERATURE FOR UP TO 5 DAYS, OR PLACE BETWEEN LAYERS OF WAXED PAPER IN AN AIRTIGHT CONTAINER AND FREEZE FOR UP TO 2 WEEKS.

THE EASIEST WAY TO FIND SOMETHING THAT'S LOST AROUND THE HOUSE IS TO BUY A REPLACEMENT.

CHOCOLATE HAZELNUT BLOSSOMS

YOUR GO-TO RECIPE WHEN YOU NEED
COOKIES IN A HURRY. CHOCOLATE HAZELNUT
SPREAD (SUCH AS NUTELLA) IS THE KEY.

1 1/2 CUPS	ALL-PURPOSE FLOUR	375 ML
1/2 CUP	GRANULATED SUGAR	125 ML
1/2 CUP	PACKED BROWN SUGAR	125 ML
1/4 CUP	UNSWEETENED COCOA POWDER, SIFTED	60 ML
1 TSP	BAKING POWDER	5 ML
1	EGG	1
1/2 CUP	CHOCOLATE HAZELNUT SPREAD (SUCH AS NUTELLA)	125 ML
1/2 CUP	UNSALTED BUTTER, SOFTENED (SEE TIP, PAGE 289)	125 ML
	ADDITIONAL GRANULATED SUGAR	
30 TO 35	CHOCOLATE ROSETTES (SEE TIP, OPPOSITE)	30 TO 35

PREHEAT OVEN TO 375°F (190°C). LIGHTLY GREASE 2 LARGE
BAKING SHEETS OR LINE WITH PARCHMENT PAPER.
IN A LARGE BOWL, BEAT FLOUR, GRANULATED SUGAR,
BROWN SUGAR, COCOA POWDER, BAKING POWDER, EGG,
CHOCOLATE HAZELNUT SPREAD AND BUTTER UNTIL WELL
COMBINED. SCOOP LEVEL TABLESPOONFULS (15 ML) OF
DOUGH AND ROLL INTO 1-INCH (2.5 CM) BALLS. ROLL IN
GRANULATED SUGAR. PLACE 2 INCHES (5 CM) APART ON
PREPARED BAKING SHEET AND USE A FORK TO FLATTEN
SLIGHTLY. BAKE, ONE SHEET AT A TIME, FOR ABOUT
8 MINUTES OR UNTIL PUFFY AND JUST SET AROUND THE
EDGES. FOR EVEN BROWNING, ROTATE THE PAN HALFWAY
THROUGH. REMOVE FROM OVEN AND IMMEDIATELY

PLACE A CHOCOLATE ROSETTE IN THE CENTER OF EACH COOKIE. LET COOL ON BAKING SHEET ON A WIRE RACK FOR 5 MINUTES, THEN TRANSFER TO RACK TO COOL COMPLETELY, ALLOWING ENOUGH TIME FOR THE ROSETTES TO SET. MAKES 30 TO 35 COOKIES.

TIP: YOU WILL FIND CHOCOLATE ROSETTES IN BOXES NEAR THE OTHER CANDIES OR IN THE BULK FOOD SECTION OF THE SUPERMARKET.

MAKE AHEAD: STORE IN AN AIRTIGHT CONTAINER AT ROOM TEMPERATURE FOR UP TO 5 DAYS, OR PLACE BETWEEN LAYERS OF WAXED PAPER IN AN AIRTIGHT CONTAINER AND FREEZE FOR UP TO 2 WEEKS.

FORGETFULNESS IS A SIGN OF GENIUS.
— I FORGET WHO SAID THIS

GOOD MORNING MOCHA COOKIES

YOUR COFFEE AND OATMEAL IN ONE!

2 TBSP	INSTANT COFFEE GRANULES	30 ML
1 TBSP	HOT WATER	15 ML
1 CUP	ALL-PURPOSE FLOUR	250 ML
1 TSP	BAKING SODA	5 ML
1/2 TSP	SALT	2 ML
1 CUP	PACKED BROWN SUGAR	250 ML
3/4 CUP	UNSALTED BUTTER, SOFTENED (SEE TIP, OPPOSITE)	175 ML
1	EGG, LIGHTLY BEATEN	1
2 CUPS	QUICK-COOKING OR OLD-FASHIONED (LARGE-FLAKE) ROLLED OATS (NOT INSTANT)	500 ML
1 CUP	CHOPPED SEMISWEET CHOCOLATE OR CHOCOLATE CHIPS	250 ML
1 CUP	CHOPPED PECANS	250 ML
1/2 CUP	RAISINS	125 ML

IN A SMALL BOWL, STIR INSTANT COFFEE INTO HOT WATER UNTIL DISSOLVED; LET COOL.

PREHEAT OVEN TO 375°F (190°C). LIGHTLY GREASE 2 LARGE BAKING SHEETS OR LINE WITH PARCHMENT PAPER. IN A BOWL, WHISK TOGETHER FLOUR, BAKING SODA AND SALT; SET ASIDE. IN A LARGE BOWL, CREAM BROWN SUGAR AND BUTTER UNTIL LIGHT AND FLUFFY. BEAT IN EGG UNTIL THOROUGHLY COMBINED. BEAT IN COFFEE MIXTURE. STIR IN FLOUR MIXTURE, OATS, CHOCOLATE, PECANS AND RAISINS UNTIL WELL COMBINED. SCOOP HEAPING TABLESPOONFULS (15 ML) OF BATTER AND ROLL INTO BALLS. (IF BATTER SEEMS STICKY, USE LIGHTLY FLOURED

HANDS.) PLACE 2 INCHES (5 CM) APART ON PREPARED BAKING SHEETS AND USE THE FLOURED BACK OF A SPOON TO FLATTEN SLIGHTLY. BAKE, ONE SHEET AT A TIME, FOR ABOUT 12 MINUTES OR UNTIL SET AT THE EDGES. FOR EVEN BROWNING, ROTATE THE PAN HALFWAY THROUGH. TRANSFER COOKIES FROM BAKING SHEET TO A WIRE RACK AND LET COOL COMPLETELY. MAKES ABOUT 30 COOKIES.

TIP: FOR THE BEST RESULTS WHEN MAKING CAKES AND COOKIES, IT'S IMPORTANT FOR THE BUTTER AND EGGS TO BE AT ROOM TEMPERATURE, AROUND 70°F (21°C). IF THE INGREDIENTS ARE TOO COLD, THE FAT WILL NOT PROPERLY COMBINE WITH THE LIQUIDS IN THE MIXTURE. THIS WILL AFFECT THE TEXTURE OF THE FINISHED CAKE.

TIP: THE HIGH SUGAR CONTENT IN COOKIES MEANS THEY SOMETIMES GET OVERLY DARK ON THE BOTTOM. TO AVOID THIS, SET THE BAKING SHEET ON TOP OF A SECOND, UNGREASED BAKING SHEET. THIS IS CALLED DOUBLE PANNING.

MAKE AHEAD: LAYER WITH WAXED PAPER IN AN AIRTIGHT CONTAINER AND STORE AT ROOM TEMPERATURE FOR UP TO 5 DAYS OR IN THE FREEZER FOR UP TO 2 WEEKS.

BUTTER VS. MARGARINE?
I TRUST COWS OVER SCIENTISTS!

GLAZED ITALIAN COOKIES

RICOTTA CHEESE (YES, WE SAID CHEESE) MAKES THESE COOKIES IRRESISTIBLY LIGHT AND CAKE-LIKE. SO EASY, SO DELICIOUS, SO ITALIAN.

2 1/4 CUPS	ALL-PURPOSE FLOUR	550 ML
1/2 TSP	BAKING SODA	2 ML
1/2 TSP	SALT	2 ML
1 CUP	GRANULATED SUGAR	250 ML
1 CUP	UNSALTED BUTTER, SOFTENED (SEE TIP, PAGE 289)	250 ML
2	EGGS, AT ROOM TEMPERATURE	2
3/4 CUP	RICOTTA CHEESE (SEE TIP, OPPOSITE)	175 ML
1 TSP	VANILLA EXTRACT	5 ML
1/3 CUP	CHOPPED SKINNED UNSALTED PISTACHIOS (SEE TIP, PAGE 44)	75 ML
1/3 CUP	DRIED CRANBERRIES	75 ML

GLAZE

1 1/2 CUPS	CONFECTIONERS' (ICING) SUGAR	375 ML
	GRATED ZEST OF 1 ORANGE	
3 TBSP	FRESHLY SQUEEZED ORANGE JUICE	45 ML

PREHEAT OVEN TO 350°F (180°C). LIGHTLY GREASE 2 LARGE BAKING SHEETS OR LINE WITH PARCHMENT PAPER. IN A BOWL, WHISK TOGETHER FLOUR, BAKING SODA AND SALT; SET ASIDE. IN A LARGE BOWL, CREAM SUGAR AND BUTTER UNTIL LIGHT AND FLUFFY. BEAT IN EGGS, ONE AT A TIME. BEAT IN RICOTTA AND VANILLA (DON'T WORRY IF THE MIXTURE LOOKS CURDLED). STIR IN FLOUR MIXTURE, PISTACHIOS AND CRANBERRIES. DROP BY HEAPING TEASPOONFULS (5 ML) ONTO PREPARED BAKING SHEETS, SPACING THEM ABOUT 2 INCHES (5 CM) APART. BAKE,

ONE SHEET AT A TIME, FOR 12 TO 14 MINUTES OR UNTIL LIGHTLY BROWNED AT THE EDGES AND ON THE BOTTOM. FOR EVEN BROWNING, ROTATE THE PAN HALFWAY THROUGH. LET COOL ON BAKING SHEETS ON A WIRE RACK FOR 10 MINUTES, THEN TRANSFER TO RACKS TO COOL COMPLETELY.

GLAZE: IN A BOWL, STIR TOGETHER CONFECTIONERS' SUGAR, ORANGE ZEST AND ORANGE JUICE UNTIL SMOOTH. DRIZZLE ABOUT 1 TSP (5 ML) GLAZE OVER EACH COOKIE. MAKES ABOUT 40 COOKIES.

TIP: RICOTTA IS A RICH, FRESH ITALIAN CHEESE THAT RESEMBLES A SMOOTHER VERSION OF COTTAGE CHEESE. YOU CAN USE EITHER THE LIGHT (5% OR 7%) OR REGULAR (10%) VERSION HERE. YOU'LL FIND RICOTTA IN THE DAIRY SECTION OF THE SUPERMARKET. TO USE UP LEFTOVER RICOTTA, MAKE OUR LEMON RICOTTA PANCAKES (PAGE 16) THIS WEEKEND.

MAKE AHEAD: LAYER WITH WAXED PAPER IN AN AIRTIGHT CONTAINER AND STORE AT ROOM TEMPERATURE FOR UP TO 2 DAYS OR IN THE FREEZER FOR UP TO 2 WEEKS.

IF I CAN'T BE A GOOD EXAMPLE,
I'LL BE A TERRIFIC WARNING.

GINGER-GLAZED SHORTBREADS

A DAINTY SPICED TREAT TO ENJOY WITH A CUP OF TEA.
OR SERVE WITH SWEET CHAI ORANGES WITH CINNAMON
CREAM (PAGE 332) AS A LIGHT DESSERT. WITH SLIGHT
VARIATIONS, THE SAME SHORTBREAD BASE IS USED TO
MAKE BLACKCURRANT LINZER SLICES (PAGE 298) AND
WHITE CHOCOLATE FIG SQUARES (PAGE 302).

BASE

I CUP	ALL-PURPOSE FLOUR	250 ML
1/4 CUP	GRANULATED SUGAR	60 ML
I TSP	GROUND GINGER	5 ML
1/2 CUP	COLD UNSALTED BUTTER, CUT INTO CUBES	125 ML

TOPPING

1/4 CUP	UNSALTED BUTTER	60 ML
I TBSP	CORN SYRUP	15 ML
2 TBSP	CONFECTIONERS' (ICING) SUGAR	30 ML
I TSP	GROUND GINGER	5 ML

FROSTING

2/3 CUP	CONFECTIONERS' (ICING) SUGAR	150 ML
I TBSP	MILK	15 ML

BASE: PREHEAT OVEN TO 350°F (180°C). GREASE AN 8-INCH
(20 CM) SQUARE BAKING PAN AND LINE WITH PARCHMENT
PAPER. IN A FOOD PROCESSOR, PULSE FLOUR, SUGAR,
GINGER AND BUTTER TO FINE CRUMBS. (YOU CAN ALSO
DO THIS IN A LARGE BOWL BY RUBBING THE MIXTURE
THROUGH YOUR FINGERS OR CUTTING THE BUTTER IN
WITH A PASTRY BLENDER.) PAT MIXTURE INTO BOTTOM
OF PREPARED PAN. BAKE FOR ABOUT 15 MINUTES OR UNTIL
BASE IS SET AND GOLDEN BROWN.

TOPPING: IN A SMALL SAUCEPAN, MELT BUTTER AND CORN SYRUP OVER LOW HEAT, STIRRING CONSTANTLY. WHISK IN CONFECTIONERS' SUGAR AND GINGER UNTIL DISSOLVED. POUR OVER BAKED BASE AND USE A SPATULA TO SPREAD EVENLY. LET COOL COMPLETELY ON A WIRE RACK.

FROSTING: IN A SMALL BOWL, STIR TOGETHER CONFECTIONERS' SUGAR AND MILK UNTIL SMOOTH. TRANSFER TO A SMALL PLASTIC SANDWICH BAG, GENTLY SQUEEZING THE FROSTING INTO ONE OF THE BOTTOM CORNERS. WITH SCISSORS, SNIP OFF A VERY SMALL CORNER OF THE BAG TO CREATE A PIPING BAG. DRIZZLE FROSTING IN DECORATIVE LINES OVER COOLED SHORTBREAD. CUT INTO SQUARES. MAKES 16 SQUARES.

MAKE AHEAD: PLACE IN A SINGLE LAYER IN A LARGE AIRTIGHT CONTAINER AND STORE IN THE REFRIGERATOR FOR UP TO 2 DAYS OR IN THE FREEZER FOR UP TO 2 WEEKS.

TEACHER: HOW CAN YOU DELAY MILK TURNING SOUR?
CHILD: KEEP IT IN THE COW.

POTATO CHIP SHORTBREAD

A SWEET AND SALTY FLAVOR YOU WILL LOVE.

1¼ TO 1½ CUPS	ALL-PURPOSE FLOUR, DIVIDED	300 TO 375 ML
½ CUP	CRUSHED PLAIN POTATO CHIPS	125 ML
¼ CUP	WHITE RICE FLOUR	60 ML
½ TSP	SALT (PREFERABLY COARSE-GRAIN), DIVIDED	2 ML
1 CUP	UNSALTED BUTTER, SOFTENED (SEE TIP, PAGE 289)	250 ML
¾ CUP	CONFECTIONERS' (ICING) SUGAR	175 ML

PREHEAT OVEN TO 325°F (160°C). IN A BOWL, WHISK TOGETHER 1 CUP (250 ML) OF THE ALL-PURPOSE FLOUR, POTATO CHIPS, RICE FLOUR AND ¼ TSP (1 ML) OF THE SALT; SET ASIDE. IN A LARGE BOWL, BEAT BUTTER UNTIL SOFT. BEAT IN CONFECTIONERS' SUGAR UNTIL LIGHT AND FLUFFY. BEAT IN FLOUR MIXTURE. TURN DOUGH OUT ONTO A FLOURED WORK SURFACE AND KNEAD, WORKING IN ENOUGH OF THE REMAINING FLOUR UNTIL DOUGH BEGINS TO CRACK. (THERE MIGHT BE A SMALL AMOUNT OF FLOUR LEFT OVER.) DIVIDE DOUGH IN HALF AND PAT INTO TWO 8-INCH (20 CM) ROUND CAKE PANS. USING A FORK, SCORE EACH INTO 12 TO 16 WEDGES AND MAKE A DECORATIVE BORDER AROUND THE EDGE. SPRINKLE WITH THE REMAINING SALT. BAKE FOR ABOUT 25 MINUTES OR UNTIL CENTERS ARE GOLDEN BROWN AND EDGES ARE SLIGHTLY DARKER. LET COOL IN PANS ON A WIRE RACK FOR 10 MINUTES, THEN CUT INTO WEDGES. LET COOL COMPLETELY IN PANS. MAKES 24 OR 32 WEDGES.

PAT-IN-THE-PAN SQUARES

A QUICK AND CHEWY FIX FOR A COOKIE CRAVING.

2 1/3 CUPS	ALL-PURPOSE FLOUR	575 ML
3 1/2 TSP	BAKING POWDER	17 ML
1/4 TSP	SALT	1 ML
1 1/2 CUPS	FIRMLY PACKED BROWN SUGAR	375 ML
1 CUP	UNSALTED BUTTER, SOFTENED (SEE TIP, PAGE 289)	250 ML
2/3 CUP	SWEETENED CONDENSED MILK	150 ML
1 1/2 CUPS	SEMISWEET, WHITE OR MINT CHOCOLATE CHIPS	375 ML

PREHEAT OVEN TO 350°F (180°C). GREASE A 13- BY 9-INCH (33 BY 23 CM) METAL BAKING PAN AND LINE WITH PARCHMENT PAPER. IN A BOWL, SIFT TOGETHER FLOUR, BAKING POWDER AND SALT; SET ASIDE. IN A LARGE BOWL, CREAM BROWN SUGAR AND BUTTER UNTIL LIGHT AND FLUFFY. STIR IN CONDENSED MILK. STIR IN FLOUR MIXTURE AND CHOCOLATE CHIPS. USE YOUR HANDS TO WORK MIXTURE INTO A SOFT DOUGH. PAT DOUGH INTO PREPARED PAN, USING THE BACK OF A LARGE SPOON TO LEVEL THE TOP. BAKE FOR ABOUT 20 MINUTES OR UNTIL BROWNED AT THE EDGES BUT STILL SOFT IN THE CENTER. FOR EVEN BROWNING, ROTATE THE PAN HALFWAY THROUGH. LET COOL COMPLETELY IN PAN ON A WIRE RACK. CUT INTO 60 SQUARES. MAKES 5 DOZEN SQUARES.

MAKE AHEAD: STORE SQUARES IN AN AIRTIGHT CONTAINER AT ROOM TEMPERATURE FOR UP TO 5 DAYS, OR PLACE BETWEEN LAYERS OF WAXED PAPER IN AN AIRTIGHT CONTAINER AND FREEZE FOR UP TO 2 WEEKS.

YOGURT BERRY BARS

LIGHT ENOUGH FOR SNACKING,
IMPRESSIVE ENOUGH FOR DESSERT.

CRUST

1½ CUPS	DIGESTIVE COOKIE OR GRAHAM CRACKER CRUMBS (ABOUT 18 COOKIES)	375 ML
¼ CUP	GRANULATED SUGAR	60 ML
⅓ CUP	UNSALTED BUTTER, MELTED	75 ML

FILLING

1	ENVELOPE (¼ OZ/7 G) UNFLAVORED GELATIN POWDER	1
¼ CUP	MILK	60 ML
1 CUP	FRESH BLUEBERRIES	250 ML
1½ CUPS	RASPBERRY- OR STRAWBERRY-FLAVORED STIRRED NATURAL YOGURT (SEE TIP, OPPOSITE)	375 ML
½ CUP	FROZEN RASPBERRY OR CRANBERRY FRUIT BEVERAGE OR COCKTAIL CONCENTRATE, THAWED	125 ML

CRUST: PREHEAT OVEN TO 350°F (180°C). LINE AN 8-INCH (20 CM) SQUARE BAKING PAN WITH FOIL, LEAVING A 1-INCH (2.5 CM) OVERHANG. IN A BOWL, COMBINE COOKIE CRUMBS, SUGAR AND BUTTER. PAT INTO BOTTOM OF PREPARED PAN. BAKE FOR 10 MINUTES OR UNTIL GOLDEN BROWN. LET COOL COMPLETELY.

FILLING: IN A SMALL SAUCEPAN, SPRINKLE GELATIN OVER MILK; LET GELATIN ABSORB MILK FOR ABOUT 1 MINUTE. PLACE OVER LOW HEAT, STIRRING UNTIL GELATIN IS DISSOLVED. LET COOL FOR A FEW MINUTES, BUT DO NOT LET SET. IN LARGE BOWL, COMBINE BLUEBERRIES, YOGURT,

RASPBERRY CONCENTRATE AND COOLED GELATIN MIXTURE, STIRRING THOROUGHLY. POUR FILLING INTO COOLED CRUST. REFRIGERATE FOR AT LEAST 4 HOURS, UNTIL SET, OR FOR UP TO 1 DAY. USING THE EDGES OF THE FOIL AS HANDLES, REMOVE FROM PAN AND TRANSFER TO A CUTTING BOARD. CUT INTO SQUARES. MAKES 16 SQUARES.

TIP: THERE'S A CONFUSING VARIETY OF YOGURTS SOLD IN SUPERMARKETS TODAY. FOR THE BEST RESULTS IN THIS RECIPE, LOOK FOR TUBS THAT SAY "STIRRED NATURAL YOGURT," CONTAINING NO GELATIN. WE PREFER THE TASTE OF YOGURTS FLAVORED WITH SUGAR RATHER THAN ARTIFICIAL SWEETENER, BUT EITHER CAN BE USED.

MAKE AHEAD: LAYER WITH WAXED PAPER IN AN AIRTIGHT CONTAINER AND REFRIGERATE FOR UP TO 3 DAYS. DO NOT FREEZE.

HOW IS IT THAT ONE CARELESS MATCH CAN START A FOREST FIRE, BUT IT TAKES A WHOLE BOX OF MATCHES TO START A CAMPFIRE?

BLACKCURRANT LINZER SLICES

A SPIN ON A CLASSIC LINZERTORTE. ALTHOUGH RASPBERRY JAM IS TRADITIONALLY USED WITH A LINZERTORTE, WE LOVE THIS COMBINATION OF SLIGHTLY TART BLACKCURRANT JAM WITH THE BUTTERY SHORTBREAD BASE. WITH SLIGHT VARIATIONS, THE SAME SHORTBREAD BASE IS USED TO MAKE WHITE CHOCOLATE FIG SQUARES (PAGE 302) AND GINGER-GLAZED SHORTBREADS (PAGE 292).

BASE

1 CUP	ALL-PURPOSE FLOUR	250 ML
1/4 CUP	GRANULATED SUGAR	60 ML
1 TSP	GROUND CINNAMON	5 ML
1/2 CUP	COLD UNSALTED BUTTER, CUT INTO CUBES	125 ML

TOPPING

1 CUP	GOOD-QUALITY BLACKCURRANT JAM (SEE TIP, OPPOSITE)	250 ML
3 TBSP	TOASTED SLICED OR SLIVERED ALMONDS (SEE TIP, PAGE 301)	45 ML
2 TSP	GRANULATED SUGAR	10 ML

BASE: PREHEAT OVEN TO 350°F (180°C). GREASE AN 8-INCH (20 CM) SQUARE BAKING PAN AND LINE WITH PARCHMENT PAPER. IN A FOOD PROCESSOR, PULSE FLOUR, SUGAR, CINNAMON AND BUTTER TO FINE CRUMBS. (YOU CAN ALSO DO THIS IN A LARGE BOWL BY RUBBING THE MIXTURE THROUGH YOUR FINGERS OR CUTTING THE BUTTER IN WITH A PASTRY BLENDER.) REMOVE 1/4 CUP (60 ML) OF THE MIXTURE AND SET ASIDE. PAT THE REMAINING MIXTURE INTO BOTTOM OF PREPARED PAN. BAKE FOR

ABOUT 15 MINUTES OR UNTIL BASE IS SET AND LIGHTLY BROWNED. REMOVE FROM OVEN, LEAVING OVEN ON.

TOPPING: PLACE JAM IN A SMALL MICROWAVE-SAFE BOWL. MICROWAVE ON HIGH FOR 20 SECONDS TO LOOSEN SLIGHTLY. SPREAD EVENLY OVER BAKED BASE. IN A SMALL BOWL, COMBINE RESERVED BASE MIXTURE AND ALMONDS. SPRINKLE OVER JAM. BAKE FOR 10 TO 15 MINUTES OR UNTIL JAM IS BUBBLING AND TOPPING IS GOLDEN. SPRINKLE WITH SUGAR. LET COOL COMPLETELY IN PAN ON A WIRE RACK. CUT INTO SQUARES. MAKES 16 SQUARES.

TIP: WE LIKE QUALITY JAMS, SUCH AS THE FRENCH BRAND ST. DALFOUR, AS THEY CONTAIN A HIGH PROPORTION OF FRUIT, ARE GENERALLY SWEETENED WITH FRUIT JUICE AND CONTAIN LITTLE OR NO ADDED SUGAR. THE JAM MIGHT ALSO BE LABELED "PRESERVES," "DELUXE SPREAD," OR "FRUIT SPREAD."

MAKE AHEAD: STORE IN AN AIRTIGHT CONTAINER AT ROOM TEMPERATURE FOR UP TO 2 DAYS, OR PLACE BETWEEN LAYERS OF WAXED PAPER IN AN AIRTIGHT CONTAINER AND FREEZE FOR UP TO 2 WEEKS.

MY GREATEST FEAR IS THAT THERE IS NO PMS
AND THIS IS MY PERSONALITY.

MUESLI BARS

GREAT FOR BREAKFAST ON THE RUN.

1/2 CUP	GRANULATED SUGAR	125 ML
1/2 CUP	UNSALTED BUTTER	125 ML
1/4 CUP	LIQUID HONEY	60 ML
1 CUP	QUICK-COOKING OR OLD-FASHIONED (LARGE-FLAKE) ROLLED OATS (NOT INSTANT)	250 ML
1 CUP	GROUND ALMONDS	250 ML
2/3 CUP	RAISINS	150 ML
1/3 CUP	DRIED CRANBERRIES	75 ML
2 TBSP	TOASTED SESAME SEEDS (SEE TIP, OPPOSITE)	30 ML
2 TBSP	ROASTED UNSALTED SUNFLOWER SEEDS (SEE TIP, BELOW)	30 ML

PREHEAT OVEN TO 350°F (180°C). GREASE AN 8- OR 9-INCH (20 OR 23 CM) SQUARE BAKING PAN AND LINE WITH PARCHMENT PAPER. IN A LARGE SAUCEPAN, COMBINE SUGAR, BUTTER AND HONEY. HEAT OVER MEDIUM HEAT, STIRRING OFTEN, UNTIL BUTTER IS MELTED. STIR IN OATS, ALMONDS, RAISINS, CRANBERRIES, SESAME SEEDS AND SUNFLOWER SEEDS. SPREAD IN PREPARED PAN, PRESSING EVENLY. BAKE FOR 20 TO 25 MINUTES OR UNTIL FIRM TO THE TOUCH AND GOLDEN BROWN. (IF THE TOP STARTS TO BROWN TOO QUICKLY, LOOSELY COVER THE PAN WITH FOIL.) LET COOL COMPLETELY IN PAN ON A WIRE RACK. REMOVE FROM PAN TO A CUTTING BOARD AND CUT INTO BARS. MAKES 12 BARS.

TIP: SUNFLOWER SEEDS, WHICH ARE COMMONLY FOUND IN THE BULK FOOD SECTION OF THE SUPERMARKET, ARE

AVAILABLE RAW, ROASTED AND SALTED, OR ROASTED
BUT UNSALTED. FOR THIS RECIPE, WE RECOMMEND THE
ROASTED BUT UNSALTED TYPE.

TIP: TOASTING NUTS, SEEDS AND SHREDDED COCONUT
HELPS TO BRING OUT THEIR FLAVOR. ALTHOUGH YOU CAN
TOAST THEM IN THE OVEN, WE HAVE MORE SUCCESS —
AND FEWER BURNT NUTS — ON THE STOVETOP. SPREAD
NUTS, SEEDS OR COCONUT IN A DRY NONSTICK SKILLET
AND COOK OVER MEDIUM HEAT, SHAKING OR STIRRING
FREQUENTLY, FOR 4 TO 5 MINUTES OR UNTIL FRAGRANT
AND LIGHTLY BROWNED. TIP NUTS ONTO A COLD PLATE TO
STOP THE COOKING PROCESS AND LET COOL COMPLETELY.

MAKE AHEAD: LAYER WITH WAXED PAPER IN AN AIRTIGHT
CONTAINER AND STORE AT ROOM TEMPERATURE FOR UP
TO 5 DAYS OR IN THE FREEZER FOR UP TO 2 WEEKS.

VARIATION: SUBSTITUTE OTHER DRIED FRUITS, SEEDS
AND CHOPPED TOASTED NUTS, USING THE SAME TOTAL
VOLUME AS THOSE CALLED FOR. CHOPPED DRIED APRICOTS
AND DRIED CHERRIES ARE PARTICULARLY GOOD HERE.

MEN WITH PIERCED EARS ARE BETTER PREPARED
FOR MARRIAGE — THEY'VE EXPERIENCED PAIN
AND BOUGHT JEWELRY.

WHITE CHOCOLATE FIG SQUARES

MOIST, CHEWY AND WITH JUST THE RIGHT DEGREE OF SWEETNESS. A MUST FOR YOUR CHRISTMAS BAKING LIST OR ANY TIME OF YEAR.

BASE

1 CUP	ALL-PURPOSE FLOUR	250 ML
1/4 CUP	GRANULATED SUGAR	60 ML
1/2 CUP	COLD UNSALTED BUTTER, CUT INTO CUBES	125 ML

TOPPING

1 1/2 CUPS	CHOPPED DRIED FIGS (ABOUT 8 OZ/250 G)	375 ML
3 TBSP	RUM, BRANDY OR UNSWEETENED APPLE JUICE	45 ML
2 TBSP	COLD WATER	30 ML
1/3 CUP	ALL-PURPOSE FLOUR	75 ML
1 TSP	GROUND CINNAMON	5 ML
1/2 TSP	BAKING POWDER	2 ML
1/4 TSP	SALT	1 ML
1 CUP	PACKED BROWN SUGAR	250 ML
2	EGGS	2
1 TSP	VANILLA EXTRACT	5 ML
1 CUP	CHOPPED TOASTED PECANS (SEE TIP, PAGE 301)	250 ML
1/2 CUP	WHITE CHOCOLATE CHIPS	125 ML

BASE: PREHEAT OVEN TO 350°F (180°C). GREASE AN 8-INCH (20 CM) SQUARE BAKING PAN AND LINE WITH PARCHMENT PAPER. IN A FOOD PROCESSOR, PULSE FLOUR, SUGAR AND BUTTER TO FINE CRUMBS. (YOU CAN ALSO DO THIS IN A LARGE BOWL BY RUBBING THE MIXTURE THROUGH YOUR FINGERS OR CUTTING THE BUTTER IN WITH A PASTRY

BLENDER.) PAT MIXTURE INTO BOTTOM OF PREPARED PAN. BAKE FOR ABOUT 15 MINUTES OR UNTIL BASE IS SET AND GOLDEN BROWN. REMOVE FROM OVEN, LEAVING OVEN ON, AND LET COOL FOR 10 MINUTES.

TOPPING: IN A MEDIUM SAUCEPAN, COMBINE FIGS, RUM AND WATER. BRING TO A BOIL OVER MEDIUM-HIGH HEAT. REDUCE HEAT AND SIMMER FOR 5 MINUTES OR UNTIL LIQUID IS ABSORBED. (WATCH TO MAKE SURE IT DOESN'T BURN.) LET COOL SLIGHTLY.

IN A BOWL, WHISK TOGETHER FLOUR, CINNAMON, BAKING POWDER AND SALT. IN ANOTHER BOWL, WHISK TOGETHER BROWN SUGAR, EGGS AND VANILLA. STIR EGG MIXTURE INTO FLOUR MIXTURE. STIR IN COOLED FIG MIXTURE AND PECANS UNTIL JUST COMBINED. POUR OVER BAKED BASE AND USE A SPATULA TO SPREAD EVENLY. BAKE FOR 30 TO 40 MINUTES OR UNTIL A TESTER INSERTED IN THE CENTER COMES OUT CLEAN. (IF THE TOP STARTS TO BROWN TOO QUICKLY, LOOSELY COVER THE PAN WITH FOIL.) IMMEDIATELY SPRINKLE CHOCOLATE CHIPS OVER TOP AND LET STAND FOR 2 OR 3 MINUTES OR UNTIL SOFTENED. RUN A FORK THROUGH CHOCOLATE TO GIVE IT A SWIRLY EFFECT. LET COOL COMPLETELY IN PAN ON A WIRE RACK. REMOVE FROM PAN TO A CUTTING BOARD AND, USING A SHARP KNIFE, CUT INTO SQUARES. MAKES 16 SQUARES OR 32 SMALL BARS.

MAKE AHEAD: LAYER WITH WAXED PAPER IN AN AIRTIGHT CONTAINER AND STORE AT ROOM TEMPERATURE FOR UP TO 5 DAYS OR IN THE FREEZER FOR UP TO 2 WEEKS.

SARAH SUNSHINE'S CRANBERRY FUDGE

WHEN OUR CREATIVE AND DELIGHTFULLY NAMED NEIGHBOR, SARAH SUNSHINE DEEN, PRESENTED THIS DELICIOUS FUDGE TO US AT CHRISTMAS, WE SAID, "WELL, THIS RECIPE HAS TO GO IN THE BOOK!" PACKAGE IN PLAIN CELLOPHANE PARTY FAVOR BAGS AND TIE WITH DECORATIVE RIBBON TO CREATE PERFECT HOSTESS GIFTS.

1 1/2 CUPS	DRIED CRANBERRIES	375 ML
1 1/2 CUPS	WATER	375 ML
1 1/2 CUPS	GRANULATED SUGAR	375 ML
1	JAR (7 OZ/198 G) MARSHMALLOW CREME	1
2/3 CUP	EVAPORATED MILK	150 ML
1/2 CUP	UNSALTED BUTTER, CUT INTO CUBES	125 ML
8 OZ	SEMISWEET CHOCOLATE, CHOPPED	250 G

LINE A 9-INCH (23 CM) SQUARE BAKING PAN WITH FOIL. IN A LARGE SAUCEPAN, BRING CRANBERRIES AND WATER TO A BOIL OVER MEDIUM-HIGH HEAT. REMOVE FROM HEAT AND LET STAND FOR 10 MINUTES. DRAIN AND BLOT DRY ON PAPER TOWELS. IN THE SAME SAUCEPAN, COMBINE SUGAR, MARSHMALLOW CREME, EVAPORATED MILK AND BUTTER. BRING TO A BOIL OVER MEDIUM-HIGH HEAT, STIRRING CONSTANTLY. BOIL, STIRRING, FOR 5 MINUTES. REMOVE FROM HEAT AND STIR IN CHOCOLATE UNTIL MELTED. STIR IN CRANBERRIES. POUR INTO PREPARED PAN. COVER AND REFRIGERATE OVERNIGHT. CUT INTO 72 PIECES. MAKES 6 DOZEN.

MAKE AHEAD: LAYER WITH WAXED PAPER IN AN AIRTIGHT CONTAINER AND STORE IN THE REFRIGERATOR FOR UP TO 2 WEEKS OR THE FREEZER FOR UP TO 2 MONTHS.

F'REVERS

THE KIDS HAVE LOVED THEM FOREVER!

3 CUPS	SWEETENED FLAKED COCONUT	750 ML
2 CUPS	CONFECTIONERS' (ICING) SUGAR	500 ML
1/4 CUP	UNSALTED BUTTER	60 ML
1/4 CUP	HALF-AND-HALF (10%) CREAM	60 ML

CHOCOLATE DIP

1 CUP	SEMISWEET CHOCOLATE CHIPS	250 ML
2 TSP	UNSALTED BUTTER	10 ML

LINE A LARGE BAKING SHEET WITH WAXED PAPER. IN A LARGE BOWL, COMBINE COCONUT AND SUGAR; SET ASIDE. IN A SMALL SAUCEPAN, MELT BUTTER OVER MEDIUM HEAT. REDUCE HEAT AND SIMMER FOR 5 MINUTES OR UNTIL GOLDEN BROWN. (WATCH CAREFULLY TO MAKE SURE IT DOESN'T BURN.) POUR BUTTER AND CREAM OVER COCONUT MIXTURE AND STIR TO COMBINE. ROLL TEASPOONFULS (5 ML) OF MIXTURE INTO SMALL BALLS AND PLACE ON PREPARED BAKING SHEET. REFRIGERATE FOR ABOUT 30 MINUTES OR UNTIL FIRM.

CHOCOLATE DIP: PLACE CHOCOLATE CHIPS AND BUTTER IN A SMALL, DEEP AND COMPLETELY DRY MICROWAVE-SAFE BOWL. MICROWAVE ON LOW (10%) IN 15-SECOND INTERVALS, STIRRING AFTER EACH, UNTIL CHOCOLATE IS GLOSSY BUT NOT COMPLETELY MELTED. (THIS PREVENTS THE CHOCOLATE FROM SCORCHING.) STIR GENTLY UNTIL FULLY MELTED. DIP ONE SIDE OF EACH COCONUT BALL IN CHOCOLATE, THEN RETURN TO BAKING SHEET. REFRIGERATE FOR 30 MINUTES, UNTIL SET. MAKES ABOUT 30.

FRUIT JUICE JELLY SNACKS

THE KIDS LOVE THIS SNACK. THEY CALL IT
"CONCRETE JELL-O" BECAUSE THEY CAN PICK IT UP!

4 CUPS	UNSWEETENED CLEAR FRUIT JUICE (SUCH AS CRANBERRY, APPLE OR POMEGRANATE), DIVIDED	1 L
4	ENVELOPES (EACH $1/4$ OZ/7 G) UNFLAVORED GELATIN POWDER	4

PLACE 1 CUP (250 ML) OF THE JUICE IN A LARGE BOWL.
SPRINKLE GELATIN OVER TOP. AND LET STAND FOR
1 MINUTE TO SOFTEN. IN A SAUCEPAN, BRING THE
REMAINING JUICE TO A BOIL. POUR HOT JUICE OVER
GELATIN MIXTURE, STIRRING CONSTANTLY UNTIL
GELATIN IS DISSOLVED. POUR INTO AN 8-INCH (20 CM)
SQUARE GLASS BAKING DISH OR METAL PAN AND LET
COOL TO ROOM TEMPERATURE. COVER AND REFRIGERATE
OVERNIGHT. CUT INTO CUBES. MAKES 25 OR MORE PIECES.

YOU'RE NEVER TOO OLD TO LEARN SOMETHING STUPID.

Chocolate Swirl Cookies (page 284)
and Glazed Italian Cookies (page 290)

Sarah Sunshine's Cranberry Fudge (page 304)

Hummingbird Cake (page 308)

Encore! Chocolate Bread Pudding (page 328)
and Rum Pecan Caramel Sauce (page 338)

DESSERTS

HUMMINGBIRD CAKE

THIS RICH, MOIST LAYER CAKE RESEMBLES A DRESSED-UP CARROT CAKE. IT'S THOUGHT TO HAVE ORIGINATED IN THE SOUTHERN UNITED STATES — BUT NO TWITTERS ON HOW IT GOT ITS NAME. SMALL SLICES WILL SUFFICE, SO IT'S PERFECT FOR A LARGE GATHERING.

3 CUPS	ALL-PURPOSE FLOUR	750 ML
2 CUPS	GRANULATED SUGAR	500 ML
I TSP	BAKING SODA	5 ML
I TSP	CHINESE FIVE-SPICE POWDER OR GROUND CINNAMON	5 ML
1/2 TSP	SALT	2 ML
3	EGGS, AT ROOM TEMPERATURE	3
I	CAN (14 OZ/398 ML) CRUSHED PINEAPPLE, WITH JUICE	I
1 1/3 CUPS	MASHED RIPE BANANAS (ABOUT 3 MEDIUM)	325 ML
I CUP	CANOLA OR VEGETABLE OIL	250 ML
2 TSP	VANILLA EXTRACT	IO ML
I CUP	CHOPPED PECANS OR WALNUTS	250 ML
	WHITE CHOCOLATE CREAM CHEESE FROSTING (SEE RECIPE, PAGE 335)	
	SHAVED WHITE CHOCOLATE	

PREHEAT OVEN TO 350°F (180°C). GREASE TWO 9-INCH (23 CM) ROUND CAKE PANS AND LINE BOTTOMS WITH PARCHMENT PAPER. IN A LARGE BOWL, WHISK TOGETHER FLOUR, SUGAR, BAKING SODA, FIVE-SPICE POWDER AND SALT; SET ASIDE. IN ANOTHER LARGE BOWL, WHISK TOGETHER EGGS, PINEAPPLE WITH JUICE, BANANAS, OIL AND VANILLA. ADD THE EGG MIXTURE TO THE FLOUR MIXTURE, ADD PECANS AND STIR UNTIL JUST COMBINED.

DIVIDE BATTER BETWEEN PREPARED PANS, LIGHTLY LEVELING THE TOPS. BAKE FOR 30 TO 35 MINUTES OR UNTIL A TESTER INSERTED IN THE CENTER OF THE CAKES COMES OUT CLEAN AND THE CAKES ARE STARTING TO SHRINK AWAY FROM THE EDGES OF THE PANS. REMOVE FROM OVEN AND LET COOL IN PANS ON A WIRE RACK FOR 15 MINUTES. INVERT CAKES ONTO RACK, PEEL OFF PARCHMENT PAPER AND LET COOL COMPLETELY.

PLACE ONE CAKE LAYER, BOTTOM SIDE UP, ON A SERVING PLATE. SPREAD WITH ONE-THIRD OF THE FROSTING. PLACE THE SECOND CAKE LAYER ON TOP. SPREAD THE REMAINING FROSTING OVER TOP AND SIDES OF CAKE. SCATTER SHAVED WHITE CHOCOLATE OVER TOP. SERVES 10 TO 12.

TIP: WHEN BANANAS BECOME OVERLY RIPE AND ARE NO LONGER GOOD FOR EATING OUT OF HAND, PLACE THEM IN THE FREEZER, WITH THEIR SKINS STILL ON, TO USE IN BAKING RECIPES AT A LATER DATE. THAW THE BANANAS AND REMOVE SKINS BEFORE USE.

TIP: WE LIKE TO GREASE CAKE PANS BEFORE LINING WITH PARCHMENT PAPER, BECAUSE IT HELPS KEEP THE PAPER FROM SLIPPING AROUND WHEN WE SPREAD THE BATTER. ELIMINATE THE GREASING, IF YOU PREFER.

MAKE AHEAD: WRAP COOLED CAKE LAYERS INDIVIDUALLY IN PLASTIC WRAP, PLACE IN AN AIRTIGHT CONTAINER AND REFRIGERATE FOR UP TO 1 DAY, OR OVERWRAP WITH FOIL AND FREEZE FOR UP TO 2 WEEKS. LET THAW AT ROOM TEMPERATURE FOR 2 TO 3 HOURS BEFORE ASSEMBLING AND SERVING.

WHITE CHOCOLATE BLACKCURRANT LAYER CAKE

A SPECIAL OCCASION CAKE — RICH, MOIST AND MADE FROM SCRATCH.

CAKE

6 OZ	WHITE CHOCOLATE, CHOPPED	175 G
2¼ CUPS	ALL-PURPOSE FLOUR	550 ML
2¼ TSP	BAKING POWDER	11 ML
¼ TSP	SALT	1 ML
1⅓ CUPS	GRANULATED SUGAR	325 ML
⅔ CUP	UNSALTED BUTTER, SOFTENED (SEE TIP, PAGE 289)	150 ML
4	EGGS, AT ROOM TEMPERATURE	4
1 TSP	VANILLA EXTRACT	5 ML
1¼ CUPS	2% OR WHOLE MILK	300 ML

FILLING

2 CUPS	HEAVY OR WHIPPING (35%) CREAM	500 ML
2 TBSP	CONFECTIONERS' (ICING) SUGAR	30 ML
1 TSP	VANILLA EXTRACT	5 ML
1 CUP	GOOD-QUALITY BLACKCURRANT JAM	250 ML
	SHAVED OR GRATED WHITE CHOCOLATE	
	BLACKBERRIES OR RASPBERRIES	

CAKE: PREHEAT OVEN TO 350°F (180°C). GREASE THE BOTTOM OF TWO 9-INCH (23 CM) ROUND CAKE PANS AND LINE WITH PARCHMENT PAPER. IN A DOUBLE BOILER OR A HEATPROOF BOWL SET OVER A POT OF HOT, BUT NOT BOILING WATER (DO NOT LET THE BOTTOM OF THE BOWL TOUCH THE WATER), MELT WHITE CHOCOLATE, STIRRING UNTIL SMOOTH. LET COOL FOR 10 MINUTES.

IN A BOWL, WHISK TOGETHER FLOUR, BAKING POWDER AND SALT; SET ASIDE. IN A LARGE BOWL, CREAM SUGAR AND BUTTER UNTIL LIGHT AND FLUFFY. BEAT IN EGGS, ONE AT A TIME, MAKING SURE EACH ONE IS FULLY INCORPORATED BEFORE ADDING THE NEXT. BEAT IN VANILLA. STIR IN FLOUR MIXTURE ALTERNATELY WITH MILK, MAKING THREE ADDITIONS OF FLOUR AND TWO OF MILK. STIR IN COOLED MELTED CHOCOLATE UNTIL JUST COMBINED. DIVIDE BATTER BETWEEN PREPARED PANS, LIGHTLY LEVELING THE TOPS. BAKE FOR 25 TO 30 MINUTES OR UNTIL LIGHTLY BROWNED AND A TESTER INSERTED IN THE CENTER OF THE CAKES COMES OUT CLEAN. LET COOL IN PANS ON A WIRE RACK FOR 10 MINUTES. INVERT CAKES ONTO RACK, PEEL OFF PARCHMENT PAPER AND LET COOL COMPLETELY.

FILLING: IN A LARGE BOWL, BEAT CREAM, CONFECTIONERS' SUGAR AND VANILLA UNTIL SOFT PEAKS FORM.

ASSEMBLY: USING A LONG SERRATED KNIFE, CUT EACH CAKE LAYER IN HALF HORIZONTALLY, TO GIVE YOU FOUR LAYERS. PLACE ONE LAYER, CUT SIDE UP, ON A SERVING PLATE. SPREAD WITH ONE-THIRD OF THE JAM. TOP WITH THE SECOND LAYER; SPREAD WITH HALF THE REMAINING JAM AND HALF THE WHIPPED CREAM. TOP WITH THE THIRD LAYER. SPREAD WITH THE REMAINING JAM. TOP WITH THE FOURTH LAYER, CUT SIDE DOWN, AND SPREAD WITH THE REMAINING WHIPPED CREAM. SCATTER SHAVED WHITE CHOCOLATE OVER TOP. REFRIGERATE FOR AT LEAST 1 HOUR OR FOR UP TO 4 HOURS. GARNISH WITH BERRIES JUST BEFORE SERVING. SERVES 10 TO 12.

COCONUT LIME CHEESECAKE

A LIGHT ENDING FOR YOUR NEXT DINNER PARTY.
SERVE WITH CHILLED BLUEBERRY COMPOTE (PAGE 334).

CRUST

1 1/2 CUPS	DIGESTIVE COOKIE OR GRAHAM CRACKER CRUMBS (ABOUT 18 COOKIES)	375 ML
1/3 CUP	UNSWEETENED SHREDDED COCONUT	75 ML
1/4 CUP	GRANULATED SUGAR	60 ML
1 TSP	GROUND CINNAMON	5 ML
1/2 CUP	UNSALTED BUTTER, MELTED	125 ML

FILLING

1	ENVELOPE (1/4 OZ/7 G) UNFLAVORED GELATIN POWDER	1
1/4 CUP	COLD WATER	60 ML
1/4 CUP	BOILING WATER	60 ML
	FINELY GRATED ZEST OF 1 LIME	
1/2 CUP	FRESHLY SQUEEZED LIME JUICE	125 ML
8 OZ	CREAM CHEESE, SOFTENED	250 G
1 CUP	GRANULATED SUGAR	250 ML
2 CUPS	HEAVY OR WHIPPING (35%) CREAM	500 ML

CRUST: PREHEAT OVEN TO 350°F (180°C). PREPARE A 9-INCH (23 CM) SPRINGFORM PAN BY WRAPPING FOIL AROUND THE OUTSIDE — UNDER THE BOTTOM AND UP THE SIDES — TO PREVENT LEAKS. PLACE PAN ON A LARGE BAKING SHEET. IN A BOWL, COMBINE COOKIE CRUMBS, COCONUT, SUGAR AND CINNAMON. STIR IN BUTTER. PAT INTO BOTTOM OF PREPARED PAN. BAKE FOR 10 MINUTES OR UNTIL BROWNED. LET COOL COMPLETELY.

FILLING: IN A SMALL BOWL, SPRINKLE GELATIN OVER COLD WATER; LET GELATIN ABSORB WATER FOR ABOUT I MINUTE. ADD BOILING WATER, STIRRING CONSTANTLY UNTIL GELATIN IS DISSOLVED. STIR IN LIME ZEST AND LIME JUICE. LET COOL FOR A FEW MINUTES, BUT DO NOT LET SET. IN A LARGE BOWL, BEAT CREAM CHEESE AND SUGAR UNTIL VERY SMOOTH. ADD COOLED GELATIN MIXTURE, STIRRING WELL. IN ANOTHER BOWL, WHIP CREAM UNTIL STIFF PEAKS FORM. GENTLY FOLD WHIPPED CREAM INTO CHEESE MIXTURE. POUR FILLING INTO CRUST. COVER AND REFRIGERATE FOR AT LEAST 4 HOURS, UNTIL SET, OR FOR UP TO I DAY. REMOVE FROM PAN AND SERVE. SERVES 8.

TIP: TO MAKE COOKIE CRUMBS, PLACE COOKIES IN A FOOD PROCESSOR AND PULSE TO FINE CRUMBS. OR PLACE COOKIES IN A LARGE FREEZER BAG AND SQUEEZE AND THUMP THEM INTO CRUMBS.

MAKE AHEAD: REMOVE CHILLED CHEESECAKE FROM PAN, PLACE ON A BAKING SHEET AND PLACE IN FREEZER, UNCOVERED, UNTIL HARD. WRAP IN A DOUBLE LAYER OF FOIL, PLACE IN A LARGE AIRTIGHT CONTAINER AND FREEZE FOR UP TO 2 WEEKS. TO SERVE, THAW OVERNIGHT IN THE REFRIGERATOR.

WHEN TEMPTED TO FIGHT FIRE WITH FIRE, REMEMBER THAT THE FIRE DEPARTMENT USUALLY USES WATER.

FRESH RHUBARB
VANILLA CUSTARD TART

A SUPERB WAY TO SERVE FRESH RHUBARB. THIS TART IS BEST EATEN THE DAY IT'S MADE. SERVE WITH SOUR CREAM CHANTILLY CREAM (PAGE 337) OR ICE CREAM.

3 CUPS	CHOPPED RHUBARB	750 ML
2 TBSP	GRANULATED SUGAR	30 ML

CRUST

1 CUP	ALL-PURPOSE FLOUR	250 ML
1/3 CUP	GROUND ALMONDS	75 ML
1/4 CUP	GRANULATED SUGAR	60 ML
1/4 TSP	SALT	1 ML
1/2 CUP	COLD UNSALTED BUTTER, CUT INTO CUBES	125 ML
1	EGG YOLK	1
1 TO 2 TBSP	COLD WATER	15 TO 30 ML

CUSTARD

3 TBSP	GRANULATED SUGAR, DIVIDED	45 ML
3	EGGS	3
3/4 CUP	HEAVY OR WHIPPING (35%) CREAM	175 ML
2 TSP	VANILLA EXTRACT	10 ML

PREHEAT OVEN TO 375°F (190°C). LINE A LARGE BAKING SHEET WITH PARCHMENT PAPER. SPREAD RHUBARB ON PREPARED BAKING SHEET AND SPRINKLE WITH SUGAR. BAKE FOR ABOUT 8 MINUTES OR UNTIL RHUBARB IS TENDER BUT STILL HOLDS ITS SHAPE. TRANSFER TO A DISH AND LET COOL COMPLETELY. LEAVE OVEN ON.

CRUST: PLACE A 9- OR 10-INCH (23 OR 25 CM) TART PAN WITH A REMOVABLE BOTTOM ON A LARGE BAKING SHEET.

IN A FOOD PROCESSOR, COMBINE FLOUR, ALMONDS, SUGAR, SALT AND BUTTER; PROCESS UNTIL MIXTURE RESEMBLES FINE BREAD CRUMBS. ADD EGG YOLK AND 1 TBSP (15 ML) COLD WATER; PULSE, ADDING MORE WATER 1 TSP (5 ML) AT A TIME IF NECESSARY, UNTIL IT JUST STARTS TO COME TOGETHER AS A BALL OF DOUGH. TURN OUT ONTO A LIGHTLY FLOURED WORK SURFACE AND KNEAD LIGHTLY INTO A 6-INCH (15 CM) DISC. (AT THIS POINT THE DOUGH CAN BE WRAPPED IN PLASTIC WRAP AND REFRIGERATED FOR UP TO 3 DAYS. LET STAND AT ROOM TEMPERATURE FOR 15 MINUTES BEFORE ROLLING OUT.)

ROLL DOUGH OUT TO A CIRCLE ABOUT 12 INCHES (30 CM) IN DIAMETER. LIFT DOUGH INTO THE PAN (IT IS VERY PLIABLE) AND PRESS TO FIT THE BOTTOM AND SIDES. (IF THE PASTRY CRACKS, JUST PATCH IT IN THE PAN — NO ONE WILL EVER KNOW.) TRIM THE EDGES. REFRIGERATE FOR 15 MINUTES. PRICK THE BOTTOM AND SIDES OF THE PASTRY WITH A FORK. BAKE FOR 20 TO 25 MINUTES OR UNTIL LIGHTLY BROWNED. (CHECK AFTER 10 MINUTES; IF THE BOTTOM IS PUFFING UP, LIGHTLY PRICK A FEW MORE TIMES.) LET COOL COMPLETELY IN PAN ON A WIRE RACK.

CUSTARD: REDUCE OVEN TEMPERATURE TO 350°F (180°C). SPREAD COOLED RHUBARB EVENLY IN BOTTOM OF CRUST. IN A BOWL, WHISK TOGETHER 2 TBSP (30 ML) OF THE SUGAR, EGGS, CREAM AND VANILLA. POUR OVER RHUBARB. SPRINKLE WITH THE REMAINING SUGAR. BAKE FOR ABOUT 30 MINUTES OR UNTIL CUSTARD IS SET AND LIGHTLY BROWNED. LET COOL IN PAN ON RACK FOR AT LEAST 10 MINUTES BEFORE REMOVING THE TART RING. LEAVE TART ON THE PAN BASE TO SERVE. SERVES 6 TO 8.

FRESH RASPBERRY HAZELNUT TART

*SERVE WITH SIMPLE CARAMEL SAUCE
(VARIATION, PAGE 339) DRIZZLED LIGHTLY OVER TOP.*

CRUST

I CUP	ALL-PURPOSE FLOUR	250 ML
1/3 CUP	GROUND HAZELNUTS	75 ML
1/4 CUP	GRANULATED SUGAR	60 ML
1/4 TSP	SALT	I ML
1/2 CUP	COLD UNSALTED BUTTER, CUT INTO CUBES	125 ML
I	EGG YOLK	I
I TO 2 TBSP	COLD WATER	15 TO 30 ML

FILLING

1/2 CUP	SEEDLESS RASPBERRY OR RED CURRANT JELLY (NOT JAM), DIVIDED	125 ML
I CUP	MASCARPONE CHEESE, AT ROOM TEMPERATURE	250 ML
2 TBSP	CONFECTIONERS' (ICING) SUGAR	30 ML
2/3 CUP	HEAVY OR WHIPPING (35%) CREAM	150 ML
3 CUPS	RASPBERRIES	750 ML
1/3 CUP	CHOPPED TOASTED HAZELNUTS (OPTIONAL)	75 ML

CRUST: PREHEAT OVEN TO 375°F (190°C). PLACE A 10-INCH (25 CM) TART PAN WITH A REMOVABLE BOTTOM ON A LARGE BAKING SHEET. IN A FOOD PROCESSOR, COMBINE FLOUR, HAZELNUTS, SUGAR, SALT AND BUTTER; PROCESS UNTIL MIXTURE RESEMBLES FINE BREAD CRUMBS. ADD EGG YOLK AND I TBSP (15 ML) COLD WATER; PULSE, ADDING MORE WATER I TSP (5 ML) AT A TIME IF NECESSARY,

UNTIL IT JUST STARTS TO COME TOGETHER AS A BALL OF DOUGH. TURN OUT ONTO A LIGHTLY FLOURED WORK SURFACE AND KNEAD LIGHTLY INTO A 6-INCH (15 CM) DISC. (AT THIS POINT THE DOUGH CAN BE WRAPPED IN PLASTIC WRAP AND REFRIGERATED FOR UP TO 3 DAYS. LET STAND AT ROOM TEMPERATURE FOR 15 MINUTES BEFORE ROLLING OUT.)

ROLL DOUGH OUT TO A CIRCLE ABOUT 12 INCHES (30 CM) IN DIAMETER. LIFT DOUGH INTO THE PAN (IT IS VERY PLIABLE) AND PRESS TO FIT THE BOTTOM AND SIDES. (IF THE PASTRY CRACKS, JUST PATCH IT IN THE PAN — NO ONE WILL EVER KNOW.) TRIM THE EDGES. REFRIGERATE FOR 15 MINUTES. PRICK THE BOTTOM AND SIDES OF THE PASTRY WITH A FORK. BAKE FOR 20 TO 25 MINUTES OR UNTIL LIGHTLY BROWNED. CHECK AFTER 10 MINUTES; IF THE BOTTOM IS PUFFING UP, LIGHTLY PRICK A FEW MORE TIMES. LET COOL COMPLETELY IN PAN ON A WIRE RACK.

FILLING: PLACE RASPBERRY JELLY IN A MICROWAVE-SAFE BOWL. MICROWAVE ON HIGH FOR ABOUT 30 SECONDS, UNTIL MELTED. LET COOL BUT DO NOT LET RESET. IN A LARGE BOWL, BEAT MASCARPONE WITH CONFECTIONERS' SUGAR TO LOOSEN IT SLIGHTLY. STIR IN 2 TBSP (30 ML) MELTED JELLY. IN ANOTHER LARGE BOWL, WHIP CREAM UNTIL SOFT PEAKS FORM. FOLD INTO MASCARPONE MIXTURE. SPOON INTO COOLED CRUST, LEVELING TOP WITH A SPATULA OR SPOON. IN ANOTHER BOWL, TOSS RASPBERRIES WITH THE REMAINING MELTED JELLY. TUMBLE OVER TOP OF MASCARPONE MIXTURE. SPRINKLE WITH HAZELNUTS, IF DESIRED. REFRIGERATE FOR AT LEAST 1 HOUR OR FOR UP TO 4 HOURS. SERVES 8.

CRISPY BLUEBERRY PIE

AN EFFORTLESS CELEBRATION
OF FRESH SUMMER BLUEBERRIES.

I	9-INCH (23 CM) FROZEN DEEP-DISH PIE SHELL	I
1/4 CUP	PANKO (SEE TIP, OPPOSITE) OR DRY BREAD CRUMBS	60 ML

FILLING

4 CUPS	BLUEBERRIES	I L
1/3 CUP	PACKED BROWN SUGAR	75 ML
I TSP	GROUND CINNAMON	5 ML
	GRATED ZEST AND JUICE OF I LIME	

TOPPING

2/3 CUP	PANKO OR DRY BREAD CRUMBS	150 ML
1/3 CUP	ALL-PURPOSE FLOUR	75 ML
1/3 CUP	PACKED BROWN SUGAR	75 ML
1/3 CUP	UNSALTED BUTTER, MELTED	75 ML

PREHEAT OVEN TO 375°F (190°C). PLACE PIE SHELL ON A BAKING SHEET AND LET THAW FOR 15 MINUTES. PRICK BOTTOM AND SIDES WITH A FORK. BAKE FOR 8 TO 10 MINUTES OR UNTIL LIGHTLY BROWNED. LET COOL COMPLETELY. SPRINKLE PANKO OVER BASE OF COOLED CRUST. REDUCE OVEN TEMPERATURE TO 350°F (180°C).

FILLING: IN A LARGE BOWL, COMBINE BLUEBERRIES, SUGAR, CINNAMON, LIME ZEST AND LIME JUICE. SPOON OVER PANKO IN CRUST.

TOPPING: IN A LARGE BOWL, COMBINE PANKO, FLOUR, SUGAR AND BUTTER (THE MIXTURE WILL CLUMP SLIGHTLY). SPRINKLE EVENLY OVER BLUEBERRIES.

BAKE FOR 30 TO 40 MINUTES OR UNTIL FRUIT IS BUBBLING AND TOP IS NICELY BROWNED. (IF TOPPING STARTS TO BROWN TOO QUICKLY, COVER LOOSELY WITH FOIL.) LET COOL ON A WIRE RACK FOR 15 MINUTES BEFORE SERVING. SERVES 6 TO 8.

TIP: PANKO IS ALSO KNOWN AS JAPANESE BREAD CRUMBS. THE LARGE FLAKES CREATE A DELICIOUSLY CRUNCHY CRUST ON FRIED AND BAKED FOODS. LOOK FOR PANKO IN EITHER THE BAKERY SECTION, THE SEAFOOD SECTION OR THE ASIAN FOODS AISLE OF THE SUPERMARKET. A GOOD SUBSTITUTE IS DRY BREAD CRUMBS.

A WOMAN KNOWS ALL ABOUT HER CHILDREN: DENTIST APPOINTMENTS, FAVORITE FOODS, BEST FRIENDS, HOPES AND FEARS. A MAN IS VAGUELY AWARE OF SOME SHORT PEOPLE LIVING IN THE HOUSE.

EASY PEACHY PIE

THIS SUMPTUOUS SUMMER PIE WILL HAVE YOU IN AND OUT OF THE KITCHEN IN NO TIME. A FROZEN PIE SHELL CUTS DOWN ON THE WORK, WHILE PANKO BREAD CRUMBS DELIVER A CRISPY STREUSEL TOPPING. SPRINKLING PANKO IN THE BOTTOM OF THE PIE SHELL PREVENTS THE FRUIT JUICES FROM MAKING THE PASTRY SOGGY.

1	9-INCH (23 CM) FROZEN DEEP DISH-PIE SHELL	1
1/4 CUP	PANKO (SEE TIP, PAGE 319) OR DRY BREAD CRUMBS	60 ML

FILLING

6	RIPE PEACHES, PEELED (SEE TIP, OPPOSITE) AND CHOPPED	6
1/3 CUP	PACKED BROWN SUGAR	75 ML
1 TSP	FINELY GRATED GINGERROOT	5 ML
1 TBSP	FRESHLY SQUEEZED LIME JUICE	15 ML

TOPPING

2/3 CUP	PANKO OR DRY BREAD CRUMBS	150 ML
1/3 CUP	ALL-PURPOSE FLOUR	75 ML
1/3 CUP	PACKED BROWN SUGAR	75 ML
1/3 CUP	UNSALTED BUTTER, MELTED	75 ML

PREHEAT OVEN TO 375°F (190°C). PLACE PIE SHELL ON A BAKING SHEET AND LET THAW FOR 15 MINUTES. PRICK BOTTOM AND SIDES WITH A FORK. BAKE FOR 8 TO 10 MINUTES OR UNTIL LIGHTLY BROWNED. LET COOL COMPLETELY. SPRINKLE PANKO OVER BASE OF COOLED CRUST. REDUCE OVEN TEMPERATURE TO 350°F (180°C).

FILLING: IN A LARGE BOWL, COMBINE PEACHES, BROWN SUGAR, GINGER AND LIME JUICE. SPOON OVER PANKO IN CRUST.

TOPPING: IN A LARGE BOWL, COMBINE PANKO, FLOUR, BROWN SUGAR AND BUTTER (THE MIXTURE WILL CLUMP SLIGHTLY). SPRINKLE EVENLY OVER PEACHES.

BAKE FOR 30 TO 40 MINUTES OR UNTIL FRUIT IS BUBBLING AND TOP IS NICELY BROWNED. (IF TOPPING STARTS TO BROWN TOO QUICKLY, COVER LOOSELY WITH FOIL.) LET COOL ON A WIRE RACK FOR 15 MINUTES BEFORE SERVING. SERVES 6 TO 8.

TIP: TO PEEL FRESH PEACHES, PLUNGE INTO BOILING WATER FOR 20 SECONDS. DRAIN AND PLUNGE INTO A BOWL OF ICE WATER. ONCE COOL, LIGHTLY SCORE THE SKIN WITH THE POINT OF A PARING KNIFE AND PEEL AWAY THE SKIN.

EVERYTHING IS ALWAYS OKAY IN THE END. IF IT'S NOT, THEN IT'S NOT THE END.

MINI BANANA CHOCOLATE STRUDELS WITH RUM CREAM

ANOTHER ONE OF THOSE FABULOUS PHYLLO RECIPES — AND IT CAN BE MADE AHEAD. IF YOU PREFER, SERVE WITH A SCOOP OF MANGO SORBET INSTEAD OF THE RUM CREAM.

RUM CREAM

I CUP	HEAVY OR WHIPPING (35%) CREAM	250 ML
1/4 CUP	CONFECTIONERS' (ICING) SUGAR	60 ML
I TBSP	RUM, ORANGE LIQUEUR OR ORANGE JUICE	15 ML

STRUDELS

8	SHEETS FROZEN PHYLLO PASTRY (EACH 17- BY 13-INCHES/43 BY 33 CM) THAWED	8
3/4 CUP	UNSALTED BUTTER, MELTED	175 ML
1/2 CUP	PANKO (SEE TIP, PAGE 319) OR DRY BREAD CRUMBS	125 ML
3	BANANAS, PEELED AND CUT IN HALF CROSSWISE, THEN LENGTHWISE	3
3/4 CUP	CHOCOLATE HAZELNUT SPREAD (SUCH AS NUTELLA)	175 ML
3/4 CUP	CHOPPED TOASTED HAZELNUTS OR PECANS (SEE TIP, PAGE 301)	175 ML
	CONFECTIONERS' (ICING) SUGAR	

RUM CREAM: IN A LARGE BOWL, WHIP CREAM, SUGAR AND RUM UNTIL SOFT PEAKS FORM. TRANSFER TO AN AIRTIGHT CONTAINER AND REFRIGERATE FOR AT LEAST 30 MINUTES OR FOR UP TO 2 HOURS. MAKES ABOUT 2 CUPS (500 ML).

STRUDELS: PREHEAT OVEN TO 350°F (180°C). LINE 2 LARGE BAKING SHEETS WITH PARCHMENT PAPER. CAREFULLY UNROLL PHYLLO PASTRY AND COVER WITH A CLEAN TEA

TOWEL OR SHEET OF PLASTIC WRAP. PLACE ONE PHYLLO SHEET ON A WORK SURFACE, WITH A LONG EDGE CLOSEST TO YOU, AND BRUSH WITH BUTTER. TOP WITH ANOTHER PHYLLO SHEET AND BRUSH WITH BUTTER. SPRINKLE WITH ABOUT 2 TBSP (30 ML) PANKO. CUT CROSSWISE INTO 3 STRIPS, EACH ABOUT $5\frac{1}{2}$ INCHES (14 CM) WIDE. PLACE A BANANA CHUNK ABOUT $\frac{1}{2}$ INCH (I CM) FROM THE BOTTOM OF EACH STRIP. SPREAD I TBSP (15 ML) CHOCOLATE HAZELNUT SPREAD OVER EACH BANANA AND SPRINKLE WITH I TBSP (15 ML) HAZELNUTS. FOLD BOTTOM EDGE OVER BANANA; FOLD IN SIDES AND ROLL UP. REPEAT WITH THE REMAINING PHYLLO AND FILLINGS. PLACE ROLLS, SEAM SIDE DOWN, ABOUT I INCH (2.5 CM) APART ON PREPARED BAKING SHEETS. BRUSH WITH THE REMAINING BUTTER. BAKE, ONE SHEET AT A TIME, FOR 15 TO 20 MINUTES OR UNTIL GOLDEN BROWN AND CRISPY. TO SERVE, DUST EACH STRUDEL WITH CONFECTIONERS' SUGAR, CUT IN HALF AND ARRANGE ON A PLATE WITH A DOLLOP OF RUM CREAM. MAKES 12 STRUDELS.

TIP: THAW PHYLLO OVERNIGHT IN THE REFRIGERATOR. DO NOT ATTEMPT TO DEFROST IT IN THE MICROWAVE, AS THIS WILL RENDER IT UNUSABLE. BRUSHING PHYLLO WITH BUTTER OR OIL PREVENTS IT FROM DRYING OUT AND CRACKING. WHILE YOU'RE WORKING, KEEP UNUSED PHYLLO COMPLETELY COVERED WITH A CLEAN TEA TOWEL OR WITH PLASTIC WRAP TO PREVENT IT FROM DRYING OUT.

MAKE AHEAD: LET STRUDELS COOL COMPLETELY. WRAP INDIVIDUALLY IN PLASTIC WRAP AND PLACE IN AN AIRTIGHT CONTAINER. REFRIGERATE FOR UP TO I DAY. REHEAT ON A BAKING SHEET LINED WITH PARCHMENT PAPER IN A 325°F (160°C) OVEN FOR 10 TO 12 MINUTES.

OLD-FASHIONED
APPLE CHERRY CHARLOTTE

BREAD PUDDING MEETS APPLE PIE IN THIS TRADITIONAL
FRUIT-FILLED DESSERT. IT'S MOLDED IN AN OVENPROOF
BOWL. (A PYREX GLASS MIXING BOWL IS BEST, BUT
A SOUFFLÉ DISH ALSO WORKS.) WHEN TURNED OUT,
THE CHARLOTTE HAS A CRUNCHY AND BUTTERY DOME
ENCASING A GENEROUS HELPING OF TENDER APPLES
AND DRIED CHERRIES. LEAVE OUT THE CHERRIES IF YOU
PREFER. SERVE IT WARM WITH A GENEROUS DOLLOP
OF WHIPPED CREAM OR VANILLA BEAN ICE CREAM.
IMPRESSIVE, YET INCREDIBLY EASY.

FILLING

2 TBSP	UNSALTED BUTTER	30 ML
4 CUPS	THINLY SLICED PEELED TART APPLES (SUCH AS GRANNY SMITH)	1 L
1/2 CUP	DRIED CHERRIES OR RAISINS	125 ML
1/4 CUP	PACKED BROWN SUGAR	60 ML
1/2 TSP	GROUND CINNAMON	2 ML
	FINELY GRATED ZEST OF 1 ORANGE	
1/3 CUP	FRESHLY SQUEEZED ORANGE JUICE OR UNSWEETENED APPLE JUICE	75 ML
1/4 CUP	PINEAPPLE, APRICOT OR PEACH JAM	60 ML

CRUST

9 TO 10	SLICES 60% WHOLE WHEAT OR WHITE SANDWICH BREAD	9 TO 10
1/2 CUP	UNSALTED BUTTER, MELTED	125 ML
	CONFECTIONERS' (ICING) SUGAR	

FILLING: IN A LARGE NONSTICK SKILLET, MELT BUTTER
OVER MEDIUM HEAT. ADD APPLES AND TOSS TO COAT.
STIR IN CHERRIES, BROWN SUGAR, CINNAMON, ORANGE

ZEST, ORANGE JUICE AND PINEAPPLE JAM; BRING TO A BOIL. REDUCE HEAT AND SIMMER, STIRRING FREQUENTLY, FOR 15 TO 20 MINUTES OR UNTIL LIQUID HAS ALMOST EVAPORATED AND APPLES ARE TENDER. REMOVE FROM HEAT AND LET COOL TO ROOM TEMPERATURE.

CRUST: REMOVE CRUSTS FROM BREAD. CUT EACH SLICE IN HALF DIAGONALLY TO GET 2 TRIANGLES. BRUSH BOTH SIDES OF EACH PIECE OF BREAD WITH BUTTER. LINE THE BOTTOM AND THREE-QUARTERS OF THE WAY UP THE SIDES OF A 6-CUP (1.5 L) OVENPROOF BOWL OR SOUFFLÉ DISH WITH BREAD. DON'T LEAVE ANY GAPS BETWEEN PIECES — OVERLAP THEM AND PRESS FIRMLY. SPOON FILLING INTO THE LINED BOWL. TOP WITH THE REMAINING BREAD (YOU MIGHT HAVE A COUPLE OF TRIANGLES LEFT OVER). PLACE A SMALL PLATE ON TOP AND WEIGH IT DOWN WITH A LARGE CAN OF TOMATOES (OR SOMETHING SIMILAR). LET STAND FOR 20 MINUTES.

MEANWHILE, PREHEAT OVEN TO 375°F (190°C). REMOVE WEIGHT AND PLATE FROM CHARLOTTE. PLACE BOWL ON A LARGE BAKING SHEET (TO MAKE IT EASIER TO GET IN AND OUT OF THE OVEN). BAKE FOR 30 TO 35 MINUTES OR UNTIL GOLDEN BROWN AND CRISPY ON TOP. LET COOL ON A WIRE RACK FOR 10 MINUTES, THEN GENTLY INVERT ONTO A SERVING PLATE. WAIT FOR THE APPLAUSE. SERVES 4 TO 6.

MAKE AHEAD: THE COOLED FILLING CAN BE REFRIGERATED IN AN AIRTIGHT CONTAINER FOR UP TO 2 DAYS. AFTER ASSEMBLING THE CHARLOTTE, COVER THE BOWL WITH PLASTIC WRAP AND REFRIGERATE FOR UP TO 2 HOURS. REMOVE PLASTIC WRAP BEFORE BAKING.

JOLLY GOOD BREAD AND BUTTER PUDDING

WHEN IT COMES TO BREAD PUDDING, BRITS KNOW BEST! SERVE WITH CHANTILLY CREAM (PAGE 336).

1/4 CUP	UNSALTED BUTTER, SOFTENED	60 ML
8	THICK SLICES RAISIN BREAD	8
1/2 CUP	GOOD-QUALITY THICK-CUT ORANGE MARMALADE	125 ML
1/2 CUP	RAISINS	125 ML
1/4 CUP	GRANULATED SUGAR, DIVIDED	60 ML
1/4 TSP	GROUND NUTMEG	1 ML
	FINELY GRATED ZEST OF 1 ORANGE	
3	EGGS	3
1 CUP	2% OR WHOLE MILK	250 ML
1/3 CUP	HEAVY OR WHIPPING (35%) CREAM	75 ML

BUTTER AN 8-INCH (20 CM) SQUARE BAKING DISH. BUTTER ONE SIDE OF EACH BREAD SLICE, THEN SPREAD MARMALADE THICKLY OVER BUTTER. CUT EACH SLICE IN HALF DIAGONALLY TO GET 2 TRIANGLES. ARRANGE HALF THE BREAD IN PREPARED DISH, OVERLAPPING AS NECESSARY. SPRINKLE WITH RAISINS. ARRANGE THE REMAINING BREAD ON TOP. IN A BOWL, WHISK TOGETHER 2 TBSP (30 ML) OF THE SUGAR, NUTMEG, ORANGE ZEST, EGGS, MILK AND CREAM. POUR OVER BREAD, PUSHING DOWN GENTLY WITH A SPOON TO ENSURE ALL BREAD IS SUBMERGED. SPRINKLE WITH THE REMAINING SUGAR. COVER AND REFRIGERATE FOR AT LEAST 30 MINUTES OR FOR UP TO 12 HOURS TO ALLOW EGG MIXTURE TO SOAK INTO BREAD.

MEANWHILE, PREHEAT OVEN TO 350°F (180°C). BAKE, UNCOVERED, FOR 30 TO 40 MINUTES OR UNTIL GOLDEN BROWN AND PUFFY AND A TESTER INSERTED IN THE CENTER COMES OUT CLEAN. LET COOL IN DISH FOR 15 MINUTES BEFORE SLICING. SERVES 4 TO 6.

DOLPHINS ARE SO SMART THAT WITHIN A FEW WEEKS OF CAPTIVITY, THEY CAN TRAIN PEOPLE TO STAND ON THE EDGE OF THE POOL AND THROW THEM FISH.

ENCORE! CHOCOLATE BREAD PUDDING

OUR FAVORITE DESSERT IN THIS BOOK! SERVE WARM WITH RUM PECAN CARAMEL SAUCE (PAGE 338) AND A GENEROUS DOLLOP OF WHIPPED CREAM OR VANILLA ICE CREAM. YOUR GUESTS WILL FEEL COMPELLED TO PUT DOWN THEIR FORKS AND EXCLAIM "ENCORE!"

14	SLICES WHITE SANDWICH BREAD, CRUSTS REMOVED, CUT INTO $3/4$-INCH (2 CM) CUBES	14
8 OZ	SEMISWEET OR BITTERSWEET (DARK) CHOCOLATE, CHOPPED	250 G
$1/2$ CUP	GRANULATED SUGAR	125 ML
I TSP	GROUND CINNAMON	5 ML
6	EGGS	6
I TSP	VANILLA EXTRACT	5 ML
$2^1/2$ CUPS	HALF-AND-HALF (10%) CREAM	625 ML

PREHEAT OVEN TO 450°F (230°C). SPREAD BREAD CUBES IN A SINGLE LAYER ON 2 LARGE RIMMED BAKING SHEETS. BAKE, TURNING BREAD SEVERAL TIMES AND ROTATING PANS ONCE, FOR 10 TO 12 MINUTES OR UNTIL GOLDEN BROWN. LET COOL COMPLETELY.

BUTTER A 12-CUP (3 L) SHALLOW CASSEROLE DISH. PLACE CHOCOLATE IN A LARGE BOWL. IN ANOTHER BOWL, WHISK TOGETHER SUGAR, CINNAMON, EGGS AND VANILLA; SET ASIDE. IN A LARGE, HEAVY-BOTTOMED SAUCEPAN, HEAT CREAM TO JUST BELOW BOILING OVER MEDIUM HEAT. POUR CREAM OVER CHOCOLATE AND LET STAND FOR 3 TO 4 MINUTES OR UNTIL CHOCOLATE HAS MELTED. STIR UNTIL SMOOTH. SLOWLY (AND WE MEAN VERY SLOWLY) LADLE ABOUT $1/2$ CUP (125 ML) OF THE WARM CHOCOLATE

MIXTURE INTO THE EGG MIXTURE WITH ONE HAND WHILE CONSTANTLY STIRRING THE EGG MIXTURE WITH THE OTHER. (THIS METHOD IS CALLED "TEMPERING" AND PREVENTS THE CREAM MIXTURE FROM SCRAMBLING THE EGGS.) GRADUALLY STIR IN THE REMAINING CHOCOLATE MIXTURE. STIR IN BAKED BREAD CUBES, PRESSING DOWN GENTLY WITH A SPATULA TO HELP THE BREAD SOAK UP THE LIQUID. TRANSFER TO PREPARED CASSEROLE DISH. COVER AND REFRIGERATE FOR AT LEAST 4 HOURS OR FOR UP TO 12 HOURS.

PREHEAT OVEN TO 325°F (160°C). BAKE, UNCOVERED, FOR 30 TO 45 MINUTES OR UNTIL PUDDING IS PUFFY AND A TESTER INSERTED IN THE CENTER COMES OUT WITH A FEW MOIST CRUMBS ATTACHED. SERVES 6 TO 8.

MAKE AHEAD: THE BAKED PUDDING WILL KEEP, COVERED, IN THE REFRIGERATOR FOR UP TO 3 DAYS. IT'S YUMMY COLD OR REHEATED IN PORTIONS IN THE MICROWAVE.

TIP: TRY ONE OF THESE ALTERNATIVE SERVING SUGGESTIONS OR DISH IT UP WITH YOUR OWN STYLE — THERE IS NO WRONG WAY TO EAT THIS PUDDING.

* SERVE WITH A SCOOP OF COCONUT ICE CREAM AND A SCATTERING OF CHOPPED MACADAMIA NUTS.

* SERVE WITH WHIPPED CREAM FLAVORED WITH MINT LIQUEUR, TOPPED WITH A FEW CHOCOLATE SHAVINGS AND SOME TOASTED SLIVERED ALMONDS.

* SERVE WITH PITTED CHERRIES MARINATED FOR 1 HOUR IN CHERRY LIQUEUR, VODKA OR CRANBERRY JUICE, ALONG WITH CHOCOLATE SUNDAE SAUCE AND A DOLLOP OF SOUR CREAM.

THE FABLED LEMON FINALE

WHETHER THE LADIES ARE COMING FOR LUNCH OR THE GIRLS ARE HEADED OVER FOR MARGARITAS AND A MOVIE, SERVE THIS DROP-DEAD EASY TREAT AND THEY'LL ASK FOR THE RECIPE. IT SETS JUST LIKE A LEMON MOUSSE, WITH A LOT LESS FUSS. SERVE WITH BLACKCURRANT LINZER SLICES (PAGE 298), THIN GINGER COOKIES OR YOUR FAVORITE CRISP COOKIE.

3/4 CUP	GRANULATED SUGAR	175 ML
2 CUPS	HEAVY OR WHIPPING (35%) CREAM	500 ML
	FINELY GRATED ZEST OF 1 LEMON	
1/3 CUP	FRESHLY SQUEEZED LEMON JUICE (SEE TIP, BELOW)	75 ML
	RASPBERRIES, BLACKBERRIES OR BLUEBERRIES, OR A COMBINATION	

IN A HEAVY-BOTTOMED SAUCEPAN, COMBINE SUGAR, CREAM AND LEMON ZEST. BRING TO A BOIL OVER MEDIUM-HIGH HEAT, STIRRING CONSTANTLY. REDUCE HEAT AND SIMMER, STIRRING OCCASIONALLY, FOR 3 MINUTES. REMOVE FROM HEAT AND STIR IN LEMON JUICE. LET COOL SLIGHTLY. POUR INTO 4 SMALL WINE GLASSES OR RAMEKINS. COVER AND REFRIGERATE OVERNIGHT, UNTIL SET. GARNISH WITH BERRIES. SERVES 4.

TIP: WHEN SQUEEZING JUICE FROM LEMONS, LIMES AND ORANGES, TRY TO HAVE THE FRUIT AT ROOM TEMPERATURE — IT WILL GIVE UP JUICE MORE EASILY THAN IF SQUEEZED STRAIGHT FROM THE REFRIGERATOR. IF YOU FORGET TO REMOVE IT FROM THE FRIDGE AHEAD OF TIME, PRICK THE CITRUS FRUIT WITH A FORK AND MICROWAVE ON HIGH FOR ABOUT 20 SECONDS TO WARM IT SLIGHTLY.

PATIO FRUIT PACKETS

FRUIT AND BOOZE WRAPPED AND COOKED IN INDIVIDUAL FOIL PACKETS ON THE BARBECUE — HOW EASY IS THAT?

2 TO 3 TBSP	BUTTER, MELTED	30 TO 45 ML
8	RED OR BLACK PLUMS, PITTED AND CUT INTO QUARTERS	8
1 CUP	BLACK OR RED CHERRIES, PITTED	250 ML
1/4 CUP	PACKED BROWN SUGAR	60 ML
2 TBSP	PORT, ORANGE LIQUEUR, ORANGE JUICE OR CRANBERRY JUICE	30 ML
1 TSP	GROUND CINNAMON	5 ML
	FINELY GRATED ZEST OF 1 ORANGE (OPTIONAL)	
4	THIN GINGER COOKIES (2 TO 3 INCHES/5 TO 7.5 CM IN DIAMETER), CRUMBLED	4
	WHIPPED CREAM OR ICE CREAM	

PREHEAT BARBECUE GRILL TO MEDIUM. CUT 4 LENGTHS OF FOIL, EACH ABOUT 20 BY 12 INCHES (50 BY 30 CM). FOLD IN HALF CROSSWISE TO MAKE 12- BY 10-INCH (30 BY 25 CM) RECTANGLES. BRUSH EACH RECTANGLE TO THE EDGES WITH BUTTER. IN A LARGE BOWL, COMBINE PLUMS, CHERRIES, BROWN SUGAR, PORT, CINNAMON AND ORANGE ZEST. DIVIDE AMONG FOIL RECTANGLES. FOLD UP EDGES OF FOIL OVER FRUIT TO ENCLOSE AND SCRUNCH EDGES TOGETHER TO SEAL. GRILL FOR ABOUT 10 MINUTES OR UNTIL FRUIT IS JUICY AND SOFTENED BUT NOT MUSHY. USING TONGS, REMOVE PACKETS FROM GRILL AND LET COOL UNTIL COOL ENOUGH TO HANDLE. OPEN TOPS OF PACKETS, SPRINKLE CRUMBLED COOKIES OVER TOP AND ADD A DOLLOP OF WHIPPED CREAM. SERVES 4.

SWEET CHAI ORANGES WITH CINNAMON

THE PERFECT ENDING TO A CURRY DINNER.

I CUP	WATER	250 ML
2	CHAI TEA BAGS	2
2/3 CUP	GRANULATED SUGAR	150 ML
4	NAVEL ORANGES, PEELED AND SLICED INTO THIN ROUNDS (SEE TIP, OPPOSITE)	4

CINNAMON CREAM

1/2 CUP	HEAVY OR WHIPPING (35%) CREAM	125 ML
I TSP	CONFECTIONERS' (ICING) SUGAR	5 ML
1/4 TSP	GROUND CINNAMON	I ML

IN A SMALL SAUCEPAN, BRING WATER TO A BOIL OVER HIGH HEAT. TURN OFF HEAT, ADD TEA BAGS, COVER AND STEEP FOR 20 MINUTES. DISCARD TEA BAGS, SQUEEZING GENTLY. STIR SUGAR INTO TEA. BRING TO A BOIL, REDUCE HEAT AND SIMMER, STIRRING OCCASIONALLY, FOR ABOUT 15 MINUTES OR UNTIL SLIGHTLY THICKENED AND SYRUPY. (THE SYRUP IS READY WHEN IT LIGHTLY COATS THE BACK OF A TEASPOON WHEN IT'S QUICKLY DIPPED IN AND OUT.)

MEANWHILE, ARRANGE ORANGE SLICES, SLIGHTLY OVERLAPPING, IN A SERVING DISH LARGE ENOUGH TO ACCOMMODATE THE FRUIT IN A SINGLE LAYER. POUR WARM SYRUP OVER ORANGES. LET COOL COMPLETELY. COVER AND REFRIGERATE FOR AT LEAST I HOUR OR FOR UP TO I DAY.

CINNAMON CREAM: IN A LARGE BOWL, WHIP CREAM, SUGAR AND CINNAMON UNTIL SOFT PEAKS FORM. TRANSFER TO

AN AIRTIGHT CONTAINER AND REFRIGERATE FOR AT LEAST 30 MINUTES OR FOR UP TO 2 HOURS. MAKES ABOUT 1 CUP (250 ML).

SERVE ORANGES WITH A GENEROUS DOLLOP OF CINNAMON CREAM. SERVES 4.

TIP: ORANGES LOOK AND TASTE BETTER IN DESSERTS AND FRUIT SALADS WHEN BOTH THE SKIN AND THE WHITE PITH ARE REMOVED. WITH A SHARP KNIFE, CUT BOTH ENDS OFF THE ORANGE. SET ONE END FLAT ON THE CHOPPING BOARD AND, USING THE MID-SECTION OF THE KNIFE BLADE, FOLLOW THE NATURAL CURVE OF THE FRUIT TO CUT OFF THE SKIN AND PITH IN ONE MOVE. DON'T WORRY IF A LITTLE ORANGE FLESH COMES AWAY WITH THE SKIN, BUT BE CAREFUL NOT TO REMOVE TOO MUCH. MAKE REPEATED CUTS AROUND THE ORANGE UNTIL IT IS PEELED. SLICE OR CHOP THE FRUIT AS DESIRED.

MAKE AHEAD: COOL THE SYRUP, TRANSFER TO AN AIRTIGHT CONTAINER AND REFRIGERATE FOR UP TO 3 DAYS. WHEN READY TO SERVE, SIMPLY DRIZZLE OVER THE SLICED ORANGES.

VARIATION: USE OTHER TYPES OF FLAVORED TEA, SUCH AS MINT, LEMON GINGER OR ORANGE SPICE, TO CREATE A VARIETY OF EXCITING SYRUPS THAT ARE DELICIOUS POURED OVER FRUIT, PANCAKES OR ICE CREAM.

WHY BE DIFFICULT? PUT SOME EFFORT INTO IT AND BE IMPOSSIBLE.

BLUEBERRY COMPOTE

"COMPOTE" (NOT COMPOST!) IS A FANCY WORD FOR
A SIMPLE DISH OF FRUIT SIMMERED WITH SUGAR.
IT'S THE PERFECT ACCOMPANIMENT TO COCONUT
LIME CHEESECAKE (PAGE 312), A BOWL OF ICE CREAM
OR A PILE OF FLUFFY PANCAKES.

1 LB	FRESH OR FROZEN BLUEBERRIES (ABOUT 3 CUPS/750 ML)	500 G
1/2 CUP	GRANULATED SUGAR	125 ML
1 TSP	GROUND CINNAMON	5 ML
1 TO 2 TBSP	FRESHLY SQUEEZED LIME JUICE	15 TO 30 ML
2 TSP	CORNSTARCH	10 ML
2 TSP	COLD WATER	10 ML

IN A SAUCEPAN, COMBINE BLUEBERRIES, SUGAR,
CINNAMON AND LIME JUICE. BRING TO A SIMMER OVER
MEDIUM HEAT. REDUCE HEAT TO LOW AND SIMMER,
STIRRING OCCASIONALLY, FOR 2 TO 3 MINUTES OR UNTIL
SUGAR IS DISSOLVED. IN A SMALL BOWL, COMBINE
CORNSTARCH AND COLD WATER. GRADUALLY STIR INTO
THE SIMMERING COMPOTE, ADDING JUST ENOUGH
TO LIGHTLY THICKEN THE FRUIT MIXTURE. TRANSFER
TO A LARGE BOWL AND LET COOL. SERVE AT ROOM
TEMPERATURE OR REFRIGERATE UNTIL CHILLED. MAKES
ABOUT 3 CUPS (750 ML).

TIP: THERE IS NO NEED TO THAW FROZEN BLUEBERRIES
BEFORE ADDING THEM TO THIS RECIPE.

MAKE AHEAD: REFRIGERATE IN AN AIRTIGHT CONTAINER FOR
UP TO 3 DAYS.

WHITE CHOCOLATE CREAM CHEESE FROSTING

THIS RICH, SMOOTH FROSTING IS PERFECT FOR OUR HUMMINGBIRD CAKE (PAGE 308) AND IS ALSO DELICIOUS SPREAD ON TOP OF CARROT CAKE.

8 OZ	WHITE CHOCOLATE, CHOPPED	250 G
8 OZ	CREAM CHEESE, SOFTENED	250 G
I CUP	UNSALTED BUTTER, SOFTENED	250 ML
I TSP	VANILLA EXTRACT	5 ML

IN A DOUBLE BOILER OR A HEATPROOF BOWL SET OVER A POT OF HOT, BUT NOT BOILING WATER, MELT WHITE CHOCOLATE, STIRRING UNTIL SMOOTH. LET COOL SLIGHTLY.

IN A LARGE BOWL, BEAT CREAM CHEESE AND BUTTER FOR 3 TO 4 MINUTES OR UNTIL SMOOTH AND LIGHT. SCRAPE DOWN THE BOWL. ADD COOLED MELTED CHOCOLATE AND VANILLA; BEAT FOR I MINUTE. MAKES ABOUT $2\frac{1}{2}$ CUPS (625 ML).

MAKE AHEAD: TRANSFER TO AN AIRTIGHT CONTAINER AND REFRIGERATE FOR UP TO 3 DAYS. BRING TO ROOM TEMPERATURE BEFORE USING.

IF I AGREED WITH YOU, WE'D BOTH BE WRONG.

CHANTILLY CREAM

HERE'S AN EASY "CHEFFY" RECIPE FOR MAKING WHIPPED CREAM EVEN MORE DELICIOUS. DOLLOP ON TOP OF YOUR FAVORITE DESSERTS!

1 CUP	HEAVY OR WHIPPING (35%) CREAM	250 ML
2 TBSP	CONFECTIONERS' (ICING) SUGAR	30 ML
1 TSP	VANILLA EXTRACT	5 ML

IN A LARGE BOWL, WHIP CREAM, SUGAR AND VANILLA UNTIL SOFT PEAKS FORM. MAKES ABOUT 2 CUPS (500 ML).

TIP: BE CAREFUL NOT TO OVER-WHIP CREAM. IF IT STARTS TO LOOK GRAINY, YOU HAVE GONE TOO FAR. YOU CAN SOMETIMES RESCUE OVER-WHIPPED CREAM BY ADDING A LITTLE MORE UNWHIPPED CREAM TO THE BOWL AND WHIPPING ON LOW SPEED.

A BUS IS A VEHICLE THAT MOVES TWICE AS FAST WHEN YOU ARE RUNNING AFTER IT AS WHEN YOU ARE IN IT.

SOUR CREAM CHANTILLY CREAM

ANOTHER TERRIFIC DESSERT TOPPING.
DOUBLE THE RECIPE TO FROST A LAYER CAKE.

1/2 CUP	SOUR CREAM	125 ML
1 CUP	HEAVY OR WHIPPING (35%) CREAM	250 ML
1 TBSP	CONFECTIONERS' (ICING) SUGAR	15 ML
1 TSP	VANILLA EXTRACT	5 ML

IN A LARGE BOWL, WHIP SOUR CREAM, WHIPPING CREAM, SUGAR AND VANILLA UNTIL SOFT PEAKS FORM. (WHIP TO STIFF PEAKS IF USING TO FROST A CAKE.) MAKES ABOUT 3 CUPS (750 ML).

VARIATION

RASPBERRY CHANTILLY CREAM: OMIT THE SUGAR AND ADD 2 TBSP (30 ML) SEEDLESS RASPBERRY JAM TO THE CREAM BEFORE WHIPPING.

LORD, KEEP YOUR ARM AROUND MY SHOULDER
AND YOUR HAND OVER MY MOUTH!

— RUM PECAN CARAMEL SAUCE —

THE ESSENTIAL TOPPING FOR CHOCOLATE BREAD
PUDDING (PAGE 328). THIS SAUCE ALSO ADDS THE
DECADENT FACTOR TO ICE CREAM, WARM BROWNIES,
SLICED BANANAS AND CRÊPES. IT KEEPS IN THE
REFRIGERATOR FOR ABOUT 2 WEEKS — IF YOU CAN
AVOID THE TEMPTATION TO EAT IT BY THE SPOONFUL!

1/2 CUP	COLD WATER	125 ML
I CUP	GRANULATED SUGAR	250 ML
I CUP	HEAVY OR WHIPPING (35%) CREAM	250 ML
2 TBSP	RUM (SEE TIP, OPPOSITE)	30 ML
1/2 TSP	VANILLA EXTRACT	2 ML
I CUP	CHOPPED TOASTED PECANS (SEE TIP, PAGE 301)	250 ML

POUR WATER INTO A HEAVY-BOTTOMED SAUCEPAN. ADD
SUGAR, BEING CAREFUL NOT TO LET IT STICK TO THE
SIDES OF THE PAN. BRING TO A BOIL OVER HIGH HEAT,
WITHOUT STIRRING. BOIL FOR 6 TO 7 MINUTES OR UNTIL
SUGAR IS DISSOLVED AND SYRUP IS A PALE GOLDEN
COLOR. REMEMBER — DON'T STIR! REDUCE HEAT TO
MEDIUM AND COOK FOR I OR 2 MINUTES OR UNTIL SYRUP
IS A DEEP AMBER COLOR. (WATCH CLOSELY, AS THE SYRUP
CAN TURN FROM TOFFEE-COLORED TO HORRIBLY BURNED
IN SECONDS.) REMOVE FROM HEAT. CAREFULLY ADD
1/4 CUP (60 ML) OF THE CREAM. THE SYRUP WILL BUBBLE
DRAMATICALLY. WHEN THE BUBBLING HAS SUBSIDED, WHISK
IN THE REMAINING CREAM, RUM AND VANILLA. (IF THE
SAUCE LOOKS A BIT LUMPY, HEAT IT OVER LOW HEAT,
STIRRING CONSTANTLY, UNTIL SMOOTH.) IF USING RIGHT
AWAY, STIR IN PECANS. OTHERWISE, LET COOL, TRANSFER

TO AN AIRTIGHT CONTAINER AND REFRIGERATE FOR UP TO 2 WEEKS. REHEAT OVER LOW HEAT AND STIR IN PECANS JUST BEFORE SERVING. MAKES ABOUT $1\frac{1}{2}$ CUPS (375 ML).

TIP: DON'T BE TEMPTED TO SUBSTITUTE ARTIFICIAL RUM FLAVORING FOR THE REAL THING – IT WON'T TASTE GOOD!

TIP: THE SYRUP WILL INITIALLY TURN GOLDEN BROWN AT THE EDGES OF THE PAN. AS IT CONTINUES TO COOK, THE GOLDEN COLOR WILL "CREEP" TOWARD THE MIDDLE. ONCE THE SYRUP IN THE CENTER OF THE PAN TURNS GOLDEN, REDUCE THE HEAT TO MEDIUM.

VARIATION
SIMPLE CARAMEL SAUCE: OMIT THE RUM AND PECANS.

TRULY FABULOUS PEOPLE NEVER GET DRESSED
BEFORE LUNCHTIME.

Library and Archives Canada Cataloguing in Publication

Fan fare! Best of Bridge cookbook : 200 all new recipes : brand-new volume, brand-new recipes.

Includes index.
ISBN 978-0-7788-0276-1

1. Cooking. 2. Cookbooks.

TX714.F35 2011   641.5   C2011-902995-2

INDEX